THE CAUSE OF
CHRISTIAN EDUCATION

DATE DUE

New Books

11-4-14

6/18

PRINTED IN U.S.A.

THE CAUSE OF CHRISTIAN EDUCATION

FOURTH EDITION

RICHARD J. EDLIN

DORDT COLLEGE PRESS

Cover by Rob Haan
Layout by Carla Goslinga

Printed in the United States of America.

Dordt College Press   www.dordt.edu/DCPcatalog
498 Fourth Avenue NE
Sioux Center, Iowa 51250
United States of America

ISBN: 978-1-940567-09-9

The Library of Congress Cataloging-in-Publication Data is on file with the Library of Congress, Washington, D.C.

Library of Congress Control Number: 2014947617

TABLE OF CONTENTS

perspective that is ridiculed by contemporary society. It is, using the definition that I love the most, to challenge students with the celebration of the lordship of Christ over all of creation.

To summarize therefore, this book seeks to assist Christians who have a concern about schooling at any level, and who want to be deliberate and faithful to their calling to love God with all their heart and mind, and their neighbors as themselves, as they consider schooling choices for themselves and/or for those for whom they care. As you become more informed through reading these pages, you may at the same time be both emboldened and challenged. Such is the lot of those who seek to follow Jesus Christ. My concern is that many of us, even dedicated Christians, sometimes drift along with the world around us in how we make decisions in life for ourselves and our loved ones. Many of our pagan neighbors make decisions based upon their secularist religious commitment to self-advantage and the primacy of personal economic gain as the road to living life to the fullest – and we as Christians often drift along with the flow, in the process unconsciously repudiating the Lord whom we desire to serve. Inculcation into this enticing but vain way of living is nurtured and perpetuated in what is taught, and how it is taught, in secular schools.

This book hopes to expose the school for the powerful and dangerous institution that it is, and intends to assist Christians to make educational choices that honor God and are for the very best for their children. Though Christian schooling and all other forms of schooling are based upon firmly-held beliefs and ideas, the goal of the Christian school is quite different from that of the secular school – our aim is to help students learn that you cannot properly understand anything, including yourself, mathematics, language, science, and history, without understanding God's world God's way. The Christian school studies every subject and relationship in the light that God provides. It is truly radical and countercultural.

A biblical theology of God's kingdom, beginning with God's explosive commitment at the beginning of human history, is foundational to this book, with Jesus Christ front and center. God's first amazing decision, after declaring that he wanted to make man in his own image, was to bestow upon humanity God's own capacity of caring creativity – in our case, to form culture (Genesis 1:26–29). Forming culture means how we use our creative capacities when we name things, make things, communicate with each other, or design cultural patterns though elections. Forming culture means how we make love and war. It means how we cook in the kitchen and how we re-create in the wilderness or on the internet. It means how we write an essay, or explore the languages of mathematics, science, and words. It means how we paint a painting, open our homes and neighborhoods to strangers and the dispossessed, or select a replacement washing machine.

Understanding God's world God's way is what God's kingdom is all about – and this is at the heart of faithful Christian schooling. It is not extra or tangential to the gospel, but rather is a part of it. It does not demean the importance of personal conversion, but is integral to it as a part of God's big story. Helping children to understand themselves and their world is what Christian schools are all about. Christians are called to view how they do all things as spiritual acts of worship, doing them (i.e., shaping culture) in a God-related manner that displays a conscious obedience to God's character and rule rather than a conformation to secular patterns of belief and behavior (Romans 12). The meaning of the Cross of Christ is pivotal to all of this – remember that God so loved *the world* that he sent his only begotten son to die and rise again. Eternal life, says Jesus in his high priestly prayer in John 17, is not only a hope for a precious existence with him after we die. Eternal life is knowing Jesus both now and for eternity in all that we do (John 17:3). Again, this is what Christian schooling is all about. It is about being God's salt-and-light ambassadors, it's about God making his appeal through us (2 Corinthians 5:20) as we play our part in the cry of the Lord's Prayer of "Thy kingdom come on earth, as it is in heaven."

This book is not for the faint-hearted. If your commitment to Jesus Christ is in place because owning him is what your culture's norm expects of you, or if your commitment is punctuated with qualifications (i.e., where you are, what Dr. Kenda Creasy Dean from Princeton Theological Seminary calls, "almost Christian"), then lay this book aside. It is too unsettling and dangerous for your postmodern worldview and way of life. But if you humbly and at times falteringly, and always relying upon the power of the Holy Spirit in the light of the truth of God's Word and the all-of-life encompassing authority of the gospel of Jesus Christ, seek to live life now and for eternity as fulfilled worship and service to God and others, then this book might just help you to carry out your vision in the area of education and schooling. So open its dangerous pages with hope, and anticipation.

As you read this book, you will come to realize that I reject the dichotomy identified by some, between instruction and practice. Those terms describe two sides of the same coin. As any parent will tell you,

Finally, my prayer for every Christian reader is not that you necessarily agree with everything written here, but that, as you chart your own course of seeking to live faithfully before God, your love for the Lord "may abound more and more in knowledge and depth of insight, so that you may be able to discern what is best and may be pure and blameless for the day of Christ, filled with the fruit of righteousness that comes through Jesus Christ – to the glory and praise of God" (Philippians 1:9–11).

Richard J. Edlin
April 2014

Chapter 1

No Neutrality and Why It Matters

THE PURPOSE OF SCHOOLING

As I write this fourth edition of *The Cause of Christian Education*, my adopted country is going through an election campaign to select the national government for the next three years. High on the agenda of all politicians as they seek election is the necessity of declaring their commitment to providing access for all citizens to high quality schooling. Despite economic uncertainty, it is the kiss of death for any politician or political party to dare to suggest that funding be reduced to the multi-billion dollar education industry. Everybody, it seems, wants more spending on schools, not less. Everybody, it seems, is not only content with subjecting our children to ten years or so of compulsory schooling for five days per week for forty or so weeks per year, but there are even many calls to extend this compulsory education for an extra two or three years. What is it that makes schooling so important? Why do we give it such a high place in the nurture of our children for such a long period of years? Why do we so willingly place our most precious young ones in the instructional care for such extended periods of time, to people who would otherwise be complete strangers? What takes place in schools that makes schooling to be of such profound, unquestioned importance?

In short, before we examine the characteristics of Christian schooling, it is pertinent that we reflect upon the fundamental purpose of schooling in the first place. Only then can we begin to examine the dynamics and structure of what schools actually do. This is because purpose shapes practice. If I believe that the purpose of a motor vehicle is to provide a means of transportation from one place to another, then I am going to ensure that any vehicle that I buy has a good history of reliability; whereas if I believe that a key purpose of a motor vehicle is to display my wealth and social status, then I am going to choose a vehicle that is known to be expensive and fitted with ostentatious extras. Our reasons for doing something shape the actual something that we end up doing.

In the course of this book, the terms "education" and "schooling" are often used interchangeably. Though education is a much broader term than schooling, the principles and practices discussed in these pages apply to both contexts. It is important also to realize that the "Christian education" referred to in the book's title and in its pages does not refer to the important area of teaching Bible in the context of institutional churches on Sundays, in youth group activities, etc. Though there are obvious similarities, the mission and task of the local church are different from the mission and task of the Christian school. What we are discussing in this book is the day-school activity that usually takes place Monday through Friday for at least five hours per day for around forty or so weeks per year.

So what is the purpose of schooling? Writing about education 300 years before Jesus Christ, Aristotle concluded as follows:

> All do not share the same view about what should be learned by the young, with a view to goodness or to the best life; nor is opinion clear whether education should be directed mainly to the understanding, or mainly to moral character. If we look at actual practice, the result is confusing; it throws no light on the problem whether there should be training in those pursuits which are useful in life, or those which make for goodness, or those which go beyond the ordinary run (of knowledge). (Aristotle *Politics*, 1337a33)

Somewhat more recently, Lawrence Stenhouse (1967, 1) reflected a widespread belief when he opined that the purpose of education, including schooling, is, "the transmission of culture from generation to generation."

More recently still, in 2010, a report commissioned by the government in Queensland, Australia, investigated stated aims for schooling in sixteen different developed Western and Asian countries, and concluded that the only two purposes explicitly shared across all of them were "the aim of individual development and the aim of citizenship/community/ democracy" (Schofield 2010, 17).

In the political campaign referred to earlier, there seemed to be four broadly accepted foci for schooling, which Stemler and Bebell (2012) also identify in their publication on the subject. These four conjoined schooling purposes relate to:

- the intellect (basic numeracy and literacy);
- citizenship (assimilation into the beliefs and values of the prevailing culture);
- economics (equipping for vocation); and
- social responsibility.

In terms of this book, we offer two parallel suggestions concerning the purpose of schooling. The first is that schooling is designed to transmit and enrich culture, and facilitate educands' successful participation in it. Our second definition is also simple and to the point: the purpose of schooling is to help students learn about the world and their places and tasks in it.

The above two definitions could be expanded in many ways. The following description, while adding complexity, also identifies the foundational role of belief or worldview, which is central to this book's exploration of the cause of Christian education. This expanded definition also allows for the vital paradigm-shifting, teleological concept of student formation in addition to mere information-gathering, which Smith and Smith (2011b) and others have highlighted in recent years as being implicit in all pedagogy: Education is the careful and deliberate engagement of perspectives, materials, and experiences with an eye to nurturing a view of the world and of human capacities that responds to students' sensitivities and abilities and that addresses prevailing cultural norms and worldviews; thereby enabling students to interpret reality in a manner consistent with the beliefs of their mentors, all the while also equipping them with the capacity to function as fulfilled and productive members of society in the light of their comprehensive framework of basic beliefs about things.

THE MYTH OF NEUTRALITY

At first glance, schooling that adheres to the two definitions above might seem to be relatively uncontroversial. With the provision of dedicated and well-trained teachers, coupled with well-resourced classrooms in which students are encouraged to care for each other, some might contend that schooling should be a very constructive and certainly harmless activity. While there are differing religious views in the community at large, this type of education, focusing on basic competency in numeracy and literacy might hardly be seen to offend the sensibilities of any mainstream societal group. Especially with government schools in most countries attempting to be (relatively) free, secular, and compulsory, there might appear to be little need for private schools. In fact, in that they claim to teach from a perspective linked to narrow sectional interests in the culture (usually of either a religious or ethnic nature), these private schools are seen by some to be positively destructive and working against tolerance and social cohesion.

It does not take long, however, to shatter this myth of religious neutrality in the schooling of the young, wherever it takes place. Schooling is not and can never be neutral. Because schooling seeks to shape children with certain outcomes in mind of what it means to be an educated citizen, schools select resources, teaching methods, and curriculum perspectives that pursue those objectives. This is the answer to the question raised earlier about why do we value schooling so much. Intuitively, parents realize that the dissemination in schools of information and skills, such as numeracy and literacy, is inexorably wrapped up in a nurturing package that shapes who children are and how they understand the world. As Jamie Smith (2009, 26) has correctly commented, "Education is not primarily a heady project concerned with providing information; rather, education is most fundamentally a matter of formation, a task of shaping and creating a certain kind of people."

This makes schools bed-partners with parents, and gives teachers enormous influence over who our children will finally become. Jesus Christ confirmed this perspective in his parable recorded in Luke 6:39–40, when he did not say that students become like their curriculum, but Jesus said that students, when they are fully trained, become like their teachers! An implication of Jesus' comment is that parents should carefully look at the beliefs and lifestyles of their children's teachers, since this is a good indication of what our children will be like in later life. As Hekman (2007, 17) suggests, as he encourages Christian schools to become communities of grace, "How teachers behave themselves is even more important than what they say."

In retrospect, it seems obvious that education can never be neutral in terms of the activities and outcomes of what occurs in the classroom, including numeracy and literacy. Classroom activities and outcomes are based upon beliefs, and chosen pedagogies seek deliberately to shape the perspectives, vocational choices, and the general lifestyles of our children. If schools deal with how children understand the world and their places and tasks in it, then of course it is impossible for them to be neutral.

For example, as we will see in more detail later, a secular view of the child and classroom instruction (perhaps apart from ethics or religion class) assumes the irrelevancy of the divine in human life – we are little more than the products of chance biochemical interactions over time, just like all other animals and plants. Consequently, the social mores that we surround ourselves with, such as laws, family structure, and so on, are socially-determined constructions of the human mind. On the other hand, for the Christian parent, divine revelation, divine interaction, and divine accountability are at the core of understanding who we are and this requires the exploration of Christian beliefs when we seek to understand ourselves, the world, and our places and tasks in it. In both of these two cases, there is no neutrality. One position in general education is based upon a belief in the irrelevance and probably non-existence of a creator-sustainer God; the other position is based upon the exact opposite – a belief in the centrality of a creator-sustainer God in understanding humans and our world. The positions could not be further apart.

George Counts, a famous American educator and social reformer, put it this way:

> The formulation of an educational program is a . . . long series of complex creative acts . . . embracing analysis, selection, and synthesis. It likewise involves the affirmation of values and the framing of both individual and social purposes. Inevitably, education conveys to the young responses to the most profound questions of life – questions of truth and falsehood, of beauty and ugliness, of good and evil. These affirmations may be expressed in what an education fails to do as well as in what it does, in what it rejects as well as in what it adopts. (Counts 1952, 36)

> To a very large degree, education was actually the handmaiden or midwife of catastrophe. . . . [Education] may serve any cause. . . . [I]t may serve tyranny as well as freedom, ignorance as well as enlightenment, falsehood as well as truth, war as well as peace, death as well as life. It may lead men and women to think they are free even as it rivets upon them the chains of bondage. (28–29)

Though the Christian world rightly rejects the uncertainties of postmodernity, it seems that one of the positive fruits of a postmodern ethic has been the growth in the acknowledgement of non-neutrality. Just a handful of decades ago, when most scholars and educators thought within a modernist or positivist framework and therefore tried to maintain the objectivity of human knowing, few of those shaping educational theory and practice openly accepted the perspective that education was not neutral. Today however, assisted by the afterglow of postmodern thinking with its rejection of metanarratives, the acknowledgement of the faith-committedness of education is commonplace, perhaps even the norm, among scholars (Lincoln & Guba 2013). The reality of this position has permeated down to the popular level in varying degrees in different settings. Therefore, in order to assist in the widespread acceptance of this perspective, a few examples of relevant comments relating to the non-neutrality of education are provided below. Some of the examples are from Christian thinkers, some from non-Christian thinkers:

Teachers . . . teach us facts and shared values, but they inevitably do that from within the context of certain interpretations which are derived from their own particular beliefs about what it means to be human. (Cooling 2010, 33)

Curriculum and agents (including stakeholders and actants) involved in curriculum can never be neutral... [curriculum] is intensely historical, political, racial, gendered, phenomenological, autobiographical, aesthetic, theological and international. (Dinan-Thomas 2005, 145)

All learning and education in every field of study, whether philosophy or mathematics, theology or physics, takes place in light of a set of commitments and assumptions that a person brings to the learning task. . . . Whether a person brings Marxist, Darwinist, or Christian faith assumptions to their learning, religious assumptions always shape learning. (Johnson 2003, 124)

This is one thing we cannot deny – that is, that our understanding of an objective existence is affected by our subjective understanding of it. . . . Value neutrality itself is a value. A belief in value neutrality cannot transcend ideology. . . . Value neutrality is a myth. (Wang & Li 2011, 1)

To claim to be free of philosophical presuppositions is simply to be unaware of them. (Bartholomew 2000, 12)

Facts can never be isolated from the domain of values or removed from some form of ideological inscription. (Lynch 2001, 354)

There is no sphere of life that is neutral; rather, our practices and institutions are always and ultimately shaped and informed by faith commitments. (Smith 2013a, 42)

Any choice of pedagogical practice implies a conception of the learner and may, in time, be adopted by him or her as the appropriate way of thinking about the learning process. For a choice of pedagogy inevitably communicates a conception of the learning process and the learner. Pedagogy is never innocent. It is a medium that carries its own message. (Bruner 1996, 63)

All knowledge claims are necessarily "contaminated" by the perspective of the knower and the knowing community. (Wright 2013, 4)

To suggest that there is any kind of knowing or thinking, let alone a particularly reliable or prestigious one, which is somehow exempt from the pervasive call to serve God in Christ, and which in fact deliberately seeks to be free of all religious commitment, is nothing short of biblical nonsense. The Bible does not countenance religious neutrality. (Wolters 2007, 72)

The central, distinguishing characteristic of humanity is not rationality or moral consciousness or creativity. These are aspects of our human uniqueness, but the heart and core of that uniqueness is our response relation to God. Here the whole of human life, in all its aspects and dimensions, is focused. There is no "natural" area, no religiously neutral area, that lies outside the scope of this religious focus. (Fowler 1980a, 10)

The Decision "Not to mention God in the classroom" Is Not Neutrality

The assumption is often made, as in the separation of church and state argument, that as long as God is not being mentioned, then Christianity is not being defamed. Nothing could be further from the truth. Much of the effective ideological indoctrination against Christianity that takes place in western culture occurs by the deliberate act of leaving God out. By not mentioning God and his claims of Lordship over every aspect of creation, public school programs constantly reinforce the impression that God is not relevant in the world in which we live. Omission of a biblical worldview is not neutrality. It is a carefully calculated religious position that claims that God may be relevant to private spiritual matters, but that over the vast range of learning and life's experiences, God is just not relevant. This is not neutrality.

For example, examine the "Survival" simulation in Figure 1 on the next page. It is frequently used in schools in social studies and liberal arts programs. God is not mentioned anywhere, but it certainly is not religiously neutral. It can be an exciting activity with lots of student group work and interaction, but it is strongly non-Christian. Also known as "Lifeboats," an acceptance of the pre-suppositions in this activity unconsciously reinforces in the minds of impressionable youngsters the belief that people have value primarily according to the job that they do, since this is the only information that the students are given upon which to decide who in the lifeboat should live and who should die. In the second place, the simulation assumes that we, as people, have the right to "play God."

Despite the fact that God is not mentioned, "Survival" is a potent and silent reinforcer in schools of powerful non-Christian principles. Lamentably, such is our blindness as Christians today, in the many situations where the author has shown this simulation exercise to educators who are Christians, often up to 80 percent of them have not been able to detect the dangers, including the non-Christian presuppositions, that the simulation contains. This is just one example of many resources with specific non-Christian presuppositional and subliminal messages that children are confronted with continually in public education. If adult

Christian teachers can't detect the bias, then how can we expect our children to do so?

SURVIVORS ROLE PLAY

World War III is over. There are 16 adult survivors. The little group is adrift in a life raft somewhere on the Pacific Ocean. A few days previously, they had set out in the last plane in the world, trying to escape nuclear radiation and contamination. The one piece of news that had encouraged them had been the announcement of the discovery of an unknown land. It has minerals, mountains, no human inhabitants, and all the resources that humanity would need for survival. The radiation danger does not exist there.

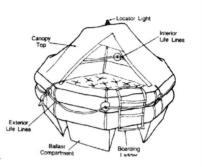

They have now been adrift in their raft on the ocean for FIVE days because their rescue plane crashed. Food and drink are in desperately short supply on the raft. It is estimated that the new land is still EIGHT days away.

YOU now come into the picture. You are not on the raft but you are in complete control of it. To ensure that at least some people survive to reach the new land, and because of the food and water shortage, you face the unfortunate necessity of throwing overboard FOUR people. Sadly, some will have to die so that the rest can live.

TASK: In your group, select the FOUR people from the list below who have to be **thrown overboard**. Your group's decision must be unanimous.

These are the people on the boat from whom you have to make your choice:			
POLITICIAN	DRUG ADDICT	UNION LEADER	SCIENTIST
TEACHER	POLICEMAN	APPRENTICE MECHANIC	PILOT
HOUSEWIFE	FARMER	TEENAGE GIRL	ARTIST
POET	POP SINGER	SCHOOLBOY (HIGHSCHOOL)	DOCTOR

What We Choose to Include in the Classroom, and What We Choose Not to Include, also Reflects our Beliefs

Another area of pedagogy that demonstrates no neutrality is the selection of resources for the classroom. It is not possible to teach everything, or to expose students to every possible resource. Accordingly, textbook publishers and teachers carefully select the resources for teaching, and the information that will be taught. These selections are made based upon what the selectors *believe* to be the most important resources and experiences. There it is again: we cannot escape the reality that beliefs are central in shaping students' learning experience. There is no neutrality. Stronks and Blomberg extend this point with a hint of amusement by using the analogy of supermarket shopping:

> The choices we make will be limited by the options we see before us. If the supermarket shelves do not stock a certain range of products or a particular brand of that product, then our choices are that much constrained. . . . We take for granted that the world is structured in a certain way, without acknowledging the extent to which it is constructed by prior human decisions. (Stronks & Blomberg 1993, 192)

The Example of Science as a Religious Activity

Consider the example of science. Science is a wonderful tool that helps us understand the physical, chemical, and biological properties and processes in the world in which we live. Scientists have made amazing discoveries that have improved the quality of human existence – though science has also been used to develop the most horrendous devices and practices. Science has contributed to both environmental degradation and environmental cleansing. But the misguided claim that science is the objective rendering of reality is little more than ideological fundamentalism masquerading as neutrality. As Miller (2010) has noted, "to hold science up as the One and Only Truth is a kind of fundamentalism in itself."

Science, like Christianity, secular rationalism, Confucianism, Islam, psychology, and all other interpretive lenses, has its own belief system to which its believers adhere, and which subject the perspectives of alternative paradigms to science's own over-riding dogma. Christians admit their bias. They admit that they believe Jesus Christ when he says that he is the way, the truth, and the life; that he is the essential interpretive key for reality; and that fulfilled life now and forever can only be found through him. Though many in the contemporary world refuse to recognize it, a commitment to science as the ultimate key to truth (we call this scientism – "if it's scientific you can really believe it; if it's not scientific then it's just opinion") also is a belief system based upon its own super-lative claims. The issue is not religion versus science as has often been claimed, because both science and Christianity are religious in nature. The issue really should be defined as the religion of science versus the religion of Christianity.

This contention that superlative science, like Christianity, is essentially religious may be supported firstly by understanding what religion actually is, and secondly by examining some of the belief claims of leading scientists about their discipline.

According to the Oxford English Dictionary (2013), religion may be defined as "a particular system of faith and worship." The Merriam-Webster Dictionary (2013) parallels this definition with its own which states that religion is "a cause, principle, or system of beliefs held with ardor and faith." The Australian government bases its understanding of religion upon a ruling from their High Court that religion is "a complex of beliefs and practices which point to a set of values and an understanding of the meaning of existence (Australian Bureau of Statistics, 2004). Central to these definitions is the perspective that religion is a cause fervently believed in by its adherents, to the extent that they view it as the ultimate interpreter of reality, contending that all other belief categories are subservient to it. Once again, Christians readily acknowledge that this is a reasonable description of their position. It can also be easily demonstrated that science is a belief structure or religion in exactly the same way. The difference is that whereas Christianity is a theistic religion, scientism is an a-theistic religion.

Consider for example, the clear faith assumptions made in his approach to science by Harvard endowed chair of biology, Professor Richard Lewontin. In the following extract, he is reviewing a book written by his friend Carl Sagan, and is moved to make the reflection that true science insists upon a purely materialistic interpretation of reality (that is, there is nothing beyond our senses and the concept of a supernatural God is ridiculous), even if this faith commitment does not always cohere with human experience:

> Our willingness to accept scientific claims that are against common sense is the key to an understanding of the real struggle between science and the supernatural. We take the side of science *in spite* of the patent absurdity of some of its constructs, *in spite* of its failure to fulfill many of its extravagant promises of health and life, *in spite* of the tolerance of the scientific community for unsubstantiated just-so stories, because we have a prior commitment, a commitment to materialism. It is not that the methods and institutions of science somehow compel us to accept a material explanation

of the phenomenal world, but, on the contrary, that we are forced by our *a priori* adherence to material causes to create an apparatus of investigation and a set of concepts that produce material explanations, no matter how counter-intuitive, no matter how mystifying to the uninitiated. Moreover, that materialism is absolute, for we cannot allow a Divine Foot in the door. . . . To appeal to an omnipotent deity is to allow that at any moment the regularities of nature may be ruptured, that miracles may happen. (Lewontin 1997, 7)

Earlier in the same article, Lewontin claimed that his perceptions outlined above were consistent with the beliefs of most scientists.

Another notable scientist, a world-famous paleontologist of his day, was Professor David Watson. He died in 1975, but for thirty years he was Jodrell Professor of Zoology and Comparative Anatomy at University College, London. As a strong believer in the value of the fossil record in supporting the theory of evolution, Watson revealed the extent of his commitment to the religion of science in a paper prepared for the British Association for the Advancement of Science. Concerning evolution, he recognized that it was ". . . a theory universally accepted, not because it can be proved by logically coherent evidence to be true, but because the only alternative, special creation, is clearly incredible" (Watson 1926, 95).

Francis Crick, famous for his brilliant co-discovery of the molecular structure of DNA, provides our third example. Writing in 1994 he hypothesized that, "'You,' your joys and your sorrows, your memories and your ambitions, your sense of personal identity and free will, are in fact no more than the behavior of a vast assembly of nerve cells and their associated molecules. . . . 'You're nothing but a pack of neurons'" (Crick 1994, 3). This eschewing of anything supernatural, and Crick's perspective-shaping prior commitment to the belief that science is the omniscient measure of all things, is revealed later in the same book (258) when he asserted that the only way to accept as true the idea of eternal life is to subject it to scientific analysis.

A profound example of the epistemological or religious challenge that reality poses for non-theists is the transparent musings of noted atheist philosopher Thomas Nagel. Nagel's reflection that "One of the things that drives the various reductionist [i.e., evolutionary] programs about mind, value, and meaning, in spite of their inherent implausibility, is the lack of any comprehensive alternative" (Nagel 2012, 15) is a clear case in point. Furthermore, the religious fervor of scientism zealots has been obvious in their frenzied reaction to Nagel's questioning of some of science's hallowed presuppositional beliefs (Zammito 2013). They view as blasphemy Nagel's frank admission that contemporary evolutionary science defies common sense in how it deals with the notion of consciousness. They regard it as heretical that any atheist like Nagel should conclude that, "the dominance of materialistic naturalism is nearing its end. . . . [W]e must start out from a larger conception of what has to be understood in order to make sense of the natural world" (Nagel 2012, 15–16).

The strengths and limitations of reductionistic science were demonstrated in the early 1990's when popular magazines such as *Time* and *US News and World Report* (Toufexis 1993) ran stories where scientists were quoted as claiming that human love was primarily a function of biochemistry, especially the responses triggered by phenylethylamine (PEA) in the human body. A discerning reader responded by noting that one could indeed describe the Mona Lisa in terms of the chemical composition of the paint, but to limit oneself to this would be to miss the whole point of the painting! The painting's ultimate meaning is beyond the reach of chemical enquiry.

So what does all this show? It reveals that, according to key scientists (Lewontin 1997), "real" scientists subject their exploration of reality to a set of presuppositions or beliefs that reject all truth claims that are derived from any position other than those based upon a singular belief in materialism or natural causes. This "cause or system of belief held with ardor and faith" against all odds, as the dictionary puts it, clearly is a religious position. It cannot claim to be neutral; it cannot claim to be unbiased. Like Christianity, science is the product of faith commitments. It is a religion. We could even call scholars like Lewinton, Watson, Hitchens, Hawkins, Crick, and others who take a public role in defending scientific orthodoxy its prophets and archbishops.

We should not misconstrue these comments as an attack upon science itself, defined as the systematic and evidentiary study of the physical and "natural" world. Christians need to take science seriously, and need to humbly acknowledge, for example, that there are fervent Christian scientists on both sides of the age-of-the-earth debate. From a Christian perspective, as many scientists throughout the ages have testified, scientific investigation, when used correctly, is a wonderful rational tool that God has given us as we explore and develop aspects of his world. When placed in subjection to the omnipotent God, scientific investigation reveals God's glory and can be used by men and women as good stewards for the betterment of humankind. Christians enjoy and appreciate authentic science. But science itself is faith-committed with its own dogmas, and it is not God. It is perspectival, and is based upon belief assumptions. Misguidedly taken as the ultimate key to truth, legitimate, belief-based science becomes blind faith scientism; in this totalitarian form, Christians believe that science is a false and misleading religion.

In an opinion piece in the *New York Times*, Wax (2013) puts it this way:

> Those who condemn[ed creationists] believe science is the only reliable way to discover truth. But this belief in science collapses on itself: there is no scientific evidence to prove that science is the only reliable way to discover truth. Once we take unproven hypotheses and dogmatize them, we have moved beyond scientific evidence into philosophical reflection on truth and the scientific method. Naturalist or not, when it comes to the world's origins, we are all in the realm of faith.

In a similar vein, Dr. Arthur Jones, who has written useful materials that examine science from a Christian worldview perspective rather than from a purely naturalistic perspective, makes the following point: "That which is presented as a scientific conclusion based upon the rational analysis of empirical evidence, may, largely and primarily, flow from (unrecognised) philosophical and religious commitments" (Jones 1998, 133–134).

Christian educators gleefully embrace authentic science, and hope that many graduates from Christian schools will excel in this important field of enquiry. What we do reject are scientism's omnipotent claims upon truth, and the determination of many of its adherents to so indoctrinate modern culture that alternative perspectives about truth and reality are given little credence. As Lincoln and Gurba (1985) have commented,

> We are all so imbued with the tenets of science that we take its assumptions utterly for granted, so much so that we almost cannot comprehend the possibility that there might be other ways of thinking. And when other ways are suggested, we are inclined to shut our ears, feeling that merely to listen to them is, quite literally, a heresy. (Lincoln and Guba 1985, 8–9)

WORLDVIEW AS AN ALTERNATIVE TERM FOR RELIGION

The discussion about the universality of religion in all of life, including education, may be assisted by replacing the word "religion" with the word "worldview." Though there are differences between the two terms, they both describe foundational, heart-commitment beliefs that shape how people understand and live in the world. Many books and articles have been written in recent years by both Christian and non-Christian scholars about the concept of worldview. Its faith foundations, its presuppositional character, and its determining influence on life have been well described. Like religion, worldview is not just a set of beliefs but is a core perspective of the heart of every human being that is lived and breathed (even if not consciously articulated) by its adherents. These foundational notions mean that a person's mental structures and ways of seeing and being in the world, according to Kanitz (2005, 105), always occur in a "deeply populated intellectual ground with various worldviews firmly entrenched and with others competing for space."

Further aspects of worldview, and in particular the notion of dualism, are explored in this book in chapter three, dealing with why we think the way that we do. In particular, through an explication of the dynamic possibilities for Christians of a reformed critical realist perspective, that chapter provides a cogent alternative to contemporary secular worldviews. However, it is not our purpose here to examine the concept of worldview in any depth. Suffice it to repeat that for many purposes the terms worldview and religion can be interchanged if this facilitates discussion with other educators, policy-makers, or parents who share a concern about the nature of contemporary schooling.

Here are some suggestions for further reading to gain a deeper understanding of worldview: Goheen and Bartholomew (2008) have written wisely and clearly on the concept of worldview from a Christian perspective, as have Plantinga (2002), Sire (2009), and Wolters (2005). J. K. A. Smith (2009) issues a timely reminder against viewing worldview as merely a cerebral construction. Edlin (2008a) has written elsewhere about the underpinning role that worldview plays in education. The work of Fernhout (1997) in exploring the relationship between worldview and schooling is particularly instructive.

SECULARISM IS NOT NEUTRALITY – IT IS A POWERFUL FAITH/WORLDVIEW POSITION OF ITS OWN

In many countries, government-provided education is championed as being secular. The general understanding of this term is that secular schools do not promote one form of religion over another. They are not opposed to religion or faith, but because secular schools cater for children from many different faith backgrounds, they construct learning in a context where religion or discussion about God is excluded from the curriculum in most classes, with the exception of religious instruction classes. Therefore, mention of a deity or God-related perspectives are rigorously excluded from the science classroom, and "religious" ceremonies such as Christmas or "religious" documents such as the Ten Commandments may be banned. Puzzlingly, other faith perspectives such as humanism, atheism, or economic rationalism seem to be acceptable topics for inclusion, but not Christianity. Books that openly view life from a Christian perspective, such as the Bible, have even been banned from school libraries, so as to maintain the secular environment.

For example, in a ruling on December 17, 1990 (Roberts 1990, 1056) the U.S. Court of Appeals considered a case where a fifth-grade public school teacher was ordered by his administrator to remove two books – *The Bible in Pictures* and *The Story of Jesus* – from a 239-book classroom library. Other books dealing with Greek gods and goddesses and American Indian religions were not ordered to be removed. In this case, known as Roberts v. Madigan, the court ruled that the selective removal of only Christian religious books from the library was completely in order. Furthermore, it was accepted by the court that the school administrator was not acting improperly in banning the teacher from displaying or silently reading the Bible during a class "silent reading" period. Incredibly, however, the court said that it was permissible to display and read from a book about the life of Buddha during that time! The court ruled (Roberts 1990, 1056) that "We discern no anti-Christian message here." It should be noted that in a lengthy dissenting opinion, Senior Court Judge Barnett dissociated himself from the court's judgment and claimed that the public school's actions (Roberts 1990, 1056) "were acts of intolerance, lack of accommodation and hostility toward the Christian religion."

There are many comments that could be made about the Roberts v. Madigan example. At this point however, the key issue to understand is that a commitment to secularism in schooling is not neutrality. It is the clear imposition of a belief system on teaching and learning. It is the application of the belief, religion, worldview, or faith assumption that dealing with God and how he understands the world and our places and tasks in it is irrelevant to teaching and learning. Our point here is not to agree or disagree with the faith of secularism (we shall consider the Christian faith position and its impact on schooling in the rest of this book!). The point here is that a secular approach to education is just as much a faith commitment, is just as real a religion (defined earlier as "a cause, principle, or system of beliefs held with ardor and faith") as is Christianity or Islam. Secularism does not equal neutrality. Furthermore, the attempt to impose a secular regime upon government schools is the championing of one religious perspective over another and is a clear, intolerant, and outrageous breach of religious freedom.

One lesson from this situation is the misleading nature of the term "faith-based schools." The term is often used to separate private denominational schools from government-operated secular schools. This discussion has shown that all schools, including secular schools, are indubitably faith-based. There is no such thing as a non-faith-based school. The term is unhelpful and we should desist from its use.

THE CHALLENGE FOR RELIGIOUS EDUCATION (RE) PROGRAMS IN SCHOOLS

A similar concern lies behind the term and concept of RE or religious education in school. We will use the United Kingdom as an example, though the challenges facing "ethics" classes in many other countries are similarly problematic. RE is a compulsory subject in schools in England and Wales, and refers to a specific time in a school's program when faith issues are discussed in a comparative manner. Currently, despite increasing pressure for change, Christianity is required to be given special emphasis in RE classes in government schools, as an historical foundation plank of UK culture.

Many good things can be done in an RE class when the goal is, as stated by the RE Council of England and Wales, to provoke "challenging questions about the ultimate meaning and purpose of life, beliefs about God or ultimate reality, issues of right and wrong and what it means to be human" (Orchard 2013, 3). Scholars, educators, and parents in organizations such as the Stapleford Centre (www.stapleford-centre.org) are to be highly commended for their tireless work in providing significant resources to schools that enhance the Christian character of their RE programs – including guided discussion about other religious traditions such as Islam, secularism, and socialism.

However, there are two substantial concerns about RE from a Christian perspective. First, powerful secular religious groups such as the British Humanist Association are determined to reduce all RE classes merely to a comparative religions program as "an inclusive, impartial, objective, fair, balanced and relevant subject allowing pupils to explore a variety of religions and non-religious worldviews" (*Religious Education* 2013, 1). Such an approach is not only logically impossible, given the faith-committed nature of all knowledge, but it de-prioritizes the faiths of parent groups in favor of a secular smorgasbord of ideas with all positions being given equal validity.

Our major concern, however, is that the whole concept of RE may be used to perpetuate the falsehood that some of the curriculum is shaped by religion and belief, and that the rest of it is not. "There is religious education, and there is the rest of the curriculum, which is not religious education." If RE unconsciously embeds this secular presupposition in the impressionable minds of children, it is in fact inculcating them into a secular religious perspective. Similarly, consigning "ethics" to a particular class may create the similar misconception that some things are impacted by ethics, but many others such as science, mathematics, and literacy are ethically neutral.

This same challenge confronts Christian schools in their "Christian education" or "Bible" classes. Extreme care needs to be taken to ensure that the perspective and content of these classes supports and underpins the religious foundations of every subject, rather than degenerating into an unintended replacement of the recognition of the role of belief in all key learning areas and in every aspect of the life of the school community. It is partly for this reason that the place of the Bible in the Christian school is explored in an entire chapter in this book – though once again, this is meant to confirm, not replace, the faith commitments that exist in all the other chapters!

THE NON-NEUTRALITY OF MAINSTREAM EDUCATIONAL LEADERSHIP

The situation where secularism has become the entrenched religion in many government schools around the world has not occurred by accident. It has been a deliberate goal of many of the fathers of modern education.

Horace Mann and John Dewey have both made enormous contributions to the shape of contemporary public education in North America, the rest of the Western world, and now permeating into non-western regions as well. Some of the contributions of Mann and Dewey, such as the encouragement of an inquiring spirit in education, have been valuable. Nevertheless, both men are typical of the founders of modern education who, unbeknown to many evangelical Christian parents, deliberately have laid a basis for our modern schools that leads children down a path that is away from God and away from a God-honoring perspective of the world.

Mann was active in educational developments in Massachusetts from 1827 until his death in 1859. Although he vehemently opposed state funding for private schools and argued for a taxpayer-funded education in government-controlled schools, he never claimed that this government education system bore any concept of moral neutrality. According to Richard Baer (1987) from Cornell University, Mann wrote in the *Common School Journal* of August 1, 1840, that books that omit clear direction as to what the authors believe to be true were seriously flawed. He claimed that clear sectarian messages were very important in educational materials such as, for example, civics texts.

The fundamental problem for Christians is that the beliefs and values that Mann sought to espouse in his educational system inculcated those beliefs that were not just different from a Christian world and life view, but were fundamentally opposed to it. Baer (1987) has commented that:

> Horace Mann and other proponents of public education were intent on reforming society by changing the values of children. Mann had little sympathy for Calvinists or Catholics, and he was determined to use every legal means – including state coercion in schooling – to ensure that other people's children were taught the truth as he understood it. (Baer 1987, 39)

In more recent decades, John Dewey was an even more influential educational philosopher whose anti-Christian beliefs have been a bulwark of curriculum development. It would be incorrect to say that Dewey gave nothing of enduring value to education. By God's mercy, and through the exercise of common grace, Dewey was able to awaken many educators to the uniqueness of the individual and the inquiring mind that is a part of what it means to be made in God's image. Nevertheless, as we shall see, the fundamental principles that he espoused and that today are central to the presuppositions that control modern public education are distinctly secular, humanist, and anti-God.

Dewey made no secret of his intolerance of Christianity. As first president of the American Humanist Association, he signed the 1933 Humanist Manifesto, which declared that there was no God and no place for a belief in anything outside of ourselves in modern thinking. His whole approach to education was predicated upon the belief that the child, not God, is the center of education: "The child [is] the sun about which the appliances of education revolve; he is the center about which they are organized" (Dewey 1976 [1899], 23).

Richard Riley was US Secretary of Education from 1993 until 2001. According to Elliott (2012), Riley also has been unapologetic about using education to persuade students to commit to a non-Christian, constructivist belief system in understanding the world. "Knowledge would only be knowledge when the approved leadership of education (the NEA and the Administration) so declared it to be knowledge and teachers would thereby be commanded to 'lead' youngsters into 'creating that knowledge' within themselves" (Elliott 2012, 5).

Richard Rorty, who taught at various times at Princeton, Stanford, and the University of Virginia before his death in 2007, was a vehement postmodernist. He was also a prominent voice in shaping contemporary education. Like Dewey, Rorty made no secret of his abhorrence of faith positions that advocated a clear view of truth, such as bible-believing Christianity. He openly declared that a key goal in education should be to dispel such faith-committed perspectives and to work at inculcating a postmodern faith perspective in students. In the following quotation replace his term "fundamentalist" with any religion, such as Christianity or Islam, that believes in external truth and you will understand Rorty's dramatic opposition to Christianity and his dogmatic faith commitment to organizing teaching and learning around the faith of radical constructivism and postmodernity:

> I, like most Americans who teach humanities or social science in colleges and universities . . . try to arrange things so that students who enter as bigoted, homophobic, religious fundamentalists will leave college with views more like our own. . . . The fundamentalist parents of our fundamentalist students think that the entire "American liberal establishment" is engaged in a conspiracy. The parents have a point. . . . [W]e are going to go right on trying to discredit you in the eyes of your children, trying to strip your fundamentalist religious community of dignity, trying to make your views seem silly rather than discussable. We are not so inclusivist as to tolerate intolerance such as yours. . . . I think those students are lucky to find themselves under the benevolent *Herrschaft* [domination] of people like me, and to have escaped the grip of their frightening, vicious, dangerous parents. (Rorty, 2000, 21–22)

An Alternative Core Perspective from Athens

Paul's address to the Athenians, as recorded in Acts 17, is one of the most famous sermons in the Bible. After being upset by all the idols that he had seen in Athens, Paul spoke in the Areopagus about the God who doesn't live in human constructions. He then proceeded to explain that the God of heaven and earth "made the world and everything in it." This same God also set people on the earth ". . . so that they would seek him and perhaps reach out for him and find him" (verse 27). This is one of the most momentous claims of the Bible. Not only did God create everyone, but also he created us all as God-seekers! Paul was claiming that all people, Jews and Greeks alike, are God-seekers (as the Athenians were unconsciously demonstrating), whether they acknowledge it or not. If being religious, then, is defined as seeking after God, this means that we are all religious, whether we admit it or not.

In this context, the assertion of Paul in another passage, Romans

1:25, takes on a startling perspective: "They [people] exchanged the truth about God for a lie, and worshiped and served the created things rather than the Creator." Note the choice here. There is no choice about worshiping and serving. We *must* worship and serve because God made us this way. The only choice in the Romans passage is the *object* of our worship and service: the creature or the Creator. In this profound commentary on modern-day secularism or humanism (seeking fulfillment in worshiping and serving the creature rather than the Creator), the Bible reminds us that all of life is religious, and that, sadly, Satan has diverted humankind's God-ordained worship instinct away from its true object and towards the god-substitute of autonomous humanity.

Core principles of a *Christian* understanding of education will be explored in the next chapter of this book, but it is important at this point to firmly appreciate the universal inevitability of worship in the human spirit, since the universality of this concept is a core component of a Christian understanding of the world. Plantinga (2002) puts it this way:

> . . . in a famous prayer at the beginning of his *Confessions*, Augustine addressed the *summun bonum* of the world: "O Lord," prayed Augustine, "you have made us for yourself, and our heart is restless until it rests in you."
>
> What Augustine knew is that human beings want God. In fact, humans want union with God: they want to get "in" God, as Jesus prays in John 17:21. Until it's suppressed, this longing for God arises in every human soul because it is part of the soul's standard equipment. We have been endowed by our Creator with a *sensus divinitatis* (a "sense of divinity"), wrote John Calvin, and everywhere in the world, even when it expresses itself as idolatry, the sense of divinity is the seed of religion. God has *made* us for himself. Our sense of God runs in us like a stream, even though we divert it toward other objects. We human beings want God even when we think that what we really want is a green valley, or a good time from our past, or a loved one. Of course we *do* want these things and persons, but we also want what lies behind them. Our "inconsolable secret," says C. S Lewis, is that we are full of yearnings, sometimes shy and sometimes passionate, that point us beyond the things of earth to the ultimate reality of God. (Plantinga 2002, 6–7)

We need to see education, like all other human activities, in this biblical light. Whatever our occupation, we are involved in worship. There is no such thing as religious neutrality in human endeavor. The human endeavor of education is a religious activity, and the practice of it will be an expression of worship either of the Creator or the creature.

Some decades ago, a very interesting and popular movie called *Dead*

Poets Society was released. It explored the conflict that occurred in the lives of students in a high school where the educational perspectives of child-centered education and content-centered education clashed severely. Whatever film-goers may have thought of the movie (and it was great entertainment), they had to agree that it highlighted this key factor about education: the nature of education offered to children will be determined by the beliefs (or worldview or religious perspective) of those involved in determining the patterns of instruction. In identifying this motif, *Dead Poets Society* unwittingly acknowledged the biblical perspective that education is a religious activity that results from and reinforces worship either of God or a god-substitute.

On the basis of this discussion, we must affirm that government schools are not religiously neutral institutions. Typically, they function according to a design that says that God is not relevant to education. While insisting that they are religiously neutral ("being deluded by a lie"), they proceed rigorously to maintain ideological structures and curricula that assert that mankind is the ultimate determiner of truth and reality.

We lament the secular religious idolatry of much state education, and Christians should always take the opportunity, following Paul's pattern in Athens, to gently persuade public educators of the true religious nature of the educational task. Nevertheless, we cannot remove from others the right to choose the god whom they will worship (and whom they will encourage students to worship) in education. This right to choose the object of our worship is a God-given right. It is not ours to remove. Enforced proselytism denies the right and responsibility of each mature person to make his or her own moral choices. What we can champion, however, is the right for parents to choose for their children the type of education that conforms to their own belief structures. This primary parental right, which in practice is repudiated by much state-supported secular education, is enshrined in Article 26(3) of the United Nations Declaration of Human Rights (1948), which declares that, "Parents have a prior right to choose the kind of education that shall be given to their children."

A Christian approach to schooling and a secular approach to schooling are both served by teams of dedicated and well-meaning teachers who, by and large, enjoy the craft of teaching and relate constructively with their students. Both approaches fervently desire to equip children with the capacities to function effectively and with satisfaction in later life. One does this from the dogmatic faith position that God is at the center of this task; the other does this from the dogmatic faith position that God and traditional religions have little to contribute to learning about ourselves, our world, and our places and tasks in it, and that the alternative faith of the paramountcy of human wisdom alone is the key to success and fulfillment. The two positions stand in stark contrast to each other. Both cannot be right. Both cannot share the same classroom. Though they may share some common techniques, fundamentally the two positions are diametrically opposed to each other. Some secular educators, as is the case with John Dunphy (1983) in the comment below, even go so far as to claim that the distinctions between the practices and outcomes of these two positions are so stark as to suggest that they are in fact outright enemies of each other (note that Dunphy has subsequently re-affirmed his position in later discussions):

> I am convinced that the battle for humankind's future must be waged in the public school classroom by teachers who correctly perceive their role as the proselytizers of a new faith: a religion of humanity that recognizes and respects the spark of what theologians call divinity in every human being. These teachers must embody the same selfless dedication as the most rabid, fundamentalist preachers for they will be ministers of another sort utilizing a classroom instead of a pulpit, to convey humanist values in whatever subject they teach, regardless of the educational level: pre-school, daycare, or large state universities. The classroom must, and will become, an arena of conflict between the old and the new, the rotting corpse of Christianity together with all its adjacent evils and misery and the new faith of humanism resplendent in its promise of a world in which the never realized Christian ideal of love thy neighbor will finally be achieved. . . . It will undoubtedly be a long, arduous, painful struggle, replete with much sorrow and many tears, but humanism will emerge triumphant. It must if the family of humankind is to survive. (Dunphy 1983, 24)

IMPLICATIONS OF THE UNIVERSALITY OF RELIGION IN EDUCATION –
FOR GOVERNMENTS

At the same time as postmodern thinking has led to an increased recognition of the non-existence of neutrality, Becker (2013) confirms that the social reality of plurality is upon us. That is, it is widely accepted that, particularly in a globally-connected world, most modern nations are comprised of citizens with a smorgasbord of differing belief perspectives, whose adherents desire that their children be nurtured in a manner consistent with those often diametrically opposed belief systems. Therefore, attempts to inflict a singular (usually secular) religious perspective upon nations in their government-funded school systems are increasingly being recognized as being forlorn and misguided. Teaching in a government-supported state education system that is committed to a secular faith perspective will only appease one group – those parents who share this secular worldview. Attempts to satisfy everyone in one monolithic school system when society is populated by diverse groups, all of which have their own competing claims about truth, will not really satisfy anybody. Citizens increasingly are becoming alert to the danger that John Stuart Mill noted almost two hundred years ago,

> A general state education is a mere contrivance for moulding people to be exactly like one another: and as the mould in which it casts them is that which pleases the predominant power in the government . . . it establishes a despotism over the mind, leading by natural tendency to [despotism] over one's body. (Mill 1859, 89)

In different locations around the world, democratic governments are exploring diversity in government-funded approaches to schooling, and many parents are welcoming these non-traditional independent options. Following the well-established patterns that have existed in Belgium and the Netherlands for many decades, other governments are trialing government-funded schooling alternatives that allow sectional interest groups to offer educational programs that reflect their belief systems. They do this while still maintaining some degree of government oversight to ensure that basic standards are met and that children are being well-equipped for productive life in cohesive, pluralistic cultures.

- In England, there are the new "free schools" funded by government but shaped by local community groups rather than centralized bureaucracy.

- In Australia, there are parent-controlled schools that are partially government funded. Despite the extra financial burden on parents of enrolling children in non-government schools in the Australian state of New South Wales, the percentage of children enrolled in these types of schools there has risen from 19.2 percent in 1931, to 34.5 percent in 2012 (Tovey 2013).

- In New Zealand, there are "special character schools" existing alongside secular state schools. Both are funded by the government, but the special character schools have an approach shaped by the beliefs of their local communities to which the government holds them accountable.

- Charter schools and voucher-based school experiments in some states in the USA could also been seen as examples of this growing phenomenon.

In an article entitled "Disestablishing our Secular Schools," Charles Glenn (2012), Professor of Educational Administration and Policy at Boston University, writes in support of this development:

> Critics of the present [mono-religious school] system, like their predecessors, are falsely accused of being enemies of education, or of wanting to destroy the public school. Unhealthy obsession with defending the status quo obscures the dysfunctional character of the present arrangements, particularly in urban districts where decisions that affect millions of students – and their teachers – are made through bureaucratic processes that have little to do with education and, all too often, are indeed anti-educational. . . .
>
> Government should play a significant role, setting standards for essential outcomes on which there is a societal consensus and ensuring that family circumstances never prevent a child from receiving an adequate education, but public education should be no more synonymous with government-operated schools than public health is with government-operated hospitals. Parents should be free to choose the school their children attend without financial penalty.
>
> This is only possible if we give up the fruitless effort to make public education "neutral," as though anything so intimately associated with the shaping of human beings could ever avoid choices among alternative views of human flourishing. The sort of lowest common denominator schooling into which public schools have been forced, the "defensive teaching" in which their teachers engage to avoid controversy, can never provide a rich educational environment. Indeed, the false belief in neutrality has fostered an idea of teachers as a kind of secular clergy.

A fear sometimes raised when the proliferation of schools based upon belief systems is mentioned is the possibility that such schools will fragment society and, like some of the militant Islamic Madras schools in troublesome parts of the world, the concern is that they will actually contribute to social and political disintegration. Though understandable, when governments still exercise a broad watching brief to ensure that justice and generally accepted societal norms are upheld, this fear has proven to be unfounded.

- The Netherlands, already identified as a nation that permits state-funded schooling plurality, is very multi-cultural but is also one of the most politically stable and socially responsive countries in Europe.

- In a major study by the Centre for Independent Studies in Australia, Buckingham (2010) notes that for Muslims in the

Australian community education can never be separated from faith, and that for them "schooling is not an academic exercise with a side-serving of faith" (15). She concludes that attempting to achieve social harmony and prevent intolerance by denying people's freedom to choose a school is unquestionably authoritarian and undemocratic. It is highly unlikely that public schools could ever meet the ideal of a social and cultural "melting pot" without sacrificing other core liberal ideals (17).

In fact, Buckingham uses the Australian Survey of Social Attitudes, conducted in 2005 by the Australian National University, to demonstrate that citizens in Australia who have attended non-government schools have a statistically higher sense of social responsibility and involvement than do their peers who have attended government schools, and that "There is no evidence that religious schools make their students less tolerant of difference" (Buckingham 2010, 20).

Etherington (2008) also provides a convincing rejoinder to what have proven to be misplaced and at times spurious criticisms of the place of Christian schooling in western pluralistic democracies. He joins with D. A. Carson (2012) in raising legitimate concerns about the radical constructivist redefinition of tolerance by Rorty and many others. Rorty and company's postmodern perspective encourages intolerance towards any position that claims moral certitude. "This new form of 'tolerance' is completely intolerant of the viewpoint that other viewpoints can be morally wrong" (Etherington 2008, 126).

Research conducted by the Cardus organization in North America supports the conclusion that there are higher-than-normal rates of social commitment and community involvement in students who have graduated from protestant and catholic schools:

> Independent schools don't simply churn out ultra-rich snobs and religious hardliners, but valuable members of society, a new study suggests.
>
> A sweeping survey of graduates from religious and independent schools shows students are more generous and engaged in their communities than their peers at publicly-funded schools.
>
> The Cardus Education Survey polled more than 2,000 former students between the ages of 24 and 39 from separate Catholic, Evangelical Protestant, private and Christian schools on a wide variety of issues ranging from charitable donations to civic involvement and employment prospects.
>
> The study concludes alternative school graduates are as likely, if not more so, to be valuable contributors to the "public good." (Aubury 2012).

Ch'ng (2012) notes quite properly that in many other important areas communities allow for diversity without the fear that this pluralism will cause societal disintegration, but rather out of the recognition that it is the actual diversity that brings about cohesion. For example, he notes that political parties in Australia are permitted to conduct employment discrimination, selecting potential workers on the basis of their political compatibility with the political party concerned. The same is true, he claims, for "single-sex, age-specific and minority culture clubs [that] can exclude from membership people who are not of the same sex, age or culture" (Ch'ng 2012, 2). How ridiculous it would be, for example, for a university to employ a misogynist as the primary lecturer in its women's studies program, or a believer in intelligent design as a professor in its evolutionary science department.

Diverse political or religious groups can live together in relative civic harmony, and this process is not hindered by allowing for a proliferation of schools that reflect the faith perspective of their parent communities. We urge legislators to abandon the biased practice of supporting secularism in education since this displays favoritism towards one religious perspective, and instead to develop policies and strategies that encourage the provision of a range of schools that respond to the diverse worldviews or faith sensibilities of all of their citizens.

IMPLICATIONS OF THE UNIVERSALITY OF RELIGION IN EDUCATION –
FOR PARENTS

Although schools in many countries originally began as enterprises of the church, the success of modernity in the nineteenth century and its marginalization of theistic religions (as opposed to secular ones) to the edges of society meant that churches saw little reason to continue to be involved in schooling. For their part, as John Stuart Mill observed earlier, governments were only too happy to assume responsibility for education, because it gave them the opportunity to mold the upcoming generation in a way that endorsed existing power structures and turned schooling into vocational training centers. Thus, for example, the United Kingdom passed the Forster's Act of 1870 and New Zealand passed the Education Act of 1877, both of which began the move towards compulsory and secular education controlled by central government. Though some parochial (church-operated) schools continued to exist, there was a global trend in many countries for parents to come to assume that education was a state responsibility, that it would be paid for largely through taxation, and that it would be innocuous enough not to offend the sensibilities of most social groups.

By the mid-twentieth century, some parents were beginning to re-alize that education was not religiously neutral, and that they needed to found their own alternative schools that explored the world and our places and tasks in it in a manner that was consistent with their own beliefs and not the state's dogma of humanistic secularism. Noll's sober analysis has become increasingly recognized – namely, "to the extent that we seek to educate the hearts and minds of our students, we are invading their private spaces as much as do psychotherapists and surgeons" (Noll 2012, 94).

In the early decades of the twenty-first century, this realization has grown from a gentle tidal surge into a grand tidal wave. Parents have begun to realize the central importance of schooling in shaping children's lives. Some have joined the homeschooling movement, and truly demo-cratic governments are beginning to respond to the demands of their parents by supporting alternative schooling patterns. Parochial schools, which had continued offering educational choice but which for some time had seen little difference between their curriculum and classroom practices and those of government schools, have been rediscovering the idea that their religious distinctives should shape everything that they do.

In 2011, a partnership of Irish Catholic educators affirmed that "there are no value-neutral schools, and thus parents must choose what particular ethos and vision they want their children to learn" (*Zenit News Bulletin* 2011, 1). In the Southern Baptist denomination in the USA, key leaders have become quite outspoken about the non-neutrality of secular education and its clear opposition to Christianity, and the consequen-tial need for church members to consider alternative schools for their children. Dr. Al Mohler, president of the Southern Baptist Theological Seminary in Louisville, Kentucky, supports an exit strategy for Christians from public education. He is quoted as maintaining that, "There is no such thing as neutrality. Every worldview is predicated on certain found-ing assumptions, and those of Christianity are incompatible with those undergirding the secular humanist worldview" (Worthen 2010, 3).

The import of this growing perspective is that the time has passed when parents could assume that state secular schooling would automati-cally satisfy their desires for their children. The time has come for all parents to re-assert control over the education of their children. No lon-ger bewitched by the myth of educational neutrality, authentic parenting requires parents to identify the faith perspective that they wish to see in their children's key learning areas, classroom patterns, discipline patterns, student interactions, teacher behaviors, and schooling outcomes. In the light of this, the call is for parents to then lobby for and choose educational options that celebrate their chosen faith perspectives.

For Christian parents, the Bible does not specifically stipulate that they should send their children to Christian schools. Nevertheless, there are biblical principles that can guide parents as they consider schooling options for their children. Here a just three of many examples:

- The Scriptures remind parents to bring up their children in the nurture and instruction of the Lord (Ephesians 6:4).

- Jesus clearly said that students, when they are fully trained, will become like their teachers (Luke 6:39–40).

- Paul, writing to the Christians in Colossae, reminded them not to be led astray by philosophy (or religion) based upon human wisdom (Colossians 2:8–10).

The collective wisdom of these principles should be of great assistance to Christian parents when they consider the type of schooling that they choose for their children.

IMPLICATIONS OF THE UNIVERSALITY OF RELIGION IN EDUCATION –
FOR TEACHERS

The vast majority of teachers recognize the strategic nature of their profession. Most put in long hours and work hard at establishing warm relationships with their students, very aware of the impact that they can have on their young charges. And yet research (Glanzer & Talbert 2005) suggests that some of them still seem unaware of the significance of their own views of the world in shaping how their students in turn see the world, an insight that has led even Jerome Bruner (1996, 84) to declare, in remarkably ecclesiastical terms, that "the teacher is the vicar of the culture at large."

The reality is that schools are increasingly being recognized as worldview-nurturing institutions. Alongside the global drive for higher test scores is the parallel determination in many jurisdictions that schools will inculcate values and perspectives. Despite the power of economic rationalism and its insatiable quest for child sacrifice, the essential religious nature of the human spirit refuses to succumb to the indifference of evolutionary determinism in schooling. Mills concurs by opining:

> There is now a widespread rejection of school cultures that are dominated by the reduction of human beings to mere quantities, to movable and interchangeable parts in the system. Secular discourse regarding school cul-

ture is becoming a fundamental arena for the emphasis on moral agency, value, and human fulfillment. (Mills 2003, 153)

Minor, Onwuegbuzie, Witcher, and James (2002) reviewed recent research and put it this way: "A substantial body of evidence has emerged . . . suggesting that teacher beliefs drive instructional pedagogy" (6). In the light of this rediscovered reality of the non-neutrality of education, teachers are beginning to recognize that they have an obligation to inform their parent communities and their students, at levels appropriate to their maturity, of the distinctive faith characteristics of their view of the child and of the purpose and nature of education. For example, in his curriculum document on human growth and development, secular educator Dr. Charles Harris (2009) in Virginia prefaces his teaching resources by acknowledging the nature and impact of his faith commitment to a Vygotsky-style social constructivism.

Contemporary authentic schooling, also within the secular community, behooves schools and their teachers to clearly and unapologetically articulate their belief structures and to demonstrate how these structures are reflected in teaching and learning. Perhaps in a manner that is too strident for contemporary ears, Counts openly encouraged this approach decades ago:

> [It is my firm conviction t]hat teachers should deliberately reach for power and then make the most of their conquest. . . . To the extent that they are permitted to fashion the curriculum and the procedures of the school, they will definitely . . . influence the social attitudes, ideals, and behavior of the coming generation. . . . [I]nstead of shunning power, the profession should rather seek power and then strive to use that power fully and wisely in the interests of the great masses of the people. (Counts 1932, 45)

Neil Postman, in his book *The End of Education*, is a little less strident, but he makes a similar point: not only is neutrality impossible; worldview commitment is a necessary precondition for satisfactory human existence in order that we may be guided through the complexities of life – and teachers have a central plank in helping children to develop it.

Another implication of the recognition by teachers of the non-neutrality of schooling is that they should take a much less passive role in employment interviews. Teachers have a right to know the religious direction that a potential employer desires to be inculcated in their classrooms. They should resist the now-discredited attempts of some appointment committees to insist on secularism as an objective pedagogical style with its associated intolerance towards all alternative perspectives. We have seen already that secularism imposes clear belief structures of its own, and that its so-called tolerance is correctly summarized by D. A. Carson when he says that "The new tolerance is the social commitment to treat all ideas and people as equally right, save for those people who disagree with this view of tolerance" (Carson 2012, 98).

All is not doom and gloom however. When postmodernists (also called radical constructivists in educational jargon) attempt to act consistently with their worldview, their belief that no perspective can claim a universally applicable understanding of truth logically leads to the conclusion that as many perspectives on reality as possible be presented to students so that young people can make their own informed choices. It was the presentation of this argument that in part (there were economic issues as well) convinced a large secular, government university in Australia to allow this author and others for several years to teach undergraduate education courses (including school leadership, curriculum design, and educational philosophy) on campus from a Christian worldview perspective. After all, Christianity is a widespread belief system in the Australian context, and so from a postmodern perspective students deserved the right to be exposed to Christianity and its schooling implications, alongside the other secular and rationalistic belief structures that were taught by tenured professors.

Differing faith perspectives will encourage teachers to apply their beliefs in different ways as they seek to shape the children under their care. Evangelical Christian educators come to this issue with their own clear set of beliefs, which are all-embracing and are self-consciously rooted in Jesus Christ as disclosed to us through biblical revelation. A biblically-shaped understanding of the world and our places and tasks in it is the Christian educator's starting point, and this shapes everything that the Christian teacher does. Christian schooling, defined this way, is all about challenging students with the celebration of the lordship of Christ over all of life. In so doing, students can discover the infinite value of who they are, the wonderfully creative gifts that God has given them in the world, the impact of sin upon everyone and everything, and the all-of-life-impacting redemptive claims of Jesus Christ. They can discover the nature of their various callings in a diverse world that is not random or out of control, but that is upheld moment by moment through God's creative, redeeming, and sustaining power. In its own way, the rest of this book is devoted to exploring the meaning for schooling of this foundational faith perspective.

Implications of the Universality of Religion in Education –
For Students

The primary implication for students of the non-neutrality of schooling is quite clear: schooling will always seek to initiate children into a belief-based understanding of the world. It is as inevitable as it is unavoidable. In totalitarian nations such as North Korea, this occurs overtly rather than covertly. In many democratic nations, because of the widespread misunderstanding of the worldview of secularism, this often occurs covertly more than it does overtly. In both cases indoctrination is occurring as children are taught about the world and their places and tasks in it in the light of particular beliefs about life.

This inculcation impacts students from three main directions:

- firstly, from the teacher since the teacher is the main textbook that the students will read. As Hegeman, Edgell, and Jochemsen (2011, 120) claim, "the moral profile of the teacher is . . . the narrative that the student reads";

- secondly, from the delivery environment of the classroom and school, with its relational and pedagogical structure and priorities; and

- thirdly from the content material of the school's programs. These sources often are shaped by powerful political and economic agendas.

An observable difference between contemporary teens and their predecessors half a century ago seems to be the reduction in idealism today, as expressed in the decline of student protest movements. During the time of the Vietnam War or apartheid South Africa, young people were prominent in public displays of concern. Today, in a context of equally important global issues, such as extreme environmental degradation and the outrageous use of chemical weapons against innocent civilians in the Middle East, the degree of idealistic concern and hope for change is much more diluted among young people. Perhaps the reduction of the purpose of schooling from the concept of the civilized person to pragmatic skill acquisition for employment has something to do with this. Perhaps also, a postmodern perspective that there are no big causes any more because morality is individually determined has also contributed to this malaise. We suggest that these factors are at least in part the consequence of a full flowering of a secularized, self-centered worldview in which many government schools nurture children.

Collins (personal communication, August 2013), the CEO of a

well-respected Christian ethos school, reports that an increasing number of parents who approach him are desperately concerned for their teenagers who seem to have lost all motivation and have succumbed to the fleeting security of drug abuse. Collins asks the young people themselves if they have thought about the future, to which they invariably respond in the negative. "They have no career thoughts, no aims and no ambitions," said Collins. But is it any wonder that this is the case, when these young people (and perhaps some of their parents as well) have been nurtured in a postmodern, media-saturated culture that tells them that there is no such thing as "the future" in any sense other than the prospect of a random, soul-destroying purposelessness? Consequently, the only activity worth engaging in is a narcissistic living for today. As Nike advertisements like to proclaim, "Just Do It!"

The listlessness that results from postmodern moral ambiguity is well expressed in a clever but very sad poem, penned by Edna St. Vincent Millay. It was originally published in 1939 in the shadow of a looming world war. Though these were the decades well before the term "postmodern" had been coined, the poem anticipated postmodernity's forlorn agenda. In the poem, she notes that we live in an age of unprecedented access to information, but in which, according to her, there exists no coherent system of belief to comprehend that information and thus there is no capacity to learn how to be wise. Millay's poem is insightful but tragic. It unwittingly supports the contention that under the domination of a postmodern ethic, the idealism of youth dies prematurely in a sea of apathy and confusion.

> Upon this age, that never speaks its mind,
> This furtive age, this age endowed with power
> To wake the moon with footsteps, fit an oar
> Into the rowlocks of the wind, and find
> What swims before his prow, what swirls behind –
> Upon this gifted age, in its dark hour,
> Rains from the sky a meteoric shower
> Of facts . . . they lie unquestioned, uncombined.
> Wisdom enough to leech us of our ill
> Is daily spun; but there exists no loom
> To weave it into fabric; undefiled
> Proceeds pure Science, and has her say; but still
> Upon this world from the collective womb
> Is spewed all day the red triumphant child.
> (Millay [1939] 1988, 140)

The contrast between the hopelessness of a postmodern approach to life and education as evidenced in the above material on the one hand, and the hopefulness of a Christian approach to life and education on the other, could not be greater. In losing ourselves in Jesus Christ, we find out who we really are. In looking at God's world God's way in the home, church, and classroom, we embrace purpose and meaning, and become participants in communities of grace and truth. As Cooling (personal communication, 22 July 2013) comments, "The gospel message is a vision of what human life could be if lived in the way God intended." It is this perspective that forms the framework for Christian education and that provides the cornerstone for an examination of education in the remaining chapters of this book.

Schools exist to assist parents in the nurture of their children. Therefore, at the time of enrollment, parents should interrogate potential schools to ensure that the faith into which the schools are inducting their children is consistent with that of the home.

Over time, children grow and mature, and develop a faith allegiance of their own. In ways consistent with their unfolding maturity, they too must be given the opportunity to understand the worldview behind their schooling, and also be given the opportunity to assent to it or defect from it.

Though there may be an important place in Christian schools for children from other faith backgrounds, the impact of schooling on children from Christian homes is of special importance in the context of this book. In the light of schooling's non-neutrality and the relativistic faith assumptions of a secular worldview, Christian parents (and their supporters such as grandparents, fellow church-members, etc.) are faced with the dilemma of how to select a nurturing context for their children that shapes them for several hours per day, forty weeks per year, in a manner that is consistent with their own faith perspective and is faithful to the calling from Scripture to bring their children up in the nurture and instruction of the Lord (Ephesians 6:4). It is clear that this would be problematic in a state-controlled secular education system. This is why systematic theologian Louis Berkhof (1990) concluded that, after appropriate deliberation,

> [A Christian] who believes that the child is the image-bearer of God, naturally proceeds on the assumption that that most fundamental truth may not be ignored in any part of his education, *and especially not in his school education.* . . . Can Christian parents reasonably expect their children to be imbued with a spirit of true religion if they persist in sending them to a school where for twenty-four hours per week they are taught in a spirit that is fundamentally irreligious, if not positively anti-Christian? The answer can only be a decided negative. (Berkhof 1990, 33)

An inconsistent witness between the Christian home and the secular government school is one factor contributing to the tragic pattern among many contemporary young people of what Dean (2010) calls the "almost Christian" generation.

Reactionary reasons alone, however, do not make for well-informed choices. There must be a corresponding proactive comprehension of the value and purpose of the Christian faith-based school, where communities of children, teachers, and parents become intoxicated with awe and wonder about God's world and their places and tasks in it, and where young people are compelled by a clear sense of joy and purpose as they become equipped to live hope-filled lives in this world and beyond. These schools provide a radical alternative to their secular counterparts.

As Christians, we respond to Edna Millay by proclaiming that in fact there is a loom to weave it into a fabric – God's all-encompassing story in Jesus Christ! In the Christian school, children may at times become uncomfortable as they look beyond themselves to a God-driven concern for others and for the welfare of the city in which they live (Jeremiah 29:7). Their classrooms also will be centers of academic robustness, hope, purpose, and genuine enquiry based upon a biblically faithful worldview. Humbly, and undoubtedly making mistakes along the way, their teachers will aim to live a Christian worldview in their thinking, speaking, and actions as they interact with students, administration, parents, the curriculum, and society at large. It is to this choice of distinctively Christian education, either in a home setting or, more particularly here, in an institutional school setting, that this book now turns.

A CONCLUDING STORY

> The influential approach that treats religious beliefs as irrelevant clutter in *education* is unhelpful, both because it is unfair and because it is a misunderstanding of the nature of human knowledge. . . . The opposite is true, namely that beliefs, including religious beliefs, are integral to human knowing and therefore education. (Cooling 2010, 37)

Perhaps a little brief true story is the best way to illustrate the point and the urgency of the impact of the myth of neutrality, and of the cause of Christian education. Some time ago, an interview was shown on television between a group of teenage students and the editor of *Forum*, a sex magazine produced in America. Most of the teenagers in the interview came from Christian homes but attended government, secular schools.

At the commencement of the interview, the *Forum* editor asked the teenagers if, as a foundation point for their discussions, they would accept the principle that people should have the right to do what they wanted to do as long as it didn't hurt anyone else. After some thought, the students unanimously accepted this concept, and the discussion proceeded. After a time, they began to discuss issues concerning human sexuality. The editor explained that he had been living in a situation that he termed "open marriage" with a female companion for a number of years. That is, they agreed to live together without making any public marriage commitment to each other, exercising the freedom at times to explore their sexuality with other people.

He said that he and his partner both loved each other and found this relationship to be most suitable. They had no children, and if and when they felt that they should end their relationship, they could split up and go their separate ways without any legal or other complications. He then asked these Christian youngsters to comment upon this situation.

Immediately, several of the young people drew the *Forum* editor's attention to the words of Scripture and the instruction there concerning fidelity and the character of marriage. They did not get very far, however. The editor stopped them and referred them back to the premise that they had all accepted at the beginning about people having the freedom to do what they think is right as long as it doesn't hurt others. If this statement was true, he said, then obviously their Bible was in conflict with it. This apparent inconsistency quickly took on major proportions in the discussion. These Christian youngsters wanted to bring the Word of the Lord to bear in this situation of "open marriage," but they felt unable to do so because it conflicted with the opening assumption upon which they had all agreed. Their dilemma was obvious and painful to watch. They were confused, impotent to speak in a Christian way about the real life situation presented to them.

Why did this conflict arise? It arose because the students accepted the principle of autonomy right at the beginning of the discussion, a principle that is completely foreign to the Scriptural view of humanity. Just what the students *could* have said might be the subject of some discussion, but at this point we need to recognize and accept the real confusion that these young Christians felt. It is a confusion that many others share that all too often over a period of time leads people to be deluded by Satan into thinking that Christianity doesn't speak about the nitty-gritty situations of life.

The core of the problem, as we have noted, is that these youngsters accepted the secular worldview principle propounded by the *Forum* editor at the start of their discussion – that in day-to-day living, we have the right to do whatever we want as long as it doesn't hurt others. This principle is consistent with Rorty's postmodern way of understanding the world, and sounds so tolerant and reasonable. As we now know, a secular education system nurtures children in this autonomous perspective. It doesn't appear to preach against God as such, it just makes him irrelevant when thinking and studying about the world and our places and tasks in it. A key dogma underlying social studies, science, and language studies – to name but a few subjects – is that we need to be considerate, but within this personally-defined constraint, we need not recognize any outside limits or authority upon what we decide to do. True to Dewey's constructivist curriculum principles, we need just to help children create their own view of truth, unfettered by outmoded theistic fallacies.

In other words, humankind is the central point of the world and the sole determiner of what is real and true. Putting it another way, this secular view of the world, which is basic to our state schools, claims that truth is individually determined rather than existing outside of ourselves. Furthermore, this philosophy often subliminally claims that people have the legitimate, autonomous right to implement their own view of truth as long as they allow others to arrive at and work out their ideas of truth as well. As it undergirded the education of the students in the interview, this unspoken, but regulatory principle affirmed that all guides to human conduct are best determined by unfettered human freedom – hence the acceptance of the state-school-educated Christian youngsters of the legitimacy of the *Forum* editor's commencing premise and its application in open marriage. Despite the obvious lessons of history and human nature, it is assumed that if people are simply unshackled from phobias, ignorance, and poverty, then they will make wise, selfless choices that are for the good of all and will lead inevitably to the improvement of the world in which we live.

The Christian view of the nature of human beings, and of the divine origin of laws, rules, norms, and values for human conduct is radically different. This alternative way of understanding the world is founded on the declared, directive, and sustaining power of God, the Creator, and his Word as he upholds his creation. It has as its central point not the blind limitations of human thinking, but the gospel of Jesus Christ in its all-of-life encompassing and discerning fullness. However, the students in the interview had learned to consign this way of thinking to their own private spirituality, having been trained to view God-related concepts as being irrelevant to the real world.

The implications of the unbiblical worldview position in which the students were nurtured in the secular school system are clear. First, it leads youngsters to accept human reasoning as the foundation principle of their lives – an acceptance that ultimately leads to hopelessness and despair. Second, it leads to conflict for those who have been exposed to Christianity because Christianity seems (wrongly) to be an impotent belief system when examined from this perspective. Third, it allows Satan increased opportunity to tempt particularly young Christians to repudiate their Christian faith (Dean's "almost Christian"), as they feel compelled to choose between two apparently mutually exclusive views of life and of life's purpose.

Although we should all feel distress for the Christian youngsters referred to in the above interview, it is a typical outcome of contemporary secular education. The constant, but impossible, call to be "morally neutral" in the classroom is as frequent as a downpour in a tropical rain forest. Yet, surely it's not the desire of Christians to have our own youngsters, who are no different from the ones in the interview, absorb this view of life through their education which leads them away from the Lord and which has them view the world as a place in which Christianity is irrelevant.

There is a better way. As should always be the case, it does not start with us and what we think is right, but with God and what he has revealed to us through Jesus Christ and his Word. With this as our starting point, we will see that authentic Christian nurture means shaping our children to understand and live a worldview that declares that life in its entirety will be lived either in obedience or disobedience to the Lord (not to man) who alone made, redeemed, and continually upholds this world, a world that in all its facets (or subjects, as they are called at school) can, therefore, only be properly understood in relationship to this Creator/redeemer/sustainer God. God is gracious, and all sovereign. He can use even a pagan Pharaoh to do his will, and he certainly can work out his will in secular settings such as the public school where Christian teachers seek to serve him faithfully (see chapter 14). Nevertheless, schools that are dedicated to the lordship of Christ in every aspect remain the primary context in which a discerning, biblical worldview can be systematically nurtured in every subject and in every interaction between students and teachers.

Chapter 2

Foundations of Christian Schooling

THE RELIGIOUS NATURE OF CLASSROOM LAYOUT

What a crazy place to start a chapter about the distinctive characteristics of Christian schooling – by talking about furniture. "Surely religion has nothing to do with furniture layout or classroom design," one might say. But wait, because talking about classroom furniture helps make a key point. A delightful professional development activity for teachers is to place them in groups and then ask them to design their ideal classroom by drawing their design on a large sheet of paper and then sharing it with their colleagues. The results are often very creative and intriguing. Some layouts focus upon a theme – the environment, for example – so that the desks and furniture are arranged with areas like "the reading rain forest," "the coral reef library," and so on. Other designs may group desks in clusters, others placing desks in ordered single rows all facing the front, and still others may arrange the furniture in a double horseshoe with an activity space in the middle. In every case, teachers are thoughtful and deliberate about the process, and they usually enjoy the opportunity to share their plans with fellow educators.

Then comes the crunch: teachers are asked to explain *why* they chose the design that they did. Why did they group the furniture in a certain way? Why did they design the classroom with large windows? Why did they include computers or iPads with internet access? Why did they prioritize wall space for the display of student work? Why did they put the teacher's desk and electronic whiteboard in a central location? As teachers respond to these questions, they begin to express their passionate beliefs about education and the nature of the teaching/learning situation.

It soon becomes very clear that even how furniture is arranged in a classroom is the deliberate result of beliefs and ideas. Some teachers believe that collaborative learning is a key to good pedagogy, so in their designs they grouped desks and children in interactive clusters to facilitate this belief. Others (especially in Asia) believed that good teaching and learning is primarily direct instruction with the teacher being the director and source of knowledge, so they arrange the furniture in individual, solo placements to discourage student interaction and to focus attention on the teacher up front. Still others may be unsure about their preferred pattern and choose to adopt a classroom layout that reflects what they experienced when they were at school or what they were taught was the ideal pattern when they were at teachers training college.

What is the point? The point is that even how furniture is set out in a classroom is not neutral. Whether teachers realize it or not, even furniture placement, or the size of classroom windows, or where and how you design the faculty lounge or school entranceway, these all are the result of the application of a whole set of beliefs and ideas about what makes for good education. Beliefs shape what a teacher understands about the nature of the child, about how children learn, about community and relationships, about abstract versus concrete instruction, about evaluation and assessment, about discipline, about collegiality, about environmental stewardship, and about leadership models, just to name a few examples. Sometimes consciously, and often unconsciously, all of these educational concerns are built upon beliefs that reflect teachers' personal worldviews – their core beliefs or guiding principles of life . . . or their religious commitment.

It could well be argued that classroom designs and furniture placements are acts of worship, embodying the same core faith commitment that is displayed in a school's chapel service or in giving thanks before a meal at a parent-teacher meeting. By their very nature as culture shaping activities, they are declarations of belief about education and are a testimony to the worldview or religious commitment that drives teachers' thinking and living.

Christian parents and teachers want the beliefs that direct education and mold children to be faithful to God as he has revealed himself through his three-fold Word – in Christ, in the scriptures, and in his creation. This requires a renewed and exciting (and at times unsettling) exploration of every aspect of schooling in the light of a Christian worldview.

Imagine the arguments that would occur, for example, if Christian schools stopped trying to measure their teacher salary rates against state schools patterns, and suggested that younger married teachers get paid more (to allow one partner to stay at home and nurture family life) and principals or administrators (who now mostly have paid off their mortgages and have reduced financial liabilities) get paid much less!

In chapter one, we explored the fact that there is no such thing as neutrality, and that every worldview presupposes a certain set of beliefs. Christianity is no exception. While Christianity openly tolerates the existence of other beliefs in society, since God gives to all people the capacity and responsibility to make moral choices, Christianity itself claims exclusivity in being the only pathway to God and the only true basis for understanding the world and our place and task in it. Worthen (2010, 3) reminds us that "Every worldview is predicated on certain founding assumptions, and those of Christianity are incompatible with those undergirding the secular humanist worldview."

The activities of Christian education need to be deliberately Christian, even though the resulting patterns at times may also be held in common with people from other religious faiths. This being the case, in any study of the cause of Christian education, it's a vital preliminary that we clearly understand Christianity's foundational beliefs for education. After reaffirming two defining characteristics of a Christian worldview as they apply to education or schooling, we will turn our attention to exploring vital biblical principles that give direction and meaning to those characteristics.

Defining Characteristics for Christian Education

First Defining Characteristic: *Schooling from a Christian perspective involves challenging children with the celebration of the lordship of Christ over all of creation.*

Second Defining Characteristic: *Christian education does not spend all its time looking at the Son; instead, it looks at the world and our places and tasks in it in the light that the Son provides.*

The glory of the life of a Christian is the realization that there is a Creator God who made the world, sustains it moment by moment through his word of power, who redeemed it in Jesus Christ, who has drawn his people back to himself, and who empowers us to live in this world as creative stewards, to the praise of his glorious grace. That's the fundamental Christian confession and Christians desire it to be the cornerstone for everything that we think, say, and do – including education. Whether we are teachers, parents, board members, or students, *schooling from a Christian perspective involves challenging children with the celebration of the lordship of Christ over all of creation.* That is our first defining characteristic. This purpose statement lies at the heart of this book and each chapter seeks to explore its meaning in particular aspects of the life of a school. It has the goal of ensuring that discussions about everything from the nature of knowledge to understanding curriculum – even including furniture layout – reflects the lordship of Christ and empowers everyone in Christian schools to celebrate God's goodness as they become equipped to serve and honor him in all that they do.

Challenging children with a celebration of the lordship of Christ over all creation as the core responsibility of the Christian school should not be confused with traditional evangelism, which encourages students in a personal faith encounter with Jesus Christ – traditionally known as conversion. It is to be hoped, and openly acknowledged, that all children in a Christian school will come to a saving faith in Jesus Christ, but the school is not an evangelistic hothouse in that sense. Rather, by exploring God's world God's way, the expectation is that the children will understand their creator, themselves, and the world in which they live, in the very best way possible, and become dynamically equipped to function fully and effectively in the world of the twenty-first century. This is true every bit as much for their math, science, and literature classes, as it is for their Bible or social studies classes.

This brings us to our second defining characteristic: *Christian education does not spend all its time looking at the Son; instead, it looks at the world and our places and tasks in it in the light that the Son provides*

A fundamental principle of the Bible is that this world – all of it – was and is God's. He made it, and it declares his glory (Psalm 19). This has dramatic implications for how Christians do education. Douglas Wilson (1991), building on the insights of R. L. Dabney, puts it this way:

> Every line of true knowledge must find its completeness as it converges on God, just as every beam of daylight leads the eye to the sun. [quoted from Dabney. Wilson then continues] The Christian educator's job is not to require the students to spend all their time gazing at the sun. Rather, we want them to examine everything else in the light the sun provides. (62)

Noll (2011), Fernhout (1997), Van Dyk (1985), and Colson and Pearcey (1999) make a similar point:

> The light of Christ illuminates the laboratory, his speech is the fount of communication, he makes possible the study of humans in all their interactions, he is the source of all life, he provides the wherewithal for every achievement of human civilization, he is the telos of all that is beautiful. He is, among his many other titles, the Christ of the Academic Road. (Noll 2011, 22)

> A Christian school is a place where Christian educators refuse to be satisfied with providing only factual knowledge, high exam scores, and marketable skills. Rather, teachers in a Christian school seek to transform all activities and studies into an expression of biblical wisdom, training the

students to walk as disciples of Jesus Christ. (Van Dyk 1985)

The Christian school not only shapes everything that happens within its walls in the light of the biblical story, but it also celebrates the Christian story in the way students are taught to engage the world round them. The students' whole walk of life is to be missionally shaped by their identity as committed followers of Jesus, citizens of His kingdom here on earth. (Fernhout 1997, 75–76, some adaptation by this author)

Many believers fail to understand that Scripture is intended to be the basis for all of life. In the past centuries, the secular world asserted a dichotomy between science and religion, between fact and value, between objective knowledge and subjective feeling. Evangelicals have been particularly vulnerable to this narrow view because of our emphasis on personal commitment. . . . [But] genuine Christianity is more than a relationship with Jesus, as expressed in personal piety, church attendance, Bible study, and works of charity. Genuine Christianity is a way of seeing and comprehending all reality. . . . In every topic we investigate, from ethics to economics to ecology, the truth is found only in relationship to God and his revelation. (Colson 1999, 14–16)

Although dissatisfaction about values or the quality of instruction in other schools may be a factor in leading Christians to choose Christian schooling for their children, Christian schools are not primarily a reaction to what occurs elsewhere. In fact, if the Christian school remains a collection of parents who are disaffected with what they have experienced in other schools, the Christian school has little prospect of being able to carry out its task. The Christian school should primarily be proactive, not reactive. It should be the consequence of a humble and at times uncertain yet determined commitment by Christians to seek to apply the foundations of God's Word for all of life. It is an attempt to be faithful to the calling of bringing up one's children in the nurture and instruction of the Lord (Ephesians 6:4) and to share this wonderful hope with surrounding communities.

Schools of all religious persuasions, Christian, secular, or whatever, provide protective environments, carefully nurturing children in a worldview that reflects each school's aims, objectives, and vision for fulfilled living. To be protective and nurturing of the young is not a bad thing. This is done so that, as they gradually mature, students will grow to be able to function effectively in the less controlled and at times hostile climate of the world at large. Given this proactive and protective context, the rest of this chapter is now dedicated to exploring biblical directions for Christian education that give meaning to the two defining characteristics noted above.

Biblical Directions for Education

Schools are social institutions in which students learn about the world and their places and tasks in it. This widely accepted statement of the purpose of schools was introduced in chapter one. Schools as such are seldom referred to in the Bible. In pre-modern times when literacy, for example, was of much less relevance, formal schooling wasn't seen as being important nor was it available for most children. So, like some other modern institutions (e.g., hospitals), there is no clear picture of a school in the Scriptures. However, God's Word has much to say about the *purpose* of schools. This means that by studying what the Bible says about the world and the place of people in it, we should begin to catch a glimpse of what biblically oriented education is. That is, we won't find much about the term "school" in the Bible, but we will find much concerning what should go on in our schools.

We don't need to start with human philosophies or human wisdom to know what education is about, but we can, and must, start with the Word of God and, as the Holy Spirit interprets it to us, allow the Lord to show us the type of education to which we should expose our children. After all, Christians will one day have to give account to God for how they have carried out the task of bringing up their children in the fear and admonition of the Lord. It behooves all Christians, therefore, to seek his guidance and to give biblically faithful effect to his entrustment in the education of their children. Let us, therefore, examine the Scriptures.

This Is God's World

> The earth is the LORD's, and everything in it,
>   the world, and all who live in it;
> for he founded it on the seas
>   and established it on the waters. (Psalm 24:1–2)

Christians agree that this is God's world. As the Psalmist says, and other Scriptures repeatedly celebrate, the Lord God made the earth and all therein. If we have an education system that proclaims otherwise, or just doesn't say anything about the origins of the earth or people or trees or animals, then it is expressing a religion that is contrary to the Scriptures. If God did make the world, then any knowledge of that world seems to be, at the very least, deficient if it attempts to explain the world apart from God. It is like attempting to bring democracy to the Middle East, for example, without an appreciation of the Middle Eastern peoples and their heritage, and also without understanding the cultural origins,

to preserve the earth for future generations (though this is important), but because people have been given authority to shape and use the earth as God's stewards with a loving accountability to him for how we do it.

The fact that the creation brings glory to God (Psalm 19) is not limited to the so-called natural world. Psalm 104 reminds us that human discretionary creative capacities (part of God's image bearing in us) are also to be employed in such a way as to reflect God's glory. So an aesthetically pleasing and functional computer, a marvelous feat of engineering, a socially constructive economic model, an honorable form of government, a well-written novel, a child's painting, or a student's thesis all have as a core reality (even though their human creators may not recognize it) the task of bringing praise to God. The Christian school should approach its teaching in this light. Maybe we could start in music class by adding a few verses to that wonderful old hymn *How Great Thou Art* and extol the God-honoring wonders not just of trees and rivers, but of good buildings and rightly-used technology as well!

A further aspect of image bearing is the capacity to live in and shape relationships. Christians are not "people of the book" in the way that some other religions can be described. Fundamentally, God has revealed himself to us through his Son, and even the purpose of Christian scriptures is to point us to Jesus (John 5:39–40). True life is not to be found in following rules or written regulations delineated in a sacred text, but in a relationship with God through Christ. Obedience to a moral code is an expression of love for God (1 Thessalonians 1:3), rather than being a means of gaining salvation. Deep relationships modeled upon those demonstrated in the biblical metanarrative, which reflect trust and interdependence, should also characterize relationships within the Christian school – whether they are relationships between students, between students and teachers, between teachers and school leaders, or between teachers and parents. Several authors – for example, Van Brummelen (2009) and Graham (2003) – helpfully explore image-bearing relationships between people in the school community by using the biblical concepts of prophet, shepherdly priest, and king. This perspective will be expanded further in later chapters in this book.

A STUDY OF THE WORLD SHOULD LEAD TO THE PRAISE OF GOD

In Psalm 147 above, the Psalmist doesn't stop at recognizing the Law of God in his world, but he goes on to praise God as a result of this. Verses 1, 12, and 13 of that psalm express this. So, too, does Psalm 104. It is well worth reading the entire psalm. It points toward all the wonderful things that God in his wisdom is doing in his creation. It is full of "o-oohs" and "aahs" over the diversity of God's creatures.

In the same breath, the Psalmist praises God for the cultural and material products that have resulted from humanity's use of the talents that God has given. The writer gazes in awe at the sea around him and also at the human creations (boats) that sail over its surface: "How many are your works, Lord! In wisdom you made them all; . . . May the glory of the Lord endure forever; may the Lord rejoice in his works" (Psalm 104:24 and 31).

We have said that schools are social institutions in which students learn about the world and their places and tasks in it. The Scriptures have shown that such learning about the world should be built upon the evident base that this is God's world, which he has made, redeemed, and sustains – a study that should reflect God the Creator within the context of the actual study, and that should lead to the praise and worship of the God of all the earth. Anything else does not give God his honor and due, and is educating students to serve a god substitute, usually ourselves, since man is seen as the center of things, the determiner of truth, in most education systems today.

The contemporary cultural perspective (be it modern, postmodern, or radical constructivist) in which humanity is encouraged to attempt to usurp God's place is the subject of the compelling book *Hope in Troubled Times* by Goudzwaard, Vander Vennen, and Van Heemst (2007). They conclude that, rather than giving humanity more control, this "modern project" moves the ability to influence events further away from us.

> Clearly there are influences at work, particularly in Western society, which morph into paralyzing and seemingly autonomous powers. By themselves, there is nothing evil about technology, the economy, money, the market, and the exercise of power . . . but the modern project of creating a malleable society, organized to suit our goals, has given them an exalted status. Their enthronement process has gone so far that we begin to see these forces as living, self-propelling powers. We then follow them as gods wherever they go, initially because we expect their progress over time to deliver only good things, but later because we find it difficult to escape their almost hypnotic influence. From that point on, we may feel that the ability to chart our own future has been whisked out of our hands. There seems to be no recourse, no ability to withdraw us from where these dynamic powers and forces could ultimately bring us. And then a sense of betrayal and paralysis creeps in. (Goudzwaard, Vander Vennen, & Van Heemst 2007, 12)

Far be it that Christian schooling should reflect such hopeless powerlessness. Thankfully, God, and therefore Christian schooling, does not leave humanity in despair. Evil is not the sovereign superpower. Its limited authority has been overtaken by the hope of the cross. The explosive assertion of the gospel and the profound privilege of Christian education is to recognize God and humanity in their rightful places and so provide a framework for fulfillment and life – both now on this earth and for eternity in the renewed earth that we will experience after Christ's return.

A Study of the World Should Lead to Salt-And-Light Missional Service

Christians are not called to serve themselves. As a part of sharing the gospel, their service to God includes seeking the welfare of the city in which they live (Jeremiah 29:7). This is what Christians are asking for when we repeat Jesus' words that "your kingdom come, your will be done, on earth as it is in heaven" (Matthew 6:10). Promoting justice, being concerned for the outcast, seeking peace, caring for the environment, creating machines, structures, and symbols that improve society – these gospel tasks exist alongside (and as a part of) the charge to proclaim the need for personal salvation through Christ, which is the kingdom work for every Christian. It is in this sense that writers such as Bartholomew, Goheen, and others rightly highlight Lesslie Newbigin's idea of the missional nature of the gospel. Not just that Christian nurture is aimed at preparing a small, select group of Christians to go and convert the heathen (valuable and worthy as this is), but that Christian schooling has as its goal the nurturing and equipping of all young people, as they respond in faith to Jesus Christ, to live as hope-filled, God-enthroning ambassadors in every aspect of life and culture. Without accepting an Arminian universalist doctrine, Bartholomew and Goheen (2004, 12) make a compelling observation: "The biblical story does not move toward the destruction of the world and our own 'rescue' to heaven. Instead, it culminates in the restoration of the entire creation to its original goodness."

Hekman describes the missional task of the Christian school both inside and outside the school gates this way:

> [Christians] are called to the work of restoring what sin and the Fall have corrupted, including their life together in school. A mission-driven school sees its work in relationship to the ongoing vision of the coming to fullness of the kingdom of God on the earth, completed by Christ's return. A mission-driven school looks outward at the world's need for healing and redemption. A mission-driven school knows that it has God's work to do and is constantly reminding its members . . . that even the young can be a blessing to hurting people. (Heckman 2007, 12–13)

The missional calling of the Christian school may also be described in terms of the cultural engagement calling to be salt and light, which is a recurring theme throughout this book. Jesus referred to himself as the light of the world (John 8:12), but then in the Sermon on the Mount (Matthew 5:13–16) he clearly transfers this concept and its calling to his followers. Teachers first of all teach people, not subjects. They teach children about the world and their place and task in it, so that as students learn about creation and their own giftedness, and as they see their teachers model a Christian understanding of the world and a Christian lifestyle before them, they will come to grasp and be empowered for themselves to bear witness to the lordship of Jesus over every Key Learning Area (KLA) and in every relationship.

The Christian school is not meant to be an introverted, sanctified huddle. As a holy people, as those redeemed in Christ, his followers are called to be the proclaimers of the glory of the gospel of Jesus Christ in all of life – and Christian schools have an important task in equipping God's people for this task: "But you are a chosen people, a royal priesthood, a holy nation, God's special possession, that you may declare the praises of him who called you out of darkness into his wonderful light" (1 Peter 2:9).

Christian education is about the task of preparing young people, whether they become captains of industry or day laborers, to be salt and light in how they think about and understand their vocations, how they approach work and social life, and in how they live in relationship to others around them. The Christian school's task is to equip children to be obedient to Jesus' command: "let your light shine before others, that they may see your good deeds and glorify your Father in heaven" (Mathew 5:16).

The issue of the missional task of the Christian school is reflected in a statement from Redeemer University College (2002) in Canada. Amended to reflect the priorities of this book and the setting of the Christian school, it could read:

> We are called to witness to the victory of Jesus Christ in our whole lives, to make known the good news of God's renewed reign over creation (1 Corinthians 10:31; Colossians 3:17). Since the kingly authority of our risen Lord extends to the whole world, the mission of his people is equally comprehensive: [to teach our children about the world and their places and tasks in it in such a way that we] embody the rule of Christ over marriage and family, business and politics, art and athletics, [science and history,] leisure and scholarship (Matthew 28:18–30; Romans 12). Thus the work of [the Christian school] must be understood as a part of the call of God to

[learn about and] proclaim [the all-of-creation breadth of] the good news of his kingdom; [a kingdom with the exclusive, reconciling cross of Jesus Christ at the centre;] a kingdom which is in our own day both present and yet-to-come. (Redeemer University College, 9)

This could well be a part of the mission statement for any Christian school.

Equipping students winsomely and fearlessly to be able to engage the culture as salt and light for Jesus Christ is no small task, and neither is it without substantial challenges. It calls for a preparedness to be counter-cultural, to face opposition and even mistrust, to be misunderstood and at times ostracized by one's peers. In some contexts, it may even be life-threatening. A classical biblical example is that of Daniel's three friends Shadrach, Meshach, and Abednego, whose countercultural stand against idolatry caused them to be thrown into a fiery furnace (Daniel chapter 3). The White Rose story is another sobering example, this time from the twentieth century.

THE WHITE ROSE STORY

The story of the young Christians who led a non-violent resistance to Adolf Hitler during World War II, and who were brutally guillotined by the authorities for their cultural engagement and their faithfulness to God, reminds us of the potential cost of Christian salt-and-light disciple-ship that we are calling our students to embrace in Christian schooling. A number of Christian young people in Hitler's Germany, and some non-Christians too, shared a common social conscience, and they came to-gether in what became known as the "White Rose" group. They initiated a letter-writing campaign, in which they stood up for truth and justice in the face of the Nazi oppression of Jews and other minorities. These young people were put on trial for their "traitorous" activities of writing letters protesting government injustice, and several were executed. For many of the White Rose martyrs, it was their primary allegiance to Christ and the value that Christians are called upon to place on all human life that led these young people to act in such a counter-cultural manner. In their show trial, they were accused of being unpatriotic, and of not conform-ing to socially acceptable patterns of behavior and belief, and so they were condemned to death and pitilessly executed in the prime of their lives.

The story of Sophie Scholl and her White Rose friends is hauntingly told in the movie *Sophie Scholl: The Final Days*. A viewing of the movie, an examination of resources relating to the White Rose story available on the internet, a discussion of these young people's worldview and motivation in the face of apathy and injustice, with an eye to drawing lessons for Christian cultural engagement today (e.g., how do we respond to the contemporary situation concerning asylum seekers or the lack of access by some to basic medical care), should be a mandatory case study for all senior classes in Christian high schools and in biblically-grounded worldview courses at Christian universities.

Salt-and-light discipleship is not cheap. In human terms, it may be very costly.

Christian cultural engagement is not an alternative to the gospel. It is a part of the gospel. It should never become the Kuyperian secularism that Jamie Smith (2013b) quite rightly warns against. It is a proactive and winsome calling for all Christians that delight in the majesty of God over his creation and the creative and stewardly lordship that he has given to humankind over the world. And it places the cross of Christ at the center of all of life. Christian schools seek to prepare students for this type of cultural engagement. Horton (1992) puts it this way:

> [When] we return to the rich soil of Scripture, which takes this world very seriously (both in its created and fallen reality), we have the potential not only to prepare the way for a new generation of Christian leadership in the culture, but to prepare the way for a renewed interest in the gospel as well. (Horton, 2009, para. 36)

A BIBLICAL VIEW OF WISDOM AND KNOWLEDGE

All parents hope that their children at school will come to know what is the wise and proper way to understand our world. Here, too, the Scriptures clearly show that any wisdom or knowledge gathered apart from the Lord is not telling the full story. Since we are all made in God's image, a secular attempt to know wisdom apart from God will have some insights into what is real and true, and Christians should willingly and discerningly study all scholarship, whatever the worldview of its author. Ultimately, however, secular scholarly endeavor provides only a partial explanation of the world and is an incomplete guide for students as to how they should live in the world. This is because it attempts to explain things from the perspective of autonomous human reasoning and independent of God's revelation in Christ, in the Scriptures, and in creation. The declaration of the Christian is that in Jesus Christ "are hidden all the treasures of wisdom and knowledge" (Colossians 2:3).

Psalm 110:10 and Proverbs 1:7 remind us that "The fear of the LORD is the beginning of knowledge. . . ." This means that the foundation of true wisdom is nothing less than bowing in our hearts in a humble fear of the Lord. Education that is not founded on commitment to the Lord is bound to be distorted.

Many will agree that God's Word contains wisdom and knowledge for one's *spiritual* life, but hardly for the day-to-day living in the world of the home, commerce, industry, politics, or schooling. Surely, it is claimed, one will not find wisdom in the Bible for the study of athletics, reading, home economics, or the computer, for example. We have already begun to address this issue in the section above, and will return to it in the next chapter on human knowing when we will consider the origins and impact of dualism. However, at this point, it is again fruitful to briefly refer to the Scriptures.

Consider the examples of Joseph (Genesis 41 and 47) and Bezalel (Exodus 31:1–5). As the late Rev. Alan Kerr liked to remind his parishioners, both men were said to have their wisdom from the Lord. However, this was not just "spiritual" wisdom. Joseph had wisdom to run a food conservation program that carried Egypt and the surrounding countries through a seven-year famine. Bezalel had artistic crafting skills to build the curtained shrine of the Israelites in the desert. Also consider Daniel and his friends, of whom it was said, "God gave [them] knowledge and understanding of all kinds of literature and learning" (Daniel 1:17). Then there was the promise of Jesus to give his followers wisdom in speech, which their detractors would be powerless to contradict (Luke 21:15). In none of these examples is wisdom, insight, or ability limited just to a so-called other-worldly, spiritual idea.

Therefore, contrary to much of today's thought (even among Christians), the Scriptures testify that all true knowledge and wisdom can only fully be found in the context of a heart commitment to Jesus Christ. Any learning by teachers or their students about the world and their place in it that is attempted apart from this context will be much less than satisfying. Remember the second principle at the start of this chapter: *Christian education does not spend all its time looking at the Son; instead, it looks at the world and our places and tasks in it in the light that the Son provides.*

The Christian community is called to be obedient to the Word of the Lord in all of life. The challenge is that we not be deluded by the false neutrality claims of what is predominantly a humanist, self-serving, God-dishonoring, public education system, despite the vital salt-of-the-earth witness of many Christian teachers in these schools. Christians are called to consider all things, including the education of their children, in terms of the Word of the Lord and obedience to his will. As Paul said in his letter to Christians in Rome, "Do not conform to the pattern of this world, but be transformed by the renewing of your mind. Then you will be able to test and approve what God's will is – his good, pleasing and perfect will" (Romans 12:2–3). Paul leads the way (Philippians 1:9-11) in reminding us (teachers and parents) that the capacity to "discern what is best" is one of the primary goals of Christian nurture.

THE ROMANS 14 PRINCIPLE

If education is not neutral, may anyone demand that Christians must either homeschool or send their children to a Christian school? By no means! Although such a position may be(come) the strong *conviction* of individual parents, which they adopt for their own children and explain passionately to others, there is no biblical warranty to condemn other believers for taking alternative positions. Instead, on disputable matters such as this, about which there is no direct biblical pronouncement, the faithful calling is for Christians to remonstrate together in love, so that each parent can be convinced in their own mind of the faithfulness of their chosen position.

Francis Schaeffer used to remind his listeners about the difference between biblical proclamations, such as the divinity of Jesus or the fact that Jesus is the only mediator between God and humanity, and convictions, regarding, e.g., issues such as baptism or the vagaries of some eschatological beliefs. Both claim faithfulness to Scripture, but only the former have the status of pronouncements that are universally binding on all Christians. The latter represent diverse but firmly held conclusions/interpretations based on their reading of the Bible as to what it means to think and live faithfully in the area under discussion. Their commitment to Christian education falls into this category.

Although the Bible has much to say about nurturing our children, there is no commandment or edict in God's Word that says, "You shall send your children to Christian schools." Of course, many Christians have reached this conclusion, but it is a response that they arrive at as they seek to understand and apply the Bible to all of life, not an explicit requirement of God's people that can be supported by chapter and verse. In a spirit of appropriate epistemic humility, proponents of Christian education need to admit that their interpretation of scripture to support Christian schooling is a fallible, human response to God's Word and should not be given the same universal timelessness as the Word itself.

In his letter to Christians in Rome, Paul provides a great example of how Christians should deal with important but divisive issues that seem at least to some not to be clear in Scripture. Paul commences his comments by encouraging Christians not to be divided about disputable matters (Romans 14:1). Instead, he exhorts Christians to study the Word so that they can know what they believe and the foundations for it, as they ultimately will be called to give account to God for the choices that they have made. He illustrates his contention by talking about unclean food (and elsewhere he discusses food offered to idols in the same way). His point is that he himself has a strong personal conviction (that it's okay to eat such food), but not one that he wants to force upon others. Once again, the key point is not that we all agree, but that we know what we believe regarding divisive non-core faith matters; that we know why we believe it; that we are accountable to God for what we believe; and that we should not let these beliefs fracture the body of Christ.

Therefore, it is not permissible to say that the only faithful response on the divisive issue of education is the construction that demands that all Christians choose Christian schooling for their children. However, neither is it acceptable to just follow the crowd. The calling is to pray, study the scriptures, and meditate deeply about the matter – leading to a course of action that one can explain from a biblically faithful perspective. The focus of the discussion between Christians on any side of the argument about Christian schooling is not "You are wrong and I am right." Rather it should be:

> This is an important issue. I have reached a certain position that is a construction based upon my understanding of scripture. Your construction seems to have led you to a different conclusion. Let's discuss the matter in Christian love because I might be mistaken (or you might be). Let's firmly but humbly share how our understanding of God's Word has led us to our conclusions, and let's have as the goal of our discussions and fellowship the desire to see each of us live and nurture our children more faithfully before the Lord every day.

However much some Christians committed to Christian schooling might like to say so, it is inappropriate to insist that Christian schooling is the only way. Rather, they could remind their friends of things like the non-neutrality of education and of Jesus' comment that, "The student is not above the teacher, but everyone who is fully trained will be like their teacher" (Luke 6:40). Next, they can invite their friends to visit a local Christian school, read books such as this one in the light of the Word of God, and then remonstrate with them to help them determine for themselves what is a faithful response before the Lord in the nurture of children.

The Message in the Report Cards

One measure of the degree to which a Christian school has been able to apply this perspective may be found in the tone and priorities of a school's report card system. For example:

- Do these notifications of progress that are sent home to parents reflect a competitive or a collaborative spirit?

- Do they focus on ranking and grades, or is effort (or how a child's gifts are actually being used) given a significant place?

- Is there a formative as well as a summative character to the document?

- Does the report card encourage or inhibit interaction between school, student, and home?

The best measure of the faithfulness of a Christian school lies in its graduates. They are its *living* report cards. The witness of young people graduating from a Christian school should be able to go beyond being thankful for caring and trustworthy teachers – many teachers in secular schools could be commended for the same qualities. Listen to Christian school graduates. As they share more deeply about what they have learned about themselves and this world, in the light of God's revelation, you should hear how this has been equipping them to view all of life through a biblically faithful worldview, and has been preparing them as Christ's ambassadors for the challenges of a pluralistic and largely secular culture.

Conclusion

This chapter has identified some of the key foundations upon which genuine Christian education must be based. It identifies core Christian worldview propositions that are derived from Scripture and that should be the ultimate guide for the decisions at every Christian school Board of Governors meeting, in every principal's office, at every Parent-Teacher Association meeting, in every faculty lounge, in every student counseling session, and in every school classroom. Though student outcomes are never certain or guaranteed, the following list of goals suggests outcomes in the lives of students that might reasonably be anticipated (and prayed over) as a consequence of becoming involved in Christian schooling:

Christian schooling seeks to equip students in the following ways:

- Challenge them with a celebration of the lordship of Christ over all of life (a response to the First Commandment [Exodus 20:3; Deuteronomy 6:5], the Greatest Commandment [Matthew 28:37–39; Luke 10:27; 1st question in Westminster Shorter Catechism).
- Equip them to be constructive, involved salt-and-light citizens for the good of society, enabling them to engage culture constructively for Christ, as his agents of shalom.
- Provide students with a joyful life-long passion for thinking and learning.
- Instilling in them discerning capacities so that they are able to identify the personal, cultural, intellectual, and economic idolatries of contemporary post-Christian culture (Keller, 2009).
- Develop in them godly wisdom to help them make wise choices in life – vocation, relationships, recreation, etc., thus enabling them to be creative and faithful exponents of the cultural mandate as worthy stewards.
- Deepen their own personal relationship with Jesus Christ and their grasp of the vast extent of the glory and impact of the gospel, now and for eternity.
- Look at God's world God's gospel-centered way by approaching every curriculum area from a biblically faithful worldview perspective.
- Discover and develop their own gifts and talents in a God-honoring, hope-filled, interdependent way.
- Enable children to use their intellect to the fullest and be well prepared for future academic options according to their ability.
- Learn in a safe, compassionate, rigorous, expansive, discovery, nurturing, and supportive Christian environment.
- Be provided with Godly mentoring examples.
- Learn how to deal with sin and blessing, and failure and success, in themselves, their peers, and their teachers, in a God-honoring manner.
- Mix with peers from homes with similar values and goals (1 Corinthians 15:33).
- Mature into discerning citizens and wise parents themselves.
- Know how to critique and respond faithfully to the beguiling worldviews and gods of our age (technology, sex, secular humanism, economic rationalism, etc.).
- Become equipped to be godly in every vocation and calling and defend truth.
- Be strong and articulate in understanding and defending their faith.
- Operate in support of, and partnership with, the home and the church.

A significant event occurred at a Christian college in the United States in July 2013, which confirms the strategic importance of Christian schools being deliberate and overt in the Christian foundation of their salt-and-light cultural engagement; for many secular institutions also encourage their students to be involved in social improvement activities. In this case, Wheaton College reframed its conceptual framework for its teacher education program so as to ensure that its call for students to be "agents of change" and promoters of "social justice" was not a reflection of secular perspectives but was firmly rooted in the person and work of Jesus Christ. The revision also called faculty to embody justice in their own lives as examples to their students. Roys (2013) reflects that the new document, "instead of drawing on Marxist models . . . points to Christ. . . . Jesus exemplified justice by respecting all people; welcoming the poor, objecting to unjust practices; and recognizing individual responsibility" (Roys 2013, 1).

A particularly moving and encouraging reflection about the Christian school experience was penned by Mr. Glenn Oeland in May 2012. His daughter was just about to graduate from a Christian high school and was preparing to go to university for the next step in her education. Oeland's letter reeks of the hopes – and fears – of most Christian parents, and it reflects poignantly upon the blessings and sacrifices of Christian schooling. Oeland has given permission for his powerful letter to be included as Appendix One in this book. The author encourages all Christian parents and students to turn to it, read it aloud, and discuss its contents – with a box of paper tissues at hand!

Chapter 3

Why We Think The Way We Do

THE PERVASIVE PROBLEM OF DUALISM

Education is concerned with shaping the intellect or the patterns of the mind, so as to give direction to how we act and live. Early in this book therefore, it is appropriate that attention is given to the forces that have shaped twenty-first century patterns of thinking, followed by some initial reflections upon the contours of a biblically-informed pattern of thinking that points to the exciting concept of reformed critical realism.

Chapter One of this book suggested that a primary reason for the pervasiveness of the myth of neutrality in education has to do with the way that many contemporary people think about things – or perhaps, because of our cultural conditioning, how we *don't* think about things. Dualism is charged with being the intellectual construct that is at the heart of this error.

Dualism is an approach to the world that suggests that matters relating to faith, opinion, and emotion are subjective and not based on facts and so exist in the realm of individual belief, religion, and private conviction. These are "sacred" matters and have little place in the public realm. On the other hand, however, it is argued that "secular" things such as science, observation, and rationality are sensual, measurable, and objective and so can be held to be examined and found to be true or false by scientific investigation in a manner that makes the findings valid for everyone. The sacred area of faith or religiosity is personal and is not considered to be an appropriate component of the curriculum for state schools. The secular realm is observable and provable and so, like reading, writing, and arithmetic, is religiously neutral and provides the proper type of material that can be studied in schools without reference to the faith-based qualitative notions of the sacred area. That is dualism or what some call the sacred – secular divide.

Dualism is a component of worldview. Worldview is our way of seeing and being in the world. The first chapter raised the issue of worldview and its impact on education. Our purpose here is to consider why we think the way that we do, which as we will see is grounded in dualism – a perspective that is wrong in concept and in substance, and which has given rise to contemporary worldviews among Christians that allow many to erroneously dismiss the claims and impact of non-neutrality in education.

One of the key challenges in confronting dualism is the fact that most people are unaware that they hold to this philosophical position. To them, the way they think is "just the way things are" – it is one's natural way of doing things, the result of neither calculation nor effort, but just the natural order of things. We intend to examine this fallacy in this chapter – that "the way things are" is somehow unplanned and devoid of faith foundations. These ideas have been explored elsewhere (Edlin 2006b; Goheen & Bartholomew 2008), but it is important to review them here since they play such an important part in shaping how Christians understand (and misunderstand) the cause of Christian education.[1]

So then, why do we think the way that we do? In one sense, this may seem to be a silly question. "We just do!" one might be tempted to respond. But that is not the case – we don't just do. How we think (which is an important governor in what we think) is not a neutral, naïve activity. It reflects particular powerful beliefs about the world and our place and task in it. It is a rich and complicated process, developed and honed over centuries of reflection, conditioning, and reinforcement. As Kanitz (2005) has commented, in our thinking "We are starting with [an unacknowledged] densely populated intellectual ground with various worldviews firmly entrenched and others competing for space" (105). The fact that we today are largely unaware of this only adds to its power and authority over us.

A RUGBY EXAMPLE

Let's start with an illustration from the sport of rugby union. My friend Ken was a rugby union player in his youth. In those days in the last century, Don Clark was a great fullback in New Zealand's famous All

---

1   It also should be noted that the contents of this chapter relate primarily to Western patterns of thinking. This is because classical Western philosophy, from its Greek origins, through the Renaissance, the Enlightenment, and on to postmodernity, has been a primary shaper of contemporary thinking patterns. When translated in other languages, it might be appropriate to replace this chapter with material more reflective of those cultures' philosophical heritages. For example, in Asia discussion of the historical development of thinking patterns and their educational consequences would need to focus on the very strong shaping influence of Confucianism and neo-Confucianism. This would be a very worthwhile discussion, but it is beyond the parameters of this English-language chapter.

Black rugby team. Clark typified for Ken and every contemporary rugby player what effective goal kicking looked like. Clark would line himself up on the ball, pause, and then run straight in and kick the ball over the goalposts and lead his New Zealand team to yet another inevitable victory over the hapless Wallabies team from Australia. In those days, no-one thought to question Clark's style. The way he did it was the way good goal kicking was done. That's just the way it was.

Today, rugby goal kickers use a substantially different kicking style. Kickers run in onto the ball from an angle (called round-the-corner kicking). However much Clark is revered in the twenty-first century as one of the greats of rugby history, someone using Clark's kicking style today would be laughed out of the stadium. Today, ask any rugby-playing youngster how to kick a good goal, and he'll show you round-the-corner kicking. There is no question. That's how it's done. That's the natural way. That's the way things are.

How did this change come about? The answer is that at some forgotten point in the past, someone stopped assuming that the way Clark kicked was the way things were. Someone recognized that the Clark style was based on a set of assumptions about ball kicking that could be challenged and even replaced by a superior style based upon different assumptions.

Can you see the link between this analogy and an exploration of why we think the way we do? In order to inhabit the mind field in an authentic Christian manner, which exposes dualism and the myth of neutrality, we need to recognize, critique, and biblically ground the formative influences that shape how we think. As we do this, our response to why we think the way we do will not be "because that's the way things are." Neither will it be because of an unconscious but idolatrous commitment to Greek beliefs or beliefs of any other pagan philosophical epoch. Instead, we will work at shaping the foundations of why we think the way we think, and formulate the educational processes that are a product of this thinking, as the fallen and humble yet genuine and dynamic reflections of the character and mind of God.

A Biblical Calling to be Made New in our Minds

As we seek to bring every thought into captivity to Jesus Christ (2 Corinthians 10:5), God's Word urges us, as an act of worship to God, to be much more deliberate and vigilant in proactively reforming patterns of the mind including why we think the way that we do. In his letter to his friends in Colossae, Paul urged them not to be led astray by ideas and thought-patterns based on human ideas, but to base their ideas and thought-patterns on the revelation of Jesus Christ, through whom all things hold together (Colossians 1:8). Paul also urged his readers to work hard at not being conformed to the prevailing secular culture, but to be "transformed by the renewing of your mind" (Romans 12:1–2).

Finally, consider what Paul said when writing to Christians in Ephesus, that city already famous in Paul's day for great philosophers like Heraclitus. Paul challenged them to be different from the licentious and hedonistic individualism of their culture and to be like Jesus, highlighting his underlying thesis that being born again into Christ has as one of its foundation stones "to be made new in the attitude of your minds" (Ephesians 4:17–5:2).

It's crucial that we recognize the often subliminal religious assumptions inherent in why we think the way that we do. We don't consciously think about breathing, but we take several breaths each minute to sustain our bodies. Similarly, we don't usually think about how we think; yet how we think (i.e., why we think the way we do) gives form and structure to our mental processes that enable us to comprehend, discern, and interact with the world in a coherent manner.

As Christians, we seem to have failed to realize that the impact of putting ideas together may have led us to exclude biblically informed perspectives from our core decision-making. It may also be leading Christian educators to function antithetically to the very gospel that they believe. Sadly, Harry Blamires (1963, 69) comment of several decades ago still haunts Christians in education today: "We are observing the sly process by which the Christian mind de-Christianizes itself without intending to do so."

The Western Mind

What is this contemporary Western mind that is at the core of shaping our thinking? Tarnas (1991) equates "Western mind" with "worldview." Although that is helpful, "worldview" extends the notion beyond the more limited concept of cognition, which is the focus here. The term "Western mind" could usefully be considered to be the dynamic, cumulative amalgam of specific thoughts, ideas, and cognitive processes that have gained credence through the epochs of human history, progressing from ancient Greece, through Christianity, the medieval period, the renaissance and modernity, and onto the postmodernity of the twenty-first century.

Although the definition of the western mind offered above is helpful, for the Christian it remains incomplete. Philip Jackson's (1992, 12) comment that even our definitions are a part of our argument serves to remind us that definitions also are not neutral or objective, but are philosophically laden expressions of a particular point of view. For the Christian engaging cautiously in the world of ideas, our understanding must be embedded within a Christian frame of reference. To live and move and have our being in Christ means that we declare that our understanding of thinking, and why we think the way that we do, unashamedly reflects a Christian bias just as the reflections of writers from other faith perspectives such as Islam or secular humanism should reflect their biases. As Kok (1998, 23) has commented, analysis follows assumptions and confessions, and not the other way around.

To be consistent then, Christian educators seeking to understand the concept and implications of why we think the way we do in the Western world will attempt to embed their reflections within a Christian worldview. This chapter introduces the development of western philosophy in that context. Other authors such as Bartholomew and Goheen (2013) have developed these ideas at more depth but still in a very readable and decisive manner. For our part, we need to ensure that our brief reflection in this chapter does not conclude without at least an introductory attempt to explore the contours of a Christian response to a Western understanding of the life of the mind.

We start, therefore, with an acknowledgment of the creative and sustaining authority of the eternal God of the Bible over all that is. We recognize that human beings, though created perfect, marred God's creation by sin and have thus contaminated every aspect of reality (including thinking and culture). Wonderfully, and in a preordained manner, God, by the incarnation and substitutionary sacrifice and resurrection of Jesus Christ, provided a way for the world (including humanity) to be reconciled to himself. This in turn provides those who accept it with the dynamic to live now and for eternity in a personal relationship with this Creator-sustainer God as we celebrate his lordship over everything – including mental processes.

Great philosophers such as Socrates, Plato, and Aristotle discovered valuable insights from which we can learn. However, in that they did their thinking outside of a creaturely submission to the God of the Bible, their discoveries were distorted and tended to elevate one aspect of the creation (rationality, for example) to the position of ultimate authority, which belongs to God alone. This means that in our analysis of their thinking Christian educators must recognize the pre-existing and idolatrous cultural commitments of these pagan philosophers and critique their reflections accordingly.

FOCUS ON GREEK OR HELLENISTIC TRADITIONS

Many strands are woven together in the fabric that shapes why we think the way we do in the contemporary West. Because of their singular importance, the discussion in this chapter is limited to the heritage of the Greeks, and especially Socrates, Plato, and Aristotle, and the re-emergence of some of their ideas in the neoplatonic period. Although there are other vital subsequent intellectual streams such as the Renaissance, the Enlightenment, modernity, and postmodernity, they will not be discussed here. A succinct and useful overview of the place of these forces in shaping our contemporary thinking can be found in an article by Goheen (2004) in *Pointing the Way: Directions for Christian education in the new millennium*, and in a more extended manner in the book, *Christian Philosophy: A systematic and narrative introduction* (Bartholomew & Goheen 2013).

EARLY HELLENISTIC THINKING

The centuries of Homer, with his anthropomorphic view of the gods (ascribing to them human form, characteristics, and behavior), are often described as the pre-dawn of Western thought. In this period, up until around the fifth century BC, myth and legend merged into reality. This is well captured in the *Iliad* and the *Odyssey*, which Tarnas (2010) describes as "a collective primordial vision" (24). Yet, at this time, powerful intellectual forces began to appear on the stage of human history that have enduring influence today. Democritus (460–370 BC) gave us atomic theory and perhaps provided Plato 150 years later with a platform from which to develop his powerful two-worldly perception of reality (dualism). Pythagoras (582–507 BC) helped us to understand mathematical forms. Parmenides (510 BC–c. 450 BC) asserted the primacy of logic as the determiner of reality. Heraclitus (535–475 BC) recognized the uncertainty caused by change in the world but, using language similar to that of the apostle John in John chapter 1, claimed that behind that uncertainty was a rational, fiery, ordering power of the universe called the *logos*.

We should also remember the sophists and orphics who were important during this classical Greek period. The individualistic sophists reduced the purpose of debate from determining truth to the mere winning of an argument (hence the derogatory use of the term sophistry today). The incipient dualism of the orphics had a great influence on Plato and subsequent Western thought.

THE SCHOOL OF ATHENS (RAPHAEL C. 1511)

Although the aforementioned people and movements are important, there are three giants of Greek thought who have had the most enduring impact on why we think the way that we do in the modern Western world. These men are Socrates, Plato, and Aristotle. They are all depicted in Raphael's 500-year-old mural in the Vatican. At the request of Pope Julius II, the young Raphael Sanzio painted a fresco originally entitled *Knowledge of Causes* but which has been known to posterity as *The School of Athens*. The panorama (depicted below) was an attempt to bring into one place many of the famous Greek sages – even though they did not all live at the same time. Raphael also used his imagination to embellish historical records in depicting the physical appearances of his subjects (it is suggested, for example, that Heraclitus in the picture was given the face of Raphael's contemporary, Michelangelo).

The painting provides a convenient platform from which to launch a brief discussion of the central figures from Greek culture who have equipped us (for better and for worse) in the twenty-first century to think the way that we do. Raphael left no chart by which to name his assembled figures. However, by their various actions and activities in the painting, many can be identified. Socrates, Plato, and Aristotle can be recognized conclusively.

After reading this chapter, readers might like to identify our three philosophers in Raphael's picture, using the comments made about each of them in this chapter. A colored version of *The School of Athens* can be viewed on many sites on the internet.

THE INFLUENCE OF SOCRATES (C. 469–399 BC)

Most of what we know about Socrates we know through Plato, a disciple of Socrates, and the one who recorded Socrates' wisdom in his own dialogues. For Socrates, the best way to ascertain the truth of assumptions or opinions was to challenge them with a constant stream of questions, which frequently exposed the assumptions to be ignorance masquerading as wisdom. Socrates' view was that "to know virtue . . . one has to take apart, analyse, test the worth of every statement . . . in order to find its true character" (Tarnas 2010, 34). For Socrates, once one had pursued an idea vigorously enough through this technique, then insight would be attained and correct thinking and living would be the consequence. His questioning style, imbued as it was with a genuine desire to seek after truth, was not universally endorsed, particularly by some in positions of power. Ultimately, it led Socrates to be put on trial for perverting the thinking of the youth of his day. He was convicted and condemned to die by drinking a mixture laced with deadly hemlock.

Socrates' style of critical skepticism, called the Socratic method or Socratic dialectic, lives on today in the popularity of asking questions of students as a pathway to greater understanding. In pedagogical circles, we contrast direct instruction (not in vogue in the West) with the Socratic method, which is deemed to inspire the enquiring mind, give students ownership in the learning process, and help lead to an improved and more enlightened position in everything from scientific enquiry to the causes of events in history. Though frequent questioning is seen as a blight on education in some other non-Western cultures, the Socratic method is so important in Western education that whole courses in Bachelor of Education degrees are devoted to equipping teacher trainees with effective questioning skills and strategies so as to keep them from falling into the trap of continuous direct instruction. A classroom is not considered to be a good classroom unless individual children are encouraged and empowered to question as an integral part of their learning activities. This is not only true of the student. Teachers are encouraged to consider themselves to be reflective practitioners, which involves the responsibility of questioning one's own understanding and delivery style. The concept of formative evaluation as opposed to summative evaluation is predicated on teachers being reflective interrogators of their own teaching styles and content.

At this point, we are not evaluating the merits of the Socratic method. The intention here is to show that our thinking about what makes good teaching and about why we think that questioning is a good practice is not neutral or intuitive. It is not just the way things are. It is a particular individualistic pedagogical tradition and approach that is deplored in some cultures but lauded in our own, and is a heritage from the teaching and learning style made popular by Socrates. This is why Raphael in his great fresco shows Socrates remonstrating or arguing (look at the use of his hands).

THE INFLUENCE OF PLATO (C. 427–347 BC)

Plato is at the center of Greek thought. He is the father of modern dualism. He focused his thinking on the search for truth. However, he believed that it was impossible to discover this elusive reality in the imperfect and constantly changing environment of the world in which we live. The inconstant material world and our experience of it cannot be trusted. We must seek the pure form of truth in the unadulterated world of ideas or forms. We must look elsewhere, into the world of ideas, wherein exists the true reality of the forms of things that we experience in everyday life. This is why Raphael shows Plato in the fresco pointing upward, out of our own tainted, experiential situation. Furthermore, since the unseen but perfect or ideal world of ideas is the really true world, then true knowledge is theoretical knowledge, and true wisdom is the process of disengaging ourselves from the world of experience and rigorously searching for the reality that is beyond.

Two illustrations help us to comprehend Plato's position. When initially drafting this chapter, the author was looking over beautiful Lake Tarawera in New Zealand, with its majestic and currently inactive volcano looming in the background. Consider the boats that he could see in the small boat harbor in the foreground. He could see many kinds of boats: big, little, fat, sleek, fast, slow, white, red, and so on. But which one is the real boat? Plato's answer would be that none of them are. They all embody some of the realities of what it is to be a boat, but none of them is the real, perfect boat. The real, perfect form of a boat doesn't exist in the world of experience, but only in the world of ideas. Therefore, to find what it is to understand a real boat, we need to elevate our thinking from the inadequacy of experienced reality and contemplate the world of ideas – a serious and challenging task. Only then will we truly be able to understand the essence or unchanging idea or form of the boat, from which all experienced boats are derived, but of which they all are an inadequate image.

The second illustration is the famous allegory of the cave that Plato himself relates in *The Republic*. In this witty story, which anticipates in a way Orwell's *Animal Farm*, Plato tells of unenlightened people who have spent their entire lives imprisoned in a cave and who are only able to face the cave's back wall. The light of a fire projects shadows of the outside world onto the back wall. Because of their position and ignorance, the pathetic prisoners mistake the hazy shadow on the wall for the glorious reality that exists outside the cave. They spend their energies seeking to understand the shadows, rewarding those who are best at describing their form and predicting their appearance, while all the time ridiculing any suggestion of a fuller reality that exists beyond the shadows. If only they could look the other way! In Plato's analysis, our world of experience is the paltry world of shadows and real wisdom involves seeing with the mind beyond this shadowy den to the fullness of the world of ideas where one can find the real ordering principles of life.

Because real knowledge is found in this other world of ideas, and therefore knowledge and activities limited to interaction with this present world are inferior and of less value, Plato further argued that those few who engaged in the cognitive journey beyond the temporal world towards real truth could be regarded as philosopher-kings. They were worthy of elevated status and respect, and must share their wisdom with others. They also were the best choices for positions of power since they had the required insights to rule for the greater good of the rest of humanity.

The concept today that education, which informs the mind of possibilities beyond current knowledge and experience, will lead to the betterment of the individual and of society is a legacy of Plato. It is so pervasive that we can scarcely imagine education any other way. We believe that as the world of ideas in the classroom raises their horizons and understandings to better and more extended possibilities for living all children will be able to live and act in a more appropriate and fulfilling way. The perspective that intellectual pursuits and the study of ideas (white collar work) is fundamentally a better thing to do than manual labor (blue collar work) is also a product of platonic thinking. Therefore in schooling we often discourage intellectually gifted teenagers when they think about taking up an apprenticeship and counsel them to stay on at school and go to university and "so have a more fulfilling life." At least in part, our thinking is reflecting and reinforcing Plato's dualistic and hierarchical superiority of the cerebral exploration over more manual vocations.

Teaching students to engage in original thinking is considered to be a good thing in Western classrooms, and is at the core of platonic or idealist pedagogy. According to Ozmon (2012), good platonic teachers would be defined as those who encourage their students to think morally and independently, and who consider ideas and truth beyond what they see, not just limiting investigation to the minutiae of any particular situation or data set.

Neoplatonism

Although misplaced in terms of chronological order, it is appropriate at this point to consider neoplatonism, which was the re-emergence of platonic thinking from the third to the fifth century AD. With Plotinus (a Roman philosopher) as its principal protagonist, neoplatonism focused on Plato's two-world dualism and on the concept of a "mystical other" as the controlling force in the superior world of the upper realm. This Absolute Good was the transcendent removed reality from which emanated the lower, baser world inhabited by human beings. Neoplatonism continued the platonic priorities for education. It also gave the Christian church a dualistic or dichotomous view of nature and grace, which viewed the present world as inherently evil – something from which to be delivered at the return of Jesus when all Christians will be translated from the present dark world to the new perfect world somewhere else in the hereafter. This set of eschatological assumptions, reinforced and brought into the church with an Aristotelian bent by Thomas Aquinas, is a lingering infection that continues to poison much of contemporary Western Christianity.

Aristotle (484–322 BC)

"In his lifetime he was famous; since his death he has overshadowed our history" (Henderson 2003, 56).

For over twenty years Aristotle studied at Plato's feet in the Academy in Athens. After Plato's death, Aristotle left the Academy, only to return to Athens several years later and establish his own competing learning center, the Lyceum. Aristotle accepted Plato's dualism, but came to reject Plato's thesis of the importance of being other-world centered. He contended that true reality was here among us in the physical and tangible world in which we live.

Aristotle is the father of empiricism, where real knowledge (not just Plato's imperfect shadow) is gained through a reasoned and logical analysis of our five-sense experience of the world we inhabit. This is why Raphael places Aristotle alongside Plato his mentor, but with Aristotle's hands firmly stretched earthward. At the Academy one studied transcendent ideas; at the Lyceum, one experimented in the tangible world of experience.

In Aristotle, we have the origins of positivism and modernism: sensory experiences and the interpretive, logical analysis of an active intellect (he called this *nous*) are sufficient to comprehend universal truth. Though various stages of Aristotle's thinking revealed an enduring platonic component, his focus on the physical world and strong logical methodology identified the core components from which later scientific investigation could develop.

Despite the development of a contemporary postmodern perspective, most of our Western classrooms continue to reflect a primarily modernist Aristotelian stance. Good education is seen as that which helps students to use their reasoning processes to determine the facts of a matter in the light of observation and the systematic ordering of data. Issues like beliefs or opinions that are not observable or scientifically verifiable are private things based upon personal opinions and are not really useful in modern education, which should be designed to equip students to enter the workforce and make a decent contribution to the economy. So it is that the systematic approach of the scientific method has not only become the tool for discerning truth in biology or chemistry, but we have also given primacy to systems and other "neutral" quantitative approaches in geography and other disciplines. Any differing perspective often is viewed as mere conjecture or opinion when compared to the superiority of scientific, systematic processes in discovering truth.

Many modern Western educational strategists (as well as politicians and other commentators) take this perspective a step further. Since it is the relation of education to living in the real world that is important, practical, vocational, and "life-skills"-oriented courses must be given precedence in curriculum design and school timetables, with "less practical" subjects such as history and Latin having a diminishing priority. Postmodernity and platonic idealism are seen as "promoting a mindless relativism and turning schools away from teaching traditional knowledge" (Ozmon & Craver 2007, 76). Subject specialization and streaming or tracking are viewed as appropriate organizational patterns for schools. From this perspective, the best measure of the success of a school is student performance in external examinations (hence the academic league tables in the United Kingdom), or how well schools equip children with "job skills," or the degree to which its students receive an adequate foundation for tertiary education. Hence we arrive at the contemporary commitment in the West to a concept of individualistic economic rationalism that controls many educational priorities – the idea that if something is good for the economy, then it is good, and schools should primarily focus their programs on the outcomes of preparing children to be effective economic producers and consumers. Sad confirmation of the veracity of this situation came from Emeritus Professor Ivan Snook at the 2005 teacher education graduation ceremony at a government university in New Zealand when he commented that all that is now being asked of modern teachers is ". . . to prepare young people to be workers" (Snook, A5).

Impact on the Western Mind

The above criticisms should not lead us to be ignorant of the huge benefits that have come from these same Greek philosophers. Deductive reasoning, the pleasure of studying the world around us, the Socratic questioning style, a love of learning, the values of humility, generosity, transparency, and courage – these are all features of thinking and living that we see and admire in these ancient Greeks. But here is the crux of the matter: their value is not found in the fact that the Greeks discovered these concepts, but in the fact that they reflect a biblically faithful understanding of the world and our places and tasks in it. It is the foundational filtration of Scripture that enables us to separate those thought patterns that are worthy of adopting from those that Christians reject.

Socrates, Plato, and Aristotle are the giants of Greek thought. Over time their ideas have remained as driving forces in shaping how Western people think. Plato laid the foundations for the enduring dualistic and non-Christian perspective that to know something is to conceive of it in the ideal world of the mind. We are also indebted to him for that other unfortunate idea that this world is fundamentally inadequate and irretrievably evil and that we can only find "true" truth in an ascetic escape into another realm. Neoplatonism's view of the divine as a distant, impersonal, and inaccessible god, together with neoplatonism's dualistic view of nature and grace or sacred and secular still direct and warp the way we think in the Western Christian church today.

The Bible tells us a different story. Though our fall from grace through our forefather Adam has infected all of us with sin, the platonic mode of thought that this temporal body and world is somehow inherently evil finds no support in Scripture – otherwise the perfect Son of

God could never have inhabited human form.

Finally, Plato gave us the concept of intellectual elitism, discussed at the start of the chapter, that is retained in the powerful intellectual-economic stratification of the twenty-first century and in the consequential unhealthy priorities and patterns in education.

Aristotle accepted dualism, but brought our thinking patterns firmly back to earth, establishing the seeds for scientism, which wrongly asserts that the only real knowing is that which can be understood through the senses and empirical analysis. Culture formers who followed in Aristotle's footsteps extended his ideas of logic and the superiority of the practical, so that now it is a powerful building-block in economic rationalism to which contemporary education has been subordinated.

And so we return to one of the primary purposes of this chapter – to recognize that the way that we think is not just the way things are, but is an often pagan, philosophically committed, cultural adaptation of ideas from long ago. It is also a tragic example of cultural idolatry where we let cultural assumptions determine what is right and wrong, rather than insights based upon a biblical perspective. Sadly, because these great Greek thinkers denied the truth of the one true God who created and sustains the world moment by moment by his word of power, they typically ended up falling into the same trap as the pagan Romans of Paul's day who took one aspect of God's creation and worshiped it in the place of the real Creator (Romans 1:21–25).

EXAMPLES OF THE IMPACT OF GREEK PHILOSOPHICAL TRADITIONS ON THE MODERN CLASSROOM

1.   Knowing truth

When asked to explain what truth is, many of us attempt to encapsulate it in a platonic definition that focuses on accuracy of ideas. The Bible understands truth in a different way that contains but goes beyond the world of concepts and ideas. Consider that Jesus did not say "I've come to tell you about the truth"; rather he said, "I am the truth" (John 14:6). For Jesus, and the Bible, although truth obviously has a strong cognitive aspect, truth first of all is relational. If we ignore this, then we will have all sorts of trouble with Rahab, for example, who lied when telling Jericho's soldiers that the Jewish spies had run off when in fact she was hiding them in her house. In the books of Hebrews and James, because she was trothful (faithful in relationship) to her new-found God and his servants (Joshua 2; Hebrews 11:31; James 2:25), Rahab is commended for her "untruth." But many of us have trouble endorsing the Bible's commendation of Rahab because we reduce truth to cognitive concepts. Perhaps we think about truth in this limited way because of ingrained, platonic, Western cultural tendencies that are at variance with a fully flowered biblical mindset concerning truth.

2.   Examinations tell us when a student knows something

As a second example, why do Christian educators often teach as if genuine knowing can be documented by one's ability to accurately repeat a series of ideas in a written test? Ask most teachers (and most examination/qualifications agencies and politicians as well) how we are able to determine that our students know something, and we'll tell you that students demonstrate knowledge through the sitting of examinations. We often reward this abstract academic achievement in end-of-year prize-giving ceremonies. We think this way not because "That's the way things are," but because platonic conditioning has taught us so.

Conversely, a biblical concept of knowing insists that people don't really know something until they live it out in their lives in service and worship of God. Consider the biblical concept of knowing in the example of Adam and Eve. Adam *knew* his wife Eve, and they bore a son. Forgive the pun, but this knowing was much more than just a piece of knowledge conceived in Adam's head!

Christian knowing is not a dualistic conceptual activity or a hands-on activity. It involves both. As Jack Fennema (2006, 16) comments,

> Knowing in the biblical sense is more than simply cognitive mastery; it is holistic. . . . Students are "to know" with their heart, head and hands. Learning within Christian schools includes a cognitive understanding of the truth, a heartfelt commitment to the truth and an obedient response to the truth. It is hearing the Word and doing the Word; it is both revelation and response.

3.   Academic success and titles

Consider the issue of how teachers prepare children for life beyond school. Even if not stated, an assumption of our educational culture is that if a child is capable of extended abstract thought, then usually he or she should naturally consider going to university and obtaining a degree. After all, our Western world believes that this career path leads to a higher status and often higher income in the years ahead, and usually to being an all-round better person. But why do we think this way, given that our cultural commitment to the superiority of abstract academic achievement and its attendant status-level over manual labor has no biblical foundation? Despite their intellectual skills, Jesus did not demean carpentry and

Paul continued to employ his manual skill of tent making right through-out his life. The title, Doctor, may be a useful tool in procuring a comple-mentary upgrade in airline travel, but in Christian terms it is absolutely no indicator of the value or fulfillment of a person. The reason we think this way lies in the elitist view of abstract ideas and knowledge that we have inherited from that great Greek philosopher Plato.

4.   Controversy about asking questions

Finally, consider the issue of encouraging students to ask questions in class. This is one area of dramatic difference between Western pedagogy and Eastern pedagogy. In the West, students are encouraged to question, and teacher training programs are replete with instructional techniques that encourage an inquisitive environment. In Asian schools following a Confucian model, however, it is often assumed that to ask teachers questions is insulting and contrary to good relationships. Why do we in the West so highly value this instructional technique that is decried by quality educators in other cultures? Would Jesus use it he was a fellow teacher in my school? Which model more accurately reflects a biblically authentic pattern for good education?

THE DEPTH OF THE CHALLENGE OF DUALISTIC THINKING

The depth of the malaise in the western church, caused by the adoption of dualism, is a root cause of the powerlessness of the church's overall at-tempt to share the gospel in modern society. The comments by Fowler, in which secularism is seen as a modern consequence of dualistic thinking, are frightful in their implications (this author's italics):

> Modern secularism does not make any direct attack on the Gospel [or "Christian" schools]. On the contrary, it welcomes the presence of Chris-tian churches, encouraging them to contribute to society by making input on moral issues and issues of social welfare. Yet, it has done more to under-mine the life transforming power of the Gospel in Christian practice than any direct assault on Christian faith could achieve. *It has achieved this by seducing Christians into thinking of important areas of life as religiously neu-tral areas, where conformity to the prevailing culture and worldview will not involve compromise in matters of faith.* We can escape this seductive power only by a constant critical vigilance that tests all things by the Word of God. (Fowler 2006, 83)

At the Third Lausanne Congress on World Evangelization held in Cape Town in October 2010, Dr. Mark Greene (Greene 2010), from the London Institute for Contemporary Christianity, gave a seminal address on the debilitating impact of dualism (he and others call it the sacred-secular-divide). Greene's address is extremely helpful in understanding dualism and its impact on the church. The implications of what he has to say for education are clear.[2]

Dualistic thinking also has allowed Christians to be seduced by the beguiling lie of economic rationalism. This is the notion that if something is good for the economy, then it is good and all other social and cultural objectives need to be subordinated to this ultimate good. It controls political decision-making, and it means that policy-making in education prioritizes "job-skill" subjects, thus reducing schooling to job training.

Dualism and the gods that it has created in modern society are so pervasive that it seems almost profane to criticize them or escape from them. Its "reinterpretation of norms and values," as Goudzwaard (2007) puts it, "demands new sacrifices," perhaps, e.g., by academically streaming children and subjects so that schools can focus on examination attainment, which even for many Christians has become the measure of a successful school. People feel powerless to stop this "progress," and become caught up

> . . . in a disengaged universe of unreal infatuation, and the resulting narrowing of consciousness can make it extremely difficult to discover possible ways out. (Goudzwaard 2007, 34)

With dreadful inevitability, powerlessness turns into hopelessness. Decades ago, Francis Schaeffer (1982) reminded readers that the loss of certainty and control beliefs that was overcoming the modern world would lead to a state of despair where hope decays, living is without purpose, and society becomes bereft of meaningful social interaction beyond the personal level. Polish sociologist, Zygmunt Bauman (1997) powerfully expresses the contemporary malaise this way:

> There is no certainty . . . no room will be left for the pariah. What seems more plausible, however, is that the parvenu's route of escape from the pariah status will be closed. . . . tolerance of difference may well be wedded to the flat refusal of solidarity; monologic discourse, rather than giving way to a dialogic, will split into a series of soliloquies, with the speakers no more insisting on being heard, but refusing to listen into the bargain. (Bauman 1997, 81)

Writing more recently, Hart (2009) confirms the trend of the intellectual mainstreaming of postmodernity, and its bed-fellow, the New Atheism, which seems unable even to affirm its own beliefs with any vi-

---

2 For some reason, the text of Greene's address seems never to have been widely distributed. Given its seminal importance, and with the permission of the author, the entire text of Greene's short address is included as Appendix Three in this book.

able sense of commitment:

> It probably says more than is comfortable to know about the relative va-
> pidity of our culture that we have lost the capacity to produce profound
> unbelief. The best we can now hope for are arguments pursued at only the
> most vulgar of intellectual levels, couched in an infantile and carpingly
> pompous tone, and lacking all but the meagerest traces of historical erudi-
> tion or syllogistic rigor. (Hart 2009, 220)

A Christian Response – Contours of a Christian Mind

Before concluding this chapter, we must undertake one further exploration. Thus far, we have developed the idea that, in the West anyway,
not only the content of our thinking, but also our thinking styles and
processes themselves are not neutral but have been formed through traditions and processes steeped in the secular history of Western culture,
originating with the Greeks and progressing through the Renaissance,
the Enlightenment, and contemporary postmodernity. This realization
by itself should be sufficient to produce a significant response in twenty-
first century Christians. Although we are people of our age who have
been influenced by our past, fundamentally we want to identify ourselves
in all that we do (including our thinking) as people of the God of the
Bible who live in the culturally rich but fallen context of the twenty-first
century West. Christians are the people of God's gracious choosing, for
whom Christ died. We are those who seek to live in the light of the gospel
narrative that we read in Scripture and who seek to celebrate the lordship
of Jesus Christ (and not Plato or Aristotle) over all of creation – including
the formative characteristics of why we think the way that we do today –
as we live for Christ and prepare for his return, which "culminates in the
restoration of the entire creation to its original greatness" (Bartholomew
& Goheen 2005, 12).

Even if Plato, e.g., helped us to comprehend some good things that
exist in our thinking processes, it is inadequate for the Christian to accept
them just because Plato said so. By all means read Plato and meditate
upon his ideas. But what informs our thinking and what we accept as
good must be the result of wrestling with God's order (not Plato's) in his
creation, principally as revealed in the patterns and stories recorded in
the Bible. Our final exploration, then, is to suggest broad indicators as
to how we can begin to acknowledge Jesus Christ as Lord in the formation of our thinking processes. The seven contours of the Christian mind
outlined below are not exclusive or exhaustive. They merely provide a
few touchstones that we might want to consider along the way, especially

with regard to the thinking necessary to formulate a distinctively Christian understanding of education.

1.   Seek after God in all that we do

The Westminster Confession of Faith rightly declares that the chief end of man is to glorify God and enjoy him forever. Our primary goal in life is to know him better and serve him more faithfully. As Goldsworthy (2006, 63) comments, "the gospel is the hermeneutical norm for the whole of reality." Our seeking to honor God in education should be an expression of this, as we, his ambassadors, seek for his kingdom to come on earth, as we pray in the Lord's Prayer. The cause of Christian education is not an extension of the gospel, but is integral to it. Like church worship, or singing, or recreation, or anything, it is a part of God's big story. It is to be done in the light of the Kingdom of God with the nature and purpose of the incarnation as its integration point. Higton (2012) puts it this way:

> Learning – all learning worthy of the name – is a matter of being invited as disciples to know God and the fulfillment that God has for God's creatures; that it unavoidably involves being crucified and raised with Christ; that it requires the bringing-together of learners in the Body of Christ; that it is part of the work of the Spirit making us holy; and that it nevertheless takes place both in and beyond the church, and sometimes more truly beyond the church than in it. (Higton 2012, 145)

2.   Acknowledge that there is no neutrality

Every thought and every act is carried out in obedience or disobedience to God. There is no neutrality. Any statement presupposes a belief structure or thetical stance. Bringing every thought in subjection to Jesus Christ means making the deliberate choice to recognize non-neutrality and to recognize his lordship over our thinking processes.

3.   Be relentless in critiquing our thinking – championing the restoration of hope and creativity

We need to know where our thinking patterns have come from. Although this chapter has briefly considered the influence of Greek thought, we also need to examine subsequent historical epochs (especially the Enlightenment) and identify their impact on why we think the way we do. Only after identifying the problem can we then seek to put it right in a creaturely submission of our thinking patterns to the norms of the God whom we seek to serve. And then, after recognizing the despair and listlessness that is in hearts of many young people who have been nurtured in the directionless narcissism of truth-less postmodernity, we can strategize about how to nurture them in all subject areas in the light of a dynamic and purposeful biblical worldview. This will enable the restoration of hope and the wonder of a "made-in-God's-image" creativity (Genesis 1). Both are fundamental to a Christian pedagogy; both are essential if young people are to have an appropriate understanding of themselves and the world in which they live.

4. Repudiate dualism
If we are to reform our thinking along new pathways that celebrate the lordship of Christ over how we think, we must confront and eschew dualism wherever it is found (which is almost everywhere, starting with our own hearts and minds). This means that genuine Christian education starts with the assumption that God is relevant to every classroom, and to every school subject, activity, organizational structure, and relationship. Maybe we don't mention God all the time, and we certainly don't turn the classroom into an endless altar-call; but our default position, our core assumption, our basis for hope is that a proper understanding and wise discernment in everything can only be found when he is the light through which we examine the world and our places and tasks in it.

5. See Christian thinking as a new way, not an amalgam of existing patterns
The Dutch philosopher Vollenhoven articulated the thetical-critical method (Kok, 1992), which has as its starting point a humble, self-critical, and joyful commitment to a biblically authentic way of looking at and thinking about the world that spurns the uncritical extraction of insights from secular perspectives, which can only result in an ultimately unsatisfactory syncretism. In the light of this epistemological reformation, our God-honoring thetical – "this is what we stand for" – stance gives us a platform to evaluate other positions. As Paul did in Acts 17 in Athens, we will learn to recognize truth wherever it is found, and will freely accept insights of secular writers (including some of the ideas of atheist John Dewey, e.g.) – but only because these insights first of all have been critiqued and identified as legitimate components of a God-honoring way of seeing, being, and thinking and thus become a part of a genuine, Christian mind and worldview.

6. Recognize the authority of God's written Word, the Bible, as foundational
Several useful Christian-oriented worldview courses have become available for Christian study groups to help us identify and live by a Christian way of seeing and being in the world. A dynamic distinctive of the world-

view course written by Thompson (2005) is that it commences with an investigation of the Bible as foundational for Christian living. It is in Scripture that we find the stories, norms, and principles to guide us in our search for right thinking patterns. As Greidanus (1982, 147) has said, it is important to remind ourselves that our task is not to find ready-made answers in the Bible but to study reality in the light of biblical revelation. As Fowler (2006, 83) puts it quite rightly: "The place of the Bible in our task of studying creation is not [always] to give [ready-made] answers, but to guide us in our search for the answers, to be the light by whose illumination we will find the answers in the creation itself." These comments resonate with one of the defining characteristics of Christian education as outlined in Chapter Two.

One of the biggest obstacles for the twenty-first century Christian community in the West when it comes to our ability to reject dualism, recognize cultural idolatry, and develop and articulate a Christian mind is an acquaintance with the Bible that so often does not go beyond homilies and personal salvation morality. Serious, concerted efforts in churches, study groups, and Christian schools is needed in this regard lest we find ourselves more conformed to this world's ways of thinking rather than being transformed by the renewal of our minds as we seek to serve as God's agents of shalom in our societies (Romans 12).

7. Comprehend and practice a biblically literate worldview, such as Reformed Critical Realism

We need to ensure that why we think the way we do, and how we think the way we do about everything (including schooling) emanates from a biblically faithful and thus gospel-focused way of looking at the world – in other words, a Christian worldview. We must not be addicted to the pagan alternatives of modernity or naturalistic positivism on the one hand, or the equally forlorn position of skeptical postmodernity on the other. The philosophical position of reformed critical realism that is being explored by some scholars (Beech 2013, Carson 2001, and Edlin 2006b are just three examples among many) provides a cogent and satisfying intellectual framework for Christians who seek to inhabit the mind field in a faithful manner. It recognizes God's authority over all things, and the appropriateness of our own perspectival and humble attempts to live faithfully in God's world God's way in the twenty-first century. Carson (2001) and Edlin (2006b) summarize reformed critical realism this way:

> We believe there is a real world out there where it is possible to know and to know truly (hence realism), but we also believe that our theories and hypotheses about that world, and our religious presuppositions and beliefs

about reality, color and shape our capacity to know that world (hence critical realism). (Carson 2001, 14)

Reformed critical realism celebrates the empowerment of Christians to revel in the authority of the Scriptures in a way that is liberated from the bondage of the unwarranted idolatrous positivism of modernism (naïve realism) on the one hand, and the individualistic uncertainty of postmodernism (nonrealism) on the other. (Edlin 2006b, 102)

Chapter 4

The Place of the Bible
in the Christian School

The biblical story shapes us at an individual level so that it leads to personal conversion. However, it does more than that. It provides the whole context for our life and orientation. It begins with the creation and ends with the renewal of the universe. It gives meaning and shape to history. As such, this story must not only touch us as isolated individuals; it must shape the way we think and behave as we engage with the world. (Goheen 2010, 5)

INTRODUCTION

Christians start with a belief in a personal, Creator-God who reveals himself through his Word – his Word in creation, his living Word in Jesus Christ, and his written Word in the Scriptures of the Old and New Testaments. Beyond all analysis, intellectual enquiry, or council of human activity, we are unashamedly committed to the self-evident, presuppositional, and self-authenticating authority of the Bible as God's infallible, written Word. Therefore, Christians start with the belief that the Bible is the most important book in the world – outstanding, supreme, and totally unique in its authority, purpose, and impact. Any other position would place some validating mechanism above the Bible, and that validating mechanism in itself would become the ultimate authority.

So what does all this this mean for the Christian school and the Bible? First of all, let us be clear about what it tells us of our fundamental starting point. Then, let us examine what this means for the place of the Bible in the Christian school.

THE WORD OF GOD
IS THE CHRISTIAN SCHOOL'S FUNDAMENTAL STARTING POINT

Unlike some other religions such as Islam or communism, we do not worship our holy book. As Jesus intimated to the Pharisees (John 5:39), the Bible itself is not first of all a set of rules to obey, but is the real time-and-place testimony of God's big story, with the purpose of directing us

to Christ. We do not worship the Bible, or scour its pages just for regulations to live by in the vain hope that such an attempt will make us acceptable to God. No. The God of the Bible is a personal, relational God.
We hold the Bible as infallible and supremely precious and we study it
avidly not because it is an end in itself, but because it tells us about God
and directs us to Jesus Christ in whom alone is to be found full life both
now and for eternity (John 10:10). The patterns for living that we find
in the Bible we seek to follow not as a merit-earning set of behaviors, but
as a labor of love in response to our gracious Lord and Master (1 Thessalonians 1:3).

The reflections in the box below represent the commitment to the
Bible as it is represented in the pages of this book.

We take a conservative, evangelical approach to the Bible. That is, it is
incomparable, self-authenticating, complete (a closed canon), is divinely
inspired, inerrant in its original form, and is fully authoritative for all of
life, including education. It has been God-breathed and written down
by human hands over the centuries. As such, it speaks into real cultural
situations but is designed for Christ's followers in all ages and in all settings. Our hermeneutical perspective is that we and all culture (including ecclesiastical culture) live under the authority of God's Word. The
Bible is not a mere compendium of good moral principles or attractive
values. It is God's big story of Creation, Fall, Redemption, and Fulfillment, telling of God's making and redeeming a people for himself, and
of maintaining his world moment by moment by his word of power. All
humanity, made in God's image and given authority over creation, has
fallen from grace. However, redemption is made possible through the
incarnation and substitutionary sacrifice of God's son, Jesus Christ. The
Old Testament looks forward to that event and Christians in the New
Testament and beyond live meaningfully and expectantly in the light of
it. Eschatologically, we confess that God has called us, in the power of the
Holy Spirit, humbly and purposefully to live creatively in this world as his
ambassadors, reveling as good stewards in our creative capacity, seeking
the welfare of the city in which we live, and proclaiming the full message
of hope that comes through Jesus Christ. We experience the beginnings
of the renewal of his kingdom now (see the Lord's Prayer), a renewal that
will be perfectly realized one day when Christ returns to take his own to
himself, and to banish all who have rejected him to the just punishment
of eternal separation from him.

The Place of the Bible in the Christian School

As we begin to explore how the Bible functions in the life of a Christian school that is seeking to celebrate the lordship of Christ over all of creation, two introductory perspectives will be useful in further helping to establish the contours of our discussion. The first is a declaratory statement about the place of the Bible in the educational task (such as the one above) and its meaning for education. This should be found in a dynamic Christian school's core documents. The second is a simple but powerful analogy by Douglas Wilson (1991) about the same matter, reminiscent of central perspectives found in other chapters in this book.

(1)   Stating the Position in a School's Core Statement

The following statement (2011) comes from the core educational beliefs adopted by a group of Christians seeking to start a new Christian school in Korea. It provides a bold context within which the actual place or use of the Bible in the Christian school can be given specific meaning in the school's daily operations.

We confess that:

- the whole creation finds its coherence and meaning in the only begotten Son of the Father, the living Word of God through Whom all things were made and are continually upheld;
- the supreme standards for all matters of education are the inspired, infallible and inerrant Scriptures of the Old and New Testaments, God's Word written, by whose light alone we can study creation and know its God-given meaning;
- while the study of the Scriptures is no substitute for the study of God's creation, Scripture remains indispensable and determinative for our knowledge of God, of ourselves, and of the rest of creation, and thus for the whole educational task.

(2)   The Bible as Sunlight

In his advocacy for Christian schools, Douglas Wilson (1991) points to a proper platform for understanding the role of the Bible in the Christian school that builds upon the above belief statement:

> Every line of true knowledge must find its completeness as it converges on God, just as every beam of daylight leads the eye to the sun. . . . The Christian educator's job is not to require the students to spend all their time gazing at the sun. Rather, we want them to examine everything else in the light the sun provides. (63)

IMPROPER USE OF THE BIBLE SIDELINES CHRISTIANITY IN THE CHRISTIAN SCHOOL

Christian schools acknowledge the central place that the Bible should have in the life of the school. The Scriptures alone are properly championed as the source of truth and as the foundational platform for policy and curriculum. This position is right and noble. It acknowledges a faith commitment to divinely inspired external authority. Without this, there is the risk that decisions develop in a knee-jerk response to the most vocal contemporary pressure group. For Christians, God's Word shows us how to live, and we attempt to live by his Word in the Christian school.

However, there are many schools, even some that call themselves Christian, that confine the place of the Bible, and of "spiritual" matters, to a narrow segment of the life of the school. A typical school of this type, which Stephen (a pseudonym), a friend of mine attended, proudly asserted that it followed a Christian pattern. It had daily chapel for all of its students, plus compulsory religious studies classes. It had many fine Christian teachers who prayed daily for their students and who tried to set a good moral example before them. All of these things are important. However, these activities alone, without a dynamic reformation that reaches into all areas of the school curriculum, reinforce a most unfortunate, shriveled mindset about the Bible, Christianity, and the Christian school. Stephen commented that it was this same restrictive mindset, as expressed in his "Christian" school, that actually sidelined Christianity in his impressionable adolescent mind. It confined the idea of faith to apparently peripheral areas of life like chapel, while all around, nitty-gritty, "real" subjects such as math, science, history, and language were taught as if Christianity was irrelevant to them. As we saw in Chapter Three, this unfortunate split between sacred and secular is called dualism or the sacred-secular divide (SSD), and it remains a major, disempowering problem among Christians in the twenty-first century. Mark Greene's speech in Cape Town in 2010, included as Appendix Three to this book, explores the SSD issue in more detail. Referring to the situation in many traditional Christian ethos schools, Collier (2012) comments concerning chapel and traditional Religious Education (RE) classes as follows: "Chapel and Religious Education classes don't count for marks towards [examinations]. . . . Therefore students have become masters of compliant inattention – they are physically present, perfectly well-behaved, but mentally absent" (Collier 2012, 1).

In Stephen's case, his attendance at his "Christian" school, with its anemic, dualistic faith encouraged him to view Christianity as an optional extra, which could be picked up or left behind at no great risk. It served actually to alienate him from the very faith that it sought to celebrate. For many years, he left Christianity behind, partly because of his "Christian" school, until many years later when he came to reject his school's counterfeit view of the Christian life and came to a personal relationship with Jesus Christ. He is now a Christian agriculturist who is outstanding in his field (excuse the pun!) and is a public leader in developing a Christian approach to farming and agriculture generally.

The error that was presented to Stephen in a school in New Zealand is to be found world-wide. Writing about the British experience, Mark Roques (1989) comments that treatment of Christianity and other religions in the public school classroom, in fact, often marginalizes religions because, "They are only allowed to address personal or private issues" (137).

Many Christian educators will want to disassociate themselves from the sort of Christian school that my friend Stephen attended. We probably will want to agree that a secular/sacred split in our view of the world is not Christian. We will want to agree with Gordon Spykman (1977) in saying that "If we depend on chapel and daily devotionals to integrate faith and the teaching-learning process, we will be guilty of contributing to the secularization of the classroom" (2). We will want to affirm that the Christian school will aim at championing the lordship of Christ over all of creation – in every subject, in every administrative decision, and in every relationship. This is how it should be. As Ronald Chadwick (1990) has said,

> God, as He has shown Himself to us in His divine revelation, the Bible, must be at the very center or core of our curriculum. Everything that is taught or done must be brought into rightful and meaningful relationship with God and His Word. (Chadwick 1990, 179)

The Bible must never be a fancy icing on top of an otherwise rotten cake.

All Complete Knowledge is Founded on the Word of God

But what actually does it mean to say that the Christian school should offer ". . . a vital, Christ-centered, biblical interpretation of learning?" (Philosophy Statement of the Alliance Academy, Quito, Ecuador). What does it really mean in the third-grade reading curriculum, in the seventh-grade earth science program, or in the school's approach to assessment, to recognize that Christ is the Lord of education and that his word is the guide for all these activities? After all, the school is not a theological seminary. Its primary task is not biblical exegesis. Neither is the school a church in the institutional sense. How do we affirm, as we must, the centrality of the Bible in the Christian school? What does it mean to say that the final and fully authoritative standard for ruling the life of the Christian school must be the Scriptures of the Old and New Testaments? Let us turn to the Bible itself for our answer.

The Psalmist declares that "I gain understanding from your precepts [God]. . . . Your word is a lamp for my feet, a light on my path" (Psalm 119:104–05). This shows with sparkling clarity the role of the Bible in the Christian school. The lamp is the Word of God faithfully expressed in the Scriptures, and the path is the world and the Christian's walk in it. In the school setting, the light or principles opened up by the Scriptures should be used to help students learn about creation and their responsibilities to the Creator in the world. As Wilson (1991) said in the earlier quotation, everything in the Christian school can only be properly explored if it is done in the light that the Bible provides.

This is a much broader idea than considering just what happens in the classroom. Teachers who attempt to understand child development or construct curricula independent of the faith perspective of the Word of God are floundering in darkness. All of the activities of the Christian educator must be based upon the light and principles of the Word of God if she really is to know deep truth in any field that she is considering. To attempt to develop patterns for schools independent of the light of the Word of God will inevitably lead to a warped and unworthy conclusion, and an inferior preparation for life.

Does this mean that those involved in Christian schools should search the Bible for a verse that will specifically say how much play area per pupil a school should have, whether to use D'Nealian or standard cursive style to teach handwriting, or if an offending student should be punished by extra work after class or by writing a note of apology? Of course not. The light of the Bible, though, will still point to a proper understanding of a child, recreation and work, evil, the imagination, curriculum design and content, and discipline so as to enable even matters like these to be addressed in a God-honoring way. The proper way to consider these – and all issues – is to weigh them up under the scrutinizing light of Scripture and a Christian worldview that is firmly built upon a solid foundation of biblical presuppositions.

The Bible is not primarily an educational textbook although the Christian school should study it as a separate subject area as will be discussed later. The Bible is not just an example of good literature, although its poetic forms and compelling language provide useful models for us. The Bible alone, as God's written revelation, has divine authority and divine reliability. It has been written to point humankind to Jesus Christ and to reveal God's complete offer of salvation through him. This has the most profound of implications for every area of life. As Stuart Fowler (1980b) commented,

> Salvation through faith in Christ means the refocusing of our lives in God; it is the removal of our alienation, reconciling us to live in love as God's greatly loved children. This refocusing of our lives by faith . . . gives a new meaning, a new understanding to all our perceptions, our observations, our experience [and] our analysis of ourselves and our world. . . . It is a God-focused perspective on the whole world of our experience that gives us a new insight into who we are, the order of our world, and the norms for our living in the world. (134–5)

*   *   *

In the light of this rather lengthy but necessary introduction, we will now turn our attention to the three ways that the Bible should function in the life of a Christian school. These three ways are an outgrowth of our faith commitment to the Word of God. They are:

(1)   the devotional function of the Bible in the Christian school;

(2)   the foundational function of the Bible in the Christian school; and

(3)   the permeative function of the Bible in the Christian school.

First Function:
The *Devotional* Function of the Bible in the Christian School
Above all else, the Christian school is devoted to serving the Lord. This is why many schools include the term "Christian" in their very name. It is entirely appropriate, therefore, for the Bible to function in a devotional context in the life of the school. This will be apparent at several levels. First, and outside of the classroom itself, the meetings of the school's controlling authority usually will commence with devotions and time spent reflecting upon the school's vision and purpose from a Christian worldview perspective. This is not a matter of form or procedure, but it is the key way to start such meetings because it recognizes the lordship of Christ over the proceedings and the need for his blessing and guidance upon them. But don't be misled into the error of thinking that school board meetings (or any meetings of Christians for that matter) can be divided into a sacred part and then a secular part. There should be no such differentiation. Bible reading, discussion of finances, prayer, decisions on

policy, giving out diplomas, etc., should all be seen as acts of service and worship to God. The distinction between the "religious bit" at the beginning of a meeting, and then getting on with the "real business" after someone closes the first part with a prayer of benediction, is unhelpful and represents a distorted, dualistic view of the gospel.

Second, the devotional function of the Bible should be evident in the team of teachers. In order to teach in a comprehensively Christian school, teachers must all be committed Christians, and it is important that they commence their educational endeavors each day recognizing the lordship of Christ and seeking his wisdom and guidance. Many Christian schools start the day with a faculty meeting. This is a good place to corporately bring the new day to the Lord, perhaps with a brief reading from the Bible, a few comments, and prayer.

Typically, educators become consumed with matters of the day, and the tyranny of the urgent reigns supreme. It is important for teachers communally to take a few moments aside, remember that God is on the throne, and re-orient priorities before entering the rush and bustle of the rest of the school day. Jesus was so wise when he reminded his fretful disciples that they should "seek first his kingdom and his righteousness" (Matthew 6:33), and they should know that God will give wisdom in dealing with the day-to-day cares of life as well. Remember that both the faculty meeting and all subsequent activities are all acts of ongoing worship and service to God.

Third, the devotional function of the Bible should be evident in the life of the whole school community. Although it must not be assumed that all of the students in a Christian school are Christians, a percentage of them will be. This is important, even in mission-based schools. The environment needs to be created whereby the expression of Christian beliefs and practices by Christian students is affirmed and not scorned by the school culture, including the majority peer group pressure. Time should be set aside at a formal assembly or in the classroom at the beginning of the teaching day to consider and to worship the God whose creation the school's activities seek to explore, and to commit all of the learning activities to him.

Exhilarating chapels of praise and worship have a significant place in the Christian school, but we should avoid the mistake of considering the school to be a regular church in the ecclesiastical or liturgical sense. Although there is some overlap – for example, the cultic church and the Christian school may both be considered to be legitimate expressions of the Body of Christ – it is not appropriate to view students as a captive audience for the vain repetition of theological liturgies or perpetual altar-calls. Nevertheless, the Christian school is a place of humble and un-ashamed proselytization. Children are given the opportunity to exercise their God-given right to select the worldview pathway of their choosing, but the whole approach of the Christian school is to winsomely demonstrate that a commitment to Jesus Christ is the only viable and fulfilling option. Remember Wilson's image, that the job of the school is to examine everything in the light of the Son. This in itself should provide a compelling invitation to the gospel.

How exciting it is to enter a Christian school that is dynamically aware of its mission and to see its teachers communally commit each day and activity to the Lord! What a thrill it is to join with the students in worship and praise in class devotions. Consider the joy of participating in the worship and praise times of school chapel where the whole school community celebrates the lordship of God over all creation and is encouraged in the Christian walk; challenged with the call of missions; inspired for cultural engagement by Christian leaders in the community; and stimulated to be more Christ-like in daily life. Praise the Lord for these Godly devotional experiences that are part of the precious heritage of those who attend Christian schools!

For your encouragement, and as a reminder of the importance of memory, take a look on YouTube at the young boy meaningfully reciting the books of the Bible, including a comment for each book about how it focuses on our God.[1] Wonderful stuff and a great example. It's from a church setting, but it would be great in a devotional sense for every Christian school as well.

SECOND FUNCTION:
THE *FOUNDATIONAL* USE OF THE BIBLE IN THE CHRISTIAN SCHOOL

Because the function of the Bible is so foundational in the Christian school, it is proper that specific study of the Bible be an important separate subject in the academic curriculum. The Scriptures help us to see that the world around us is of God's making and that the world is upheld by God's law (Hebrews 1:3). The Bible also shows us what humankind's task is as managers or stewards of God's world and outlines the effect of the realities of the fall, sin, and redemption on all of creation. Time should be spent with the students exploring these biblical concepts in a systematic way. Wonderful passages like Psalm 8 and 47, or books such as Romans or Colossians, could also be studied exegetically. As older school

---

1 http://www.youtube.com/watch?v=OhVrcV6WmfQ

students begin to examine moral and ethical questions for themselves, the Bible teacher in the Christian school has the privilege of helping students see these issues from a Christian presuppositional perspective. The school should not hide the world from the students. When in their teen years, teachers should respond openly and sympathetically to young people wrestling with the uncertainties of life – a time that Cooling terms the years of bafflement (Collier 2010, 3). Like the Bible itself, the Christian school has the task of showing its students the world as it really is and then helping them to find God's handles to cope with that world.

One vital aspect of study that should be included in any school's Bible program is a study of the canon of Scripture. Too often evangelical Christians affirm an allegiance to the Bible as the written Word of God without appreciating how God has brought about the collection of the writings found in the Old and New Testaments. Such ignorance is very dangerous. In foundational classes about the Bible, students can also learn about the missionary journeys of Paul, or the history of God's covenant people, or the integrity of the book of Psalms, or (to quote a title used by Francis Schaeffer) Joshua and the flow of biblical history, biblical concepts for good government, the spread of the gospel during Roman times, Christian philosophical presuppositions, and many other exciting topics. Some secular opponents of Christianity like to attribute all the problems of the world to theistic religions, but a study by scholars such as the respected sociologist Rodney Stark (2011) reject this mischievous fiction. Stark's research allows history to demonstrate that Christianity, and its benevolence towards the dispossessed and even its enemies, has been one of Christianity's greatest attractions for agnostics throughout history. As David Jackson reflects, "Wherever the Bible has gone, and wherever people have had the access to read it for themselves in their heart language [and respond to it], there has followed huge social transformation and blessing" (Jackson 2011, 67). The nation of South Korea is another modern example.

An issue of considerable debate in the Christian school community today concerns the extent of the content to be covered in a school Bible (sometimes called Christian Studies) course. Some advocates go as far as to say that a more general course of religious studies or comparative religions, as is taught in state schools in the United Kingdom, would be appropriate. Such an approach risks missing the point of the commitment of the Christian school to Christianity not just as one faith among many, but as the only way, truth, and life. Students should learn about and evaluate other religious views in the Christian school. However, this should not be done in a context where all religions are presented as being of equal validity, but in a context where all societies and views of life are evaluated in the light of the Bible. Further discussion about the place of religious education classes (RE) can be found in Chapter One of this book, and insights by Brian Hill (2005) provide valuable further illumination.

We need also to heed Mark Roques' (1989) warning concerning the standard approach to religious education in schools. This is where Christianity and other religions are taught as if they have almost nothing to say in 95 percent of what we call life. Such religions (it is taught) speak to us about colorful festivals, "confirmation," special diets, and days of celebration. They may offer us guidance in our personal morality. But they have almost nothing to say about the direction of "public" areas of life: industry, politics, economics, scholarship, engineering, banking, sport, insurance, and architecture are all unfolded in the light of a humanistic worldview. This is not a proper foundational use of the Bible in the Christian school. Hill (2005) reminds us that the beliefs and values nurtured in the biblical studies class provide a Christian, as opposed to a secular, foundation for studying every other subject. Hill continues to rightly assert that students

> need to learn about the faith traditions most significant in their own upbringing and acculturation, and then be helped, as the powers of cognitive distancing and analysis develop, to interrogate their own cultural conditioning in order to acquire an owned faith, as contrasted with one inherited at an unreflective level. (Hill 2005, 15)

A dynamic example of an exciting biblical studies class is the "Livewire" program (Holland 2012, 8–9) that has been implemented in St. Andrews Cathedral School in Sydney, Australia.[2]

Jackson (2011) rightly insists that a worthwhile biblical studies program should be:

- normative – that is, based upon an authoritative acceptance of and interaction with the Bible itself;
- situational – that is, it speaks into the contemporary life experience of the students both in terms of our world's widespread biblical illiteracy and cultural despair, while also laying the foundation for a biblically faithful and hope-filled worldview in other subject areas;
- existential – that is, it penetrates to the deepest heart commit-

---

2 Details can be found at www.aec.edu.au/resources/Projects/The%20Integral%20 Project/Integral%20Dinner%20Booklet.pdf

ments of the students who have the challenge to live "in a world gone mad."

Jackson's overall aim for a biblical studies program is that it should "teach every student 'the whole counsel of God,' enabling them to have read the whole Bible with understanding by the time they have completed their schooling and by doing so, be able to make their own informed responses" (Jackson 2011, 73).

THIRD FUNCTION:
THE *PERMEATIVE* FUNCTION OF THE BIBLE IN THE CHRISTIAN SCHOOL

The foundational function of the Bible has a key place in the life of the Christian day school or homeschool, and the concepts and principles that are learned there flow over into all other aspects of the curriculum in a *permeating* manner. Students come to see that, as they study the world, they work out their studies from the perspective and presuppositions of the Bible.

Studies in most secular schools are undertaken from either a child-centered or a content-centered perspective. The first perspective's core presupposition, linked to postmodernity or radical constructivism, is that we live in an essentially meaningless world and that education enables us to give meaning to it that will satisfy our individual needs and desires. But meaninglessness cannot generate meaning. This humanist approach is non-Christian and results in all sorts of distortions. It is the malaise that is behind the despair and the loss of hope, identity, and direction in many of today's young people.

The other equally destructive view that still has sway in some schools or subjects is that the world exists in and of itself. This content-centered view, sometimes known as positivism or modernism, has generated some very useful technological and medical advances. But it also leads to the worship and service of creation (or expressions of it like mathematics or science or economics) as the ultimate truth. It is partly a product of eighteenth-century Enlightenment (a misnomer if ever there was one) thinking. It views people as mere machines and historically has led to all kinds of distortions and error. Many of the horrors of the Industrial Revolution emanated from this mechanistic worldview. Knowledge, tradition, globalized economics, and narcissistic individualism are to be drummed into students, whether they appreciate them or not, because life is to be lived in service to this modernistic god. The misguided beliefs in the inexorable development through education of progress and human improvement, and the perspective that if it's good for the economy then it's good (and to hell with environmental consequences) are tragic myths of this perspective.

The Christian school rejects both these views. Humans are not autonomous, and history shows that education can produce evil as much as it can good. In a Christian school, education takes place in a context that is subject to the Creator, in whom all things live and move and have their being. This Creator is the loving, redeeming God in whom are hid all the treasures of wisdom and knowledge. This fundamental principle will have been examined as part of the foundational function of the Bible in the Christian school, and now the students explore and apply it as it permeates the rest of the curriculum.

In mathematics, the child discovers that $1 + 1 = 2$ not because it is convenient for people to think this way or because this just happens to be always the way things are. The mathematical statement is true because God created and maintains his world and continually enables that simple equation to be true through his moment-by-moment sustaining of his world (Hebrews 1:3). Order is the result of God's ongoing, dynamic, creative activity. There is nothing back of God.

In science, the student learns that there is order and meaning in God's world, and that experimentation can help us to make sense of aspects of his creation. However, we also learn that even science provides only limited understanding. From a Christian worldview perspective, we learn in the science classroom that we may not use technology to plunder and pollute the environment, but that God has given guidelines by which his world is to be managed and that God holds us accountable for how we conduct that management. In these two brief examples, the permeative function of the Bible is inescapable as its principles are presented to the students to guide them in their studies.

In history, students learn that human activity (politics, law, music, love, sport, recreation, technology, economics, employment, etc.) throughout the ages has uncovered exhilarating possibilities because of the creative capacity with which God has imbued humanity. However, when we abandon God's way of understanding these things, destructive consequences follow. But hope endures, since direction, purpose, and joy can be rediscovered through a restored relationship with God through Christ, and a humble implementation of his view of things in how we live.

The *White Rose* story, explained briefly in Chapter Two, should be a part of every history course that explores issues relating to World War Two, highlighting as it does the challenges of biblically authentic discipleship in real-life historical settings. God's mercy in Christ is wonderfully gracious, but it is not without cost. Cheap grace is not a biblical concept.

The form of biblically faithful Christian schooling expounded in this book joins with Niebuhr in rejecting the counterfeit gospel so prevalent in the west, which he describes as "A God without wrath brought men without sin into a Kingdom without judgment through the ministrations of a Christ without a Cross" (Niebuhr 1937, 193). No. As Wolterstorff (2002, 170) comments, "The idea of the Christian school in our society is the idea of a school producing dissenters and agents of change in the name of Christ. The Christian school is a training ground for . . . dissent and reform."

Fenton and Gould-Drakeley (2002) illustrate the permeative function of the Bible in the area of language acquisition – in their case, the teaching of Indonesian in an Australian school.

A biblically faithful worldview should permeate the athletics programs in Christian schools. For example, Goheen (2006) opens up a discussion of the issue of a biblically faithful approach to competition in sport. We could also look at the excellent movie *Chariots of Fire* (1981), which tells the story of Scottish Christian Eric Liddell. Liddell won an Olympic gold medal in athletics in 1924. He became a Christian missionary schoolteacher in China, and died in a prison camp during the Second World War, despite the intervention of the British Prime Minister with his captors to seek his release (it was granted, but Liddell refused to leave and offered the amnesty to a pregnant woman instead). The movie not only explores his athletics career, but it includes the amazing confession from Liddell that "I believe God made me for a purpose, but he also made me fast. And when I run I feel his pleasure." Liddell saw his athletics as an act of joyful worship to God. A study of Liddell's life and his biblically-grounded worldview as applied to athletics, including enjoying *Chariots of Fire*, should be a part of every Christian school's athletics program. This is using the Bible permeatively, and it is how we should teach athletics in the Christian school.

The late Chuck Colson (1999), renowned Christian speaker, summed up the matter this way:

> Many believers fail to understand that Scripture is intended to be the basis for all of life. In the past centuries, the secular world asserted a dichotomy between science and religion, between fact and value, between objective knowledge and subjective feeling. Evangelicals have been particularly vulnerable to this narrow view because of our emphasis on personal commitment. . . . [But] genuine Christianity is more than a relationship with

Jesus, as expressed in personal piety, church attendance, Bible study, and works of charity. Genuine Christianity is a way of seeing and comprehending all reality. . . . In every topic we investigate, from ethics to economics to ecology, the truth is found only in relationship to God and his revelation. (Colson & Pearcey 1999, 14–16)

Stephens (2012) celebrates the permeative function of the Bible in the Christian school this way (with some words added in parentheses by this author):

The Church is at present filled with powerful culture-makers, but they make culture according to a different story than the one they sing about on Sundays. And it's not because they are being wilfully sinful. It's just nobody told them that they could glorify God as a banker. . . . [I]magine Christian institutions which taught students how to be God's culture-makers, by making them both great disciples and great musicians, both great disciples and great athletes, both great disciples and great physicists [– doing both of these things simultaneously, with one aspect seamlessly interwoven into the other]. For in teaching them to do both, we teach them how to fully image God to the world, such that people will see through the culture we make, to ultimately behold the generous Father who stands behind all things. (Stephens 2012, 10)

The permeative function of the Bible doesn't mean that Scripture is used as the formal textbook in each subject. It does not replace the chemistry text or the technical drawing table. Rather, what it does do is give us the perspective we need to understand and explore chemistry and industrial design and their relationship to cultural formation in a faithful, God-honoring manner. Unashamedly, the Bible is our guide. As in the above examples, it provides us with our core perspectives, our learning distinctives, and our outcome attitudes. Again, in the Psalmist's terms, and reflecting Wilson's comment, the Bible is the lamp that provides God's light to interpret the various subjects in the curriculum. It does not mean that the teacher finds any and every excuse to bring Bible verses into his lesson. The Bible is not frosting on an otherwise unaltered humanist cake. It needs to be the leaven in the educational loaf, shaping the entire curriculum from its base up as it permeates through the whole school program. Note that further practical steps involved in implementing this permeative perspective are outlined in Chapter Eight, dealing with foundations for curriculum.

CONCLUSION

This book shamelessly recognizes its religious roots by celebrating an un-abashed commitment to the self-authenticating written Word of God encapsulated in the scriptures of the Old and New Testaments. From that basis, a three-fold picture has emerged of the place of the Bible in the Christian school – its devotional role, its foundational role, and its per-meative role. We believe that such an approach, when guided by the Holy Spirit, will go a long way towards achieving what must be the primary desire for Christian parents when sending their children to a Christian school, as recorded by Paul in Philippians 1:9–11:

> And this is my prayer: that your love may abound more and more in knowledge and depth of insight, so that you may be able to discern what is best and may be pure and blameless for the day of Christ, filled with the fruit of righteousness that comes through Jesus Christ – to the glory and praise of God.

Chapter 5

The Integrity and Vision of the Christian School

The Need for a Vision

Some time ago, I gave a series of addresses to a Christian Teachers' conference in the United Kingdom. I was impressed by the dedication and sacrifice of so many of the Christian teachers and administrators who were present. They had given up higher paid positions in the state sector so as to serve the Lord in Christian schools. They were opposed to the secular and amoral atmosphere of many state schools and sought to devote their energies to providing a Christian education alternative. Some of them, after having perceived the need for Christian schools, had proceeded to start one – and they were always searching for clearer and fresh ways to articulate what actually is meant by the concept of "a Christian school."

In the course of my presentations to these conscientious educators, one of the questions that we considered was that of maintaining the vision of their fledgling Christian schools. An obvious but important consensus emerged among the assembled educators: it is impossible to *maintain* a vision unless you have a clear understanding of exactly what that vision is in the first place!

In Proverbs 29:18, we read that God's people perish through the lack of vision. That is, if we are not decisively clear about what we believe and where we are going, then we seriously risk being diverted from the correct course into a worthless by-path meadow. In a similar vein, Paul in Ephesians 4:14, was concerned that immature thinking (in this case, not really knowing what we believe) leads Christians to be "tossed back and forth by the waves, and blown here and there by every wind of teaching and by the cunning and craftiness of people in their deceitful scheming." As Christians involved in education, we must have a clear concept of what we are involved in and of where we are heading. We must realize the radical distinctiveness of our educational goal of challenging children to celebrate the lordship of Christ over all of creation. We must be able to flesh out our assertion that Christian schools exist to assist families in helping their sons and daughters to learn about the world and their places and tasks in it as God's responsible stewards and image bearers. In short, if we are going to maintain the biblical integrity of our Christian schools, then our school communities must have a precisely articulated and broadly shared vision of what they are about. This applies not only to the founding generation of parents and teachers, but to every subsequent generation as well.

The goals of the Christian school are distinctively Christian. The view of education that they hold is not shared by the secular world. But, sadly, it seems that some educators, parents, or school board members in the Christian schools movement have insufficient insight even to verbalize their goals, let alone explain or defend them. In 1982, Jay E. Adams wrote a book entitled *Back to the Blackboard: Design for a biblical Christian school*. We may not all agree with everything that Adams suggests in it, but he makes some points that, decades later, are still worthy of careful consideration. Adams comments:

> Why is it that parents don't make a distinctively Christian education their first concern? Why is it that the greatest complaint I hear from Christian teachers is that they don't know how to teach in a distinctively Christian manner and are most disappointed when they recognize that apart from [Christian fellowship among teachers, the opportunities to pray, to read the Bible, and to talk about Christ], what they are doing is not appreciably different from what goes on at the pagan school down the street? And why is it that students graduating from Christian schools do not make a greater impact for Christ on their communities, at their jobs and in their churches? Why is it that among them there is so often an "if-this-is-Christian-education-so-what?" attitude rather than a recognition that they are involved in something very special, uniquely preparing them to assume roles in this world for Jesus Christ? Why do you seldom meet a graduate from a Christian school who has a sense of destiny? In short, why aren't teachers, administrators, and parents *excited* about Christian education? . . . I must answer all of these questions with one response: It is because of a lack of vision – the lack of a truly Biblical vision – that there is so little excitement in Christian education. (Adams 1982, 10)

Over the years, it has been my privilege to serve on Christian school Boards of Governors in three continents, and to have been involved in the lives of many more. I can only concur with Adam's comments. The Christian community in general, including many well-intentioned people involved in Christian schools, has unwittingly jettisoned a biblical view of education with a degree of carefree abandon that is unparalleled in the recent history of Christian thought. Or rather, perhaps it would be more correct to claim that many of us as Christians have never really taken the time to develop a comprehensive Christian view or vision of education in the first place.

For some people in Christian schools, their basic reason for involvement is escapism. In the 1960's, the "enemy" in the United States of America that many unjustly sought to flee was racial integration. In much of the western world today, the Christian school is seen as an escape from falling academic or moral standards or as a refuge from the alarming increase in drugs and violence in public schools. The one thing that has been notable by its absence in many cases is any real understanding not just of what the Christian school is against, but of what it stands *for*. In other words, as Adams claims, there is an abject lack of vision! And Christian schools risk quickly losing their integrity and running off the rails when there is this lack of an articulated vision.

THE IMPORTANCE OF THE CHURCH

Adams implicitly blames the Christian schools themselves for not possessing the sense of direction and purpose that is necessary to maintain a dynamic education that continues to excite children with the challenge to celebrate the lordship of Christ over all of creation. Perhaps this analysis is not completely just. Rather, it is first of all the churches and then the Christian education departments of Christian colleges that we should hold accountable for not instilling this perspective in the parents of children and in the teachers who teach at Christian schools. The gospel often is reduced to an inoffensive, self-centered mantra, producing "almost Christians" (Dean 2010), where, as Niebuhr once commented (1937, 193), the gospel is defined as "A God without wrath brought men without sin into a Kingdom without judgment through the ministrations of a Christ without a Cross."

Christian churches often seem to be immersed in an amorphous mass of "warm fuzzies" and a bubble-and-froth Christianity that has little real substance and lacks the fiber, substance, and total world and life view that are needed to help those in the pews appreciate the dynamic all-of-life perspective of the gospel of Jesus Christ. Because the Christian school may be seen to be exclusivist, separatist, judgmental, and certainly controversial, the pulpit sometimes is the very place from which the Christian school is condemned.

THE IMPORTANCE OF CHRISTIAN COLLEGES AND UNIVERSITIES

It is to some Christian colleges that we must also issue a very strong charge.

In many countries, such as the United States, Canada, and India, and to a degree in Korea, Australia, and New Zealand, they are the institutions that train our future teachers. They give student teachers the mindset and framework, and then the methodologies and skills, for teaching. Though there are some wonderful exceptions, in my experience, as I visit these institutions, I do not always see education programs that grapple with basic issues of what education is all about from a Christian perspective. But it should be right there, in these so-called Christian halls of learning, that our teacher trainees should become excited by the distinctives of Christian education. It is here that they should be challenged to ask "Why?" about all aspects of education and then, under the guidance of biblical norms and informed professors, develop a rich Christian *vision* for education that will drive them, inspire them, and envision them as they move into our Christian schools. All too often they come away empty-handed. Glanzer and Talbert (2005) concluded from their research into students in a Christian teacher training program that "most students did not perceive their faith or worldview directly informing their pedagogical methods or curriculum" (Glanzer & Talbert 2005, 25).

One response from Christian colleges to this issue has been "Well, we are preparing the bulk of our students to teach in the public school system and so the issue of a Christian perspective on education is not relevant for them. They need to be well prepared in the secular way of looking at things." Such a view is a travesty. In a special way, the Christian teacher going into a public school is entering a battlefield. She must become aware of the non-neutrality of education, of the religious and idolatrous vision of secular education, and of how a Christian teacher can work in a dramatic salt-and-light way in this unique mission field (see Chapter 14). This can only be done from the basis of a carefully articulated and dynamic Christian philosophy of education.

We need continually to be in supportive prayer for those who teach in Christian colleges, that they will carry out their charge faithfully before the Lord. They must live and give to their students an exciting sense of destiny and purpose as they help shape trainee teachers' visions of Christian education – irrespective of the type of school in which these students finally will teach. In North America, some Christian colleges with teacher education programs, such as Dordt College, Trinity Western, Covenant College, Calvin College, Redeemer, to name just a few, are very successful at doing this.

Christian schools generally will rise to the top in many measurements of academic performance because of the dedication of their faculties and the involved commitment of many of their parents. But we must emphasize that these measurements do not reveal the true distinctive of the Christian school. If they did, then Christian schools should be seen as little more than academically rigorous, alternative private secular schools. Belz (1993) makes a similar point:

> Christian schools will be found overall to have done a very good job in terms of general education, but will be disappointing in terms of instilling in their graduates a profound sense of discipleship. On basic skills tests, SAT scores, and other standardized measurements, Christian school graduates will increasingly outperform their counterparts from public education. But in terms of a radical adoption of a Christian perspective on life, the differences . . . will be disappointing. (Belz 1993, 1)

Sadly, even in in the present day, we still have schools that claim to be genuinely Christian, telling their constituencies in writing that "the purpose of attending Christian college is to achieve academically" (2013, source withheld). No. Academic achievement is a worthy outcome, but it is not the foundational purpose. The true distinctive of the Christian school lies in the application of a vision and purpose that provide for the cultivation of radical discipleship – or, as Wolterstorff (2012) claims, as a training ground for discerning dissent and reform in the name of Christ. And if this vision and purpose are not carefully fostered and nurtured so that they are the primary vital commitment that the board, parents, and faculty (and ultimately, the students) can articulate with passion, then the school might as well close its doors. Good academics and a strong record in job placement are not evil. They represent legitimate aspects of college life. But they do not provide an adequate organizing fulcrum for the Christian school.

A worthy vision for a Christian school is the goal of Christian Heritage College in Brisbane, Australia, of transforming and equipping students to transform their world by pursuing truth from a Christian worldview perspective (2013, Christian Heritage College). When this vision, either in word or in practice, is replaced by worthwhile but subsidiary goals that become ends in themselves, then the school has lost its Christian integrity and could be doing more harm than good. Every Christian school needs regular external audits to ensure that it is continuing to be true to its vision and purpose (see Chapter 13's discussion about a critical friend consultancy).

An Educational Confession or Creed Expresses Vision and Purpose

Because of the fundamental importance of the issue of vision for the integrity and survival of Christian schools, we need to spend some time outlining the key elements of a faithful vision. This starts with an articulation of core beliefs that will determine the vision statement. In the context of a Christian educational institution, this articulation is sometimes called a school's educational creed or confession.

Drafting an educational creed or confession is different from writing a carefully argued philosophy of Christian education. Rather, here we are dealing with simple statements of fundamental issues about things such as our common faith, humankind, the task of parents, the task of the school, the nature of children, our understanding of the world, and the effect that these perspectives will have upon the educational task. What we *believe* about these issues should provide us with our presuppositions, philosophy, and vision. What we believe should give us direction for the content of our mission and purpose statements. It is important for all Christian schools to state and continually stress their distinctive belief statements about these key doctrinal issues. They must be living documents – not buried in a publication or accreditation report somewhere and forgotten, but believed, consulted, and acted upon, providing the touchstone for decision and action.

If a school does not articulate a confession or creedal statement (sometimes given a less controversial name, such as school pillars) of the basic belief position that drives the whole philosophy, methodology, and practice of the Christian school, then an important foundation stone is missing. In biblical terms, it is similar to the house that was built upon the sand, which eventually came tumbling down because it had no firm attachment to anything. These beliefs also will be more than just a re-expression of a guiding church's doctrinal statement. There will be similarities, because the Christian church and the Christian school share the same faith and have a common commitment to the Word of God. But a denomination's creedal statement expresses an ecclesiastical confession concerning the people of God functioning as an institutional church. A Christian school's creedal statement expresses an educational confession concerning the people of God functioning in the area of pedagogy.

The term "confession" is preferable to the term "creed," because the term "creed" has a major drawback: it is a word that describes a *state of affairs* rather than an *action*. It is a noun whereas the term describing what is involved here should be able to be used as a verb. A creed is something that exists **out there**, but what needs to be expressed here is something that primarily proclaims the heart commitment or conviction of the people involved. For this reason, the term educational **confession** is preferred to the term educational creed. A confession is more readily seen as something that people **do** – something that they **confess** together. The term 'creed' cannot be used in English in the same way. It is essential that an educational confession is something that its adherents **do** – that is, something that they confess and act upon.

A school's confession should be the humble, fervent expression of what the community that chooses the school's Board of Directors believe in their hearts in response to the Word of the Lord in the area of education. Only secondarily does it become words written on paper. It must be said believingly in the same way that the Apostle's Creed should be recited, and not become just familiar sentences that are repeated as mere dry-bones incantation.

ELEMENTS OF AN EDUCATIONAL CONFESSION

An educational confession should address key areas such as education itself, the world, and the child, with whom education is concerned. It is the link between the Scriptures and the educational process, and gives vision to the shape and direction of activities in the school. In order to do this, the confession should include statements concerning the following elements.

First, a confession will include a statement of the central core faith common to all Christian confessions. It has already been said that this is not an ecclesiastical creed, so that the statements here will express the authoritative position of the Scriptures and the common faith of Christians in a relatively short series of key affirmations. Some people would accept an expanded version of the Apostle's Creed here. The example given in the sample constitution in the following few pages is a little more detailed. This section declares the basic common belief of all those involved, is applicable to all aspects of the life of the church, and expresses the corporate core commitment that separates off the people involved as being Christians from those who seek to serve a god-substitute.

Second, the educational confession will consider the purpose of the Christian school in society as a cultural endeavor in a specifically nal context. This will involve a definition of a school. The last section entitled "Man's Life and Task" provides such a constitution. Other acceptable definitions are book.

nfession should include a statement of the god's creation, of history as the unfolding of as the stage of Christian witness and action.

The next matter to be addressed in the confession will be the nature of the educational process. Here the following points need to be considered:

(i) What is a child?

(ii) The biblical context of child growth, development, responsibility, and calling in which education occurs.

(iii) The effect of sin and redemption on the educational process.

(iv) The specific task of the teacher, and of the team of teachers, within the school.

(v) The relation between parents and the school.

Finally, the confession should lay out presuppositions and principles guiding the education curriculum. These include:

(i) Each child, as a creative image-bearer of the Lord, is a responsible person who must be accepted for who s/he is and as s/he is. This will run counter to the content-centered approach of many conservative private schools.

(ii) Creation is ordered by the Word of God and is thus the meaningful context of education. This will run counter to the popular child-centered approach of many modern schools and their curricula in which we are seen as the creator instead of as the unfolder of God's creation.

(iii) The authority of the teacher, given by God, is for the sake of the responsible freedom of the students. The teacher is to guide and lead them so that they come to the redemptive acknowledgment of the all-inclusive nature of God's Kingdom. This is not to suggest that the school is an evangelistic center constantly urging students to become Christians. A school's task is educational not evangelistic in the traditional sense. But the school should bring the students to see the requirements that God places before all people for the various sectors of his Kingdom, with the Cross of Jesus Christ providing meaning and coherence to everything as the center point of God's big story. In this way, if they are Christians or become so later, students will have been prepared to participate meaningfully and obediently in society as God's representatives.

(iv) Because the school is a place where pupils are led, everything including matters such as discipline and dress code, for example, must have educative significance. The details of these particular matters would not be worked out in the actual confession, but in the school's policies and procedures manuals.

A Worked Example

The sample confession of faith that follows is one that was developed a few years ago in the Christian community in Dunedin, New Zealand, as concerned parents and supporters worked towards the establishment of a Christian school. That school now exists – Liberton Christian School – and has been functioning vibrantly and faithfully for many years. This confession has been amended over the years as the school community has sought to keep it a living document that is shared, believed, and acted upon by new generations of parents.

A SAMPLE CONFESSION

In response to the Scriptures in which the Lord God reveals to his people principles intensely relevant to education, we confess:

a. **Our Common Faith**

(i) We believe in one God, eternal in three persons, Father, Son and Holy Spirit, the only living and true God, the Creator of Heaven and Earth.

(ii) We believe that the Holy Scriptures of the Old and New Testaments are the only inspired and infallible written revelation of God to man, and are the supreme authority in all matters of life and faith.

(iii) We believe in the universal sovereignty of God over all that He has created and maintains.

(iv) We believe in the providence of God, whereby He sustains the universe, governs the world, supplies the needs of His people and brings His will to pass.

(v) We believe that man was created in the image and likeness of God, to have dominion over the earth and to do all things to the glory of God.

(vi) We believe in man's universal fall into sin through Adam's transgression and in his subsequent disobedience, guilt, condemnation and judgment before God.

(vii) We believe that God by His grace, and according to His good pleasure, restores to Himself and to His service, all who in true faith call on the Name of Jesus Christ.

(viii) We believe in Jesus Christ, the only begotten Son of the Father; that He was conceived of the Holy Spirit, born of a virgin, crucified as a ransom for many, died and was buried, was raised from the dead and ascended into heaven.

(ix) He is presently at the right hand of God the Father, and will personally return to earth in power and glory to judge the living and the dead, executing God's just condemnation on the impenitent and receiving the redeemed to eternal glory.

(x) We believe in the necessity of the work of the Holy Spirit to apply the benefits of Christ's redemption to individual sinners, working in them regeneration, faith, repentance, sanctification and glorification.

(xi) We believe in one holy and universal church which Christ the Lord and Head, gathers, preserves and defends for Himself by His Spirit and Word, out of the whole human race.

b. **Confessing Christ in Education**

(i) MAN'S LIFE AND TASK

WE CONFESS that all things are created by God and as His creation remain under His rule, are upheld by His power and exist for His glory;

that mankind, as the creature uniquely made in God's image, is given dominion over creation to rule it and develop it under God;

that human life in its entirety is religion, unfolding in service to the one true God or of a God-substitute;

that man can never be a meaning-maker in God's creation but is instead called to experience and confess creation's God-given order and meaning;

that in fulfillment of his task, man is called to discern the many ways in which God calls each of His creatures to serve Him, so that man may cultivate creation in all its richness in obedience to God's commands and in harmony with the laws by which God in His faithfulness maintains His creation;

that education is the process of nurturing and directing the child, as a creature made in God's image, to the responsible and obedient exercise of this dominion, in fulfillment of His calling under God.

(ii) THE WORD OF GOD

WE CONFESS that the whole creation finds its coherence and meaning in the only begotten Son of the Father, the living Word of God through Whom all things were made and are continually upheld;

that the supreme standards for all matters of education shall be the written word of God, known as the Old and New Testaments, as these open our eyes to the activity of God in originating and ordering His creation through His Word and Spirit, and leads us to confess Jesus Christ as the Word incarnate;

that while the study of the Scriptures is no substitute for the study of God's creation, Scripture remains indispensable and determinative for our knowledge of God, of ourselves and of the rest of creation, and thus for the whole educational task.

(iii) SIN

WE CONFESS that in sin man has repudiated God in favour of God-substitutes, and has therefore cut himself off from all true knowledge of God, of himself, and of the meaning of creation, so that the light that he supposes he has is darkness and his wisdom is folly;

that no area of human knowledge is free from this sinful falsifying;

that apart from the one sinless man, Christ Jesus, all men alike grope in darkness;

that disobedience to God is inherently destructive of man and of the creation over which man has been given dominion, but that the creation remains continually upheld in grace in subjection to God's law;

that no human activity, including the educational task, can enable man of himself to fulfill his destiny or bring himself to salvation, but the redemption and renewal of human life lie in the power of the blood and Spirit of Christ alone;

that true education is possible only where the fear of God is re-established by God's grace in the heart of man, as the indispensable foundation of all wisdom and knowledge.

(iv) REDEMPTION IN CHRIST

WE CONFESS that God in Christ by the Cross has restored the whole creation to harmony with Himself, making all things new in Christ;

that although the fulfilment of this restoration awaits the future revelation of Christ in glory, yet, in principle, by the present work of the Holy Spirit in the world, it is a present reality to be reckoned with in faith in every area of life;

that Christ in His redemption, by the Holy Spirit, is creating from among the old humanity in Adam a new humanity in Christ, united in the Church which is His body, the covenant community bound to Him as Head;

that the covenant community is God's appointed means, through the power of the Holy Spirit within the community, for communicating the redemption of Christ to the world;

that although by the grace of God, men who reject the Word of God as the ordering principle of life provide many valuable insights into the structure of reality, yet, because the religious direction of their thought remains radically opposed to that of the covenant community in Christ, there can be no possibility of a synthesis of their systems of thought with the Scripturally-directed thought which Christ's covenant community is called to pursue.

(v) THE SPECIAL TASK OF PARENTS

WE CONFESS that God has given parents the responsibility for the nurture of their children by discipline and instruction according to the Word of the Lord;

that in accordance with this responsibility, God has given parents authority over their children to guide and direct them in the way of righteousness;

that God has given children on their part a corresponding responsibility to honour, respect and obey their parents in the Lord;

that faithful training of children means instructing them in the covenant revealed in Scripture by which God binds His people to Himself in whole-hearted love, which covenant is the key to the fulfillment of all man's life;

that while parents may invite others to share with them in the nurture of their children, the responsibility for this nurture remains the responsibility of the parents, whose task it always remains to determine the character and religious direction of their children in every aspect.

The Christian School's Mission and Purpose Statement

The school's confession can now be used to provide the context for the development and nurturing of its mission and purpose statement. Usually, this consists of just one or two sentences. For example, the mission statement of Bellevue Christian School in Seattle, reads, "Our goal is to prepare young people to live fully for God in a rapidly changing world with the ability to understand, evaluate and transform the world from the foundation of God's unchanging values" (Our goal, 2013). Similarly, Covenant Christian School in Sydney has a mission statement which says that, "Our desire is to be part of God's plan to unite all things in heaven and on earth under the lordship of Jesus Christ by assisting parents in the nurture of their children, providing a Christ-centered, biblically grounded, culturally engaging and academically rigorous education which equips children to live for God's glory" (Our desire, 2013).

Stemler and Bebell (2012) have investigated patterns and rationales for different school mission statements in North America. Their research is useful, and they suggest strategies for the development of such statements that can reflect a number of primary and secondary emphases. Potential foci that they consider include emotional development, cognitive development, a civics emphasis, social development, and vocational preparation. Unfortunately, they appear not to recognize the determinative, underlying *worldview* characteristics of all foci, which leads them to a dualistic consideration of "spiritual development" as just one parallel feature among many. For this reason, their material, though useful, should be used with discernment.

Maintaining the Integrity and Vision

The articulation of a clear vision or confessional statement is not the end of the matter. In fact, it is just the beginning. We cannot overstress the importance of the contention that as much effort needs to go into keeping the vision alive, as went into developing it in the first place. The integrity of a school's direction will be violated if its sense of purpose is not nurtured as the touchstone to which all major decisions and policies are referred. All structural and directional questions in the life of the school need to be considered by examining them in the light of the vision statement. Decisions about buildings, school fees, uniforms, staffing appointments, school audits, to name just a few, should never be made without foundational and overt reference to the school's vision and purpose statements. It is only when this is done that the school community can be confident that the course charted by the school is faithful to the school's intent and purpose.

This approach also gives the school confidence that potentially difficult questions can be answered. For example, when a Christian school has developed and upholds its vision statement, based upon a clearly articulated confessional commitment, then there is a basis for dealing with issues such as:

- The suggestion from a parent at the PTA meeting that the school should focus upon being a college preparatory school.
- Is it appropriate for the church pastor to be the chairman of the school board?
- Shouldn't we offer manual arts courses just to the less academically able students, since they will go to community/technical college whereas the brighter ones will go on to university?
- What is wrong with saying that an outside publishing company determines our curriculum, as long as it is a Christian company?
- Why do we pay different salaries to high school teachers from those paid to equivalently qualified grade school teachers?
- Should we or should we not have uniforms?
- What is a good balance between Christian and non-Christian children in our student population?
- What is our basis for giving prizes at the end of the year?
- Why do some people object to outcomes-based education?
- What is the significance of the notion (Smith, 2009) that we are involved in "forming" as much as "informing" in the Christian school?
- What should our report cards look like?
- Should we require all children to attend chapel?
- What should we do when some parents and teachers object to a "spiritual emphasis" week?
- Should we accept government financial aid – isn't this "accepting money from Caesar"?

The pattern that checks decisions and direction against the school's vision statement needs to be instituted at all levels of the school community – the Board, the faculty, the parent community, and the student body. What follows are some suggestions as to how to maintain the integrity of the vision at each of these levels. It must be said that each suggestion involves work – hard analytical work by the people involved. As Christians, we have often been accused of shying away from applying our minds to the biblical integration of faith and learning. But Christianity is not a mindless religion. In Romans 12:2, Paul did not say "Do not conform to the pattern of this world, but be transformed by the **removal** of your mind." He exhorted us to be transformed by the **renewal** of our minds. We need to live as if we believe this. Prayerfully thinking issues through, so as to establish a biblical, firm foundation for our life's work, is not a luxury-optional extra. It is a fundamental requirement for all Christians who want to be able to give an answer for the faith that lies within them and who wants to be able to be sure that their actions are a true reflection of what they believe. Let us then explore some of the work that should happen at the various levels in the Christian school so as to maintain the integrity of the school's vision.

MAINTAINING THE VISION ON THE BOARD OF DIRECTORS
In his article entitled "Patterns of Organization and Procedure for Christian School Boards," Kienel (1988) comments that prospective board members of Christian schools must "be fully aware of the school's mission, organizational structure, the school's history, the legal and fiscal responsibilities of board members, the time commitment, and the administrative style of the school's chief executive officer."

Many would be tempted to say that Kienel is expecting too much and that he is not living in the real world if he expects prospective board members to be as informed as he suggests. For example, in some settings it is parents who elect board members, so how can you ensure that the people that parents vote onto the board meet Kienel's requirements?

Kienel is not being unrealistic. The school Board of Directors, or Council, is the prime policy-making body for most Christian schools. The men and women on the board will chart the course of the school during their terms of office as directors. It is important that appropriate business, management, and other professional skills exist on the board, but it is absolutely imperative that all board members can agree with and supportively articulate the school's vision. How can they chart a course that maintains the direction and integrity of the school if they do not personally understand and echo the school's vision?

To be sure, specialist qualities such as financial acumen, etc., are needed on a school board, but all appointees, whatever other talents they bring, must have a prior commitment to the school's vision and purpose. Board membership must be limited to those who share the school's vision. This is possible even where boards are elected by parents. All that needs to occur is that the list of nominees submitted by parents for consideration as directors be screened prior to the election taking place, so that each prospective member is pre-vetted for suitability in this important area of vision. A provision that establishes this course of action can be included in the school's constitution.

As with other members of the school community, steps may well need to be taken to assist board members, individually and collectively, to comprehend the school vision, so that when they review school activities or set policies for the future, they can carry out their primary task of ensuring fidelity with the vision in a responsible way. Board retreats, presentations to the board by staff members (arranged through the headmaster) of classroom activities, a section of each board meeting reviewing a section of school policy, are just three ways that boards can give attention to this most important task.

Maintaining the Vision Among Faculty

Considerable attention must be given to maintaining the integrity of a school's vision among its administrators and teachers. These are the ones primarily responsible for implementing the school's vision of education in the classroom and thus they ultimately will determine the success or failure of the vision's implementation. Time should be devoted during the teacher conference at the start of the school year, for both new teachers and old, to experience an explanation and exploration of the school confession that embodies the school's vision. There are many ways of doing this, such as using returning staff to lead a discussion, or directing discussion that results from the viewing of a film such as *Dead Poets Society*, or studying a book together, or inviting in outside speakers.

Of course, effective, targeted professional development is vital to this task. Without adequately equipped (and ongoing re-equipping) of faculty and staff, the vision and aligned practice of the Christian school can never be secure. This is one of the reasons why an entire chapter later in this book is devoted to the strategic area of teacher professional development.

A new means to maintaining vision among faculty has been made available by groups such as Edserv International (www.edservinternational.org) and the Square Inch Group (www.squareinchgroup.com). It is called a critical friend consultancy. This is where a sympathetic and knowledgeable outsider is given access to the school, its personnel, and its activities, in order to carry out an identity audit. In particular, the alignment between the school's vision and mission on the one hand, and its practice on the other, is reported upon in a non-evaluative context (i.e., it is not a part of an accreditation or licensing process). Vardy (2011), and Butler (2011) and colleagues provide guidelines for this strategy, which is discussed in some detail in the chapter 13.

MAINTAINING THE VISION AMONG THE PARENT COMMUNITY

Christian schools should not be mere recipients of children – such that the school is viewed as a separate world from the family – as if children are sent to the school at the start of the day, and return from it at the end of that day, with the two worlds rarely meeting. In fact, the Christian school is partly an extension of the home. It exists to assist families in the nurture of their children. Parents enlist the help of doctors and nurses to ensure the medical wellbeing of their children. In the same sense, parents enlist the help of teachers in schools to assist in the educational wellbeing and nurture of their children. Consequently, much attention must be given to ensuring that the vision of education and nurture that the school possesses conforms to the vision of education and nurture that the family possesses.

If the visions of the school and the home are in conflict, then there exists the possibility that the school's initial vision will lose its integrity as it becomes changed to conform to that of the parents – or vice versa. Schools exist all over the world today that were started by men and women with a real vision for Christian education, but which have degenerated into little more than elitist college preparatory institutions. Why? Often because insufficient attention was given to maintaining the integrity of the school's vision throughout the parent community. Ongoing parent vision conferences, for all parents, should be just as important as teacher professional development in the life of the Christian school.

IMPLICATIONS FOR ENROLLMENT

This raises the thorny issue of enrollment policies for the Christian school. Ronald P. Chadwick has commented that "In my conversations with many Christian school administrators across America today, the unanimous conclusion is that the strength of the Christian school is in direct proportion to the Christian home or homes that are represented in the school family" (Chadwick 1990, 175). Some Christian educators have a firm commitment to limiting enrollment only to children from Christian homes, on the basis that the key function of the Christian school is to nurture the children of the family of God. Other Christian educators welcome children from non-Christian homes. They do this on the basis of not hiding their light under a bushel and wanting the Christian school to be a community that acts as salt and light in a lost and needy world.

Whichever side of the debate Christians come down on, they must first be sure that the school's vision statement, and the policies that implement it, address the question of the foundation and goals of the school. Second, they must ensure that all new families are aware of the school's vision and are prepared if not to support it, then at least not to oppose it. Families need to know the sort of environment that exists in the school, where teachers and school supporters pray every day that their students will come to put their trust in Jesus Christ. The Christian worldview being nurtured in the school is worthless without this initial commitment. If it is a situation where children from non-Christian families are encouraged to enroll, then time must be spent ensuring that these parents understand the dichotomy between their position and that of the school. In the same way that a secular school hopes children will embrace its secular religious perspective, parents sending their children to the Christian school also must be prepared to acknowledge the school's Christian worldview character, and be prepared for the reality that the school's deliberate hope is that their children will embrace the school's Christian commitment for themselves.

MAINTAINING THE VISION AMONG THE STUDENT BODY

The students too need to know what the school is all about, and why they spend so many hours there. Teachers need to ensure that their total teaching environment – classroom, curriculum, lifestyle and attitudes, assessment procedures, discipline policies, to name but a few of its components, is challenging and meaningful for the students in a way that conforms to the school's vision and also provokes the students to personalize that vision and seek to give effect to it in their own lives.

Curriculum design and content are central to this issue, as are organizational matters in the school such as discipline and assessment. These are addressed specifically in later chapters. If a teacher is motivated and excited by the school's vision, then she, as the molder of the dreams of her students, will excite them with this vision as well.

If a vision similar to that which was outlined in the sample confession earlier in this chapter is the living foundation of the Christian school, then we can joyfully anticipate that the school's graduates will become vital members of society, seeking the welfare of the city in which they live. They will realize God's peace and fulfillment in their own lives, and be effective ambassadors of God's grace and wisdom to those around them. In turn, modeled on their teachers, they will become exciting messengers of reconciliation to others in every facet of existence into which they venture. This, and nothing less, is the true vision of Christian education.

Chapter 6

Responsibilities and Relationships
in the Christian School

THE STATE, PARENTS, AND TEACHERS

This chapter deals with two important issues that arise in the life of all Christian schools: the relationship of the Christian school with the state, and relationships between parents and teachers in the Christian school community. When adequate consideration is not given to principles regarding these issues at an earlier date, administrators and teachers can end up in crisis situations making quick-fire decisions that are regretted afterwards. However, when problems are addressed in a context where principles have been determined previously, away from the heat of conflict, then there is a heightened expectation for a God-honoring, consistent resolution.

As with the topics addressed in other chapters, the key concerns here will be to establish a biblical framework for each issue, to encourage the foundation for this framework to be portrayed in the school's foundational documents, and to advocate a greater awareness of this framework for all existing and prospective members of the school community. From this basis, the structural handles that schools should use to deal with controversial matters can be developed in ways that are responsive to the individual situations of each Christian school.

THE RESPONSIBILITY OF THE CHRISTIAN SCHOOL IN ITS RELATIONSHIP WITH THE STATE (GOVERNMENT)

Christians in many countries in the modern post-Christian West are becoming increasingly vocal in their discussions about the involvement of the government/state in society in general, and in education in particular. These discussions usually fall into one of two categories. The first view is characterized by the oft-repeated comment that "The government must do more to. . . ." The second view is characterized by the frequent remark that "The government should not be involved in. . . ."

The purpose of this section is to bring the light of the Word of God to bear on the whole question of the task of the government or state in society, and especially in education. To do this, we will outline in more detail the two views of the state held by many Christians, and we will point to a biblical perspective of the state. Also, we will consider parental responsibility in education so that, finally, we will have an adequate foundation from which to address the issue of the task of the government *in education*.

TWO VIEWS OF THE TASK OF THE GOVERNMENT
"The Government must do more. . . ."

Christians who hold this view recognize that we live in an increasingly complex age, a time in the world's history when technological developments have greatly increased humanity's ability to improve the general physical wellbeing of all people – as well as to annihilate humanity's very existence. These people urge governments to become more and more involved in regulating society in order to improve the state of all people and reduce the possibility of destruction. Education is seen as a key in this process, and these Christians join with others, such as acclaimed secular educator Dr. Paul Brock, in encouraging governments to be much more involved in education. Says Brock:

> Where will we find the foundations of wisdom to identify and expose contemporary intellectual, religious or spiritual ignorance wherever manifestations of such ignorance flourish? What will guide and encourage us to seek, identify and reject political leadership of deceit, of cowardice, of humbug, of corruption – wherever such leadership may be flourishing in the First, Second, Third or any other World?
>
> What forces will protect us from the evils imposed on and within society under the banner of terrorism on the one hand, or under the banner of protecting us from terrorism on the other?
>
> . . . What forces will sustain democratic civilization from the attacks upon our individual, collective, and indeed national security on the one hand; and upon our liberty, privacy, fraternity, equality, mutual respect on the other . . . ?
>
> To what can we look today? Surely it must be to education. (Brock, 2006)

On a national level, government is encouraged to ensure that its educational system deals responsibly with current social issues like unemployment and the redistribution of wealth that developments such as computer technology have helped to bring about.

Perhaps one obvious example has been the loud call that many of these Christians have made urging the government to ensure that programs promoting irresponsible sexual attitudes do not become part of school curricula. George Counts (1889–1974), already mentioned in Chapter One for his open recognition of the non-neutrality of education, was a social reconstructionist who firmly believed that the political system should shape education, enabling it to be a key catalyst in social change.

"The Government should not be involved in. . . ."
On the other hand, there is another group of Christians, perhaps smaller but no less dedicated or concerned than the first, who insist that the government has far too much to say in our society. According to this view, governments have asserted controls (or unwittingly been given them by an unthinking population over the years) over the lives of their people that are excessive and unbiblical. Education is often highlighted as a case in point. It is affirmed that it is entirely against the Word of God for the state to be involved in education. The Bible instructs parents, not the state, to supervise the discipline and instruction of children. Therefore, the claim is made that Christians who develop Christian schools have the support of Scripture in ignoring what are seen as illegitimate government regulations concerning education.

It is possible to have some sympathy with both of these positions concerning the task of the state in education. Although they hold opposite points of view, they both appear to have some merit. How should a Christian respond in such a situation? Which group should receive one's allegiance? The way to an answer does not lie in a detailed analysis of each of these positions and then allying oneself to either one of them. The answer, as always, must lie first in the study of the Scriptures: "[In Christ] are hidden all the treasures of wisdom and knowledge" (Colossians 2:3). It is only in the God of the Scriptures that wisdom in anything, including the issue of the role of the state in education, will fully be found. We need to consider the Scriptural view of the state and the Scriptural view of who is responsible for education of children, so that the principles of the Word of God concerning the role of the state in education can then be understood.

A Biblical Perspective of the State
The God-given task of governing and adjudicating society has existed throughout history. The nature of the particular societies in which this task has been carried out has developed from the relatively simple family

structures of early biblical societies to the highly complex and differentiated patterns of today.

Nevertheless, whatever the social context, the God-given task of governing and adjudicating the affairs of humankind has involved the following factors: (1) the establishment and maintenance of relationships with foreign communities and the protection of the home society from assault by them; (2) the establishment and maintenance of order in society so that its citizens are as free as possible to carry out their self-appointed tasks; (3) the establishment and maintenance of laws to ensure fair dealings between individuals, families, and organizations, enabling them to develop and fulfill their various tasks like gathering food and maintaining shelter, commerce, cultural traditions, and education. The book of Isaiah for example, urges protecting the unprotected, such as widows and the fatherless.

This three-fold concept of the task of government is perhaps best expressed in the idea of *justice* in limited societal contexts. Chaplin (2010) details the biblical foundations for this perspective, and summarizes the case this way:

> It is easy to say that governments should pursue justice, but not so easy to say what the actual content of justice is. We can certainly offer some general implications: shielding the weak from the abuse of power by the strong; protecting those institutions necessary to human flourishing such as marriage, family, and local community; creating a public infrastructure for social life; supporting those who cannot meet their own basic human needs. (Chaplin 2010, 2)

The history of Israel in the Old Testament, when functioning faithfully, illustrates this point. Israel began as a simple tribal community under the patriarchal leadership of Abraham. After God chose Israel as a special covenant people, Abraham's children developed into twelve tribes. Laws and regulations were implemented for the fledgling nation, and its societal patterns differentiated into four authority structures: the family, the priesthood, the civil authority, and the prophets.

In Israel the responsibility of the civil authority, whether under Moses or later under the judges or the kings, was to maintain justice and to see to it that citizens were dealt with fairly. In Exodus 18:13 we read, "Moses took his seat to serve as judge for the people, and they stood around him from morning till evening." Here he was exercising one of the tasks of government in maintaining justice and order and correcting oppression among the people. According to the very next verse the pattern of government changed when, on Jethro's advice, Moses appointed other leaders to relieve him of the more minor claims for justice that arose. However, the basic role of government, maintaining justice and correcting oppression, continued.

While the biblical narrative brings us from the Ten Commandments via the God-appointed judges to the kings, we find that although the culturally based *form* of government changed, the *function* of government remained the same – to exercise God-given authority over the affairs of the people so as to maintain justice in society. The witness of the prophets in the Old Testament clearly emphasizes this. Time and time again, these prophets witnessed against and appealed to the governing authorities to return to or maintain justice among the people of God (see, e.g., Micah 3:1–12 and Hosea 7:1–16).

This theme carries into the New Testament as well, even though the actual type of government again was different. In the context of an oppressive Roman occupation, the Scriptures affirm that government exists as a God-ordained authority to uphold justice. Thus Christians are called generally to be obedient to it even in a despotic context (see, e.g., Romans 13:1–7, 1 Peter 2:13–14, and Matthew 22:15–22).

Establishing the biblical pattern of the role of government as a God-ordained one to maintain justice and correct oppression is only the beginning. We must now go on to see what this means and then consider its implications for education.

The first point is that this biblical view of the state establishes that the state's authority is God-given, and as such, it ought to be obeyed. Second, government is neither autonomous, nor the ultimate authority. It has a charge from God and must exercise this charge in obedience to his laws and commands and not necessarily in response to the whims of the masses or contemporary societal aberrations. Pilate did not recognize this when, for example, "wanting to satisfy the crowd," he released Barabbas and delivered Jesus to be crucified (Mark 15:8–15). Third, the state should not be a master but a servant to assist in the maintenance of justice (Mark 9:35).

A fourth implication of the biblical perspective of the state is that the state's authority is limited. Government in the Scriptures has clear and real authority in the area of justice, but its mandate doesn't allow it to usurp all authority over other social institutions. The family, marriage, education, economic institutions, church, and medical agencies are all examples of institutions that have their own integrity and authority. They are not mere expressions of the state. In 1 Peter 2:11–25, Peter exhorted his readers to be subject for the Lord's sake to every human institution.

He then went on to mention some of them such as the master-servant business relationship. Government was only one among a number of examples he gave. Government is only part of God's order for society, not the whole.

A real problem in society today is that many Christians and non-Christians have an unbiblical view of the state. They see it having an umbrella-type authority that extends over and may regulate all social institutions (except, perhaps, the institutional church). In the light of the egalitarian social welfare mentality that is increasing its hold in many Western countries, the result is that health, social welfare, commerce, and, in particular, education are all seen as arms of the state. Citizens look to the state for disaster relief, pre-tax pension or superannuation plans, accident compensation, and for near total control of the economy. We have also looked to the state to educate our children. This is contrary to the Word of God. The state's God-given authority is for maintaining justice. As we shall see later, this function necessarily involves the state in a limited way in other social institutions, like the family or education, as the upholder of justice, but this doesn't mean that the state has the authority to take them over. Rather, government is charged to maintain a just pattern in society such that these other institutions are free to exercise authority in their own areas in response to the Word of the Lord.

Given what has been said, it should be clear that if an issue of justice in education arises, then this is an area of limited legitimate government concern. Owning and operating the education system, though, is outside the sphere of legitimate government activity. Before this is examined in detail, however, there is another matter that must be addressed: if the state is not primarily responsible for education, who then is?

A Biblical Perspective of Parental Responsibility in Education

The Scriptures, in both the Old and the New Testament, affirm that parents are responsible for the nurture of their children. The famous passage in Deuteronomy 6:1–9 solemnly charges parents of God's chosen people to diligently instruct their children in all the ways of the Lord. Because our world belongs to God, studying it is an aspect of this study of the ways of the Lord. So, yes, parents have the responsibility for the education of their children. In Psalm 78:1–8, the Psalmist entreats parents to tell their children of the glorious deeds of the Lord so that "they would put their trust in God and would not forget his deeds." Paul, in Ephesians 6:4, instructs fathers to bring up their children "in the training and instruction of the Lord."

In our society this parental charge goes largely unheeded by many Christians, or if they do consider it, they limit it to a false "spiritual" Sunday School context rather than seeing it in the all-of-life context of the Bible. But the evidence of the Scriptures is clear. The state has not been given the responsibility for education, and it is not even the teacher who primarily will be called to give account at the end time by the Lord for educating the children. Rather it is the parents who must answer to God for their exercise of this responsibility. They rightly may enlist the support of others such as the church community to assist them in this task, but they always retain the primary charge and authority for this responsibility.

School education is an aspect of the nurture of children that originates and extends from the context of the home and family. In our specialized, technological society parents find it necessary to delegate some of that educational task to the school just as they delegate medical treatment to doctors. This is legitimate and necessary, but delegation doesn't remove responsibility. It is the Christian parents who are responsible for ensuring that the nurturing in the schools to which they send their children is truly Christian. It should be an education that strengthens and deepens what children learn at home and at church, and because education is never neutral, this can only occur coherently in a Christian school.

In 1948, 48 countries signed the United Nations Universal Declaration of Human Rights – there were no objections, and just eight abstentions. The Declaration strongly asserts the principle of parental control by declaring that "Parents have a prior right to choose the kind of education that shall be given to their children" (UN Universal Charter, Clause 26(3)). Unfortunately, many parents, including Christians, have yielded this right to, and perhaps even thrust it upon, the state. It is the United Nation's statement, not the contemporary situation, that best describes the biblical position.

RESPONSIBILITY OF THE STATE IN EDUCATION

Now that the biblical perspective of the state (justice) and the role of the parent in education (the responsibility is theirs) have been affirmed, we may return to the key question of the responsibility of the government in education. We can now reconsider the two points of view (pro-state and anti-state) outlined at the start of this chapter. The biblical perspectives on the responsibility of the state and the responsibilities of parents as outlined above don't support either of those two positions.

To say that the state must become more and more involved in all human institutions including education is unbiblical and will not solve the problems that its proponents are concerned about. In Kuyperian and Dooyeweerdian terms, this extended control of the state over multiple aspects of the lives of its citizens contravenes the principle of sphere sovereignty. As Baus (2008) explains, sphere sovereignty is the perspective that each sector of life (called modality) has its own God-given area of influence, within which it has authority to act, and wherein it can be held responsible for those actions. The family, the institutional church, business, government, and the arts are examples of sovereign such relatively independent spheres. Monolithic state involvement and control exceeds the state's sovereign sphere and encourages an unacceptable new totalitarianism.

The concept of sphere sovereignty, with its differentiated authority and responsibility, is not perfect, and it is not without its critics. However, as a general principle, and recognizing that there are areas of symbiotic interaction between spheres, the concept is a useful one in understanding a proper ordering of society in general, and the special place of schooling and parental rights in particular.

On the other hand, however, to say that parents are responsible for the education of their children is not to say that Christian education should exist completely independent of legitimate, justice-ensuring government. The biblical position is that the state ought to be the upholder of justice. It is charged to exercise this authority over all of society. Thus, the state necessarily does have a limited, legitimate involvement with other social institutions, while still respecting their integrity.

Moses is an example of a godly leader exercising justice in all matters of life for the people of Israel. Solomon sought the wisdom of the Lord in order to exercise justice in all of society in his day. Hence, we see him involved in quarrels over injustice involving social welfare and the family. This was an exercise that maintained justice within specific social institutions, but still respected the integrity and authority of those institutions. The same applies to education.

It is the task of the government to maintain justice in education so as to allow parents the right to exercise their God-given authority and responsibility in determining the character of the nurture, education, and schooling that their children will receive. Unfortunately, dualism in the church in the nineteenth century saw denominations forgo their support of parents in education, yielding this responsibility to governments, which, realizing the powerful molding nature of schooling, they often have only been too happy to take up.

It is in this context alone that the two elements, the role of the state and the role for the parent, can come together in a biblically obedient manner.

IMPLICATIONS FOR RELATIONSHIPS BETWEEN CHRISTIAN SCHOOLS AND THE STATE

Christians should seek for justice in the education of their children. This involves calling the government to allow Christians, without undue hindrance, to establish and maintain Christian schools if they believe that this is what the Lord requires of them. Christians also champion this right for parents of other religious persuasions. It also means acknowledging a general but limited legitimate role of the state to ensure that children within its boundaries are receiving genuine education, broadly defined as a preparation to function effectively in the culture. Third, this seeking of justice for Christian education requires that Christians maintain a wary and vigilant eye over legislators and legislation so as to protect and enhance their God-ordained responsibilities in education.

A study of court decisions (Furst 1992) in the United States is illuminating with regard to this issue. On a number of occasions, especially in the last 100 years, various interest groups have asked the U.S. court system to remove the privileges previously granted to Christian and parochial schools. Up until relatively recent times, the courts generally have upheld the view that the state has a legitimate interest in the proper education of its children, but that this interest should not conflict with the just prerogative of parents to direct the education of their children. The 1925 case of *Pierce v. Society of Sisters* in Oregon is a notable example of this principle. Even as late as 1979, as in the Kentucky case of *Kentucky State Board v. Rudasill*, courts across the U.S. have shown general sympathy with the rights of parents to choose the direction of their children's education.

However, much of the affirmation of these parental rights has come as a result of court cases where state educational authorities have sought to diminish the operational independence of Christian and other non-government schools. If anything, this trend of state interference has accelerated in recent years as debates about unilateral, state-imposed, outcome-based educational programs have raged across the U.S. and elsewhere. The issue of government interference has been exacerbated by secularism's convenient re-definition of the concept of tolerance – we tolerate anything that agrees with our position, but we will not tolerate claims by others to objective truth (Carson, 2012). Several jurisdictions seem sympathetic to the idea of removing the legal exemptions that allow Christian schools (especially those that accept government funding assistance) to discriminate in employment, taking away the right to ensure that our teachers adhere to a Christian confession and code of conduct. Catholic lawyer Adam Ch'ng's (2012) useful response to this secular attack on Christianity is worth reading.

Where government regulations and requirements for starting and maintaining schools are designed to ensure that the children in those schools are dealt with justly (for example, health regulations, staff training, a properly considered and developed, but not state-mandated, curriculum), then these regulations are well-founded and should be respected and adhered to. Many state education department officials, although perhaps not able to articulate it, do exercise their authority to ensure children are dealt with justly in school. Many of these officials are not deliberately attempting to subvert Christian education, but are carrying out their proper biblical function. Christians should be subject to them when their proper use of authority does not demand actions that clearly contravene God's written Word.

Nevertheless, the Christian education community must be vigilant in analyzing current trends and developments in education in order to confront those that are improper and then to provide the legal and moral force that mitigates against unjust intrusions by the state into education.

IMPLICATIONS FOR THE FUNDING OF CHRISTIAN SCHOOLS

Because government taxes its citizens and distributes some of this taxation money for education, many Christians believe it to be appropriate to call on the government to disperse these resources justly and without fear or favor. Parents who choose a Christian education for their children, compared with those who choose the state-funded secular humanist education, are often expected to pay twice for the education of their children: once through taxes and then once again through the fees that the Christian schools are forced to levy. This is unjust because it involves government fiscal endorsement of one religious perspective (secular humanism) over others. Furthermore, it increases the possibility of elitism in Christian schools because only those who can afford to pay twice can meet the fees that most schools have to charge.

Some Christian schools in various parts of the world have overcome this elitist trap by developing a school tuition structure based upon a proportion of family income. For example, the tuition level for an individual child could be set at 5 percent of a family's earnings. Thus, if the child came from the family of a high income earner such as a doctor, the dollar amount paid for tuition for the child would be quite high. On the other hand, the dollar amount for the child of a shop assistant would be much lower if the percentage of income concept was the basis of tuition calculation. It has even been demonstrated that children of unemployed people are able to attend a Christian school using this principle. The percentage of income method of calculating tuition can be a real demonstration of the interdependent, community nature of the Christian school and offers a dynamic salt-and-light alternative to secular concepts of funding while also overcoming the criticism of elitism in the Christian school movement.

Another perspective is that Christian schools should be funded on the same proportional basis as any other "state" school. Some warn that this approach opens the door to extended government interference on the basis of "he who pays the piper calls the tune." Each school needs to develop its own mission-faithful approach to this issue. It is encouraging to note that in New Zealand that Christian schools that have accepted significant government money and others that have only accepted minimal government help both live together fairly harmoniously in Christian fellowship in the same organization – the New Zealand Association of Christian Schools (NZACS).

RESPONSIBILITY OF PARENTS AND TEACHERS
Parents . . . Parents . . . Parents
Some time ago, I was asked to assist a Christian school in Europe that was experiencing challenges and division. The school was in its first few years of existence, and many of the parents whose children attended the school had previously taught their own children in a home schooling situation. The school board, quite properly, had established a number of committees to recommend policy in areas such as discipline, finance, and development. They also had appointed an education committee that was charged with the responsibility of developing the curriculum for the ̣ool. However, there were no teachers involved in any of these com-
parents were convinced of the biblical mandate that they
ate their children, and they felt that it was irrespon-
structure and shape that learning process.
ost puppet-like extensions of the home,
selected buttons in a pre-determined pro-
ded from any ownership.
at the teachers felt uncomfortable with this

situation, which is repeated to some degree in many Christian schools around the world. Some Christian schools have experienced deep conflict, and even division, as vitally concerned parents have sought to call teachers to task. Parents may feel that certain aspects of their school's program don't match with their own concept of Christian education. Therefore, they try to "bring the teachers to heel."

For their part, the teachers feel uncomfortable with this criticism. At times, it may appear to be ill-considered and based on hearsay; e.g., on the concerns of one parent who perhaps has never visited the school, observed classes at work, and become involved in the actual program of the school. At other times, a parent's comments may be accurate but may indicate an individual parent's desire for a pattern for the school that is different from the firmly held convictions of the teacher. It also may be that one group of parents is encouraging the school to move in a certain direction and another group is suggesting a move in an entirely different direction.

Teachers . . . Teachers . . . Teachers

On the other hand, educators are not immune from creating an atmosphere, even in Christian schools, that tends to disenfranchise parents. This is vividly displayed in the public arena when the leaders of the teaching fraternity's commitment to political correctness allows them to assume that they have the right to inculcate their view of the ideal society even if this contravenes the views of parents. John Leo (1992), a columnist for *U.S. News & World Report*, has reported on this issue. He provided evidence from many parts of the United States to support his contention that the educational establishment often views parents as an awkward encumbrance in the lives of public schools. He describes the conventional attitude among educational bureaucrats as suggesting that "We are the professionals; parents are the amateurs to be mollified or brushed aside."

Many parents, conditioned by often subliminal reassurances from educators that they are really superfluous in education, and weakened by their own lack of understanding of the biblical position of the family, have come to accept being passed over or excluded from educational decision-making. The few parents who do make an effort to become involved sometimes have to overcome many barriers, including the jargon and mystique with which some educators at all levels surround the teaching process. Consequently, they often find their participation limited such activities as fund-raising or helping in the school lunch p

These are worthy and important activities, but they have little to do with helping to shape the educational process.

Happily, the state of affairs above does not represent the situation in many Christian schools. The parents' actual decision to take their children out of the "free" public education system already indicates that they have a vital, concerned awareness for their children's education. P.T.A. meetings at Christian schools are often attended by a majority of the parent community. They may be lively, dynamic affairs, where any aspect of school life is discussed. Yet, tensions between parents and teachers continue to exist. Talks on this topic at Christian education conferences are often very well-attended.

How do we find a way through the minefield of this issue? As has been the case in all sections of this book, we need to affirm again that the answer doesn't lie initially in presenting a whole range of strategies. The answer lies first in developing a biblical understanding of the issue and then developing courses of action that respond to this understanding. A beautiful feature of the Christian school situation is that most of the parents and teachers involved take seriously their responsibility and authority in education. Our purpose here is to discover how these various responsibilities and authorities mesh together in a grace-filled school community to benefit the student and to bring glory of God. One way to enlarge our understanding of this issue is to consider the concept of "office."

THE CONCEPT OF OFFICE

Much of the rest of this chapter is devoted to exploring the nature of and interaction between parents and teachers in the school setting. Both parties are deeply committed to the wellbeing of the children involved, and yet this relationship at times can be fraught with challenges. It is very common for each party to feel that the other has "overstepped their authority" and has insufficient respect for the other. But if schooling is to truly work in the best interest of the student, it is important that there be harmony between these most important stakeholders.

Assuming a humble and cooperative spirit, three things are vital if the relationship between home and school is to be harmonious. The first is a shared worldview. This issue has already been discussed at length in earlier chapters. The second is a commitment to work in community, with an openness to at times subordinate individual preferences to those of the group. We will return to the importance of a collaborative community later. The third prerequisite is a shared appreciation for the concept of office.

Office, in this context, does not refer to a physical place. "Office" refers to the authority and obligations pertaining to a recognized position or agency, with the rights and privileges pertaining to it. Christian catechisms talk about Jesus' offices of prophet, priest, and king. The idea of the priesthood of all believers is also expressing the concept of office. The term is used in this sense when a person seeking election to government is described as "running for *office*." In a similar sense, the secretary, chairperson, and treasurer in an organization are referred to as its officeholders. Spykman (1985) suggests that the language of John Calvin in his *Institutes* is strongly reflective of the concept of office, and that Kuyper built on this in the Stone Lectures that he delivered in Princeton in 1898. As early as the seventeenth century, in an anonymous booklet entitled *The Office of Christian Parent*, the term office was used to describe the calling and tasks of the office of parenthood. Schrotenboer (1989) provides a comprehensive explication of the biblical foundation for the term office, summarizing it as the way God uses people to administer his world.

Just as in governmental and commercial enterprises, so too in a school, key stakeholders hold different offices, with contingent rights and responsibilities that they can exercise within the boundaries of their office. Parents and teachers have an office. There also is an office of student, and an office of board member. For example, during a school board meeting, a board member may quite appropriately consider matters of staff discipline when referred to the board by the headmaster or appropriate sub-committee. However, if that same board member discusses staff discipline matters with other parents in the school car park or via the telephone or internet, the board member could quickly exceed the boundaries of his or her office.

From a Christian perspective, the concept of office is inescapably linked with calling. In Ephesians 4, Paul talks about God calling some to be apostles, some prophets, some pastors, and some teachers. The basic assumption here is that parents, teachers, students, board members, etc., all occupy different offices and that each has been called by God to that office. Appointment – that is, the formal granting of an office – should follow, not precede, the calling. Spykman (1985) links this aspect of office with the notion of divinely delegated authority that grants someone the responsibility (note the core word of response here) to carry out the stewardly tasks of a particular office. And along with responsibility comes service and accountability, completing the circle by recognizing that the authority of an officeholder is not absolute but is a calling originating in God, who is the only absolute authority.

As with any calling, gifting that equips a person to faithfully carry out an office, parallels the calling. God equips those whom he calls. A key mentoring role of fellow believers is to assist Christian friends in identifying their gifts, and providing humble counsel to ensure that gifting, calling, and assumption of office are all appropriately aligned.

In the context of a school the student, e.g., has the office (the rights and responsibilities) of a learner. She has the right to be taught well, and the responsibility to learn in community. She has the right to be assisted by both teachers and parents in helping her to discover her gifts so that later she can be encouraged to explore suitable career opportunities (calling and office). In addition, she has the responsibility to use the rights of the office of student in a stewardly manner, studying diligently and cooperatively, and not behaving in a disruptive manner that could in turn deny others the opportunity to carry out their student office responsibilities.

Young (2007) and Van Dyk (2000) in their discussions about the healthy Christian school community, find it helpful to ground their reflections in the concept of a stewardly exercise of office. Young (2007, 309) provides a helpful table that identifies five offices or agencies associated with the life of a school (though he has chosen not to include the office of student). Alongside each office he describes the legitimate areas of involvement pertaining that office. Van Dyk (2000), in his readable and informative style, highlights the divine equipping, the authority, the responsibility, and the limitations (in terms of sphere sovereignty) of each office. He makes the following comment:

> Our classroom authority is a direct consequence of our office. . . . Authority is inseparably attached to office. This reality is true for all forms of office. My authority as father, for example, is to be attributed to my *office* as father rather than to my size, age, or accumulated wisdom. . . . All authority [or office] possesses power. In fact, authority *must* possess power. In schools it is sometimes forgotten that the authorization to teach requires *empowerment* to teach.
>
> Power without authority [or responsibility] – and without office consciousness – deteriorates into brute force. (46)

In considering the following material, readers should bear in mind the concept of office. Many of the relational challenges that arise between stakeholders in Christian education occur because of an inadequate appreciation of the nature and boundaries of office in the context of an interdependent community.

Responsibility of Parents and
The Christian Community in Education

Earlier sections in this chapter have sought to establish the biblical basis of parental responsibility for the education of their children. In the Old Testament nation of Israel, parents were specifically charged to instruct their children in such a way that the young ones would see the lordship of God in the world and their responsibility to that same Lord as they matured in his creation. (Deuteronomy 4:9–10 and Psalm 78:1–72 are just a couple of examples.) In the New Testament, Paul reminds Christian parents that it remains their responsibility to bring their children up "in the training and instruction of the Lord" (Ephesians 6:4) who has made the world, who upholds the world, and who has given to people the task of exercising dominion over the world as God's responsible servants.

In a child's early years, there is no structural difficulty in following this biblical principle. Parents are responsible for the nurture of their children, and most of it occurs within the home. It is there that the infant learns how to smile, how to drink from a cup, and how to begin to control her own feelings in the context of family life. It is in the home that the toddler learns to crawl and walk or finds out that certain things may be played with but that mother's beautiful ornaments should be left alone. Here she may first learn through story, song, and parental (and grandparental) examples about the loving, Creator God. Within the nurture of the family, children learn how to behave in the company of others and to adopt the patterns of courtesy that are expected in the culture in which the child will grow up. Christian parents willingly accept these nurturing responsibilities of their children as part of their calling before the Lord.

This commitment to the family must be held in very high esteem in the Christian school. John Taylor Gatto, New York City Teacher of the Year in 1990, affirmed this commitment. Gatto writes:

> Family is the main engine of education. If we use schooling to break children away from parents – and make no mistake, that has been the central function of schools since John Cotton announced it as the purpose of the Bay Colony Schools in 1650 and Horace Mann announced it as the purpose of Massachusetts schools in 1850 – we're going to continue to have the horror show (in education) we have right now. (Gatto 2005, 33)

The institutional church also plays its part in this nurturing process. One aspect of infant baptism or infant dedication is the declared intention of the wider church family that all in that congregation will seek, before the Lord, to do what they can to assist the parents in their nurture of the children in their midst. The desire of all involved is that as the children come to learn about the world, they may come to recognize that it has been made, redeemed, and is sustained by the triune God, and that we are all, young and old alike, called to live lives of repentant, obedient worship and service to him.

Most parents, Christian or not, are effective "nurturers" or teachers of children in their early, most important years. It is a myth that most teaching and learning takes place in schools. Most of it takes place in the home before a child reaches school age and then continues in the home, school, and elsewhere after that. It is also a myth to suggest that parents are not effective teachers. Although many modern parents and families neglect a biblically based nurturing of their children, they nevertheless nurture and educate their children in their own particular family values and lifestyles. Most families do an efficient job of transferring their understanding of their culture and the world to their children.

For Christian parents then, the repeated biblical commands to bring children up in a way that shows God at work in his world, and that reveals the need to be obedient to the Lord, are carried out initially in the home. All parents are involved in this nurture of their young, but the Christian parent is aware that this is a God-given responsibility. The Christian father and/or mother prayerfully takes this office of parenthood very seriously. They realize that their children are not their own possession, but are entrusted to them from the Lord. Just as he has given them the wonderful blessing of children, so too he will call them one day to give an account of how they have exercised the nurturing responsibilities that accompany this blessing.

This explains Christian parents' commitment to the Christian school and their lively involvement in things like the P.T.A. They realize that their responsibility for the nurture or education of their children doesn't stop when they go to school but continues at least until the child reaches adulthood. The parents have recognized that in a society such as ours, there are many things that their children need to learn about God's world that they themselves don't have the in-depth understanding, nor the time, to teach their children. They have begun to open their children's eyes to the beauty of the landscape, the idea of number, basic traffic rules, the fact that people elsewhere live differently, and that it is possible to make pleasant and unpleasant sounds on a piano. However, they recognize that in these areas of art, mathematics, social studies, geography, music, and others, they don't have the time or competence to nurture fully their children's understanding of these aspects of God's creation. They realize that other people have studied these varied aspects of creation and thus can speak with authority about them. They desire that their children come to learn these things in a way that helps them to see God at work in his world and that will lead the youngsters to be able to respond in obedient service to God in these various subjects. Consequently, they enroll their children in a Christian school.

Christian parents who send their children to a Christian school recognize the office, that is the expertise and authority, of the teachers, but they don't give up their personal responsibility for their children's education. This responsibility is a charge that they have from God. It is not theirs to give up. They may take part in the community of a Christian school, but this doesn't diminish the responsibility that God has given to them, and to a lesser extent to the Christian community, for their children's nurture and development. They may seek to enlist the help of the Christian school, but they retain the office of parent and remain responsible for their children before God.

AUTHORITY OF THE CHRISTIAN TEACHER

If it's true that parents are responsible, then what is the task and office of the teacher in the Christian school? Is the teacher primarily an extension of the parent? Should teacher be puppet-like in their responses to the requests of parents? Does parental responsibility mean that teachers should frequently forward their schemes of work and scope and sequences for the parents to examine and approve before implementing them in the classroom? Does the teacher have any authority other than that given to him or her by the parents?

In order to address issues such as these, we should recall the biblical position of the teacher. It is assumed that readers have already rejected the prevailing secular notion that teachers, as autonomous authorities, have specialized training and that they should be left to get on with the job of education in the school. Christians reject this humanistic idea. No lawyer, plumber, pilot, housewife, mechanic, or teacher is totally independent and their authority is never entirely their own. Our talents and our very jobs are gifts from the Lord, and we are all accountable first to the Lord and second to the community for how we use them.

There are three aspects to the office of the teacher in the Christian school. First, she is responsible to the Lord. Second, she is responsible to the school administrator/principal whom that the board has chosen to lead the team of teachers within the school. Third, through the principal she is responsible to the school board that has appointed her.

First, the Christian teacher, as is true for every Christian, is responsible to the Lord. The Christian teacher is able to exercise teaching authority because this is a talent the Lord has given to her. The Bible talks in a general way about the source of the abilities and talents that people have. In Psalm 8:3–9 we read that humankind's authority in creation is God-given. In Colossians 2:9 we read that the source and head of all authority is Christ, and in Romans 11:36 we read that "from him and through him are all things." Whatever ability that the Christian teacher has is a gift from God, to be used for God's glory, under God's authority.

The Bible talks also in a specific way about the source, responsibility, and authority that we have in relation to the gifts, abilities, and expertise that God has given to us. The parable that Jesus tells us about the talents is recorded in Matthew 25:14–30. Jesus clearly shows there that he is the origin of gifts and abilities and that these should be used in a wise, stewardly manner, as he has authorized us to do. In Daniel 1:17, we read that "God gave knowledge and understanding of all kinds of literature and learning" to Daniel and his friends.

In Ephesians 3:7, Paul acknowledges that God is the source of his apostolic abilities. In the following chapter, Ephesians 4:11–13, Paul lists a number of specific gifts or offices, pointing to their divine origin, authority, purpose, and accountability. In like fashion, a teacher's ability and authority come first of all from the Lord. She exercises this ability in obedience to the Lord. The teacher is not autonomous in the use of her ability, but she is accountable to God for how she uses her gifts in her service to the Lord. As Paul says in Romans 14:12, "So then, each of us will give account of ourselves to God."

Second, the teacher in the Christian school has authority from, and is responsible to, the headmaster/administrator. This is the person appointed by the board to have oversight over the educational tasks of the school. The administrator has authority from, and is responsible to, first the Lord and then the board. He will assign classes and delegate responsibilities and tasks to the team of teachers of which he is leader. These include such things as schemes of work in the classroom in relation to a unified curriculum, assessment and discipline criteria, school administration, and relevant relationships with accrediting authorities. When a teacher is given tasks in these areas by the headmaster/administrator, she has the authority to carry them out and is responsible to the headmaster/principal for her actions. Her authority in each particular school community comes from the board through the headmaster/administrator. Therefore, although she works as a support to the home, her primary human accountability partner is the principal/administrator and not the parents.

Third, the teacher in the Christian school is responsible to, and has authority from, the school's controlling body, usually its council or board of governors. The board has recognized the competence and talents of the teacher and so has appointed her to teach in the school. Within the context of the particular school in which she is working, therefore, the community of parents need to recognize the teacher's authority as given to her by the board. The board is the body charged with determining policy that reflects the perspective of the community it serves. Under the oversight of the administrator or headmaster, the teacher is charged to teach in accordance with school policy and procedure. This means that here too the teacher cannot use her legitimate authority autonomously. She must ensure that her programs of work adhere to the religious perspective outlined in the school's guiding documents. It is the task of the board and administrator to ensure that this is done.

The teacher is not a puppet-like extension of the parent. She needs to recognize God-given parental responsibility for the education of the children under her care. She needs to know the liberty of the authority that she has in the classroom and also the accountability and boundaries that accompany this liberty. The teacher must be careful not to act as if he or she is the actual parent of the child in the classroom. Teachers, in a legitimate and affectionate way, often refer to their students as "my children." In one sense this is true, and the *in loco parentis* concept is a very appropriate one in some contexts at school. In an overall sense, however, the teacher is not the actual parent. Teachers do not have the primary responsibility for the total nurture of the children in their care.

INTERACTION OF PARENTAL RESPONSIBILITY AND TEACHER AUTHORITY

Human life is rich and diverse. Parents have the God-given responsibility for the entire nurture of their children. In exercising this responsibility, parents often make use of people and institutions outside the home. It may be the sporting expertise of the neighborhood hockey club, the musical expertise of the local piano teacher, the outdoors expertise of the Boy Scouts or Girls' Brigade, the medical ability of the family doctor and hospital staff, or the educational expertise of the local school. By using these groups or people, parents are not giving up their God-given responsibility. Rather, they are exercising their parental office in wisely choosing appropriate avenues of help in the nurturing of their children. They recognize and choose to use the authority and skill that others have for the good of their children. This means that within the context of

the significance of the relationship to the lives of the protégés" (Parkway 2013, 444).

One of the most compelling sets of studies that indicate the importance in the lives of students of mentoring and role modeling comes from qualitative research that provides actual student responses concerning their teachers. For example, in 1995, Nancy McCabe reported on a summary of high school juniors' evaluations of their best teachers. She noted that effective teachers were those who were able to reach their students both cognitively and affectively – that is, teachers who cared about their students, who had high expectations, and became involved in their students' lives. The study indicated clearly the crucial role-model impact that the teacher can have on students long after they have graduated from his or her class.

BIBLICAL EXAMPLES AND NORMS FOR MENTORING AND ROLE MODELING

The obvious example for evangelical Christian teachers who seek to be effective role models and mentors is Jesus Christ. That is why the next section of this chapter focuses on him alone. As an introduction, it is worthwhile to spend time considering a selection (this is not a comprehensive list) of eight characteristics and qualities from Scripture that are components of Christian mentorship and role modeling.

1. *Loving Paternalism*

In modern terms, the word "paternalism" may have negative connotations, but Paul uses paternalistic concepts (in a masculine and feminine sense) to describe his relationship with young Christians in Thessalonica who were under his ministering care (1 Thessalonians 1:5–12). He described his attitude to them as being like a mother caring for her children (gentle, emotional, selfless, dedicated) and like a father caring for his children (encouraging, comforting, envisioning).

Paul demonstrates in this passage the attractive blend of the cognitive and affective domains in the mentor that were commented upon so positively by the students in McCabe's study above. A sense of deep concern and interest is evident here. This is the Christian concept of love that the mentor should have for the mentee – the desire to impact students' lives in a manner that is in their best interests and for God's glory, with little regard to the cost to the mentor.

Loving paternalism includes accountability. In fact, as discussions concerning dysfunctional families have indicated, the lack of accountability may indicate a lack of concern on the part of the caregivers. Accountability includes reproof, admonition, and correction. Nurturing discipline that is lovingly administered by the mentor has the goal of the improvement of those who are disciplined. As such, accountability is not constraining but is fundamentally liberating and empowering to those who are held accountable. An analogy from our service in Latin America comes to mind. At times during our years as missionary educators in Bolivia, my wife, our young children, and I would go on small treks into the hinterland. This occasionally involved walking along very narrow mountain paths that clung to the sides of vertical cliffs with a steep, perilous drop off to one side. When these paths had a guiding rail to hold on to, we felt much more secure and could make progress with a degree of confidence. When there was no guiding and protecting rail, we could feel our hearts pound, and each step seemed to take forever as we inched our way tentatively forward along the cliff-side. Likewise, loving discipline provides the boundaries and guiderails that steady us in the course of life and assist us to progress with confidence down life's path.

2. *"As unto the Lord"*

The students and the parents do not provide the primary accountability framework for the Christian teacher. Neither do the principal or state regulations. To be sure, they have an important role to play, but they are all subordinate to the primary responsibility that the Christian mentor has to his Lord, who is Jesus Christ. Paul highlighted this by telling his Thessalonian friends that in his mentoring of them, he was "not trying to please people but God".

God is our primary audience. This is a powerful concept because God sees our heart motivations and it is to him that our highest allegiance is due. Thus, as Dick Keyes states in his book, *True Heroism in a World of Celebrity Counterfeits*, our role modeling and mentoring will not be "built on surpassing our contemporaries in some currency of competitive success, but by living out the imitation of Christ" (Keyes 1995, 118) as we interact with our students. Spykman (1985), with his affirmation of the dual concepts of the absolute transcendence of God and the delegated authority of humanity, makes a similar point.

3. *Enthusiasm for Teaching*

McCabe's students confirmed once again that the best teachers are enthusiastic about their vocation and subject. They are lifelong learners along with their students as together they celebrate the lordship of Christ over every aspect of the curriculum that they explore. For the Christian teacher mentor, teaching may be time-consuming and exhausting, but it is not a chore. It is a delight – an incredible mystery package to be unwrapped with students; full of the "oohs" and "aahs" of the psalmist in Psalm 104 where he positively delights in the thrill of studying God's creation.

Taking Jesus as his example, the effective Christian teacher does not just teach from the head, but from the head and the heart. There is a commitment, even a passion, in the way that content material is used to shed a new light on the world and our places and tasks in it. Information is not an end in itself, but is explored with the students in a way that leads both students and teacher to see how each little bit of knowledge compounds on each other bit to help us understand God's world and the creative opportunities that he has given us to be his stewards in that world.

4. *Conveying a Sense of Hope and Purpose*
This book has already discussed the strategic importance of good teaching in enabling contemporary young people to rediscover hope in a world that they are taught, through the media and other educational sources, is just a purposeless, random result of arbitrary, colliding neurons. The Christian teacher mentor conveys a strong sense of purpose throughout the teaching task. Students are not left drifting as if they have to attempt to make meaning out of an otherwise meaningless world. That is secular humanism, not Christianity. For the Christian teacher, there is an empowering sense of creative hope and ultimate meaning that comes from exploring every subject area as a part of God's purposeful gift to humankind. History is not going nowhere; stewardship in environmental studies is not based upon pantheism or personal self-interest; gender issues are not defined by subjective cultural anachronisms; science is not rooted in an amoral, despairing, neo-Darwinian, metaphysical naturalism. There is purpose and fulfillment in life, in our unique, creative capacities, and in the study of the world around us. The Christian mentor, more than any other mentor, has the opportunity and credentials to convey this visionary sense of hope and purpose in the classroom in every aspect of the curriculum and in every student interaction.

5. *Knowledgeable and Interrogatory*
The Christian mentor will not be the source of all knowledge in the classroom – but she will be knowledgeable. That is, the Christian teacher role model needs to be equipped with the skills pertaining to her subject, knowing its fundamental presuppositions and knowing how to guide her students in their own discovery. She will encourage guided exploration

where students use Information and Communication Technology (ICT) to bring insight and new information to bear on classroom enquiries. Like Paul in his missionary ministry to other cultures (e.g., in Acts 17 in Athens), she will be able to view learning from the perspective of the learner. She will probe. She will make the question "Why?" a focus of her classroom – a question that my favorite teacher, in my youth in a secular high school, asked repeatedly in his history class. It infuriated me, challenged me to go beyond my present understanding, assisted in making the social sciences exciting and exceptionally fulfilling, and helped me to develop and mature my own understanding of myself and the world.

As William Teale of the University of Illinois puts it, the mentor teacher will be able to "see learning through children's eyes" (Teale 1996). In part, this means being an effective listener so that one can really understand each child academically, socially, culturally, and spiritually, and so that the teacher can comprehend what students are thinking, as well as understand the implications of each student's learning style. This much overlooked concept of effective listening is very important. According to Borich and Tombari (1997), poor listening is one of the most common causes of frustration in the educational process. Through careful listening, and viewing education from children's perspectives, the teacher mentor can fire students' imaginations as they aspire to discover what is true and do what is right.

Knowledgeability includes mentors being competent in their understanding of educational worldviews and perspectives that differ from their own. Christianity is outward looking and relational. As such, the Christian teacher needs to model and foster an authoritative understanding of concepts and content that derive from non-Christian foundations. Otherwise, it will be impossible to critique them – and it will be impossible to mentor students to do the same. This is why Paul, when speaking at the Areopagus, was able to quote their own philosophers to the Epicurean scholars to whom he was speaking. As Carl F. Henry put it,

> If ever this generation is to become a generation of virtue, it needs to be dramatically confronted by those who smell the acrid, enveloping smoke of our pagan age, and who will share the incomparable realities and rewards of new life in Christ that alone can lift the pall of darkness. (Henry 2012, 55)

6. *The Possibility for Defection*

In its initial context, the word "indoctrinate" was not a bad word. It referred to the process of in-doctrinating, or equipping the uninitiated with a vital set of perspectives upon which they can base future belief and action. Today, however, to indoctrinate has come to mean the intolerant forcing of a perspective upon someone as if it were absolute truth, without considering whether or not the recipient understands or agrees with that perspective or body of knowledge. Modern scientism, with its imperialistic, ideological fundamentalism masquerading as neutrality, is one example of indoctrination in many schools. In the contemporary sense, the Christian teacher mentor does not indoctrinate. However, as the initial chapters in this book have already shown, there is no neutrality in education. Therefore, education in the Christian school will study the world from the perspective of a Christian world and life view, just as a public school does the same from a secular worldview where the unimportance of theism in most curricular areas is the assumed starting point. However, unlike many secular instructors, the Christian teacher mentor does not demand conformity of belief from her students. The ability to make moral choices is a God-given right that teachers should not attempt to deny. They will seek to expose all the developing worldviews in the classroom (including their own) to the searchlight of the Christian guiding principles of the school. The winsomeness of a Christian perspective also should be evident in teachers' lives, but teachers must not attempt to coerce a personal commitment to Christianity from their students. This is a matter of personal heart commitment as children make their own accountable choices about who they are, what they are learning, and what they understand about the world and their places and tasks in it.

Once again, Jesus is the master example. His teaching was more compelling and effective than ours can ever hope to be. Yet the supreme teacher did not attempt to create followers by coercion. He passionately presented an inviting message, but he also allowed his hearers the opportunity to decide for themselves whether or not they would commit themselves to what he was saying. Despite the fact that Jesus could have called upon legions of angels who would have been his instruments to command instant and total obedience and acceptance, many of the notable leaders in the contemporary community rejected and denounced Jesus' teachings. The master teacher recognized that his hearers had the God-given right to do this – and to endure the ultimately disastrous consequences of this calamitous choice.

7. Frailty

One of the great affinities that we have with biblical characters like David in the Old Testament or Peter in the New Testament is our identification with their imperfect humanity. They made mistakes. David allowed passions to rule at times, with dire consequences. Peter blurted out responses that occasionally were profound, but which on another occasion had his master turn and say to him, "Get behind me Satan." The attraction of these frail heroes of the faith is not in their errors or sins, but in the repentance that they showed, the forgiveness that they knew from God, and the way that they were able to be nurtured through their character failures and still maintain extremely effective and fulfilling vocations.

Students are close observers of their teachers. They are disillusioned with the ones who cannot admit fault or who deal with it inadequately. They need role models who acknowledge their frailty and finiteness, and who even enlist the assistance of the community of students in the classroom to overcome them. Such finiteness may be demonstrated in not knowing the answer to a question and seeking out that answer in cooperation with students, or in being prepared to admit that one has graded a test question wrongly and in taking the time and effort to apologize and put it right.

An awareness of personal frailty should make the Christian mentor teacher a person of prayer – both to present petitions to God seeking his wisdom in dealing with the myriad issues that daily confront the classroom teacher, and in commending to God's care the precious lives for which the teacher is responsible. What better way to begin working through an issue in the classroom – whether it involves being thankful for the glorious world that we are able to explore or seeking guidance on a perplexing concern relating to students – than to seek wisdom from the Creator and dynamic Sustainer of all life?

8.   *Humility*

When the Christian teacher mentor recognizes frailty as a personal characteristic, then humility before students should not be difficult. The knowledge that we operate under the gaze of a loving and omniscient heavenly Father reinforces this trait. As Keyes suggests,

> If God is our primary audience, that brings two changes. We can be assured of being accepted and loved by him – apart from public admiration – as we come to him in humility and faith. Also, he unmasks our attempts at impression management. . . . He can bring us both deep confidence in his love and also a powerful incentive for our own integrity. (Keyes 1995, 111)

There is no room for arrogance or self-sufficiency in the Christian role model. In fact, Jesus (Matthew 5) advocates characteristics antithetical to these in the Sermon on the Mount – characteristics that are countercultural, all too often invisible in those in leadership, but essentially very attractive and appropriate: "Blessed are the poor in spirit [i.e., blessed are those who know that their reliance is on their heavenly Father], for theirs is the kingdom of heaven" and "Blessed are the meek [i.e., those humble before God], for they will inherit the earth." True epistemic humility is an engaging strength. It allows the mentor to be herself before her students, to be "real" and approachable.

For the Christian mentor, humility is seen in its fullest perspective when viewed in relationship to Jesus Christ. This is because as the Christian teacher mentors students, essentially she is desirous of them modeling not her, but Christ who lives in her by faith. Paul (1 Corinthians 11:1) emphasized this point with his Corinthian protégés when he encouraged them to be imitators of him as he sought to be an imitator of Christ. The Christian mentor is not saying "Look at how great I am and copy me," but "Look at the characteristics of a Christ-like life that you see in me. By all means strive to make them a part of who you are, so that together we both can be more like Christ." This is what Kate B. Wilkinson was meaning when she wrote in a hymn in 1925 "May his [Christ's] beauty rest upon me as I seek the lost to win, and may they forget the channel, seeing only him."

The Christian mentor's humility does not make poor self-esteem a virtue, nor is it a form of self-flagellating docility. It is the opposite of egotistical, self-righteous pride. Its confidence comes from a sense of godly calling and capacity. It declares that we can only present a lifestyle that is attractive to others when we first acknowledge our utter dependence upon the saving grace of God in Christ, and second, when we rely on the empowering, indwelling presence of the Holy Spirit of God to guide us into wisdom as we use the manifest abilities that he has given us in the educational task.

THE ULTIMATE MENTOR: JESUS CHRIST

This brings us to Jesus Christ himself, the ultimate mentor and role model for the Christian teacher mentor, and the one who was considered by his contemporary friends and foes alike to be a superlative teacher. Reference has already been made in this book to several of the teaching characteristics of Christ. There is a discussion concerning Jesus' contextualization of his teaching to ensure that it was appropriate to the cultural backgrounds of his hearers. Chapter Nine discusses evaluation, and there too, the uniqueness of the individual is demonstrated by Christ – an important recognition that he showed once more in his dealing with Mary and Martha when their brother died.

One could write a complete book on this subject of Jesus as the consummate teacher – indeed several already exist including Horne's (1978) *Teaching Techniques of Jesus* and Zuck's (1995) *Teaching as Jesus Taught*. For Jesus, sharing with others about the world (i.e., teaching) was never a matter of neutrality. It always involved the recognition that teaching is committed to a cause – it is designed to help make the hearers and learners wise in how they think, what they commit themselves to, and how they act both now and for eternity. Whether we recognize it or not, the same is true of teachers today. There is no neutrality. The Christian teacher would do well to study the example of Jesus closely to gain a fundamental grasp of what it means to teach from a Christian perspective and to share a God-honoring world and life view in the classroom.

Apart from the notions of sinfulness and imperfection (obviously absent from the life of Jesus), all the characteristics of the effective mentor described in the earlier section of this chapter are incomparably exhibited in Jesus' life and ministry. For example, the concept of humility was profoundly demonstrated throughout his life and death and is an example to follow for Christian teachers who seek to be effective role models and mentors. This point is made explicitly in Paul's letter to his friends at Philippi:

> Do nothing out of selfish ambition or vain conceit. Rather, in humility value others above yourselves, not looking to your own interests but each of you to the interests of others. In your relationships with one another, have the same mindset as Christ Jesus: Who, being in very nature God, did not consider equality with God something to be used to his own advantage; rather he made himself nothing by taking the very nature of a servant, being made in human likeness. And being found in appearance as a man, he humbled himself by becoming obedient to death – even death on a cross! Therefore God exalted him to the highest place and gave him the name that is above every name, that at the name of Jesus every knee should bow, in heaven and on earth and under the earth. (Philippians 2:3–10)

Readers wishing a more comprehensive consideration of the teaching skills of Christ would do well to consult Zuck or Horne's books hand in hand with their study of the Old and New Testaments. Jesus was perfect, and we imperfect humans, with all our faults and our limited perspectives, can never be fully successful in emulating him. And he did not come to earth with the specific purpose of presenting a living example of effective pedagogy. Nevertheless, in addition to the earlier considerations where applicable, there are at least three extra pedagogical characteristics of Christ as mentor that will briefly be noted before we leave this topic: first, the servant king; second; his inferential teaching style; third, his unremitting love.

1. *The Servant King*

In John 13, Jesus the Master undertook the lowliest servant's chore of washing his disciples' feet that were covered with dust and grime from the unpaved Middle Eastern roadways. He is the servant king – and he calls his followers to emulate his example. Paul stressed this in his letter to the Philippians that we have just considered: "being in very nature God, did not consider equality with God something to be used to his own advantage; rather, he made himself nothing by taking the very nature of a servant, being made in human likeness."

The Christian mentor/teacher is called to live this servant attitude before his or her students. We should demonstrate that, while authority is vested in us as teachers, it is our responsibility to exercise this authority judiciously and graciously as a ministry to the children that we teach. Thus, students' respect should be won, as well as demanded, and we can hope that they will be encouraged to follow this Christ-like pattern in their own relationships with each other. The apostle Peter (1 Peter 5:2–3) put it well when he was writing to the leaders and teachers in the local Christian churches in Asia Minor: "Be shepherds of God's flock that is under your care . . . eager to serve; not lording it over those entrusted to you, but being examples to the flock."

The pattern of servant leadership is a challenge for educators in every culture, where the power that comes with authority can lead to pride, the abuse of others, and self-serving advancement. In particular however, it is a primary challenge for Christians living in a Confucian culture where status and obeisance come with leadership positions such as teachers, pastors, and professors.

2. *Inferential Teaching*

Some of Jesus' teaching followed a didactic, direct instructional style. The Lord's Prayer is one example. On many other occasions, however (and demonstrating that inquiry learning was not invented by Dewey and other progressive educational philosophers), Christ adopted an inferential mode of instruction where his followers were encouraged to ask questions and then were given stories or activities that enabled them to discover and personalize the answers to these questions for themselves. He was the quintessential communicator. His many parables served both to clarify and obscure. One of his students asked Jesus about the extent of the caring that we should demonstrate to others. Jesus' answer was rich and profound. Instead of saying, "We should be concerned about everyone," he gave to his hearer and to the world the parable of the Good Samaritan.

Ntarangwi (2013b) reminds us that Jesus frequently used cultural artifacts in his teaching, with the purpose of using a familiar object to introduce something new that he was teaching. So he talked about mustard seeds, grapevines, simple bread, and even Roman coins in his teaching.

In John 3, Jesus also used metaphor and imaginative disequilibrium as teaching strategies. Though its seems perfectly understandable to us today, the Bible clearly shows the shock and cognitive dissonance that Nicodemus initially experienced as he sought to come to terms with Jesus' comment that he must be "born again!" We will return to the issue of imagination in pedagogy later in this chapter, but at this point we recognize that Jesus shows us that the effective mentor and role model uses discovery learning as well as direct instruction to nurture his students.

3. *Unremitting Love*

Jesus' love for his disciples was unremitting. He allowed them to take responsibilities and to make mistakes, and he corrected them for their errors. He demonstrated that the effective teacher must become involved in the lives of his students – to laugh with them, to share their trials, to stimulate them, and even to cry with them. This takes time, and involves being vulnerable. On occasions, Jesus' disciples or students displeased him, but he never let their failures cloud his loving concern for them or diminish his determination to assist them to reach their full potential. This is an example for all teacher role models and mentors. There will be times that we may have cause for deep disappointment in our students – times even when they must endure unpleasant consequences for their actions. Nevertheless, the Christian teacher continues to reach out and provide another chance. As with Jesus' restoration of Peter after Peter's denial, the Christian mentor should be there like the father of the prodigal son (another of Jesus' inferential stories) to warmly welcome back even those who are recalcitrant and help them recommence building their lives on a more steady footing.

For Jesus, teaching about the world was always inextricably linked to living in the world. Therefore, as Jesus nurtured Peter, the Master used examples from Peter's previous experience to teach him – as we see wonderfully illustrated in the fatherly way that Jesus re-commissions Peter after the resurrection, using the familiar contexts of fishing and shepherding to make his point.

Berry (1989) of Roberts Wesleyan College summarizes much of what has been said about Jesus' unremitting love when she comments:

> [Jesus] cared deeply about those who had come to learn, understood their context, and lived the content of His message. He brought the audience, their context and His content into relationship. Christ invited his students to accompany Him on an educational journey in which it was okay to ask questions and mandatory to think. (Berry 1989, 92)

When considering Jesus as mentor, a word of warning is appropriate. Though Paul in the Colossians passage already referred to, and Peter in 1 Peter 2:21, remind us to follow Jesus as our example, we should beware of confusing mentorship with lordship. Yes, Jesus was the perfect mentor. However, he is also our Lord who we are called to follow and obey unreservedly. He is not just our role model. He is our master. Furthermore, his lifestyle is not a generic example for all beliefs like some ancient, trans-religious Mahatma Gandhi. His pattern of living cannot be separated from his claim that no-one comes to God but through him (Luke 14:6). Hartzell (2006) may slightly overstate the case, but her warning is sober and appropriate nevertheless:

> This subtle switch from the Lordship of Jesus Christ to the "modelship" of Christ deceptively exchanges the truth of Who He is and what He did for the principles that He lived. Thus the Gospel of faith is effectively transformed into a false gospel of works, and the Lord Jesus Christ is replaced with the universal "Christ" or "Jesus" of the counterfeit kingdom. (293)

THE PLACE OF IMAGINATION

Though some may disagree, we contend that essential in the repertoire of the effective Christian teacher is a fertile, cultural-mandate-shaped imagination. Like all human faculties, the imagination is impacted by our fallen nature. This is why renowned evangelical teacher Charles Haddon Spurgeon once claimed that, "The will is somewhat worse than the heart to bend, but there is one thing that excels the will in its naughtiness, and that is the imagination" (Spurgeon 1855).

Spurgeon's comment notwithstanding, from a biblical perspective, the imagination, and the creativity that flows from it, is an aspect of the stamp of God that he has gloriously gifted to humankind. In Genesis 1, when the triune God reached the pinnacle of his creative activity, he said "Let us make mankind in our own image." In doing exactly that, the first thing God did for this newly-created image-bearing man, was to make him creative – empowering him to experiment in the garden by naming creatures, farming the land, etc. – in other words, to make culture (hence the term cultural mandate). Therefore, creativity and imagination are an incredible aspect of God's character endowed to all men and women, boys and girls. True, we have corrupted this divine essence by our sin, but the proper response is not to deny imagination, but to redeem it and use it constructively to God's glory and the benefit of others, as is the Creator's primary intention.

In this sense, demonstrating the creative use of imagination in the classroom by the Christian teacher is an act of worship and service to God, and is an encouragement to our students to do the same. The Christian classroom should be creative and imaginative. I was always pleased when students, even at the PhD level, confessed with a sense of expectancy that they were never sure exactly what they were going to encounter when they entered my classroom. When you combine a set syllabus with unpredictable teachable moments; with the vast repository of information that flows from in-class internet access; with pre-selected resources; with the changing student dynamic; with students' diverse pre-existing worldviews; and with a vibrant external social, political, and economic culture, anything can happen! The Christian teacher's responsibility is to imaginatively and faithfully balance freedom and responsibility in directing this flow towards the achievement of appropriate outcomes. David Smith practices what he preaches in this regard. So too do people like Mark Roques, John Van Dyk, Patricia Ahlborn (see Appendix Two), and many others. As another example, Ken Meyer, in his 2013 PhD study, investigated the strategic role of imagination in teaching apprentices about electricity and ICT.

In Ephesians chapter three, Paul extravagantly encourages Christians to develop a divinely-intoxicated imagination, seasoned by a humble responsiveness to God and his purposes, when he concludes: "Now to him who is able to do immeasurably more than all we ask or imagine, according to his power that is at work within us, to him be glory in the church and in Christ Jesus throughout all generations, for ever and ever! Amen" (Ephesians 3:20–21).

Once again, Jesus, with his frequent use of story and creative metaphor (I am the vine, you are the branches . . . Nicodemus you must be born again . . . the story of the good Samaritan to illustrate our community responsibilities etc., etc.), highlights the importance of narrative and creative imagination in unpacking reality and in guiding students into wisdom and discernment.

Direct instruction, also known as "chalk-and-talk" or "the sage on the stage," has its place in any classroom. However, it should not be the primary pedagogy. Whether it be in furniture layout, classroom discussion, student guidance, evaluative instruments, or even school timetabling, imaginative instruction is a wonderful gift from God. John Dewey did not create discovery learning. God did. Let's redeem it and, with awe and wonder, use it to its full benefit in the Christian school classroom at all levels from the kindergarten to the postgraduate forum, and everywhere in-between.

IMPLICATIONS

The Biblical quotation at the beginning of this chapter reminded us of the critical importance of the classroom teacher in the lives of children. Although curricular issues are vital, they must take second place to choosing the best people to be the role models and mentors for children in the classroom since, at the end of the day, we will see much of the character, values, and worldview of their teachers mirrored in our children.

Smith and Smith (2011) lament the paucity of material written from a Christian perspective that moves beyond conceptual considerations and enters the realm of the actual nature of teaching Christianly in the classroom. They have a point. There are some very useful resources that include an exploration of classroom practice from a Christian worldview perspective at the elementary and high school levels (Doud 1990, Van Brummelen 1998, Van Dyk 2000 & 2007, Drexler 2007, Ireland, Edlin, & Dickens 2004, and Edlin & Ireland 2006 are a few useful titles that come to mind). Much less is available at the college or university level where the whole notion of teacher training and reflective classroom practice is woefully unaddressed in many institutions, Christian or secular. It remains true that unless we can show how the connection is made between the concepts of Christian education and an informed classroom practice, then we have largely wasted our time.

If the nature of the teachers who instruct children is vital, then the following considerations require sober reflection. First, we must ensure that teachers share a similar worldview perspective with parents, who are the most important teachers any child can possess. Most democratic nations in the world have endorsed the United Nations Charter of Human Rights, which acknowledges the primary right of parents to choose the direction of the education that their children will receive. Adults in countries recently released from socialistic or totalitarian tyranny realize that there is no neutrality in education. Adults in the West should not labor under the seductive illusion of the neutrality of secular schools any longer. As in Belgium and the Netherlands, parents should be allowed, without discriminatory financial penalty, to choose teachers and schools for their children that conform to their own worldview perspectives.

There is little evidence to support the notion that democracy will collapse if educational ownership passes back from the state to collections of like-minded individuals. Indeed, if contrasts are made between the Netherlands and the United States of America, for example, it seems that there is every reason to believe that diversity and community ownership of education, rather than state ownership of education, enhances individual freedom, diversity and democratic principles rather than diminishes them.

In the second place, we must be very particular about the process by which we select the teachers for our children. These people should be the crème de la crème of our cultures. The selection process – and the esteem given the teaching vocation – should ensure that only the very best offer themselves for this high calling, and that only the best of the best are finally chosen as our children's educator role models. The process of teacher selection and training in Finland is a useful model in this regard (Paksuniemi, 2013).

A third implication of the mentoring potential of the position of the teacher is that we should give our very best effort in terms of time and resources to training our teachers. It is they who will be helping to shape the next generation and, therefore, the future of our cultures. We should be expansive in our efforts to ensure that these teachers are as well-equipped as possible at the commencement of their teaching/role-modeling vocations, and that opportunity and finances are made available to help them maintain a regimen of ongoing teacher refreshment and growth during their careers.

Christianity is a relational religion – a relationship between humanity and personal divinity. It also involves the possibility of restored relationships between people based upon the finished work of Jesus Christ. Teaching, too, is a relational activity and should reflect many aspects of the relationship between God and his people. Guy Doud, a fervent Christian and one-time teacher of the year in the USA, often recites a poem in which teachers are referred to as the "gods of the young" (Doud 1990, 185). Let us choose our teachers with care, and let us help them to develop the characteristics outlined in this chapter so that they can be the very best role models in our schools. Remember that our children, when they are fully trained, will be like their teachers!

Chapter 8

Foundations for Curriculum
in the Christian School

THE RAILWAY TRAIN AND THE CURRICULUM

A fond childhood memory is of going with my mother down to the railway station when I was still a preschooler. I watched the rush and bustle on station platforms as commuter and long distance trains loaded and unloaded. I was captivated and slightly awed by the giant steam-powered monsters that hissed and roared at the head of each train. My wildest dreams seemed to come true when one engineer invited us to join him in the cab of one big black colossus, and he proudly explained the mystery of the steam engine. The sweaty stoker opened the little door and shoveled shiny black coal into the bowels of a fiery inferno. I even fancy that I was given the ultimate thrill of being able to pull on the rope that made the whistle sound, or is my memory becoming confused with fantasy in this last point? Needless to say, the stories about Thomas the Tank engine, recently making a comeback, were among my favorite childhood stories, and I could often be heard singing the little song "*Down by the Station Early in the Morning. . . .*" In later life, T.S. Eliot's poem "*Skimbleshanks the Railway Cat*" has always held a special attraction. As a classroom English teacher, I loved reading that poem aloud to my students, experiencing along with them the sensations and memories that it continues to evoke.

It should come as no surprise to learn that as my own sons grew up they had an HO scale train set that they (and their father too!) enjoyed playing with from time to time. It was not a large set, but it did have several curving sections, a tunnel, a bridge, a railway cutting, and some scale-size buildings gathered from different parts of the world. There were four different sections to the track, and the actual journey of the train was determined by the setting of the points or switches scattered around the board on which the track was laid. The boys had two different trains to choose from. There was a modern diesel locomotive that hauls freight cars and a replica steam engine (its wheels kept falling off) that hauls carriages reminiscent of the last century. A generation later, Granddad enjoys playing trains with his grandchildren when they come to visit us in the Illawarra in Australia.

With the use of a little imagination (see the previous chapter), the story of the railway train can provide a metaphor for the place of the curriculum in the battery of patterns and policies that shape the Christian school. The train itself, or more properly the passengers and freight, represent the children whose parents have entrusted them to this particular railway company (that is, the school). The twin rails are the philosophy and educational confession that provide the sure footing, foundation, and direction for the Christian school to run upon. The policy manuals that apply the philosophy and confession are the points or switches that select the path that this particular school will take as it maps out its course. Finally, the curriculum is the engine that empowers the whole process. Like Thomas and his friends, the curriculum energizes and leads the whole school in moving down the tracks and in celebrating and learning about the lordship of Christ over all creation.

THE ENGINE MUST FIT THE TRACKS, AND THE CURRICULUM MUST FIT THE PHILOSOPHY

The force of circumstances and the pressure of teaching have turned many Christian teachers into pragmatists. That is, if something works, then let's do it. The following is an oft-repeated cry:

> In my busy classroom, I, as a Christian teacher, do not have the time to waste in fanciful thought that does not help me directly with the urgent task of "What will I teach my students tomorrow?" In the twenty-first century, we teachers are not just educators, but in our classrooms we are expected to be child psychologists, guardians, policemen, nurses, referees, and so on. One of the reasons for the drop in educational achievement is that I spend much less time than I did ten years ago on actual teaching and so much more on classroom management and student counseling. It might not be perfect according to educational theory, but what I need to survive is a textbook that clearly lays out the teaching material in my subject and that I can lay before my students and basically say "Get on with it."

We need to be very sensitive to the workloads that we impose upon our teachers, especially those in Christian schools where they are often underpaid and contribute in many extra ways to the life of the school community. However, "the engine must fit the rails," or a dramatic and cataclysmic derailment will occur. That is, the curriculum of a school must follow the direction of the school's philosophy and guiding statements. If this is not so, then the school will be at war with itself, a confusion of competing theses and antitheses, that will harm the very children that it seeks to serve by leaving them ill-equipped to live and function as God's image bearers. Through programs such as teacher development days, summer teacher retreats, and subsidies for teacher re-training, schools must recapture the initiative and provide their teachers with the handles to construct curriculum patterns that are distinctively Christian and conform to the aims and goals of the school.

It is also appropriate to remember that it is not the purpose of this chapter to provide a comprehensive analysis of curriculum issues. Many issues are raised only in passing. Our purpose here is to introduce readers to curriculum from a Christian worldview perspective, and to provide some readily understood foundations for curriculum decision-making that are consistent with that perspective. Examples of how these principles may be worked out are provided, culminating in a schema that could be further explored independently for the construction of curriculum patterns. The works of other Christian educators such as Van Brummelen, Roques, Smith, and Van Dyk can be consulted as readers seek to build on the foundations provided here.

What is the Curriculum?

Whether education is viewed as a process of forming, or as a process of transforming, there is no neutrality. All educators have at least a general goal in mind for what should be the outcomes of the education that they offer in school. Parents who send their children to our schools very definitely have outcomes in mind, as do governments and potential employers. And if you have a particular outcome in mind, then you will have at least some sense of a process that you want to carry out in order to achieve that outcome. In schools, this process is called "the curriculum." It is the dynamic interplay between the worldview of the teacher, the goals of classroom learning, what will be taught, how it will be taught, how it will be evaluated, and what meaning it might have in the lives of the students.

Some resources that discuss curriculum foundations spend time exploring the variety of contexts in which the term "curriculum" is used in education. For example, there is:

- The overt, explicit, official, planned, or written curriculum. This refers to the officially-stated curriculum approach and pattern of the school, often determined by government or other external educational authorities. It refers to the curriculum guidelines given to teachers and conveyed to parents that describe the intended (though not necessarily the actual) nature of the teaching and learning being carried out in the school.

- The hidden curriculum, which is the kinds of learning and values that students absorb because of the nature and organizational structure of the school. A subject-divided approach will infer that the world is best viewed as a separate conglomeration of competing realities such as math, science, history, and literature. An integrated or integral approach will inculcate into students the belief that the world is an interactive, interdependent whole. As Auty (2008) reminds us, in the Christian school we need to ensure that even (or perhaps especially) the hidden curriculum reflects a biblically faithful worldview.

- The null curriculum refers to what schools choose not to teach. All schools thus unconsciously in-doctrinate into children a view of relevance and irrelevance about the world. Therefore, when God and theistic foundations are excluded from the science or economics classroom, the null curriculum is teaching children the secular belief that God is irrelevant to these aspects of the world around them.

- The received curriculum. Despite the best intentions of the teacher, what students actually absorb from classroom instruction and other parameters will not match exactly the specifications identified in the official documents of the school. What students experience has been called the received curriculum.

For the purposes of this chapter, although the other curriculum definitions are important, we will restrict our exploration to the first of these definitions – the purposely-designed or official approach to teaching and learning adopted by a school community. In the remaining sections of this chapter therefore, as we explore the official or planned curriculum:

1. We will offer a description of the two main patterns of planned curriculum in education today, acknowledging that simplicity often creates a caricature of the reality, and that many schools operationally reflect a blend of these two patterns.

2. Next, we will engage in a brief Christian critique of these two models.

3. This will be followed by a description of a couple of curriculum examples that reflect a Christian worldview.

4. We then will explore one approach to planning curriculum

structures from a Christian worldview perspective.

5. Finally, as a couple of examples, we will draw attention to information in the two key learning areas of language and mathematics that will assist teachers in preparing to design curricula and teach these in areas from a biblically faithful perspective.

THE PRODUCT MODEL APPROACH TO CURRICULUM
(CONTENT-ORIENTED LEARNING)

In some schools, the curriculum is shaped by an external publishing company that produces textbooks and specific, detailed, sequential, teacher guides for key learning areas. They may even produce student workbooks to accompany the textbook and teacher guide. Typically, each section of work (in the teacher guide anyway) will identify behavioral objectives that students will be expected to have achieved by the conclusion of that particular section, and that will be evaluated summatively at the section's conclusion. This is sometimes called the product model approach to curriculum. It is usually associated with the curriculum approach developed by Ralph Tyler in 1949. In terms of the movie *Dead Poets Society*, this, broadly-speaking, was the content-centered approach of Welton Academy.

Tyler's approach was a step-by-step model that could be observed and evaluated. The plan started with needs analysis, moved on to objectives, moved to the selection of learning experiences, the organization of learning experiences, and then the evaluation of student performance. It was rather like baking a cake. If you want a nice chocolate cake, then here are the required ingredients, here is the step-by-step recipe, and here is the desired outcome after the appropriate cooking time. And, as they say, the proof of the pudding (i.e., the success of the process) is in the eating!

Many adaptations of the Tyler model continue to exist today, often with helpful variations such as the inclusion of ongoing formal and informal formative evaluation during the unit of work's progress, and with a reduced rigidity in the behavioral objectives section due to the recognition that much of the person-shaping activity that takes place in the classroom is not well suited to quantitative statistical description or measurement.

Critics of Tyler (Smith 2000) suggest that a slavish adherence to his model is unrealistically linear, ignores the individuality and creativity of each student, turns teachers into technicians, reduces education to a series of minute, measurable units that have little relation to reality, and ignores the forming (as opposed to the informing) function of schooling.

Recognizing both the value and limitations of Tyler's model, some curriculum experts, such as Wiggins and McTighe (2010), have modified Tyler by starting at the end of the process. They identify desired student outcomes, and then work back to the start, so that needs analysis, learning objectives, and learning experiences are all explored with the final outcome leading the way.

THE PROCESS MODEL APPROACH TO CURRICULUM (STUDENT-ORIENTED LEARNING)

In other schools, the curriculum is shaped by general statements about skills, concepts, and content areas that students should cover in a particular school year, with teachers being given the freedom to introduce resources into the classroom, responding to student needs and interests that allow those skills, concepts, and content areas to be appropriately explored. O'Neill (2010) uses the term "process" to describe this second main approach to curriculum.

The process pattern is less concerned with the sequential acquisition of information, and is more concerned with student discovery and motivation. It fits well with the postmodern or radical constructivist approach to education (Mr. Keating in *Dead Poets Society*) where real meaning is derived by the individual interacting with his/her environment. The teacher becomes a facilitator and, in true Dewey-esk style, the student is placed at the heart of the learning process. Whereas the product model is subject-centered, the process model is learner and problem-centered. Piirto (1999) identifies Eisner, with his focus on personal relevance, social adaptation, and the denial of transcendence, as an early proponent of this alternative curriculum approach. In the first decade of the twenty-first century much of the hermeneutics of suspicion and reader-response theory in literature teaching reflected this approach to curriculum and pedagogy.

Though a little dated, the imaginary discussion provided by Cornwell and Johnson (1991) provides a fascinating reflection on the core differences between the product/traditional/positivist approach to curriculum on the one hand, and the student-centered/constructivist/process model on the other. In terms of our discussion here however, we can conclude that in both of these patterns there will be a plan of some sort that gives guidance and boundaries to the learning process. Again, this plan may be called the curriculum of the school.

A Christian Curriculum Foundation

The product and process models described above both have useful contributions to make to the development of a Christian approach to curriculum, but fundamentally, both of them are inappropriate for the Christian school, primarily due to their idolatrous core foundations. The product model is a child of Enlightenment thinking that embeds truth in rationality, and fits comfortably into the secular worldview mindset that denies the reality of God and his claims upon humanity in curriculum design and execution. It is unrealistically linear, and also tends to underplay the creative capacities that God has given to children and their teachers, and the interdependent interplay that should occur between what goes on in the classroom and the world outside.

On the other hand, the process model often is captive to postmodern thinking, denying the existence of truth other than that produced by the provisional conjunction of thinking and experience on the part of each individual student.

In their book, *The Bible and the Task of Teaching*, Smith and Shortt (2002) critique the main curriculum approaches of today by using the metaphor of story. They acknowledge how significant educational writers such as Kieran Egan and Neil Postman have described education as a process that inculcates a story or grand narrative in the minds and hearts of children. Smith and Shortt suggest that any curriculum critique must identify not just a linear flow of objectives, teaching resources, evaluation, etc., but any curriculum critique also must elucidate the primary characteristics of the story that the curriculum nurtures. What Smith and Shortt are saying is that the stories or the worldview perspectives of the product and process models are inadequate from the point of view of the Christian story. They rightly assert that

> The Bible's story is both a mirror in which we see truth about ourselves and a window through which we see God and God's world out there, past, present and future. It is this biblical big true story, the metanarrative of creation, fall and redemption . . . with which we are concerned in relating the Bible to education. (Smith & Shortt 2002, 82–83)

What this means is that the story (or worldview) being told through a Christian approach to curriculum needs to reflect perspectives such as: a biblical view of the child; a biblical understanding of human creative capacity and stewardship; a biblical perspective on history, wisdom, meaning and purpose; a biblical concept of what it means to know; a biblical understanding of community and cultural engagement; and the centrality of the gospel and the cross of Christ for all of life. Without these components being visible in the curriculum, the curriculum story will not be Christian.

Van Brummelen (2002, 44) expands on some of these ideas, and then summarizes this approach by contending that a Christian approach to curriculum involves "understanding and unfolding God's revelation through experience, conceptualization, and application" in such a way as to "foster students' positive responses toward God, their fellow creatures, society, and themselves." This is what Stronks and Blomberg call "responsive discipleship" (Stronks & Blomberg 1993), and which Blomberg (2007) later reflects can best be achieved by a curricular orientation focused on play, problem-posing, and purposeful response.

The purpose of education for the Christian is not the accumulation of bits of information, nor is it the process by which minds are set free to create their own truth. The Christian educator desires that his curriculum engine will lead his students to discover knowledge and wisdom, which come only in the context of God's revelation and which lead to committed service. This point has already been illustrated in Chapter 1 in the lives of Joseph and Daniel.

Curriculum design and implementation in the area of grammar provides us with a useful educational example here. I well remember the day when, as headmaster, I was looking over the end-of-semester English examination of one of my high school English teachers. She was new to my school and had come to us from a very conservative textbook-bound Christian school in California. She believed that grammar was really important and had conscientiously taught it to all of her classes, including these capable high school students who had, in fact, been taught the same essentials of grammar years before. However, the teaching of grammar for this teacher was actually an end in itself. The goal of knowing one's parts of speech was the achievement of knowing one's parts of speech. The goal of accurate sentence diagramming was the ability to be accurate in sentence diagramming. Her curriculum planning and actions demonstrated this, as did her exam, at which I was looking. One of her key tenth-grade test questions was "List the 35 prepositions." How sad and demeaning to the beauty, glory, and structure of language, which is one tool that God has given us to explore and describe his creation. It is good to know a preposition from an adverb, but not for its own sake. We need to know about prepositions so that we can use this understanding to communicate more effectively and, ultimately, to know God better.

It is sad today to see students spending many hours learning how to diagram convoluted sentences when the application of this abstract linguistics exercise is lost on them. We are not condemning the teaching of grammar, but rather the extended focusing on it that occurs in the curricula and curriculum materials of some Christian schools where little attempt is made to relate it to the reality of God's world and our purpose in that world. Note how Van Brummelen helpfully addresses this same issue:

> Why and how should Christians teach grammar? If we teach grammar as an end in itself, as one set of workbook exercises after another, evaluating the learning that has taken place on the basis of the student's recall of parts of speech and sentence types, then we are not doing justice to our task as Christian teachers. Nor does teaching grammar Christianly mean that we use Bible texts or moral maxims to recognize parts of speech or analyse sentences.
>
> Rather, the teacher of grammar must [have the curricular goal of helping] students develop their ability to listen and communicate in a responsible and creative way. We first use the students' own language experiences to indicate to them the need for learning about grammar. Next, our teaching of precise, specific grammar concepts must point to God as the Creator of the underlying structural laws for language, laws that allow us to communicate. . . . Students are given many opportunities for personal response. They apply what they have learned in oral and written communication that strives to enrich the . . . community both within the classroom and beyond. (Van Brummelen 2009, 90)

The curriculum provides the engine that determines how our students will learn about God's world and their places and tasks in it. It is the written instructional program that explains what is to be taught in the school and how it is to be taught. It must not be based on sets of rails (assumptions) that have conflicting gauges (set of religious assumptions). The result will be confusion and disaster. A Christian curriculum must recognize a godly foundation as its core and purpose and must be structured to help students learn about God's world so that they grow in understanding and discernment, and also grow in their ability to love and serve God as they live in his world.

A Christian Curriculum Model:
God and Knowing Him Are at the Core

Let us begin to construct a model that can help us understand how we as Christians should develop curriculum. The first step is easy. We have been acknowledging it all along: as in everything, the center and focus of our curriculum model and development should be God and his creative, redemptive, and sustaining activity in his creation. We can express this in a circular model by placing God and the Bible, his written Word, at the hub of our curriculum. This is the point of origin, definition, and purpose of all aspects of the curriculum. It declares that nothing in the curriculum is neutral, but that the whole focus of the learning activities of the school is to equip students to live lives of fulfilled worship and service to God in all that they do and learn about.

Mark Roques (1989) has chronicled some of the exciting developments that have taken place in the United Kingdom with regard to Christian curriculum development. In his book *Curriculum Unmasked*, Roques explains the pattern developed by Oak Hill School, a Christian school in England. The curriculum model in Figure 1 comes from that school and builds upon the thinking and writing of Christian educators in Australasia and North America.

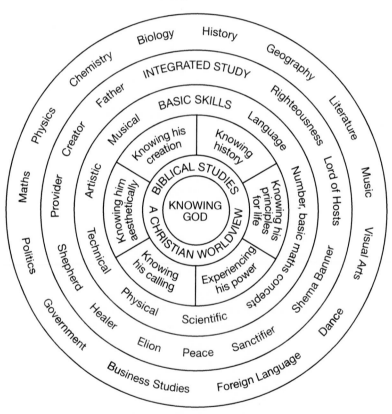

Figure 1. Oak Hill School Curriculum Model

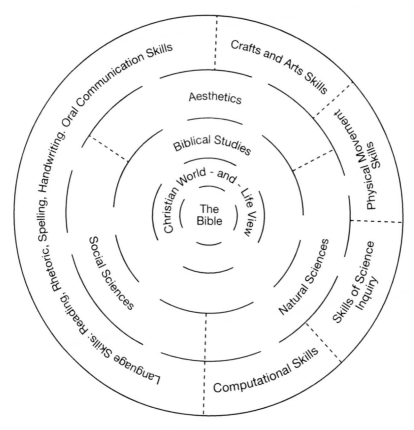

Figure 2. Steensma and Van Brummelen Model

In an excellent but now out-of-print book, Geraldine Steensma and Van Brummelen (1977) present a similar model, as per Figure 2. This model is less specific than that presented by Roques. It has broken concentric circles, reinforcing a strong commitment to an integral view of the world.

Notice how the circular nature of the Steensma and Van Brummelen model allows for the centrality of God to be recognized in all areas of study. There is no false nature/grace distinction here. Furthermore, in this model teachers can see that all knowledge is not just the intellectual accumulation of information, nor is it the child-directed search for meaning in an otherwise meaningless world. In both models, real knowledge starts with a revelatory God, involves all of life, is not limited to the intellectual realm, and provides for a commitment or response as students and teachers recognize the impact of this knowledge upon their lives.

Steensma and Van Brummelen structure their model to demonstrate the directing role of God's revelation in the Bible for the whole curriculum and to show that biblical studies is the focus. in the school as the leading discipline. The social sciences, aesthetics, and the natural sciences are the three core units at the next level, from which integrated units can be constructed, especially in the primary or elementary school.

A Christian Curriculum Should Promote Subject Integration

Grade school teachers have long been skilled at developing integrated units that bring together material and perspectives from many of the traditional disciplines or subject areas. They do this because intuitively they seem to recognize that children view the world the way God created it, which is as an integrated, interactive whole. Thus, the grade school teacher's planbook often will focus on concepts or themes such as "my family" or "sports" or "the way of life in Japan." The material will be carefully constructed to ensure that all the necessary skills of language, math, and other areas are covered, but in an integrated way that reflects the unity of the whole, and that points to the centrality of a heart commitment to God in how we deal with his manifold creation.

Increasingly, as students move toward higher grade levels, this integration gives way to compartmentalization or specialization. There is some legitimacy in this change. Ideas and materials become more complex, and skills and methods of inquiry are developed that have relevance in some areas and not in others. However, the rigidity of boundaries between subjects that exist in the middle school and high school at times is more a product of teacher training than it is the child of necessity. High school teachers are trained in specific disciplines, often in complete isolation from the concepts and patterns of other "subjects," even though there may well be a strong correlation between them. We do our students a disservice by maintaining these rigid boundaries unnecessarily.

The areas of language and social studies provide an obvious example. The social studies teacher encourages her students to go to the library or internet and conduct research using books, magazines, and online written and visual materials. These involve very important language and reading skills. She gives her students an assignment to express their perspectives and findings in written reports, essays, and perhaps even oral presentations. Although she is the social studies teacher, she again is teaching important language and reading skills.

For his part, the language teacher requires his students to be able to summarize written material. He also insists that his students support generalizations about a novel or a play with evidence that corroborates those generalizations. These are not just language skills, but they are very important social studies skills as well. The language teacher's comprehension exercises may be based upon stories of Greek civilization. His Shakespearean study of Julius Caesar will involve the historical consideration of the life and times of the Roman Empire. Here again we have the language teacher dealing with material that clearly falls into the social studies and/or civics realm. It makes excellent sense to bring these two subjects together.

Language and social studies are just two subject areas that are obvious examples of where we have allowed teacher training mechanisms to impose an unnecessary, unhelpful, and wasteful fragmentation upon the curricula in Christian schools. We would do well to carefully examine subject distinctions in order to maximize the opportunities for integrated or integral learning. We should develop separate subject instruction when we see that it is appropriate and not because other factors such as tradition or teacher training mechanisms attempt to force it upon us. As Blomberg (1991) suggests, we should start with the assumption of an integrated wholeness that may at times need exploring in different aspects, rather than starting from the point of fragmentation and trying to grasp for isolated examples of integration.

Blomberg's analogy of a slice of cake gives clarity to what is meant here. He makes the point that the difference between these two approaches is similar to the difference between having a slice of chocolate cake on the one hand (the integral approach), and individually eating the flour, cocoa, baking powder, egg, and so on, on the other (the fragmented approach). When we eat the slice, with all the ingredients interacting properly together, we have the pleasant sensation of what a chocolate cake really tastes like. If we were just to go to the shelf, though, and separately eat a portion of the various individual ingredients, we would have a far from pleasant experience and would develop an instant dislike for chocolate cake! Have you tried eating a spoonful of butter or a spoonful of flour or a teaspoon of vanilla essence recently?

AN INTEGRATION CELEBRATION: THEME WEEK
One of the most exciting and creative experiences that has been demonstrated in Christian schools all over the world has been the gradual movement by teachers into experimenting with an integrated or integral curriculum. At first, it often has been attempted hesitantly and in a spirit of some trepidation, but on almost every occasion it also has been very

successful and beneficial to the whole school program. One vehicle that teams of teachers worldwide have used to commence an exploration of an integrated teaching approach has been "Theme Week." This is where teachers decide that just for a week they will devote the whole school program, extending over all grade levels, to one particular theme.

These theme weeks are different from the traditional "spiritual emphasis week" activities common in many Christian schools. Typical themes for the concept explored here come from our interaction with God's world around us. A glance at the internet in 2013 revealed that recent theme week themes in Christian schools have included rainforest (even resulting in Covenant Christian School in Indiana being featured on the television news!), heroes, weather, vocation, faith, water, exercise, and community.

"Theme Week" is an experience that has a limited timeframe, so that teachers who initially may be fearful of the process of integration know that "it will all be over" in just five days. Everyone does it together so that if one teacher fails, then they all fail. However, the opposite is true as well! It is a cooperative effort, since in the planning stages, all teachers focus on gathering resources and teaching ideas for the theme. For example, if the theme chosen for Theme Week was "Space and Aviation," then there are 25 or so teachers gathering resources and teaching ideas for that theme. If each teacher comes up with just three ideas, then suddenly a battery of 75 ideas and/or resources becomes available to the whole faculty.

By working together, teachers help each other and even become in-volved in each other's classrooms. They learn that they don't need to rely exclusively on pre-prepared, packaged teaching guides (which is a special problem of teachers in some Christian schools) but that they themselves actually can use their God-given creativity and teaching skills to design appropriate classroom patterns of their own. They learn how to find re-sources of their own and use textbooks to support their programs, rather than having others determine them. They also learn that the selection of appropriate and creative instructional methods is as important a task for them as the selection of appropriate content material. This all occurs within the context of the specific philosophy and aims that the school has developed for its learning community.

"Theme Week" need not be presented as an unnecessary addition to an already crowded teaching agenda. The exercise should be presented in the context of teachers identifying skills and concepts that they want to be teaching their children during that week anyway and then selecting resources and cooperative activities that link into the chosen theme.

There are some legitimate criticisms that can be leveled at a "Theme Week" approach, but the benefits of this idea as a way of moving into creative, integrated, and cooperative teaching are enormous. Tried once, it's almost guaranteed to become an annual event that is eagerly anticipated by the whole school community, even by the math teacher who might have claimed that "Math is math, and it cannot be integrated into other subjects!" More importantly, it gives teachers the confidence to know that they can teach in an integrated manner, and thus it lends credibility and acceptance to the curriculum styles that this book is encouraging teachers to adopt.

Even when subject categorization becomes necessary, and it does, there are still mechanisms available to help students view the world in an integrated way. Some subjects, such as ecology, for example, lend themselves to inter-subject study. The science teacher, math teacher, English teacher, social studies teacher, music teacher, and Bible teacher could all do well to come together and develop an integrated approach to ecology, while still meeting the skills and concepts goals that are important to their own individual subject areas.

The way that this integration is carried out will point to the fundamental curricular perspective of the school. It will indicate the "big picture" of education that the school possesses and will reflect the school's basic beliefs about education. As Stronks and Blomberg (1993) have commented,

> It is in the overarching curricular framework that we will detect the religious vision of the school, for it is in such a context that the various details of schooling . . . find their meaning. (190)

A word of warning is necessary here. Some proponents of an integrated or thematic approach have implicitly suggested that the implementation of this curriculum pattern into a school program will create Christian education. This is not true. Many non-Christian educators have developed creative, integrated curricula. However, due to the fact that their basic philosophical assumptions are still non-Christian, their curriculum product remains non-Christian as well. It can still point our students away from God. We need to beware of the very simplistic and incorrect assumption that equates an integrated approach to curriculum with a Christian approach to education.

AN INTEGRATED EXAMPLE: POND LIFE IN A TANK

Roques (1989) provides a simple but excellent example of an integrated approach by relating the story of a grade school classroom in London.

The teacher had brought a fish tank to her class of 30 eager young students. It captured their attention right away, and the students were always looking in the tank to see when changes were occurring. One day, to their delight, the children discovered a whole clump of baby snails. On another, they saw a water tiger eat a tadpole, and so on. The teacher used these experiences to focus the students' learning in the core curriculum areas.

The teacher was delighted at the outcomes of these learning experiences. The students developed a sense of awe and wonder at creation in a context that led them to glorify God in their own way. "God must be very clever!" commented one child. The teacher concluded her remarks with the following:

> One prayer of a seven-year-old sums up for me the effect such a study had on his spiritual understanding. It was similar to this: "Oh God, how can you think and live and move? How can you do all that you do? Oh God, you're great!" (Roques 1989, 219)

An integrated approach to teaching requires creativity and a special approach to textbooks and resources. This latter issue is explored in Chapter 10. An integrated approach also requires a commitment, expressed in the curriculum, to recognize the wholeness of God's world.

It is important now to take time and develop practical handles for planning the type of curriculum that has been described in this chapter. The approach described here allows for the development of integrated patterns as well as recognizing that there will be much curriculum development work done in schools that focus on specific subject areas. This will be especially true at senior levels and particularly with regard to skills and content acquisition.

PLANNING THE CURRICULUM

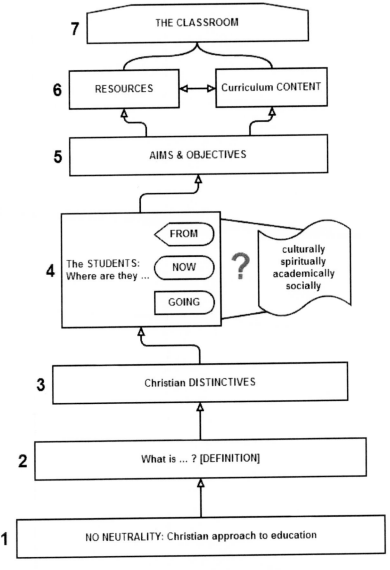

Figure 3. Curriculum Development Flowchart (Edlin)

In this section, we will be addressing the practical heart of curriculum development, which is the specific steps that need to be taken by the teachers in a school in order to develop a God-honoring, dynamic curriculum for their Christian school.

The Starting Point

The curriculum development model that is suggested in this book is found in Figure 3. It is designed to be read and implemented from the bottom up to the top and is non-traditional in many ways. One key difference is that it starts several layers below the starting point of some traditional curriculum development models. For some models found in curriculum planning texts today the starting point is step 5, Aims and Objectives – although some do include environmental factors such as the nature of the students in step 4. Our point is that, whether it is acknowledged or not, all curriculum models presuppose and flow out of a certain view of the world that proponents believe. This view (worldview again) shapes how they define the curriculum process, and determine the desired outcomes that they wish to see in the minds and hearts of students after they have been exposed to the particular curriculum approach. This is true for Christians and non-Christians. One of the benefits of living in a postmodern age is that educators are now much more willing than in the past to acknowledge these belief foundations. They give different names to it. MacDonald and Purpel (1987), for example, call this inescapable presuppositional worldview orientation a "platform." Lewis (2004) openly acknowledges the impact of faith in postmodernity as a primary curriculum-shaping force in contemporary education. Levin (2007) and research by Roehrig and Kruse (2005) openly recognize the central place of values in shaping curriculum. Practitioners like Harris (2009) increasingly are identifying their curriculum faith commitments at the beginning of their courses.

Therefore, the curriculum model being suggested in Figure 3, through steps 1, 2, 3 and 4, attempts to bring these worldview presuppositions and goals out into the open and deliberately includes them in the curriculum development process. Yet, for the Christian teacher involved in the curriculum development process, there really should be no other starting point than the foundations expressed in this model.

For example, Keenan's ACSI publication (1993) concerning curriculum development spends some time considering the way that a school's philosophy should be reflected in its curriculum design. However, he assumes a biblically faithful foundation and focuses most of his attention in the curriculum construction process at levels 5 through 7. He develops the concepts of course objectives and works through the important scope and sequence components of unit objectives, concepts, skills, content, lesson planning, resources, and evaluation. These steps are all very important, and Keenan assists the Christian teacher by providing sample templates that could be used in the process. However, the material presented in this book prioritizes the necessity for Christian educators to concentrate their curriculum development process on laying a sure foundation first, without which all of the vital structure that is built upon it will be inadequate and unstable.

STEP ONE: NO NEUTRALITY – CHRISTIAN APPROACH TO EDUCATION

Curriculum development starts with the recognition of the common bond that Christians have in Christ, a recognition of the religious nature of the task that curriculum developers are involved in and with an acceptance of the calling to prepare material for Christian schools that leads to the worship and service of God the Creator, and not worship of the creature or creation. The details of this step form the basis of the first two chapters of this book. We could, for example, remind our curriculum team, *as a part of the curriculum development process*, of Paul's stirring sermon in Athens, recorded in Acts 17:16–32. There the Word of God clearly shows us that all people are religious, that we are all worshippers in life, whether we like it or not, because God has made us that way. Paul again reminds us that most people have been deceived in this worship, however, and serve the creature rather than the Creator (Romans 1:25).

We cannot choose whether to worship or not, but what we can choose is the object of our worship. Thus, in our curriculum construction, we must actively choose to build a structure that challenges students with the worship and service of the Lord, for there is no neutrality. If our curriculum doesn't recognize and espouse the glory of God in his world, then it is leading to the worship and glory of a barren, god-substitute, usually mankind himself; which is exactly opposite to the purpose of the Christian school. As Frank Gaebelein (1954) commented many years ago,

> No man teaches out of a philosophical vacuum. In one way or another every teacher [and his curriculum] expresses the convictions he lives by, whether they be spiritually positive or negative. (37)

This first step of the curriculum development process in the Christian school must not be overlooked. It lays the foundation for all that follows. The foundation must be biblically strong and secure, and must be refreshed through regular professional development, if the structure that is built upon it is to survive and flourish.

STEP TWO: WHAT IS . . . ? – OUR DEFINITIONS ARE IMPORTANT

Definitions are important and are no more neutral than any other area of life. For example, ask a Christian for a definition of "truth" and you will get a very different answer than the one you will get from a relativist or from a secular humanist. The same applies to how we define the study areas of our curriculum. Common grace means that there may be a considerable degree of agreement at times, but as Christian educators we should not just accept the definition of an area of inquiry that happens to be in vogue around us. Even definitions reflect faith assumptions and presuppositions. We must be careful to develop distinctive definitions that reflect what Christians believe in the curriculum development process. Social studies provides us with an illustration of this.

If you consult your standard social studies manual, you'll find social studies defined as something like "those portions of the social science disciplines of anthropology, sociology, economics, psychology, political science, history, and geography that have been selected for teaching purposes." Some help!

A more meaningful general definition may be "the study of the 'behavior' of humanity" or "the study of people in community in a particular time and place."

The last definition may be the most helpful for some, but it does not yet indicate a distinctively Christian understanding of the study. In particular, it defines social studies strictly in terms of people. The foundational perspective that this book has stressed, that the center of real education is God and his creating, redeeming, and sustaining hand, is completely ignored. Perhaps an acceptable definition for Christians could be the following:

> *Social studies is the study of mankind carrying out the cultural mandate given by God, in community and relationship, in a particular time and place.*

This definition is distinctively Christian, as opposed to the distinctively secular ones above. This one reflects a worldview that only Christians will appreciate. Exactly what is meant by this definition will become more apparent as we consider the next step of the curriculum development model.

STEP THREE: CHRISTIAN DISTINCTIVES

Time needs to be spent articulating the Christian faith assumptions that apply to social studies. This process also will help identify faith assumptions that are residual in the minds of the teachers – some of which are not appropriate. Here again, the dynamic Christian commitment to an ordered God involved in his world will be startlingly apparent. The Christian distinctives will be very different from the set of faith assumptions that form the often unspoken (but, nevertheless, determinative) presuppositions and distinctives that characterize how secular educators view this subject area.

For example, in a science curriculum statement the Christian distinctives will probably identify right up front that the scientific method is an appropriate tool given by God to explore his world, but that it is not the *sole* measure that Christians should use, as if the scientific method of itself always will determine what is true or not true. If this were so (and many school science departments function as if this was the case), then the scientific method, or scientism, would be our god. The Christian school science curriculum would probably also want to make some sort of primary distinctive statement about its view of science in the light of the prevailing secular faith commitment to a view that believes the world to be ultimately random, evolutionary, and without defined purpose.

Let us return to social studies and consider what might be appropriate distinctives that Christians want to identify and have percolate through this curriculum area. We will want these perspectives to direct our understanding of this subject and to direct our selection of the objectives, skills, content, resources, and evaluation that will be components of the teaching of this subject in our school:

1. God created and upholds the heavens and the earth as ordered forms (Genesis 1:1–31; Hebrews 1:3; Colossians 1:16–17). He gave mankind a special place in this creation (Genesis 1:26–8; Psalms 8:1–9). Mankind, under God's guidance and norms, has been placed in charge of God's creation – to discover, explore, and unfold it. Social studies is the study of humanity's exercise of this stewardship.

2. Human beings are not autonomous meaning-makers in an otherwise meaningless world. We live in relationship to God, to our selves, to others, and to the rest of creation. These relationships are carried out either in obedience or disobedience to God.

3. In the Fall, mankind disobeyed God and thus became alienated from God, from himself, from the rest of humanity, and from the rest of creation. However, in Christ, the restoration of fellowship in relationships and community is possible, though these will only achieve their ultimate "fulfillment" when Christ comes again. In the present, Christians of all ages are called to engage culture and seek the welfare of the cities in which we live, as God's purposeful, graceful, salt and light ambassadors in our communities and relationships.

4. Christianity cannot be imposed, and neither can a commitment by

students to follow a Christian walk. A social studies program needs to encourage in students an open and inquiring spirit, just as Jesus did with his disciples. Students need to be challenged to understand and evaluate the faith assumptions that they explore in their own and other cultures, as well as to evaluate their own developing personal understanding of the world in the light of the principles and patterns of God's Word.

5. God has created his world as an ordered whole. It often is useful, for the purposes of study, to distinguish differences within creation so that we can focus upon certain aspects of that whole. Concepts, skills, and content in social studies often have their own unique perspectives that differ from emphases considered appropriate in some other subjects. However, our social studies will endeavor to present to the students a perspective that recognizes the integral completeness and interrelatedness of God's world. We will "endeavor" to develop structures and approaches that show how social studies' concepts, skills, and content are important in all of life, including those aspects of creation dealt with in other subjects such as language, literature, economics, mathematics, science, and the fine arts.

In some Christian schools where an integrated approach to curriculum has been adopted, Christian virtues such as truth, justice, loving your neighbor, etc., have become the uniting concepts. In yet other schools, such as Graham's imaginary Omega Christian School (Graham 2003) themes such as stewardship, environment, or worship provide the link between subjects, where students are also expected to "show how the light of Scripture shines on their [learning] and how Scripture has informed their exploration" (220). This is the school's core orientation or distinctive that deliberately shapes curriculum decision-making, design, delivery, and evaluation.

STEP FOUR: THE STUDENTS

Any responsible educator must keenly be aware of the nature of the students in her classroom. She should not employ a content-centered approach that ignores the children. Neither should she employ a child-centered approach that views content and skills as irrelevant. A good teacher embraces "perspective consciousness" (Hanvey 1975, 4) when she becomes profoundly familiar with the world of the child (De Kool 2009). In a Christo-centric Christian school with a biblically based scope and sequence, there are three key "student" questions that need to be asked in a God-centered and child-focused curriculum development process. Each question has four dimensions to it, as in Figure 4:

The Students

Where are they from?	Culturally
Where are they now?	Spiritually
Where are they going?	Academically
	Socially

Consider these three questions in their cultural dimension. Teachers must get to know their students and families very well – especially in a multi-ethnic school (and most schools are multi-ethnic to some degree these days). They must learn where their students come from culturally and what expectations they bring with them. They must find ways of making the classroom lessons relevant to their students' geographical and cultural settings so that whenever possible learning is concrete and not abstract. They must learn about the ethnic composition of the area in which the school is located in order to give a local context to content and skills and thus help the students appreciate and relate to the culture where God has called them and their parents to live. Then, the teachers should find out the geographical, academic, social, and vocational aspirations of their students and structure the students' courses to prepare them for these, within a Christian worldview context. Effective teachers will be able to view the classroom and the curriculum from the perspective of the learner.

For example, in social studies in US Christian schools, it will be important to foster curriculum perspectives that study and evaluate the backgrounds and contributions of the Pilgrim fathers and also of other immigrant populations such as African-Americans, Hispanics, Irish, and Asians. Classroom expectations and learning styles also will differ for students coming from shame-and-honor Asian cultures, compared to students raised in the rampant individualism of many western cultures.

A classical, sad example of the failure to contextualize the curriculum appropriately in the light of the students in the classroom was illustrated in a Christian school that I visited in the southern United States. I accompanied a grade school class on a social studies field trip to Tannehill, a local state park. Tannehill is the site of an iron foundry that was established during the US Civil War in order to produce weapons for the Confederate soldiers. Field trips are great experiences. The children thoroughly enjoyed themselves during the visit. They learned the details of early iron-making and other interesting historical facts. One of the park volunteers was dressed up in a Confederate uniform. He explained to the children how a musket was loaded and fired, and then he actually carried out the procedure. We all jumped back because of the noise as the musket fired! During another part of the visit to Tannehill, the children saw a model schoolroom of the Civil War era where a park member played the part of the stern schoolmistress with the children. She explained that this is what they would have experienced if they had been alive during that earlier period of history.

It was all great fun, but it was also historical revisionism. It grossly misled the children. The facts of Tannehill had been presented in a carefully selected manner, so as to convey a romantic and sanitized view of American history. The real facts of Tannehill include the reality that the whole steel-making complex was built upon the backs of black slave labor. This was ignored during the visit. There were black children in the school group I was with, and the history of this place for their culture was not romantic and beautiful. If they had been alive during Tannehill's heyday, they certainly would not have had the classroom experience portrayed for them nor would they have lived in the simple, rustic settler cottages that the class visited. Most would probably have ground out a pathetic, ill-educated existence in slave hovels (that still existed in dilapidated form in unvisited parts of the park). The original purpose of the Tannehill complex was to enable thousands of Americans to kill thousands of other Americans, but the reality of that horror was deliberately masked in the way that the students were told about the place.

The curricular model proposed in this chapter would most often quite obviously not allow for incorporating this kind of pre-formed and binding curriculum package. While it is laudable that the classroom teacher was attempting to make the teaching of historical skills, concepts, and content relevant to the actual experience of her students, pre-packaged approaches (and that also includes textbooks prepared by someone living in a different cultural and/or geographic context – see Chapter Ten) most often fail to respond adequately to this whole question of the nature of the students and their historical and contemporary situations in any given classroom. It is crucial that teachers consider the students in their classrooms and develop contextualized, creative, hands-on, educational, curricular experiences so that they can perceive the relevance of their learning. When that happens, learning becomes more vital, more effective, and more affective.

The Example of Jesus

Of course, the archetypal example of someone who was concerned about his students when he devised his teaching patterns is our Lord, Jesus Christ. Much of what is recorded in the four gospels shows Jesus educating his apostles in what was involved in the ministry of the kingdom of God. As he taught them, he contextualized his curriculum so that it reflected who his students were, where they were from, and where they were going. Several of the apostles came from rural, agrarian backgrounds. Therefore, Jesus explained his own earthly task as being like the Good Shepherd. He repeated the shepherding motif often, knowing that his student disciples would more easily be able to understand what he was saying.

Why did Jesus not use illustrations that had, e.g., to do with gold mining or motor car racing? Or why did he not say that "The kingdom of heaven is like unto a tropical rainforest?" Is it because gold mining, car racing, and jungle habitats are more ignoble than shepherding, or lend themselves less effectively to being used as illustrations? Of course not. The key factor is that they were beyond the experience of his students. No benefit would have been derived from using them as teaching tools because his disciples could not relate to them. Jesus ensured that his teaching was appropriate to the backgrounds and life experiences of his hearers.

How ridiculous it would have been if Jesus had tried to help his disciples understand who he was by saying to them "I am iCloud central" or "I am the supreme intranet controller." We today might understand these illustrations, but they would have been like a foreign language to his audience. However, are we in our schools being any less ill-advised when we try to teach mathematics as if it was just a set of symbols and do not relate it to the real experience of our students? Are we being any less asinine when in some English-language Christian schools in Asia we teach second-grade children the concept of money by using U.S. coinage instead of the local currency just because the US system is what is in the textbook? We must ensure that our curricular designs steer us in the direction of appropriate, contextualized teaching and situated cognition that recognizes the particular characteristics of the students that we have in our own (yes, unique) school, with its own special vision statement, philosophy, and confessional direction.

Some of Jesus' apostles were fishermen. Accordingly, Jesus contextualized his instruction to his students/disciples by referring to their own responsibilities as being called to be fishers of men. Likewise, when issuing a very specific challenge to Peter, Jesus built upon Peter's own name and told him that he would represent the rock upon which Christ would build his church. There was no sterile, pre-programmed, packaged curriculum here. Jesus' teaching and curriculum style clearly were in close touch with the backgrounds, present perspectives, and future goals of his students. We should follow his example in our curriculum planning and do no less.

Central to an appropriate consideration of "the students" is the approach taken in curriculum design and implementation to the issue of student assessment and evaluation. Chapter 9 deals with this matter in a general sense, but from the perspective of this chapter, curriculum decisions will be impacted by the philosophy of testing that is adopted. Faithful Christian educators will need some insight into the debate that continues to rage concerning tracking or streaming on the one hand, and mixed-ability classes on the other. Teachers need to be given professional development release time to research these options, and to be cognizant of alternative approaches. One such approach is the Joplin Plan with its selective, multi-grade ability grouping that is advocated by Robert Slavin, Director of the Center for Research and Reform in Education at Johns Hopkins University in Baltimore (Slavin 2013). This model is receiving critical praise in some Canadian provinces (Alphonso 2013). Another alternative is the student differentiation model (Fischer 2004) that allows for individualized student tracking within mixed-ability classrooms but which is very complex for many teachers to manage.

Discussions on this issue, often in the light of intense parental pressure, show a creditable concern for "the student" stage in the curriculum development model espoused in this chapter. However, it is unlikely that a consensus will develop unless there is agreement upon the insights provided by the earlier steps. For example, if the core worldview has to do with school performance and outcomes being shaped by a desire to maximize individual performance, then a competitive approach to tracking, streaming, and evaluation will prevail. If however, the core worldview has to do with understanding God's world God's way, which includes using one's talents for the benefit of others in a collaborative and even to an extent self-sacrificing way, then a very different approach to these issues may emerge.

STEP FIVE: AIMS AND OBJECTIVES

And this is my prayer: that your love may abound more and more in knowledge and depth of insight, so that you may be able to discern what is best and may be pure and blameless until the day of Christ, filled with the fruit of righteousness that comes through Jesus Christ – to the glory and praise of God. (Philippians 1:9–11)

Our prayer (aims and objectives) for our students in social studies should be the same as Paul's for the Philippian Christians quoted above. We desire to develop our students' knowledge, insight, discernment, commitment, and ability to exercise obedient stewardship by teaching them about the following:

(1)   the motivating ideas or spirit of the times, and their effects upon cultural formation;

(2)   the process of cultural formation in the light of God's call to responsible stewardship;

(3)   the context within which cultural formation takes place (religious, social, historical, economic, political, and physical).

As teachers identify their aims and objectives for the Christian school social studies curriculum, the following list includes some of the factors that they will want to consider.

We want our children to:

(1)   develop a global knowledge and perspective;

(2)   develop an historical knowledge and perspective;

(3)   appreciate the patterns, processes, and directions of their heritage and of the culture in which they are living and be aware of the religious world and life views involved;

(4)   appreciate who they are as children created by God in his created order, exercising stewardship, and living increasingly from a position of heart commitment;

(5)   develop research and thinking skills appropriate to the social sciences (including mapping, resource collation and interpretation, primary and secondary information analysis and synthesis, reliable internet research capacities, report presentation, perception of bias). These same skills will be reinforced and re-examined in successive years at ever higher levels of competence and understanding (a spiral approach).

STEP SIX: RESOURCES, CONTENT, AND LESSON PLANS

At this point, we begin to move into the detail of planning teaching activities that build on the perspectives and foundations laid thus far. In some countries, Christian schools still are in control of this step.

In others, quasi-government bodies have prescribed required skill and content acquisition parameters for each particular grade or year level. As long as adequate attention has been given to steps one through five, step six often can be completed in a manner that continues to celebrate a Christian worldview while also satisfying government mandates. And help is available.

Christian school organizations in several parts of the world have developed resources to assist teams of teachers in schools prepare materials ranging from semester structures to individual lesson plans that blend together government requirements, school vision, and intended outcomes all within the context of a Christian worldview. Sometimes these patterns are incorporated into an integrated or integral approach to curriculum; in other resources they follow a more traditional subject-differentiated approach. Sometimes they are templates or models; in other resources they follow more directive and packaged-deal approach. For example:

- Some years ago, the Society of Christian Schools in British Colombia (SCSBC) produced a great 100-page curriculum development resource that moves from vision (stages 1–5 in this chapter) to process (stages 6–7) in a comprehensive manner, providing clear guidance and many alternative patterns of application. It builds on some of the curriculum insights of Harro van Brummelen and others and is one of the best resources available to Christian schools to assist in the curriculum design process (www.scsbc.ca)

- In Australia, groups such as the National Institute for Christian Education (NICE) and Morling Education provide resources and training programs in curriculum from a Christian worldview perspective

- Global and national Christian school networking groups, such as Christian Schools International (CSI), the Association of Christian Schools International (ACSI), Light Educational Ministries (LEM), Accelerated Christian Education (ACE), Christian Education National (CEN), provide resources ranging from magazines, textbooks, and curriculum packages, to school-sharing ideas exchanges that will have varying levels of appeal to different types of Christian schools as they seek to develop their own curricula and scope and sequence documents.

There are two competing trends in education. One school of thought continues to claim that schooling is largely a technical, objective activity that can be standardized, even going so far as to say in Korea, for example, that foreign language instruction can be best taught mechanically by robots rather than living teachers. This pattern of thinking also maintains that regular, quantitative standardized tests are the best measure of progress, and gives great credence to international comparative examinations in areas such as numeracy and literacy as indicators of success and value for money in education.

The other perspective places much more emphasis on tailoring educational experiences to the needs and capacities of specific students, and recognizes that qualitative as well as quantitative outcomes must be considered when evaluating the appropriateness of schools and their curricula. These divisions are reminiscent of the old divisions of content-centered learning versus child-centered learning.

To the degree that the second paradigm influences schools, there is a widespread recognition of the value-laden nature of curriculum – even in science, however much some science teachers who remain wedded to scientific ideological fundamentalism masquerading as neutrality may like to deny this reality.

The Example of Mathematics

Perhaps the most challenging area for some educators to accept as being non-neutral is the key learning area of mathematics. Thankfully, a number of resources have become available in recent years to assist teachers explore mathematical structures from a position that recognizes the deep worldview commitment of contemporary mathematics. Furthermore, there also are valuable resources prepared by insightful Christian educators that assist in devising mathematics programs for schools that celebrate the lordship of Christ over this area of creation. These resources fit well with the curriculum foundations outlined in this chapter.

- James Bradley (2011) has written helpfully on this subject on a number of occasions.
- David Smith (2008) and his team at the Kuyers Institute have provided valuable classroom materials and teacher resources that view mathematics from a Christian worldview perspective (http://www.calvin.edu/kuyers/math/index.html).
- The Stapleford Centre, through its Charis Project, has developed mathematics resources from a Christian worldview perspective, and brings a reformed critical realist dynamism (Cooling 2005, Edlin 2006b) to the shaping of curriculum. Though out of print, David Shortt has been given permis-

sion to make some Charis materials, including mathematics resources, available on his own teacher resource website (www. johnshortt.org/Pages/Charis.aspx).

- Steve Bishop has provided a wonderful service by compiling a bibliography of resources that address the issue of mathematics from a Christian worldview perspective. People can access Steve's work at http://stevebishop.blogspot.com.au/2008/06/bibliography-for-christian-approach-to.html.

- Patricia Ahlborn teaches mathematics at Delaware County Christian School. In a paper she has written, she is delightfully frank about her own struggle with the idea of "How do you teach mathematics Christianly?" She goes on to identify the discoveries that revolutionized her understanding of this issue, and finally she provides key pointers that other Christian mathematics teachers might like to consider as they develop their own mathematics curricula. So compelling is Mrs. Ahlborn's material, that in response to a special request, she has granted permission for it to be included as Appendix Two in this book – readers are sure to find her insights refreshing and illuminating.

THE EXAMPLE OF LITERATURE

The teaching of literature is one curriculum area that, over the last few decades, has been most strongly influenced by postmodern and feminist literary theory. Templar (2003) maintains that in some jurisdictions government-sanctioned curriculum police promote adherence to it. Though the power of this influence, according to Ireland (personal communication, 22 April 2013), is waning somewhat due to the fact that the perspective was too radical and failed to provide the coherent understanding of reality that most teachers and parents are looking for, many state-endorsed literature curricula are still powerfully shaped by a critical theory that, in this writer's judgment, has played a significant role in destroying hope and purpose among young people.

Critical theory perspectives such as the hermeneutics of suspicion and reader-response theory do have their uses – for example, in assisting readers to beware of manipulative texts, even though many postmodern texts at times are classic illustrations of this manipulation. However, given that this perspective on literature denies the existence of independent truth and insists that true meaning resides not in the author's intention but in each individual reader's interpretation, it is a non-Christian approach and it creates unnecessary uncertainty and confusion. Imagine, for example, if our approach to the Bible was based on this self-centered presupposition, rather than on a humble submission to Scripture as a divinely inspired text that we read for enlightenment, truth, and guidance, and not for personal interpretation and self-fulfilling satisfaction (and we should remember that children nurtured in schools captivated by critical theory have been trained to read all literature including the Bible in just this manner!).

Ireland (2004) reviewed all of the books on the Children's Book Council in Australia shortlists between 1974 and 1994. She found that the following postmodern or radical constructivist worldview themes prevailed across the vast majority of these books which are used in Australian schools:

1. An essentially malevolent universe must be fought by the individual with secrecy and cunning;
2. If there is any force controlling humankind it is sinister;
3. No institution – family, government, church, health care body – is even remotely helpful;
4. The human race is largely corrupt, with the exception of a few brave adolescents who through vigor, violence, bravado, keen persistence, intellectual acumen, magic or psychic powers win out against the evil forces;
5. Relationships have only temporary value;
6. People are fundamentally solitary: it is hardly possible to know real connectedness, only parallel solitude;
7. The best stance to adopt about life, and about the loss of innocence, is wry acceptance. (62)

In her article, Ireland recognized the concerns that even non-Christian scholars have with the negative and despairing view of life that was being presented to children. For example, the conclusion of one expert panel with which Ireland was associated concluded that:

All seven possible texts in the 2/3 Unit Related Twentieth-Century Fiction course and five of the seven for the 2 Unit General course, portray life as profoundly deterministic, frustrating or unfulfilling. They see family life as oppressive or gratuitously constraining; marriage as a form of imprisonment, a power game, or a ritual performance; human communication as doomed from the start, or at best gravely limited; aspirations for the future as illusory; and participation in the community as a waste of time or a self-centred escape from the humdrum of domesticity. . . . [A]dults play a peripheral, insufficient, or non-existent role in the lives of young people; high aspiration is usually defeated; parents and other older people responsible for the care of the young have to be deceived or side-stepped for the sake of survival and gratification; sexual intimacy, however disappointing or damaging, is a requirement of modern teenage life; and future prospects are inescapably disappointing. The vital question of what is emotionally suitable or beneficial for young adults seems never to be asked. (Ireland 2004, 64–65; citing Aitchison, Ireland, Grover, and Kingston, 1996)

Is it any wonder that the loss of hope or purpose is alarmingly prevalent among western teenagers today – they have been weaned on a literature (and other media) base that inculcates this belief!

The teaching of literature need not lead to hopelessness or despair. Some time ago, Kopple (1991) outlined some of the key foundational beliefs for Christians dealing with literature, based upon the presupposition that language is a creative, communicative gift from God. Ireland (2001) reminds us that authors are mentors, that all libraries carry out censorship (how many secular school libraries do you know that subscribe to *Christianity Today* or *Playboy*, or that allow students unrestricted access to the internet?), and that a Christian literature curriculum needs to expose children to the gritty reality of daily living in a context in which the hope and direction given by commitment to a loving creator God gives them direction and meaning in the challenging world of the twenty-first century. She encourages teachers to select resources only after a careful review of their worldviews. This does not mean that controversial materials always are excluded, but that the children are helped to critique them from a Christian worldview perspective, ensuring that the preponderance of input children receive in literature class is neither an anemic "live happily ever after" nor leaves children despairing and without hope. More is said about this issue in Chapter 10 which deals with resource selection in the Christian school.

A useful resource for Christian literature teachers is the "What If Learning" initiative, a joint endeavor of Christian educators in the United Kingdom, Australia, and the United States. The What If Learning website provides many examples of curriculum resources that Christian teachers have devised and use in their literature instruction in many parts of the world (http://www.whatiflearning.com/examples).

Conclusion

The curriculum development foundation outlined in this chapter is linear in appearance, and there is an important flow and sequence to it, but it should not be just linear in application. Curriculum development is dynamic. It is an ongoing task, and should include review and revision loops at each stage and between stages, as the school seeks to maintain a curriculum pattern that reflects both its philosophical perspective and the changing demographic, political, and historical community that it serves. On occasion, teachable moments relating to unexpected current events will break into the normal sequence. There should be an up-and-down flow of ideas, re-visiting previous stages in the light of subsequent ones, all seeking to refine the process in the light of the school's Christian worldview and vision and the changing needs and realities of the school situation.

The creation of the position of curriculum coordinator and the provision of adequate relief time to teams of teachers can help teachers engage in the task of curriculum development. Accreditation procedures can give the whole process more urgency. A critical friend visitation (see Chapter 13) can assist in the alignment between school vision and mission and curriculum design and practice.

Effective curriculum development is central to the health of a good Christian school. It is a time-consuming and continuous process, but it must also be a primary commitment of the school administration and faculty. Short-term solutions may be found in curriculum packages prepared by others. However, for a school to be authentic, responsive, engaging, dynamic, and faithful, there is no substitute for teams of teachers in Christian schools collaborating together in exploring curriculum in the light of a Christian worldview. In the process, they will develop units of work and daily lesson plans that challenge students with the lordship of Christ over all creation as they and their students explore God's world together in a God-honoring way and become equipped to function as hope-filled, purposeful shalom-sharers in a lost and needy world.

Chapter 9

Student Evaluation and Assessment in the Christian School

EVALUATION AND ASSESSMENT OCCURS ALL THROUGH LIFE

Evaluation is a constant aspect of the human experience. When a parent says "Good girl" to her young daughter for eating all the food on her plate, that parent is providing a positive and encouraging evaluation of what the child has just accomplished. When a business executive returns a piece of typing to the secretary for correction because of spelling errors, he is indicating that the standard of work initially submitted to him was unsatisfactory, and that the secretary should make more effective use of the computer's spell checker. In a room where friends are watching a televised ball game, the evaluative comments on the play shown on the screen are often colorful and extremely varied – even contradictory if there are supporters of different teams in the room! Assessment and evaluation are a part of life in which we are all involved.

Evaluation is frequent, important, and legitimate in the context of the school. Myriads of positive and negative reinforcement activities take place in classrooms every day. It may be a grade entered in a grade book for the completion of a homework activity. It may be applauding a child for an accurate verbal answer to a question. It may be asking a student to rewrite a piece of work that has obviously been produced in haste and with little care, perhaps even containing some plagiarism from off the internet. It may be adjudicating the winning team in a debate in the history class about the origins of the First World War. It may be determining the ability of students to perform the steps involved in a chemistry experiment. It may be the situation surrounding the punishment that is incurred in order to remind a recalcitrant student that the chewing of gum is not permitted on the school property.

One of the most prominent evaluation instrument in a school's evaluation and assessment repertoire is the report card. It is meant to represent the pinnacle of the assessment activities of a school, the semi-public document that is taken to be the school's ultimate evaluation of a child's school activities. Unfortunately, the report card today is often very subjective, ill-conceived, and lacking clear reference points. Even in many Christian schools they are framed with the job-market or personal advancement in mind, and bear little overt relationship to the true purpose of education – challenging students with a celebration of the lordship of Christ over all creation. More will be said about this later in the chapter.

The solution to this problem is not to *start* by tinkering with the report card, though changes may be necessary. The solution lies, once again, in examining the Word of God and searching out biblical norms for evaluation. Once this has been done, guidelines and procedures can be established for the implementation of a vibrant and creative evaluative pattern for the Christian school that covers what goes on in the classroom, as well as report cards and other home/school assessment contacts.

In the overview of student evaluation and assessment that this chapter provides, three main topics will be considered.

- First, after reflecting upon the confusion of terminology in this field, we will consider from a Christian worldview perspective a couple of illustrations that reflect some of the assessment challenges that confront educators today.
- Second, the chapter will identify some biblical principles that ought to be considered when shaping a Christian school's approach to evaluation and assessment.
- Third, the chapter will explore biblically authentic patterns when considering the purpose and shape of evaluation and assessment.

The chapter will conclude with some reflections on the Asian educational miracle, which so-called experts in many non-Asian countries are encouraging their authorities to emulate as the key to the future socio-economic success of their nations. The Asian pattern is built around cram schools (*hagwons* in Korea, or *juku* in Japan) and one major evaluative activity (*suneung* in Korea, *gaokao* in China, or *juken* in Japan). This intensely high-pressure examination occurs at the very end of a student's high school career and shapes a young person's future in ways unimaginable in western countries.

DEALING WITH THE TERMINOLOGY

The field of evaluation and assessment has its own language or jargon that experts seem to use differently. Take, e.g., the terms "evaluation" and "assessment." At times they appear to be used interchangeably, at other times they appear to describe discrete areas of the field of reflecting upon performance.

For example, the official position of Stanford University is as follows:

> Evaluation is "the systematic process of gathering, analyzing, and using information from multiple sources to judge the merit or worth of a program, project or entity" (Rossi, Lipsey, & Freedman 2004). . . . [E]valuation differs from assessment in its focus of inquiry. Evaluation serves to facilitate a program's development, implementation, and improvement by examining a variety of outcomes. Assessment serves to evaluate student performance and the overall program impact by measuring students' skill level on a variable of interest that is usually a specified level of academic performance.

From Stanford's perspective (nd), assessment seems to focus on the student, while evaluation focuses on the program. However, the definition of McMillan (2013) seems to have a different emphasis, and at the University of Washington, at least officially, the two terms are run together where evaluation is described as being "the systematic assessment . . . " (FAQ 2005, 1). Van Brummelen (2009) provides his own attempt at making sense of the terms by stating that "assessment means gathering data that gauge student achievement of learning outcomes. Evaluation interprets such data and makes resulting judgments and decisions" (139).

Confusion seems to exist over other terms as well, at least in the minds of some people. For example, statisticians are very clear about the difference between reliability and validity, but many educators seem to see the terms as being synonymous.

Another example is the term "authentic assessment." Simply-put, authentic assessment' refers to assessment activities such as simulations, portfolios, or even some desk-based tests that assess performance in relationship to the real-life experience of the student. Rote-learning activities, or passive multi-choice standardized tests are not considered to be authentic assessment. However, consider the cumbersome and confusing definition for this term provided by an Australian university:

> [A]uthentic assessment is about making visible (produce evidence of learning in some way) and measurable (to some appropriate standard) a performance that is a valid (by this we mean relevant) indicator that the identified elements of the curriculum have been learned in an integrated manner for the conditions in which they are ultimately intended to be needed or used. (Authentic Assessment 2007, 1–2)

Wow! Despite these terminology challenges, the issue of how and why Christian educators reflect and report upon student progress is of vital importance. We should not be deterred by the confusion of others from our goal of seeking to establish biblically authentic parameters in this area. Therefore, in most comments, this chapter will not seek to distinguish significantly between evaluation and assessment, but rather will focus on exploring the principles involved in monitoring and reporting on student work and progress. If readers want more information on the lexicon of evaluation and assessment, the first chapter of Brown and Abeywickrama (2010) provides a useful introduction to the syntax of the field.

THE GRADING PROBLEM

Most teachers, especially beyond the first few years of schooling, give grades to students. They normally have little choice in the matter. Their schools require that they do so. Parents seem to demand them, and they form a core factor in the school's publicity campaigns. Students seem to respond to grades, and employers and colleges demand them so that they can be used as screening tools. We may or may not agree with some of these uses for school grades, but we have to acknowledge that they all impact the way that we evaluate children and how we report that evaluation. Unfortunately, these grades are encumbered by a whole range of flaws and variables, to the extent that grades today have become of very limited value both in terms of what they are attempting to assess and the purposes for which they are being used.

In the first place, student assessment is never neutral. Like all of education, assessment and evaluation always emanate from and impose certain beliefs or worldview commitments about the world. Secular scholars Derewianka and Ehrich (2013) reflect on this matter in this way:

> All testing is based on measures which are not 'objective', but which are social constructs. That is, these measures have been constructed at a certain point in time as though they represent a valid measure of things. Such measures are really just human interpretations of certain tasks and reflect current preoccupations, priorities, values and knowledge. They have in fact been constructed by human beings who have the personal and social biases of all human beings. (Derewianka & Ehrich 2013, 8)

Secondly, grade allocation is idiosyncratic and subjective, with huge variations depending upon the part of the world being investigated. This is called grade non-equivalence. In several Asian and British Commonwealth countries, patterns of standardization and accountability exist within schools and between schools so that an evaluation given by a

master's money.

After a long time the master of those servants returned and settled accounts with them. The man who had received five bags of gold brought the other five. "Master," he said, "you entrusted me with five bags of gold. See, I have gained five more."

His master replied, "Well done, good and faithful servant! You have been faithful with a few things; I will put you in charge of many things. Come and share your master's happiness!"

The man with two bags of gold also came. "Master," he said, "you entrusted me with two bags of gold; see, I have gained two more."

His master replied, "Well done, good and faithful servant! You have been faithful with a few things; I will put you in charge of many things. Come and share your master's happiness!"

Then the man who had received one bag of gold came. "Master," he said, "I knew that you are a hard man, harvesting where you have not sown and gathering where you have not scattered seed. So I was afraid and went out and hid your gold in the ground. See, here is what belongs to you."

His master replied, "You wicked, lazy servant! So you knew that I harvest where I have not sown and gather where I have not scattered seed? Well then, you should have put my money on deposit with the bankers, so that when I returned I would have received it back with interest.

"So take the bag of gold from him and give it to the one who has ten bags. For whoever has will be given more, and they will have an abundance. Whoever does not have, even what they have will be taken from them. And throw that worthless servant outside, into the darkness, where there will be weeping and gnashing of teeth." (Matthew 25:14–30)

In this story, Jesus is giving a picture of the evaluative aspect of his Second Coming. It is very important to see what does and does not happen in the evaluation of the three servants. Their evaluation is *not* comparative. The response of the master to each servant is not influenced by the performance level of the other servants. Rather, *the key to the assessment that occurs here is a concern with how well each of the servants has used the talents that he had been given.* The Master in dealing with his servants and, by implication, Jesus in dealing with us is not concerned to have an evaluation pattern that grades according to a linear ranking. The Master and Jesus start with the talents that have been given to each of us, proceed through and look at the task that has been set, and conclude with an evaluation of us on the basis of how well we each have used our given talents to carry out the task. Whether one person concludes with a more substantial return or a less substantial return than another person is not of primary importance. The key evaluative principle is how well each person has used the talents given to him/her.

The apostle Paul reiterates this same evaluative principle in his letter to the Christians in Rome. In an attempt to help those believers to gain a proper understanding of themselves in the kingdom of God, he challenges them to a humble perspective. Notice how Paul follows the example of Jesus and recognizes the individual nature of assessment:

> Do not think of yourself more highly than you ought, but rather think of yourself with sober judgment, in accordance with the faith God has distributed to each of you. (Romans 12:3)

This biblical pattern of assessment has radical implications for evaluation in the Christian school. Secular schools today usually use performance as their basis of evaluation. Thus, report cards are full of performance grades; there are hallowed honor societies where entrance is based completely on the basis of performance; only the "best" of the student work is displayed on the classroom wall, and so on. It is true that we need to know how our output relates to that of others, as will be discussed later in this chapter, but this should not be the basis for the overall evaluation that Christian educators give to their students. It is this erroneous evaluation mentality that generates the lamentable situation that teachers and students see every day where "the smart kid" in class receives all the accolades and recognition even though his high mark may have been achieved through much less effort than the more ordinary mark of the class plodder.

Using Jesus' approach to evaluation, the class plodder would have received Jesus' approval for a modest achievement a long time before "the smart kid" who put little real effort into using his talents and scoring a high mark. Do you see the difference? Although this is expressing the point a little simplistically, it is true to say that the biblical model of evaluation highlights effort rather than achievement. We need to examine the procedures and practices in our Christian schools to ensure that we conform to this biblical model. This means, for example, that schools and their teachers need carefully to examine the report cards that they produce. Do these report cards highlight performance or effort as the primary evaluation criterion? Usually, we follow the secular model and highlight the former when the Christian perspective should be to high-light the latter. This cannot adequately be done with just a grade. The opportunity must be provided for the teacher to make written comments about the way a child is using the talents that the Lord has given to him or her. This is especially important in a schooling context where differentiated instruction and resulting authentic assessment strategies have been implemented (Ansalone 2010, Fischer 2004). A good way for any Christian school to start discussion of this issue of student evaluation from a biblical perspective might in fact be to initiate a comprehensive review of the philosophy and design of the school's report card system.

As another application, think about how the Christian teacher should respond to the casual inquiry of a parent who asks "How is Jane doing at school?" The typical response is that we say something like "She's doing well in math. She was in the top quarter of the class last week when she scored an 'A-' on the test that we just completed at the end of a unit on long division." This is an inappropriate initial response for a Christian teacher to make. It serves to reinforce to the parent that achievement is our primary evaluative criteria. This is wrong. While mother and father do need to know about the general level of Jane's mathematical ability, our primary focus when responding to the parent's question should be to follow the example of our Lord and convey how well Jane is using the mathematical talents that the Lord has given to her.

A final example that is instructive for us concerning student evaluation is the way that Jesus dealt with Mary and Martha in John 11:1–44 in the events surrounding the death and resurrection of their brother Lazarus. This passage is not normally used to help understand a biblical approach to evaluation, but one of the key concepts that Jesus illustrates in this real-life story is that we need to respond to people in terms of the individual talents and personalities that God has given each of them. As Jesus approached Mary and Martha's home after Lazarus had died, Martha came running up to him and in tears told Jesus that Lazarus would not have died if Jesus had been able to come to the house more quickly. Jesus realized her intellectual dilemma and responded to her by dealing with her question in an intellectual way. He talked encouragingly about the future resurrection of all believers, including her brother. This is what Martha needed to hear. Shortly thereafter, tearful Mary talks to Jesus with the exact same comment that Martha made, that Lazarus would not have died if Jesus had been there. In this case, Jesus did not tell Mary to stop weeping and have faith that all Christians will one day rise from the dead. No. He recognized that the talents and personality that Mary had required an emotional response to an emotional need. Therefore, Jesus wept! Jesus was demonstrating by example that our interaction with and evaluation of people should not be based on a comparative analysis but come as a response to the individual talents and makeup that the Lord has given to each of us in different measure and composition.

This is not to say that we refuse to appreciate individual performance in the Christian school. Students do need to be encouraged and know where they stand compared to other students. Genuine excellence deserves to be recognized, though we should beware of the ill-considered use of behavioral incentives (like stickers and gold stars), which deal purely with behavior rather than the heart – and thereby earn the faint praise of what controversial educator Alfie Kohn (1999) calls being "punished by rewards." From a Christian perspective the reward normally should be in the task and not some other extrinsic incentive. Appropriate honor societies can serve a useful service. Parents need to know whether or not a school that they are considering for their child has a credible record in academics, sports, and other school-related activities. However, what we are saying here is that this comparison must not be the generator of a concept of worth for children, nor must it be the evaluative prime factor on the report cards that we send home.

For example, when I was a student in sixth-grade woodworking class, we each had to construct a small coffee table. It so happened that I had to make six legs for my table before it would stand up properly – the inserts of two of the legs were cut into the wrong side! Most of the other boys in the class constructed tables that stood quite adequately after the construction of just four legs. In this situation, it probably was quite important for me to see that other students were better at making furniture than was I, if only to ensure that I did not cultivate the quite unrealistic expectation of becoming a carpenter after I left school! Giving my table a D (in the end I did have four legs that matched and the table could stand correctly) for the quality of the result, and giving some of the other boys an A for the quality of their tables was quite appropriate. However, I had worked just as hard to create my D table as some of the boys did to create their A tables. An assessment pattern should have been in place that recognized these differing achievement and effort realities.

A second point that needs to be made when we are examining biblical foundations for school evaluation is that it is inappropriate to link together evaluation and self-image. These two matters have become intertwined because of the twin unbiblical patterns of purely performance-based evaluation on the one hand, and the notion that self-image is personally derived from within a person on the other. If our self-image is derived from what we can make ourselves out to be, or even from the mediocre products that we can produce, then we would indeed be of all creatures the most miserable.

BIBLICAL SELF-IMAGE

It has been said that the problem with modern man is not that we think too little of ourselves (as modern secular psychology suggests), but that we think too highly of ourselves. The earlier examples about Western society's grade inflation certainly indicate this. If we take the Bible seriously, then any attempt to view ourselves as good, based on who we really are or on what we can do, is doomed to failure when our "goodness" is exposed to the cold hard light of reality. At creation God made mankind good and perfect, without fault or flaw. Because of the Fall, we have moved far away from that initial created state. A casual glance through the headlines of any online newspaper or ten minutes of the news on television should be sufficient to convince us of the truth of the matter. After all, the Bible tells us that because of sin, we are rotten to the core, deceitful beyond even our own comprehension, and in our own strength generating only tarnished and warped products.

Thanks be to God that we and the students in our schools do not need to wallow in the self-pitying slough of a poor perspective of ourselves. What we must do is take our eyes off our own weak selves with all our faults and failings and look to the Lord who made us and loves us, and consider how he sees us. Four biblical perspectives of who we are give us a self-image that is not only holy and uplifting, but also lasting and dynamically empowering.

First of all, the Scriptures affirm many times that mankind, and mankind alone, is made in God's own image. We cannot deny the glory of who God is, and he has taken some of his characteristics (the capacities to be creative and make moral choices, for example) and imputed them to every human being. Made in God's own image. Wow!

In the second place, despite the Fall and our resulting evil nature, we are still God's workmanship (Ephesians 2:10). God has specifically molded, shaped, and gifted each one of us. He is continually involved in the intimate affairs of the lives of people. So precious are we to him that the Bible tells us that he even knows the number of hairs on our head. Incredible!

Third, the Bible declares that God, the Creator of the universe, cares for us so much that he sent his only Son, Jesus Christ, to die for us so that a way back to God could be opened up for all who call upon his name. Just this fact alone – that the Son of the Almighty God was sacrificed in our stead – is breathtaking in its implications for how valued and precious we are from the eternal, divine perspective. This should not delude us from the reality, however, that of ourselves we are wicked sinners and incapable of doing anything to make us worthy of God's saving grace. Humanity's basic characteristic since the Fall is not that we are deprived, but that we are first of all depraved. How much more, then, is the preciousness of the hymn-writer's refrain, "Amazing grace how sweet the sound – that saved a wretch like me!"

Finally, for all people who have accepted the salvation and lordship of Jesus Christ, we are God's ambassadors. Spend a few minutes contemplating what would happen in your neighborhood if an earthly ambassador was expected to visit. Houses would be painted, roads repaired (at last!), gardens tended, streets lined with flag-waving onlookers, and so on. Consider, though, that Christians are ambassadors of the King of kings, specifically charged with carrying the most important royal pronouncement of all time, the Good News of the gospel of Jesus Christ. Awesome!

By trying to base our understanding of who we are (self-image) on something internal and on something as fickle and sinful as ourselves, we not only risk possessing a wildly fluctuating and warped self-image, but we also ignore the real wonder of who we are when seen through the eyes of our Creator. Christian educators must break the inhibiting bonds existing in much of secular education and psychology that link together human evaluation and self-image. Using the biblical principles outlined above, we are enabled to develop approaches to psychological issues and evaluation that are God honoring and that really serve the needs of our children and the families from which they come.

DEVELOPING BIBLICAL EVALUATION PATTERNS: PURPOSES OF EVALUATION

We can understand evaluation as the process by which we attach a value to student school-based activities. We then need to ask ourselves about the purposes for which we undertake evaluation in our schools. Along the way, we should remember the pithy saying repeated by Van Brummelen (2009, 140), that "not everything that counts can be counted, and not everything that can be counted counts."

When identifying purposes, and therefore patterns, for student assessment, be it formal or informal, it is important to maintain a balance between summative evaluation (the end-on evaluation usually used to summarize performance and progress) and formative assessment (the monitoring of student progress so as to re-shape instruction to current needs). A readiness to reconfigure testing patterns in the light of wash-back (intended and unintended consequences) also is important. Remember Eisner's comment that, "simply knowing the final score of the game after it is over is not very useful. What we need is a vivid rendering of how the game is played" (Eisner 1985, 131).

It is helpful to develop an evaluation and assessment rationale based upon the *key stakeholders* in the process, under the headings of: the student, the teacher, parents, and other stakeholders.

The Purposes of Evaluation and Assessment from a Student Perspective
Two key definitions of schooling have been used in this book: first, schools are social institutions in which students learn about the world and their places and tasks in it. Second, Christian schooling is all about challenging students with the lordship of Christ over all of creation. With these two definitions in mind, the following goals should be considered when looking at evaluation and assessment from the student perspective:

- Assist students to understand and self-assess their strengths (areas of giftedness) and weaknesses, thus giving them increased ownership in their own learning and hopes for the future.
- Increase students' appreciation of God's world, and what it means to live as responsive, creative stewards in that world.
- Allow students to demonstrate and celebrate competence through the use of a variety of performance activities (i.e., not just pen-and-paper cognitive tests).
- Provide students with opportunities for meaningful learning from both success, and failure, and consequently develop appropriate ongoing learning goals.
- Help students to be aware of their own growing progress and mastery of key learning areas.
- Give students opportunities to interact with real life situations so that they can demonstrate godly knowledge and depth of insight, thus being able to discern what is best in life (Philippians 1:9–11).
- Acquire meaningful documentation that they can use for future employment opportunities and/or enrolling in further educational pathways.

The Purposes of Evaluation and Assessment from a Teacher Perspective

- Monitor the appropriateness and effectiveness of instruction (an illustration of formative evaluation) as a basis for meaningful student feedback and planning future learning goals and activities.
- Maintain an awareness of student needs and student progress.
- Demonstrate a biblical blend of grace and accountability wherein assessments are designed to allow students to show what they know and can do, rather than what they don't know and can't do.
- Join with students in the joy and fulfillment of celebrating learning progress.
- Accumulate data so that the teacher can report to appropriate authorities (including principal and parents) that meaningful, God-honoring learning is taking place.

The Purposes of Evaluation and Assessment from a Parent Perspective

- Assist parents in being able to affirm that schooling and its outcomes are allowing them to be faithful in nurturing their children in the discipline and instruction of the Lord (Ephesians 6:4).
- Receive a formal report on their children's use of their talents and their actual learning achievements.
- Provide a database for interactive, student-led conferences, which have been described (as reported by Kinney 2012) as being "the biggest breakthrough in communicating about student achievement in the last century" (57).
- Provide parents with guidance for future (re)creative, vocational, and educational decision-making with their children.

The Purposes of Evaluation and Assessment for Others

Other people such as government officials, researchers, and prospective employers also have legitimate needs for data about student progress in schools. However, the report card is not primarily an employment card or a census document, and these secondary considerations should not become the primary determinants of student portfolios or other reporting structure's purpose or form.

Evaluation and assessment should be a dynamic process where patterns used vary according to the student profile in a particular class and are based on reviewing not just the results, but also the actual effectiveness of the process itself (sometimes in the literature called backwash or washback – Hughes 2013).

EVALUATION AND REPORTING

If we accept one of the general definitions, that assessment has to do with student testing, and evaluation has to do with reporting on that testing, then the nature of school reporting is a vital aspect of student evaluation. This chapter has already indicated that evaluation patterns existing in many Christian schools could benefit from a re-examination in the light of the biblical focus on effort (how talents are used) rather than mere attainment. There should also be some overt reference to how the child is demonstrating Christ-likeness in the classroom (concern for others, showing grace and mercy, being prepared to go against the flow, obedience to authority . . .) and is growing in his/her understanding of the lordship of Jesus over every aspect of the curriculum, including ICT, numeracy, literacy, performing arts, etc. This evaluation pattern probably is best implemented through a combination of traditional (though re-designed) report cards and other authentic or alternative assessments, such as portfolios of student work and student-led conferences (Lynch 2001).

Here is a useful exercise to demonstrate the degree to which a Christian school's formal report card pattern reflects biblically authentic goals and values. In teams, spend time starting with the current report cards and work backwards. In other words, assuming that we report on what we value, start with the report cards and identify what mission and goals might have generated them. Next, compare the mission and goals the group has produced, with the actual mission and goals of the school. If there is a close alignment between the report-card-generated mission and goals and the school's actual, biblically authentic mission and goals, the experience of this writer is that you would be among the minority in the global Christian school community.

EVALUATION SHOULD BE INTERACTIVE

Finally, as is well demonstrated in the Finnish education system (Ireland 2012), student evaluation in the Christian school should be interactive. Among the parties concerned with school assessment, the three identified earlier are most important: the student, the teacher, and the parent. Students should be encouraged to develop the important skill of evaluating their own work. This is how many of the activities that they will be involved in later in life will be evaluated, and they should be helped to acquire this skill while still at school. Teachers should not fear student self-evaluation. It is an activity carried out under the guidance of the teacher and will often provide insights into important perspectives and developmental levels of the students.

Interactive evaluation should also involve the parent. Once upon a time, I assumed that it was not necessary to stress the importance of involving parents in the evaluative process. I assumed that such involvement could be taken for granted in Christian schools. Needless to say, therefore, I was staggered when I was told in a Christian school that I visited that the concept of inviting parents into the school to discuss student progress was a novel one. The administrator commented that the school must consider experimenting with the idea some day! Parent-teacher conferences are an important part of evaluation. However, some schools have gone even further and routinely invite the students to join with the parents and teachers, and even lead portions of the parent-teacher conference. This is a creative way of adding a formative component to what is otherwise a summative evaluation, for the benefit of the student involved.

Consider again that worthy goal expressed by Paul in his didactic letter to the Philippians – that the love our students have for the Lord may abound more and more and may be characterized by knowledge and depth of insight so that they can discern what is best. This will only be possible when we desist from transferring secular evaluation patterns into our schools and when we help our students, their families, and society to value the worth of a job well done that recognizes the biblical pattern of assessing how well each of our students has used the talents that God has given to him or her individually. From this evaluative pattern comes true insight and the challenge to use our God-given talents in the most compelling and appropriate manner. Therefore, though we might have fundamental disagreements with some of his assumptions and conclusions, the perspectives presented by Alfie Kohn (www.alfiekohn.org) concerning rewards and evaluation deserve some investigation, filtered through a Christian worldview perspective, by teachers and parents.

Building a student evaluation and assessment structure that is deliberately (as compared to inadvertently) constructed in the light of an institution's worldview stance is recognized in the broader assessment community outside of Christian circles as being an authentic approach to this issue. For example, the five summary guidelines for grading and evaluation provided by Brown and Abeywickrama (2010, 337–8) are not comprehensive, but they could make a useful contribution to any Christian teacher's review of his/her evaluation methodology and practice:

- Develop an informed, comprehensive philosophy of grading that is consistent with your philosophy of teaching and evaluation.
- Ascertain an institution's philosophy of grading and, unless otherwise negotiated, conform to that philosophy (so that you are not out of step with others).
- Select appropriate criteria for grading and their relative weighting in calculating grades.
- Communicate criteria for grading to students at the beginning of the course and at subsequent grading periods.
- Triangulate letter grade evaluations with alternatives that are more formative and that give more washback.

THE SEDUCTIVE ILLUSION OF THE ASIAN EDUCATIONAL MIRACLE

In recent decades, reports have circulated in western educational countries such as Australia, New Zealand, the United Kingdom, the United States, and elsewhere, that recommend an emulation of the Asian educational model as a means to improve educational standards and outcomes in western schools. The Programme for International Student Assessment (PISA) test, administered by the OECD every three years, ranks national performance in reading, science, and mathematics. TIMSS (Trends in International Mathematics and Science Study) is another international leagues table, as is PIRLS (Progress in International Reading Literacy Study). Whatever one thinks about the veracity of these tests (and there are legitimate concerns), they carry enormous international prestige and political power. Credible bodies such as the Grattan Institute (Jensen, Hunter, Sonnemann, & Burns 2012) in Australia for example, use PISA data to suggest that Asian countries such as Hong Kong, Korea, Singapore, and Japan have the best education systems in the world that should be adopted by their own nations.

It is true that some Asian countries score very highly in international literacy and numeracy comparisons (though western countries such as Finland and New Zealand often also score well). Korea, for example, in many economic areas has transformed itself from an under-developed, war-torn backwater in the middle of the last century, to a global powerhouse and the producer of high quality consumer, ICT, and heavy industry products today. Its people are wonderfully polite, they revere their elderly, and they are extraordinarily industrious. Some would argue that vibrant democratic institutions are well-established there.

But the story told by the Grattan Institute concerning Korean education masks a troubling reality. This author has spent decades working in the international education industry, including five years living and working among educators at all levels in both the public and private sectors in South Korea. Very rarely have I heard informed Korean educators speak in terms other than general embarrassment when talking about the overall impact of their education system on the nation's young people.

This chapter is not the place to spend detailed time discussing Korea or Asian education, but from an evaluation perspective, the subject of this chapter, significant questions need to be asked about the historical context, purpose, and nature of Korean schooling. A key influence in all aspects of Korean life is neo-Confucianism. This worldview has evolved from a tradition where social structures are constructed to maintain order and the status quo. Elders such as parents and teachers are revered. Shame and honor concepts shape cultural expectations where people have been expected to obey strict traditional patterns. Historically, conformity and imitation were highly valued. Change and originality were not virtues. Almost the only traditional pathway to elevate one's social status (and, consequently, that of one's family) was by success in the public service examinations, for which students studied extremely diligently.

In contemporary Korean culture, reflections of this high-context worldview are apparent everywhere (Lee 2009). Many younger children still bow to older children; institutions operate on the basis of personal relationship rather than policy; educational patterns such as rote learning, imitation through plagiarism, and teacher-centered pedagogy, prevail. From an evaluation perspective, the central role of the end-of-high school exam, called the *suneung*, is deeply distressing. In preparation for this exam, starting in middle school, students spend many extra hours each day studying in cram schools (*hagwons*), at times until early in the morning. Some students even sleep on the floor in *hagwons*, to avoid "wasting" time going home to family. City governments have created special patrols to try and force late-night *hagwons* to close early – by 10pm! To do well in the *suneung* means honor to the family, entrance for the student to a high-status university, and secure future employment in one of Korea's major companies.

On the actual day of the *suneung* in October every year, final year students sit a series of examinations that purport to reflect their entire education thus far, and that determine their educational and social place in society for the future. On this one day, airports adjust their schedules so that aircraft noise is minimized during oral questions; police make themselves available to take students to school to ensure that no-one is late; pep rallies occur outside school gates as students enter for the examination; supervisors do not wear makeup so that fragrances cannot disturb students; parents pray at temples and outside school gates.

Fixation with the *suneung* and the system that produces it is unhealthy. It encourages competition rather than cooperation, and repetition rather than understanding. It forgets that education is as much about forming as it is informing. It values head knowledge over wisdom, and does little to produce the spirit of joyful hope and discernment that are at the heart of schooling from a Christian worldview perspective. If you want to make your hair really stand on end, read about the personal experience of one young adult in the *gosichon* or exam village (Glionna 2011).

One should applaud the elevated global position achieved by Korea in numeracy and literacy, and Korea also sets a fine international example concerning some aspects of teacher professional development. But these characteristics alone should not be confused with quality, all-round education. The voice of informed educators with robust, longitudinal experience both in the west and in the east (Yelland 2012), also should be heard, and the simplistic conclusions that some seem to draw from international league tables should be viewed with extreme caution.

Today, Korea educational designers are attempting to "modernize" Korean education by including more discovery learning approaches, and in some cases even providing for alternative university entrance pathways. However, Korea will not solve its educational challenges by attempting to graft western child-centered education and evaluation onto eastern content-centered education and evaluation. The issue is a deeper, worldview one, and as this entire book has maintained, educational patterns are always a consequence of worldview.

Korea, from the perspective of its young people, appears to be moving into a period of rampant, anti-authority consumerism. Autonomous decision-making and conspicuous consumption are Korea's contemporary gods, and the nation's massive, new, high-rise shopping malls are their temples. (Some of the world's biggest shopping malls today are in South Korea.) Content-centered education and its relics, such as the *suneung*, have created great stress in Korea, leading to many suicides among young people. But autonomous, postmodern, child-centered education outside of Asia, with its lack of direction and sense of hopelessness, has led to similar distress among western youth. In both places, the hope, meaning, and creative purpose that comes through a Christian worldview, and its adoption in educational goals, curricula, evaluation patterns, and outcomes, is the best way to provide the dynamic and fulfilling pattern for education that is craved in both east and west – and it is up to Christians in education, as salt-and-light ambassadors of the King, to show the way!

Chapter 10

Resource Selection in the Christian School

Reason for Suspicion of Textbooks and Other Resources

If anything has become clear in this book, it should be that nothing done in education (or in the rest of life) is religiously neutral. All activities display and are rooted in the religious beliefs of those involved in them. This holds for resource materials in schools as well. Whether we are talking about textbooks, video clips, magazines, visiting speakers, assessment instruments, or curriculum guidelines – their content and their approach reveal distinct worldview beliefs about education and the world.

Christian schools typically have been particularly concerned about the non-Christian bias of textbooks written by secular authors and have considered many of them unsuitable for schools seeking to nurture a Christian view of the world. This sensitivity is very appropriate. Even a casual glance at many textbooks and other school resources produced by non-Christians reveals their inappropriateness for the Christian school. These books will often claim a noble-sounding commitment to "open-mindedness," but they then degenerate quickly into overt or covert endorsements of the secular status quo or political correctness. For example, the view of the family in some school materials is based on the secular, non-Christian assumption that family is a construct of the state, and these resources then endorse non-biblical family patterns (Willhoite 2000, is a tragic example). It also can be seen in the exclusion of Christian religious traditions, such as family worship, from children's fiction. Christmas being re-termed "the holiday season" is another example.

A classic example of how secular texts promote non-Christian values was obvious in some social studies materials that I, as a young teacher, had to use in my state school classroom. The material was designed to be used by 13-year-old children. It explored what it meant to be human, including why human beings had become the masters of the world, as opposed to any other animal form having developed to this pre-eminent position. The textbook led children to examine characteristics that human beings and other animals had in common, such as instinctive responses, the need for shelter, nourishment, reproduction, and so on. Then children were encouraged to identify features that were distinctive to humans alone. The key differentiating factor, according to this text, was humans' enlarged brains, which had allowed people to develop sophisticated language skills that had evolved in human beings over the millennia. Language competency enabled mankind to communicate in a complex manner and so develop control patterns over other animals whose lack of elaborate language didn't enable them to organize themselves in such an intricate way. So there it was: humanity had achieved dominance because man has evolved into becoming linguistically superior. The title of this textbook, understandably enough, was *Humanity of Man, the Language Animal* (Fletcher 1971).

The offensiveness of *The Language Animal* for Christians may be thought to be obvious, but I must say that many evangelical Christians (initially including myself) appeared to be very comfortable using it as a teaching resource. Their thinking had become darkened, shaped by the worldview myth that secularism equals neutrality, and they did not see the error of what they were teaching. Christian teachers and Christian parents quite rightly are very suspicious of many secular textbooks because of the way that they can undermine the view of life espoused in the Bible, in Christian homes, and in Christian schools. Research confirming concerns in this area was considered in Chapter 8 of this book, which reported on the following conclusion concerning children's books today that was reached by an expert panel:

> "[children's books today] . . . portray life as profoundly deterministic, frustrating or unfulfilling. They see family life as oppressive or gratuitously constraining; marriage as a form of imprisonment, a power game, or a ritual performance; human communication as doomed from the start, or at best gravely limited; aspirations for the future as illusory; and participation in the community as a waste of time or a self-centred escape from the humdrum of domesticity. . . . [A]dults play a peripheral, insufficient, or non-existent role in the lives of young people; high aspiration is usually defeated; parents and other older people responsible for the care of the young have to be deceived or side-stepped for the sake of survival and gratification; sexual intimacy, however disappointing or damaging, is a requirement of modern teenage life; and future prospects are inescapably disappointing. The vital question of what is emotionally suitable or beneficial for young adults seems never to be asked." (Ireland 2004, 64–65; citing Aitchison, Ireland, Grover, and Kingston, 1996)

In many Christian schools, the solution to the bias of secular resources has been to maintain, as a basic principle, that only textbooks produced by specifically Christian publishing houses or written by Christian authors will be acceptable within the school. This is particularly the case in North America, where several large and small Christian publishing houses exist that seek to meet the needs of Christian schools. We need to thank the Lord for the efforts of these businesses, and we need to encourage their endeavors by providing feedback to them about the suitability of their materials and by purchasing their products when appropriate. However, does the fact that a business is operated by Christians mean in and of itself that such a business produces a "Christian" textbook? Does the fact that a particular book is written by a Christian mean that it is always expounding a Christian world and life view? I think not in both cases. So then, what makes a Christian textbook?

WHAT MAKES A "CHRISTIAN" TEXTBOOK CHRISTIAN?

In the Christian school movement, we may have been asking the wrong question in this whole area of resource selection. To ask the question "Is this book authored by a Christian or published by a Christian publishing house?" may in fact lead us *away* from being able to choose appropriate resource materials for our schools. Let us explore a number of possibilities to show how this is so.

1. Is a book "Christian" because it is authored by a Christian?

A few years ago, as a Christian school headmaster/administrator, I was looking for resources to use in a new course on psychology that we were developing for senior high school students. I inquired of a number of Christian colleges in North America to see what they were using. Many of them suggested the same psychology book, but some added a comment something like "It's written by a Christian, but from a non-Christian perspective." I was immediately suspicious, but bought a copy of the book anyway. Here was a textbook written by a Christian dealing with the "Who am I?" type psychology questions. Surely, for any Christian publication dealing with this issue, a fundamental proposition to espouse would be the biblical concept that human beings are made in God's image, meaning that humans have wonderful divine-originated capacities such as creativity and a moral concept. This is the Christian's starting point and shows us the real factor that differentiates us from the rest of the animal kingdom. Alas! The concept of being made in God's image and its consequences were not mentioned anywhere in the book! Neither were the concepts of the Fall or of a soul, fundamental ideas for Christians that help us to understand who we are!

Here then was a book written as a textbook by a Christian, and used in Christian colleges, that was anything but Christian. God does not need enemies when he has friends like us! Sadly, it is true that we as Christians can at times be found doing the devil's job for him. On these occasions, Jesus' admonition to Peter applies to us as well:

> Jesus turned and said to Peter, "Get behind me, Satan! You are a stumbling-block to me; you do not have in mind the things of God, but merely human concerns." (Matthew 16:23)

Clearly, just because a textbook or other school resource is written by a Christian does not mean that it is automatically suitable for us to use in our Christian schools. When our thinking processes have been captured by secular religious presuppositions, Christians lamentably are just as capable as non-Christians of producing material that leads us away from the truth. Remember Paul's counsel to his friends in Colossae:

> See to it that no one takes you captive through hollow and deceptive philosophy, which depends on human tradition and the elemental spiritual forces of this world rather than on Christ. (Colossians 2:8)

2. *Does a resource become "Christian" when it quotes the Bible?*
Surely if a resource quotes Scripture, that will make it Christian and appropriate for use in Christian schools. Here again, the answer is, "Not necessarily." Remember Satan, when he tempted Jesus in the wilderness (Luke 4:1–13). Satan quoted the Bible several times. The quotes were accurate but out of context and were designed to lead Jesus astray. "Proof texting" does not turn a resource into a Christian resource.

We need to have very clear biblical handles for what we do in a Christian school, and a biblical foundation is the only key to a correct understanding of who we are, of the world in which we live, and of our God-given tasks within that world. A biblically based framework and worldview, though, does not mean that we must provide a Bible verse to support every fact that we present to our students. Try explaining to a biology class, by quoting Scripture, the procedures for administering an epidural anesthetic! No. The insertion of biblical quotations does not necessarily turn a book into a Christian textbook. We should learn from Wilson in the vital interpretive perspective advocated earlier in this book:

> The Christian educator's job is not to require the students to spend all their time gazing at the sun. Rather, we want them to examine everything else in the light the sun provides. (Wilson 1991, 63)

One of the most distressing examples of Christians mindlessly and erroneously accepting and promoting something as "Christian" because it happens to refer to the Bible has been the way the musical works of Tim Rice and Andrew Lloyd Webber have been used in some churches and Christian schools. *Jesus Christ Superstar* treats Jesus as a somewhat deluded public figure, with Judas Iscariot being the only person able to understand accurately the temporary euphoria surrounding Jesus' public activities. There may be merit in studying *Jesus Christ Superstar* so as to be able to understand its insidious message, but this anti-Christian rock opera incredibly has been held up by many Christian clerics and educators as worthy of gospel acceptance!

Equally as distressing has been the widespread acceptance and performance of *Joseph and the Amazing Technicolor Dreamcoat* by a number of Christian schools. True, the biblical story of Joseph forms the background to this rock opera. True, also, is the fact that it is a very entertaining, lively, and superficially attractive musical event. (The appearance of pharaoh as an Elvis look-a-like is very impressive.) However, it is far from Christian. In fact, it mocks the whole idea of God's covenant faithfulness and care of his people in times of difficulty. In Rice and Lloyd Webber's musical, Joseph probably never really escapes from Pharaoh's prison at all. He only escapes in his mind by *dreaming* about leaving his dungeon cell. Even this is achieved by the implicit help of mind-bending drugs. How else do you have psychedelic dreams? And, after all, as the theme song of the musical that is the opera's final conclusion declares, "Any dream will do!" Is that what Joseph really believed? Is this really the message that we want to present to our students and school communities – that Christianity really is just another temporary, deluded escape from the harsh and forlorn realities of a punishing and hopeless existence? Based on Rice's autobiography, in which he identifies this song as one of his most important works, that any dream will do certainly seems to sum up the view of the writer of the opera's lyrics (Rice 1999). "We are still waiting" and "Any dream will do" represent a travesty of the genuine hope and good news that the Bible conveys. Yet here again we find that many of us who are Christian leaders and educators (who should know better) react with a positive knee-jerk to any mention of Bible stories or the word "Bible" in contemporary culture. We cling tenaciously to all things popular that mention our sacred book. We fail to examine them from a Christian worldview perspective and consequently (unconsciously) weaken and mock the very message that we treasure.

We should not ignore such works, like the musicals I've been describing, but, rather than uncritically adopt them, we must help students to evaluate them (as all else) from a Christian presuppositional perspective. Only then will we be challenging our students to chart a course for their lives that is fruitful, biblically based, productive, hope-filled, fulfilling, and God-honoring.

No. The use of Bible verses or its stories does not make a resource Christian.

3. *Does the use of biblical analogies turn a resource into a Christian resource?*

Some texts available to Christian schools imagine that by alluding to Christian lifestyle characteristics they are Christian resources. I remember reading a science text published by a Christian company that sought to "Christianize" its approach by using biblical analogies. Osmosis, for example, was explained by reference to the Christian doctrine of sanctification, the process of the "gradual absorption" of the characteristics of Christ. There is no way that this "Christianized" chemistry.

No. The use of biblical analogies in and of itself does not necessarily create a Christian resource.

4. *Is a textbook that reinforces "sound teaching practices" a Christian resource?*

The answer here again must be "Not necessarily." Christians differ, for example, over what is a sound teaching practice. I have heard Christians say that "Phonics is the God-given way to teach reading." But this is patently a human proposition with which many Christians disagree.

Outcome based education (OBE) is another divisive issue for some Christians. Many Christians are vehemently opposed to OBE, while others see it as an important characteristic of Christ's teaching and hence a priority for the training that goes on in Christian schools. The apostle Paul, they argue, was certainly concerned about the outcomes of what he taught the Philippians: "And this is my prayer [i.e., desired outcome]: that your love may abound more and more in knowledge and depth of insight, so that you may be able to discern what it best" (Philippians 1:9–10a). So, the lesson learned should be, I suggest: legitimate concerns about a humanistic, secularized OBE agenda that is espoused by some pagan educators ought not lead us to neglect working towards and taking stock of biblically faithful outcomes in the lives of our children in Christian schools.

It might be said that books that encourage the sound educational practice of thinking will support a Christian educational perspective. However, what "thinking" means to some Christians is anything but "thinking" to others. This was reinforced for me once when I was helping my daughter with her homework. She was reading a textbook produced by a Christian publishing house and was working through a comprehension exercise. On one side of the page was the extract and on the other side was a list of questions. The questions were divided into two sections. The first section, made up of ten questions, involved simple, open-ended questions. The second section was entitled "Thinking Questions" and was composed of two questions that started with words like "Why" and "How." These are good open-ended words for questions involving higher order thinking skills. However, the publisher had highlighted just two sections of the script in the original passage alongside, each section being a word-for-word answer to these two "thinking" questions. What a travesty! All my daughter needed to do was copy the answer. Is it any wonder that so many children do not know how to think today when they are led to understand that simple correlation exercises are advanced thinking activities?

No. The use of what some call "sound teaching practices" does not of itself create a Christian textbook.

5. *Will a book encouraging conservative values be a good Christian resource?*

Conservatism does not equal Christianity. This should go without saying, for if we look at the life of Jesus and the apostles, we see that they were anything but conservative. They challenged the status quo and rocked the establishment. Their message was so dynamic and radical that people wanted to kill them. Yancey (1995, 154) reminds us that in almost all incidents that record Jesus' interaction with women, he implicitly repudiated existing cultural norms.

Jesus' disciples called for obedience to those in authority over us but also held high the notion that Christians first of all are accountable to God for what they do and owe their primary allegiance to him and not to any political structure. Imagine my surprise, therefore, to read in a civics textbook in a Christian school in the US that the definition of a political conservative (presumed to be a Republican) is someone who believes in eternally-held values, and a political liberal (presumed to be a Democrat) is someone who does not believe in eternally-held values! Apparently, according to this "Christian" resource, it's not possible to be both a Democrat and a Christian.

Christians thank God for their national identities, and are among the foremost at seeking the welfare of the cities in which they live (Jeremiah 29:7). However, a Christian is not primarily an American or a Korean or an Australian, or a Kenyan, or an Englishman. First of all, Christians are children of Christ, and have an enduring spiritual, sibling relationship with Christians from all other ethnic groups.

Imagine my surprise, also, to read in a "Christian" textbook that the U. S. was forced to withdraw from the Vietnam War because of the actions of a small band of radicals back home, just when America was on the point of victory!

We could go on. Some assume that in order to be a Christian resource a book must present a "wholesome" view of the world. We have no argument with wholesomeness. The Scriptures encourage us to focus our attention on wholesome things, but appropriate wholesomeness should not be confused with the fictitious presentation of a sugar-coated view of reality.

The task of curriculum materials in our schools is to help our children learn about the world and their place in it in a biblically authentic way. The Bible shows the world in all its fallen-ness and gives us the handles to cope with it. It is possible to read some gruesome and unsavory things in the Bible, such as mass slaughter, a woman driving a tent peg through a man's head, and so on. We should not pretend the world is anything else than what it really is, a place lovingly made by God, affected by the Fall, and in which Christians are called to bring the redeeming and re-forming message of the Good News. This must be done with proper regard to the developmental levels of children and without destroying childhood naivety. The exclusive use of resources, though, that assume that the world is a lovely place, that "they always live happily ever after," that evil never triumphs over good in the short term, and that if you treat other people correctly they will do the same to you, presents a perverted view of the world and will not serve children well in the Christian school.

Censorship is the deliberate suppression of material that may be considered to be objectionable in some way. In schools, this infers the application of a set of beliefs about what is right and wrong, and the determination to nurture in the light of carefully selected resources. All schools practice censorship, and rightly so: no school library that I know of subscribes to *Playboy*; every quality school practices internet filtering; no teaching program could ever include everything, so decisions are made about what to include and what to exclude. "Any act of selection is simultaneously an act of exclusion" (Baer 1987, 5). Once again, there is no neutrality. Resource decisions, like all others, are driven by ideology and worldview (Farrell & Tanner 2002, Braunschweig 2012). The internet is full of examples of censorship occurring in public schools, often in a way that ostracizes Christianity but permits the celebration of secularism and other religious alternatives. In 2013, this caused a group of Christian teenagers in a public school in Idaho to produce a video protesting against anti-Christian bullying by teachers and their curriculum (Brinkman 2013).

In the Christian school, censorship should be done in a way that does not hide from children the sober realities of life (otherwise Shakespeare would never be allowed) but helps them to come to terms with it in a manner consistent with the child's maturity and consistent with the biblically authentic aims and goals of the school and parent community.

For example, while books such as *The Catcher in the Rye* might properly be considered as an inappropriate book to be used for literature study in the Christian high school, books such as *Lord of the Flies* can be very useful as set texts. The latter book was, in fact, written by a Christian – William Golding. Golding deliberately exposes the sinful nature of humankind that inevitably emerges when the thin veneer of civilization is stripped away.

From a Christian worldview perspective, Ireland (2004) endorses the gritty, authentic realism of many authors whose books are used for study in Christian schools:

> Without falsifying reality, or pretending that life is any easier than it is, . . . [these authors] cogently convey the view that life is worth all the effort. They take for granted the paradox that people who love you can be infuriating, and that just when adults seem most incomprehensible to teenagers, mutual understanding can emerge. And they proclaim without hesitation that it is a fine thing to be a human being, to face tough decisions and contradictory people, and to come through difficulty with renewed hope and confidence. (63)

We should note in passing that even the way Christian parents and teachers approach such seemingly "wholesome" things as the Disney channel on cable television needs review. Christians often can be heard giving thanks for this channel since it is the one they believe that their children can watch without adult supervision because its programs are not going to be filled with the gore, depravity, and bad language evident on other channels. However, the Disney channel is not religiously neutral. It does, indeed, screen many useful family programs. But, at times, we can allow this to lull us into a false sense of security by apparently "harmless and wholesome" stories. We need to examine the presuppositions that some children's movies subliminally encourage our children to adopt. For example, a prevailing assumption in many family films is that life is O.K. without God. Families emerge triumphant through the trials of life because of the inherent goodness of people (often the mother, as fathers regularly are presented as oppressive) and the resilience of the human spirit. They encourage the view that if people of goodwill everywhere will unite then evil will be overcome and good will triumph. They espouse the notion that even apparently bad people usually are only this way because of their circumstances and that appropriate counseling, help, education, and material benefits can enable them to rise above their former behavioral abnormalities. These are not Christian principles. We are essentially depraved, not just deprived. The world will not become a better place just because people receive education. Read the comments by George Counts earlier in this book as a reminder of this. We cannot make ourselves good by our own efforts. True lasting goodness does not exist apart from a personal relationship with Jesus Christ. Lamentably, by the exclusion of any real evidence of a faith commitment to Christianity, many children's movies teach the opposite of these biblical principles. Our children unconsciously absorb this non-Christian view of life.

This does not mean to say that our children should not watch the Disney channel – there is much enjoyment, adventure, and laughter there. However, it does mean that, as with all television viewing, we need to help our children to evaluate what they see from a biblical framework and not just accept it as if it was portraying a true and neutral view of the world.

Another example is to compare what the Bible says about the wisdom of elders with what the Muppets series implicitly tells us about the value of older people's wisdom through the constant ridicule of the two old men up in the balcony who are shown almost always to be arguing and making stupid statements.

THE USE OF "NON-CHRISTIAN" RESOURCES

On the other hand, what do we say about potential resources that are known to be authored by non-Christians? Should these be banned from the Christian school? Is it fair to assume that there is nothing useful in the work of an atheist or a secular humanist or an agnostic or of the adherent to some other pagan religion? Should we reject all of Dewey's writings because he was vehemently non-Christian? Is there nothing for us to learn in the life of Gandhi in India? Should we reject *Peterson's College Guide* or the *Oxford English Dictionary* on the basis that non-Christians may be contributing editors? The answer is no. God, in his wisdom, has given insights to all people. This is known theologically as "common grace," and we need to recognize this reality. Many of the great discoveries, advances, and even educational resources, have occurred as the result of the work of non-Christian people. We need to praise the Lord for these discoveries, and make use of that which he has revealed.

Here is the key to resource selection, which we will expand upon shortly: we should consider all material in the light of biblical norms and then make good use of that which conforms to these norms.

Although this is a very debatable position to take, some Christian school educators at times seem even to prefer texts produced by a non-Christian over an inferior pseudo-Christian text where the Christian author has not articulated or remained true to a Christian position. The reason that they give for taking this position is that at least in a book authored by a non-Christian, we should be vigilantly looking for the outworking of a secular religious perspective. On the other hand, in an inferior work by a Christian, we may well be lulled into a false sense of security. The director of one Christian school put it this way: "A better decision is a quality secular text over a poor Christian one. A good attentive Christian teacher can work around the failings of a secular text" (Hilgemann 1993).

In many of the in-service sessions that I have held with Christian teachers all over the world, I've encouraged them to view the movie *Dead Poets Society*. Although it is not a "Christian" work in the sense that it is not produced by a Christian and its key actors probably are not Christians, yet, it can be used very effectively in focusing our attention on principles of education and the key role that religious presuppositions play in how we understand education. This movie in and of itself can never provide us with our foundational beliefs, but it can be used to point us to various realities and to cause us to re-examine the biblical foundations that we wish to undergird our own educational beliefs and methodologies. In other words, resources produced by non-Christians can have an important role to play in the Christian school.

RE-DEFINING THE ISSUE

The above discussion indicates that the traditional way of viewing the question of selection of resources, which divides the matter up between "Christian resources versus non-Christian resources," is *not* the most helpful way of considering the issue. There are some resources that one would expect to be Christian but which are not, and there are other resources produced by non-Christians that are very useful. The whole issue needs to be redefined. Instead of focusing on "Christian versus non-Christian," we need to make our resource choices in terms of *what are the resources that conform to our mission statement and that will assist us most effectively to work out our educational confession and goals in the Christian school?*

In other words, we can only appropriately come to grips with resource selection in the Christian school after we have come to terms with the fundamental and foundational issues of what our particular school is all about and what are the goals that we have for our individual school. It is not possible to be coherent, articulate, and consistent in resource selection unless a school community is first of all coherent, articulate, and consistent in its Christian philosophy of education.

CONTEXTS OF RESOURCE SELECTION
Restate the School's Mission Statements and Philosophy as a Series of Questions or Guidelines for Resource Selection

The key step in establishing patterns and guidelines for resource selection is to reformulate the foundational and guiding documents of the school in such a way that they will give direction to the resource selection process. In the four examples below, words or concepts that may be fundamental to a Christian school are extracted and then put in a context where they illustrate how they should provide an evaluative filter for resource selection.

1. *The concept of "nurture" is important in the foundational statements of some Christian schools.*
The idea of nurture differs radically from the idea of inculcation. Nurture involves recognizing individuality, creativity, and guided discovery. For Christian schools valuing nurture this means that the resource selection process will weed out and exclude those resources that, except in areas of biblical authority or foundational patterns such as multiplication tables, attempt to force all students into one mold in their ways of thinking and development. A behavioristic textbook that focuses on just one possible pre-determined answer when looking at civics, for example, would be inappropriate in this school. Such rigid often jingoistic books do exist. Instead, those selecting the school's civics books, videos, games, and so on would need to ensure that the resources chosen encourage genuine thinking processes and promote opportunities for children to discover

and evaluate civics patterns in their own and other cultures from a biblical perspective. If a resource teaches that any one political pattern (such as democracy or theocracy) is the best in all circumstances, for example, without allowing this position to be challenged or fairly examined in the light of the Scriptures, then that resource would not be appropriate for uncritical use in a nurturing type of Christian school.

On the other hand, in another school, the school community may have expressed its belief through foundational statements that the inculcation of information is of primary importance. In this case, a rigid, closely structured textbook with a fully detailed and prescriptive teacher guide would probably be appropriate. In the selection of math resources for this school, for example, purchasing manipulatives would not have the same priority as in the first school mentioned. A math textbook that constantly sought to explain mathematical concepts with real world examples would be seen to be important in the nurturing-type school, but could be viewed as a distraction in the other. Of course, it could also be argued that the content-centered pattern of the school favoring rigid, closely-structured materials is not fostering genuine Christian education.

2.   *What the guiding statements say about how the school looks at the world affects resource selection.*

This book has already suggested that Christian schools should follow a biblical model and, at levels appropriate to children's maturity, help their students to look at the world in all its fallen-ness and give them the handles to cope with that world. If this is a school's foundational perspective then the environment and culture around the school will be important resources for study and exploration.

Conversely, in a school where knowledge is viewed as an abstraction and where the school's philosophy expresses its primary task as being one of continuously sheltering students from the often unfocused and at times evil characteristics of the world, then a carefully controlled and sanitized textbook need be the only resource provided for the students. This could perhaps be accompanied by a student workbook where students merely fill in the blanks and then tear out and dispose of their work pages when the next page of the book is being studied.

In the former of these two schools, an exciting pattern of Christian education is depicted. Its students will often be out in the community gathering data. History will involve oral history and primary sources, and it will attempt to use data in order to discover the prevailing "spirit of the age," which can then be evaluated against biblical norms. Science will involve constant experimentation in laboratories, beside streams, and in the surrounding examples of vegetation and animal life. Literature resources will be chosen to recognize and analyze the works of a diversity of writers from different cultural and religious perspectives and will encourage students to express themselves in ways that recognize their own perspectives compared to biblical norms. These are examples of the pattern already encouraged in previous chapters in this book, of looking at the world in the light of the Son.

3. *A foundational commitment to the lordship of Christ over all of creation will influence resource selection.*

When a Christian school declares that no area of life is religiously neutral, this should impact resource selection. It means that although some useful textbooks may claim to be "purely factual and objective," the faculty will be vigilant at unpacking with the students the religious direction and commitment of all resources and seeking a response to this elucidation.

This principle also means that perhaps the best starting point for the school in the selection of resources is to ascertain exactly what is available in the area of study that has been produced by Christians. This does not assume that the work of a Christian will automatically be adopted because, as was stated earlier, authorship by a Christian does not guarantee appropriateness. In addition, there are many areas of study that Christians have not addressed. Nevertheless, it is vital for Christian school resource selectors to be informed about what Christians are writing about in their areas of study. They need carefully to evaluate potential resources written by Christians to see if they conform to the school's guiding statements and to consider if they are appropriate to use in the classroom. Whenever possible, we should be affirming Christian scholarship, which means both encouraging it and being constructively critical of it so that with each passing period of time, it conforms more and more to the task of helping us to see the world the way that God sees it.

4. *A foundational commitment to promoting creative salt-and-light worship and service will influence resource selection.*

Some schools that claim to be Christian see the implementation of the task of being salt and light in a lost world as a responsibility of the home and not the school. Other Christian schools, in concert with their parents, have expressed in their foundational statements a commitment to challenging and assisting their students to implement the calling of Christ to carry his reconciling message of forgiveness and hope to the community in which they live. This second view is the pattern that is encouraged in this book.

Schools with this latter perspective will encourage appropriate and dynamic "activism" on the part of their students. As Wolterstorff says, "The idea of the Christian school in our society is the idea of a school producing dissenters and agents of change in the name of Christ. The Christian school is a training ground for . . . dissent and reform" (2002a, 170).

Frequently, these Christian schools will bring the community into the classroom as a resource and will reach out to the community in return. I observed a sixth-grade class operating in a creative manner in Australia. In their study of life and death, they went to a local supermarket and discerned and later discussed people's attitudes to death through the use of a questionnaire. They were even scheduled to visit a funeral home and listen to a mortician, as they considered the meaning of mortality from a Christian perspective.

In another Christian school in Asia, the teacher was using the construction and furnishing of a home as a vehicle to teach the required math skills to her students, and she looked at Christian concepts of money, materialism, and conservation along the way. This could be extended into an integrated approach where content material and skills normally considered in home economics or science are incorporated together into other lessons. As another example, a good Bible teacher may challenge his students to develop a Christian mind and to express this through an analysis of various Christian and secular society holidays or through a variety of outreach programs into the community.

When a Christian school's philosophical foundation is clearly understood and articulated, diversity and dynamic discussion can occur during the resource selection process, with the confidence that this variety can result in positive outcomes because of the touchstone of those foundational principles. As long as the pattern and content of the resources selected conform to the school's mission statements, an exciting, biblically founded potpourri of educational patterns can develop in a way that responds to the changing needs of the students. These educational patterns reflect a Christian concept of curriculum development, as was outlined in the curriculum development flowchart in Chapter 8.

"SNAKE ALLEY"– AN APPROPRIATE RESOURCE SELECTION?

An example of the selection of an unusual and haunting resource that I observed comes from a school in Asia. This Christian school was attended mainly by expatriate children from the mission and non-mission community. The faculty agreed that the school's foundational statements mandated them to develop in their students a sensitivity to the host culture around the school. Furthermore, teachers were concerned to challenge their students with the lordship of Christ over all of creation so that, as and when the children chose to live with Christ as their Lord, they would be able to share his healing Good News with the people around them. Discussion was focused on the extent to which senior year students should be made aware of the darker sides of community life and of the calling to bring God's redemptive shalom into these areas as well.

The particular "darker" side of life that was being considered as a potential resource to learn about and bring Christ's love to was known locally as "snake alley." In the company of one of the local teachers, I had walked through "snake alley" the previous evening. It was a popular tourist alley where gambling took place and men sold potions made from snakes and other creatures as aphrodisiacs. The main alley was well-lighted and lined with little stores selling tourist items and these aphrodisiacs. In one store, I noticed a large baboon sitting on and chained to a table. The baboon was wearing neat children's clothes and was quite an attraction.

Side alleys ran off the main thoroughfare. They were dark and gloomy but were brightly lit up at occasional points along them by red lights where brothels existed. The various prostitutes from these brothels (and some of them were as young as some of the students back at the Christian school) stood outside the brothel doors, beckoning customers. Apparently, they had up to fifteen "clients" each night.

As we moved back to the main alley, we became caught in a steady flow of people. Cramped up in a crowded space, it was difficult to see the ground in front of you. Therefore, as we were swept along by the crowd, I was horrified when I almost tripped over something chained to the ground in the middle of the alley's pathway. A near naked, very deformed little boy was obstructing my path. He had a hood over his face (apparently this was understood in local religious lore to protect his dignity), but the rest of him was filthy and a betrayal of humanity. Like the baboon I had seen earlier, this boy was chained to a ring and could not move. He was curled up in a semi-ball, as much as he was able to in his deformed condition. The baboon up on the counter of the man selling aphrodisiacs, in fact, was in a much better state than this boy. The baboon was safe from being trodden on, was clean, and well clothed. This boy, though, like all human beings, deserved dignity and worth as a bearer of God's own image! The stark contrast between the boy and the baboon, against the background of "snake alley's" sexual exploitation, was almost too much to bear. It was with some relief, but also with a sense of shame and horror, that we left "snake alley."

"Snake alley" was a part of the community. The Christian school that I was visiting was also a part of that community. The teachers were trying to work out what it meant for them to be preparing their twelfth-grade (form seven or year twelve) students to be sensitive to the culture around them and be salt-and-light in that community. Was this a "Christian" resource? What did this term mean with regard to "snake alley"? Did the teachers pretend that this den of horror did not exist nearby, or that their students were not mature enough to have their consciousnesses raised about it? Did they talk about "snake alley" and leave it at that? Should they take these older teenagers on a class trip down there and let them see it (though, as it turned out, many of them had walked through "snake alley" with other tourists already)? Should they invite students who so chose, with parental approval, to join the group of Christian teachers who went down "snake alley" once a month and publicly prayed and witnessed in the area? Just what should they do? How did this evil, colorful, sad, needy community resource of "snake alley" fit within the activities of the Christian school's program?

You may be interested to know the outcome of the discussion. As I stated above, the school had an articulated mission statement that desired to have its students learn about the world around them in all its fallenness at levels responsive to their maturity. The school also deliberately sought (still today) to invite its students to respond to what they see in the world and sought to challenge them about what it means to be God's ambassadors everywhere. At the point at which I left the discussion, the feeling of many teachers was that "snake alley" was a real part of life, and in a sensitive way, with parental involvement and consent, it was considered appropriate to see it as an albeit unconventional resource that the school should recognize and to which its senior students should be helped to understand, visit (accompanied by teachers), and minister into as God's shalom-bearing ambassadors.

THE POSSIBILITIES AND CHALLENGES OF TECHNOLOGY

In many schools today, tablets, smart phones, or the internet are as likely to provide learning resources as is the standard hard-copy textbook. The teacher is much more a facilitator than in the past, no longer being the repository of all information, since almost all students have dynamic access to almost unlimited information online. Research is considerably easier than a generation ago, as internet search engines locate information much more readily, and entire university courses are available online through pathways such iTunes U. However, research is much more complicated as well, requiring students to search vast amounts of data, become aware of differing levels of authenticity where all data reflect their own biases and where students need to reach for genuine understanding rather than just copy and plagiarize.

We encourage Christian schools to embrace new technology, and make use of the enlarged resource base that ICT provides. In many smaller schools and in remote settings, licensed e-learning using other schools' resources in subjects that appeal to only a few students is common. Smartboards make learning more varied and interesting, appealing to a wider range of learning styles than was possible previously – though "death by PowerPoint" remains a frequent challenge where cognitive overload can cause poorly-used ICT to be a barrier rather than an aid, to learning.

The missions community is making effective use of the internet in education.

- Online schools such as NorthStarWorldwide are providing resources and dynamic educational options in many nations.
- Australian missionaries' children (MKs or TCKs) can use computers at their MK school in the middle of the South American jungle to access up-to-date information about their home country, even including local weather forecasts and the current edition of local newspapers.
- Students can also use the web to gain information about vocational opportunities and college/university entrance costs and requirements in their homelands.
- Administrators can access the web to find out about teacher certification requirements in home states.
- Schools can use their school's web pages to make their school's needs known to prayer partners and to recruit teachers.
- Teachers and students can use the web in their classes to create virtual tours of the home countries of class members.
- Teachers can use the web to access library search engines or educational databases to conduct research for graduate education programs that they can undertake while they are still on the field.
- Schools can use the web to activate the "virtual classroom" and teach programs in subject areas that are outside of the expertise

of the current faculty.

The possible uses of the world wide web are endless. The problems of isolation and "time-lapse" that once plagued MK schools are quickly slipping into oblivion. Other technologies are also exciting, such as the development of low-cost satellite television, which can be used for news gathering and teacher-supported remote instruction. CD-ROM, USB-memory, and iCloud technology have meant that the freight costs and customs charges that came with bringing hard-copy library resources, such as general and national encyclopedias, into the MK school have been reduced. One little disc, which normally incurs minimal freight and customs charges, can replace boxes of books and shelves of storage space.

Use of the internet in schools must be conducted with the same care and concern for vision fidelity as is the case with any other resource. Students must be taught how to use the internet, not just let loose on a computer or tablet keyboard. Apart from the unsavory material available on the web, care must be taken to nurture a hermeneutics of suspicion (an insight that has been sharpened by postmodern thinking) in students concerning any online data that they access – as with what they read in their textbooks as well.

The potential for the internet to re-define reality must also be explored with students. Just consider the meaning of the term "friend" for someone born in the twentieth century, and what this means when we sing "What a Friend We Have in Jesus," compared to the meaning of the word "friend" for an IT native who understands the word in terms of the hundreds of "friends" one has in Facebook, and whose relationship can be quite casual, uncommitted, and terminated at the flick of a switch. As Chua and Edlin (2010) have commented elsewhere,

> Whilst celebrating the many positive opportunities created by the internet, we need to undertake a sober analysis of the way that the devil can use this new invention to lure us to thinking, like Adam, that we can be God. . . . For example, think of the attributes of God that the Psalmist celebrates in Psalm 139. David rejoices in God's omniscience (all-knowing), his omnipresence (everywhere) and his omnipotence (all powerful). It is the lure for humanity to possess exactly these same characteristics that seduces so many in contemporary life to spend hours each day in front of their computer altars. The 24/7 range and breadth of the internet, and the infinite body of knowledge that it enables us to possess and which we can control with a few clicks of a mouse, appeals to the fallen side of our natures which still strives to be like God rather than to worship and serve Him. And all this is possible without once having to engage in interpersonal interaction with the accountability and mutual responsibility that social intercourse

brings with it. At last, omniscience, omnipresence and omnipotence are ours at the press of a button. And the moment it becomes too challenging or stressful, we can exercise the ultimate power by switching this electronic world off! (Chua & Edlin 2010, 1–2)

Holland (2011) reflects on the powerful impact of the digital revolution in the modern classroom. Radical constructivism's abandonment of absolute truth has found a powerful ally in social media whereby traditional concepts of knowledge and learning have been replaced by sensationalism, personal opinion, and the discrediting of metanarrative.

Conclusion

Resource selection in the Christian school is no more a neutral activity than any other aspect of the life of the Christian school. The tendency of some schools to select resources by relying completely upon packages prepared by others is an understandable response to rapid change and bias in educational media. But it is no substitute for effective teacher training in worldview-based resource selection. Also, it can quickly become an abrogation of responsibility that denies the uniqueness of each school and its community. Dynamic, appropriate resource selection can only occur in a context of informed discussion, based upon a corporate understanding of the school's foundational statements and a well-versed comprehension of the important features that do and do not characterize authentic Christian education.

Chapter 11

Christians in Higher Education

INTRODUCTION

The phrase "the outrageous idea of Christian scholarship" was originally used by George Marsden in his book of the same name, published in 1998. As the title indicates, some Christian academics are ambivalent at best about the relationship between their faith and their academic life – reinforcing the modern myth that somehow scholarship is fundamentally devoid of religious roots and fruit. As Marsden asserts, nothing could be further from the truth. The purpose of this chapter is to briefly explore this dilemma of the Christian academic, and then to suggest ways that Christian scholars should function if they are to be true to their calling of looking at God's world God's way, and equipping young people to engage every aspect of the culture in a shalom, kingdom-coming manner. Of course, for our students to be able to do this, it starts with us their professors. Students probably will learn just as much from what they see us do, as from what they hear us say. So let us begin by exploring our own situations – the life and times of a Christian academic in the twenty-first century.

How does the Christian academic stay true to both his faith and the academic enterprise of the secular university in this challenging situation? Or, as Marsden (1997a) puts it, "Should a Christian scholar be forced to pose as something else, usually as a liberal humanist, to be accepted in the academy" (15)? Some of the responses offered by Christian thinkers seem to be problematic. They risk hiding the hope of the gospel from the intellectual life of our culture and also stunting the growth and causing intellectual schizophrenia in the Christians who seek to live by them.

Is William Lane Craig (2004) correct when he argues that:

> Most Christian scholars today fail to make a meaningful contribution because either they are intimidated by the hostile [secular university] environment or they have uncritically accepted a post-enlightenment liberalism where their faith at best provides only qualitative enrichment to secular ideas while ignoring the contradiction between the two. (iv)

If so, then J. Gresham Machen's (1951) rebuke rings loudly in our ears:

> We may preach with all the fervor of a reformer and yet succeed only in winning a straggler here and there, if we permit the whole collective thought of the nation or of the world to be controlled by ideas which . . . prevent Christianity from being regarded as anything more than a harmless delusion. (162)

On the other hand, there are some very illuminating insights offered by other Christians that resonate strongly with a biblically faithful meta-narrative and that provide Christian scholars with a robust scaffold for engaging the academic mind.

In this chapter, initial comments speak to the situations of Christian scholars in both Christian and secular settings. Later in the chapter, material focuses directly on the Christian academic in the Christian higher education institution.

Confronting the Complexity:
A Missiological View of Christ and Culture

Goheen and Bartholomew (2008) echo Wright and Wolters by advocating the concept of narrative as a means of describing reality. For western cultures, they identify the prevailing narrative as the Western story that is shaped by neo-Hellenism and principles of individual autonomy, epistemological dualism, material prosperity, scientism, and globalized, economic rationalism. Running across that story is the biblical narrative of creation, fall, redemption, the church, and fulfillment, with Jesus Christ and his kingdom purposes being central at every step along the road. As in the diagram below, contemporary Christians find themselves at the intersection of these two incompatible stories. At this missiological crossroads, Christians must choose which story has priority – which one gives way to the other in terms of shaping one's view of reality and life's purpose. The decision that one makes will shape how the Christian lives in his or her own culture.

Figure adapted from Goheen and Bartholomew (2008, 8)

INTELLECTUAL SCHIZOPHRENIA

There is another context in which the wide range of perspectives of Christian scholars in the academy can be viewed. This has to do with post-Enlightenment and idolatrous, prevailing cultural assumptions that have deeply infiltrated the church and provided erroneous signposts for contemporary Christians in all walks of life – including the university. In one guise or another logical positivism or modernity, as a legacy of the Enlightenment project's enthronement of reason as the only credible measure of truth, continues to deeply impact western Christianity. The view of the world nurtured within many Christian churches today is that the gospel of Christ and the work of the kingdom have only to do with personal salvation, moral uprightness, and a pious patience as we await death and our translation into a perfect eternity with Christ. Engagement with culture is either as an especially ordained church worker, minister, or missionary, who carry out personal evangelism, or as laypeople who pray for these especially consecrated believers and who put money into the church offering week by week to support their full-time ministries.

It's widely assumed and believed in the Christian circles that many scholars have grown up in and within which they worship today that the Christian faith is a personal, belief-based position that is divorced from the intellectual rigor and so-called "values-free" investigation of daily life and vocation. For its part, western secular culture tolerates – even supports – religion as long as it remains in a private realm. It is assumed that religion should not seek to give direction to commerce or political structures or international relations – or scholastic investigation, which, it is claimed, can only really be directed and measured in terms of an objective scientific paradigm.

While such a dichotomy might be incomprehensible in many non-western cultures, it is a dualistic part of mother's milk in the west, and it has pernicious consequences. Lesslie Newbigin (1986) put it this way:

> Having been badly battered in its encounter with modern science, Christianity in its Protestant form has largely accepted relegation to the private sector, where it can influence the choice of values by those who take this option. *By doing so, it has secured for itself a continuing place, at the cost of surrendering the crucial field.* In this way, the church can grow in its private sphere, and we can have government leaders defend religion in general, but at the cost of marginalisation. (19, emphasis added)

Commitment to this perspective may cause intellectual schizophrenia among Christian academics. They talk and sing hymns about following Jesus in everything, but the nurture and encouragement within the life of many churches has bred a presuppositional commitment to dualism, with its consequential belief that faithful Christian living for the Christian scholar is unconcerned with scholarly exploration outside of theology and perhaps philosophy. As Marsden (1997b) claims, until recently this view has been reinforced by supposedly objective educational institutions themselves: "The rule evolved that to be part of the mainstream academic profession one had to lay one's religious faith aside" (28), resulting in Christian scholars often being unwittingly coerced into adhering to a fundamentalist and deceptive ideology of objective scientism. Indeed, Carson (2012) reminds us that the language of academics of "tolerance" is really a deceptive mask for intolerance of anything that is not politically correct – especially a faith position like Christianity that believes in right, wrongs, and accountability.

On the academic level, it may well be that the modern form of the university, which is very different from its antecedents, mitigates against any role in encouraging the virtuous life to which Christians aspire.

The enduring passion of the opposition to Christianity on university campuses is at times ribald and unapologetic. Note, for example, the alarmist comments by one of postmodernity's greatest champions, the late Richard Rorty. In the extract below (repeated from Chapter One), Rorty's vitriol is not directed just against Christianity, but against any theistic worldview that believes in certainty and absolute truth, and whose messianic leaders make exclusivist claims like Jesus does in Luke 14:6. However, to understand how his comments impact our community, when Rorty uses "fundamentalist," we might read "bible-believing evangelical Christian":

I, like most Americans who teach humanities or social science in colleges and universities . . . try to arrange things so that students who enter as bigoted, homophobic, religious fundamentalists will leave college with views more like our own. . . . The fundamentalist parents of our fundamentalist students think that the entire "American liberal establishment" is engaged in a conspiracy. The parents have a point. . . . [W]e are going to go right on trying to discredit you in the eyes of your children, trying to strip your fundamentalist religious community of dignity, trying to make your views seem silly rather than discussable. We are not so inclusivist as to tolerate intolerance such as yours. . . . I think those students are lucky to find themselves under the benevolent *Herrschaft* [domination] of people like me, and to have escaped the grip of their frightening, vicious, dangerous parents. (Rorty, 2000, 21–22)

In a desperate attempt to secure for ourselves a place of acceptability rather than ridicule at the table of secular scholarship, some of us, even in Christian institutions around the world, can be accused of having largely abandoned the Christ-centered core of who we are, what we believe, and how we know – i.e., what may be called the theo-logical foundation of wisdom and understanding in every discipline. Let me be clear: at times we seem to have deluded ourselves into believing either that higher education is religiously neutral, and therefore we instruct from the forlorn perspective that scholarly teaching and learning in our specialties have nothing to do with faith; or we practice pre-emptive capitulation where we have become epistemic schizophrenics and deliberately cloister our cherished gospel to the Sunday corner to which our secular cultures have been successful in consigning it, while we practice an idolatrous God-denying scholarship at university in the remaining six days of the week.

In this way, wisdom has been debased, and while we worship the God of the Bible on Sundays, we unwittingly worship the god of economic rationalism, even in our "Christian" institutions of higher learning, the rest of the time. We pretend that in the production of marketplace graduates we somehow have fulfilled the calling of Christian higher education. We preach about not being conformed to this world's way of thinking and of being transformed by the renewal of our minds (Romans 12) on the one hand, but we nurture and teach in ways and with belief assumptions that are little different from our secular colleagues on the other.

Marsden (2011) expresses his extreme concern about the failure of Christian higher education and its tragedy for public life this way:

Since most of the Christian scholarship of previous generations has died out or been secularized, perhaps the principal question we should ask concerning evangelical Christian scholarship today is whether it represents simply a transitional stage in the secularization of our community. Are evangelical academics today simply introducing secular standards to our community but doing so by giving them the gloss of Christian education? (65)

The Gospel at the Center
Provides Integrality, Wholeness, and Purpose

The suggestion of this chapter, not new but often unheeded, is that the pathway to faithful Christian scholarly endeavor lies not in an attempt to reconcile the irreconcilable, but in a rediscovery of alternative foundational principles that emanate from a dynamic, biblical worldview and that celebrate the lordship of Christ over all of life and therefore give empowerment and direction for Christian cultural engagement in all of life, including academia. Gloriously, in the twilight of modernity and the emerging age of postmodernity, this perspective and its tenants as outlined below may have a greater potential to impact the academy today than in any time since the nineteenth century. "Christians can more fully participate in contemporary academic life than they could ten or twenty years ago" (Mathewes 1999, 118).

We agree with Neuhaus (1996) that, for the Christian academic in any institution, the word "Christian" is not a peripheral notion or a limiting label but is the starting point, the end point, and the guiding principle all along the way. If philosophical neutrality is the fraud that this book claims it to be, then Christians will want no part of it. Though the possibility of co-belligerency does exist, in many secular quarters ". . . gaining the secularist's approval is not possible," claims Claerbaut (2004), "because at their cores, Christianity and secularism are incompatible" (83). Nevertheless, academics with competing worldviews often work alongside each other on the campuses of government universities. Business schools have socialist professors teaching classes alongside economic rationalists. Medical schools have professors with pro- and anti-abotrtion positions in the same faculty. Being a Christian is not an anti-intellectual position, and being a Christian professor in a state university is a special opportunity for missionary service. Despite clear opposition, some fine Christian thinkers have found room to work in secular institutions, and they deserve the prayers and support of the Christian community as they encourage their peers and students to examine the consistency of their worldviews, and as they maintain a witness to the coming kingdom of God in the purportedly pluralistic environment of these government universities.

Nevertheless, dedication to the whole-hearted flowering of a Christian worldview is the preserve of the Christian institutions of higher learning, since this is their raison d'être. It is here that robust exploration of God's world takes place deliberately and overtly right across the institution. Coram Deo applies to all teaching, decision-making, and intended outcomes. It is to the practice of the craft of teaching and research at these overtly Christian institutions that the remaining comments in this chapter are directed – though they will still have some application to Christian academics in non-Christian institutions as well.

Some misunderstand the academic approach of the Christian university, thinking that it is an attempt to reduce Christian scholarly endeavor to little more than unending biblical exegesis. Not at all. Christian scholars throughout the ages have, and will continue, to investigate the world in which they live. The difference is that they do not do this with a presuppositional commitment to the absence of God as is the case with many of their secular colleagues, which has produced a pagan and often distorted scholarship. Rather, Christian scholars will conduct their research in the light of a living God who is here and who has declared himself in his Word written (in the Bible), living (in Christ), and in creation (the observable and unobservable world around us). Earlier in the book we have been reminded of Douglas Wilson's profound reflection:

> Every line of true knowledge must find its completeness as it converges on God, just as every beam of daylight leads the eye to the sun. The Christian educator's job is not to require the students to spend all their time gazing at the sun. Rather, we want them to examine everything else in the light the sun provides. (Wilson 2012, 4)

One implication of this perspective is that the Christian academic is capable of going beyond the mere exploration of technique that passes for scholarship in many universities today. "Academics face pressures toward specialization that obscure our vision of the academy as a whole and thereby facilitate disintegration . . . . Christian commitments can help resist the compartmentalization of academic research" (Mathewes 1999, 119). For example, robbed of a foundation for evaluating prime causes, it has been observed that much research inquiry at key universities in Australia avoids questions of origin and purpose. Philosophical uncertainty and radical constructivism mean that the profound question of "Why?" often has been replaced by the more technical and superficial question of "How?" This is another illustration of the loss of confidence and the loss of hope that is a product of a postmodern culture.

From a position of epistemic humility, Christian scholars can return causal issues to academic investigation. This is because they function within a worldview that goes beyond utilitarianism and sees integrality, purpose, and meaning in the disciplines of history, physics, business studies, psychology, and health sciences.

> A Christian [scholar] will settle for nothing less than a comprehensive account of reality. Not content with the what of things, [s/he] wrestles with the why of things; not content with knowing how, [s/he] asks what for . . . the Christian [scholar] cannot evade the hard questions about what it all means. (Neuhaus 1996, 3)

It may well be that a philosopher from the last century has suggested a framework for scholarly practice within the Christian university (though he encouraged it for all educational institutions irrespective of worldview). George Counts (1889–1974) was an American social reconstructionist who acknowledged the non-neutrality of education, and who exhorted educators to teach in the light of this reality:

> My thesis is that complete impartiality is utterly impossible, that the school must shape attitudes, develop tastes, and even impose ideas. It is obvious that the whole of creation cannot be brought into the school. This means that some selection must be made of teachers, curricula, architecture, methods of teaching. And in the making of the selection the dice must always be weighted in favor of this or that. (1932, 19)

> I would merely contend that as educators we must make many choices involving the development of attitudes in [students] and that we should not be afraid to acknowledge the faith that is in us or mayhap [i.e., perhaps in] the forces that compel us. (20)

> That teachers should deliberately reach for power and then make the most of their conquest is my firm conviction. To the extent that they are permitted to fashion the curriculum and the procedures of the school they will definitely and positively influence the social attitudes, ideals, and behavior of the coming generation. (28)

> We should . . . give to our [students] a vision of the possibilities which lie ahead and endeavor to enlist their loyalties and enthusiasms in the realization of the vision. (37)

OUR CALLING AS CHRISTIAN ACADEMICS IN THE CHRISTIAN UNIVERSITY

A few Christian institutions have taken the time to reflect and codify what they understand to be faithful scholarship in an authentic, Christian college or university.

For example, Dordt College (Kok 2004, 17–24) has produced an institutional guiding document based upon a dynamic, reformational theology and worldview. It

- puts the Word of God at the center;
- highlights the creativity and stewardship framework of the cultural mandate;
- requires all curriculum and teaching to be viewed through a biblically authentic lens; and
- concludes with identifying student outcomes that include learning for service, gaining in wisdom, and commitment to transforming culture.

For this chapter, with our focus upon the Christian academic, we can do no better than encourage readers to consider the following guidelines produced by Redeemer University College, Canada, in its guiding document entitled *The Cross and Our Calling*. This extended extract has merged within it some additional reflections, as noted, from the author of this book.

> [Those who seek to be Christian academics in a Christian university] are called in our teaching, research and artistic expression to witness to the victory of the cross and the lordship of the resurrected Christ. We understand the overall purpose of a Christian university education to be to equip young men and women to serve as witnesses to Christ's victory in the various vocations they will take up in society. They are to be witnesses not solely by using the opportunities for [narrowly defined] evangelism that their positions may afford, but by testifying to the transforming power of Christ in every aspect of their professional or vocational conduct as teachers, homemakers, businesspeople, lawyers, journalists or artists, or in whatever other tasks to which God may call them. [A Christian university] seeks to prepare servant leaders who dare to challenge the idols of our culture, and who in the very exercise of their callings bear witness to Christ in his gentle yet liberating rule. In formulating the purpose of [Christian] university education in this way, we [agree with Seerveld in] deliberately repudiating the mistaken conception that study is merely the handmaid of economic competitiveness [and the equally mistaken belief that a university education is primarily a pre-professional training activity]. It is good that Christian university students should become prepared in the course of their studies to become successful and productive members of society. But when social status and financial gain [often the by-product of a university education] become the principal goals of education, that good has become twisted and rendered evil. Our students' first task is, as ours, to witness to God's rule and shalom over creation. . . .
>
> In this task, [Christian universities that seek to be faithful to the Scriptures participate] in two venerable traditions. The first is the scholarly tradition

. . . stretching back [with dual roots in the academy of classical Greece and the training institutions of local cultures]; the second is the tradition of Christian participation in higher education which had its beginnings among the early church fathers, flourished in the middle ages and was refined during the Reformation and in subsequent ages. As [the twenty-first century holders of this baton, we as Christian academics] do not seek to create a Christian ghetto. . . . Instead, we week to participate in the ongoing work of scholarship from within a Christian [as opposed to a non-Christian] tradition [there is no other alternative] which seeks to carry out its academic task in the light of Scripture. More specifically, we stand in the tradition of scholarship rooted in Augustine and Calvin which has been given more recent expression [by] scholars and theologians such as Kuyper, Bavinck, Dooyeweerd, [Newbigin, Plantinga, Wolterstorff, Clouser, Goheen, Wolters, Wright, Bartholomew, Fowler, Smith and] others. Our participation in these two scholarly traditions compels us to discern the religious foundations and faith commitments that shape all theoretical work, acknowledging with thanks the creational insights they confer while seeking to identify and to reject that idolatrous twisting that can disfigure them.

In articulating the task of Christian scholarship in this way we stand against two very different idols of the mind that have had great influence[, and to which reference has already been made in the first part of this paper]. The first is rational objectivism: in this view, the academic enterprise can be religiously neutral. While some modernist scholars might once have looked upon all pre-theoretical commitments in academic work as something which compromised scientific integrity, the Christian scholar recognizes (with the postmodernist) that no academic inquiry can begin without presuppositions, that all theoretical work is shaped by foundational beliefs. The second of these idols is radical relativism: in this view, since perspectives on reality have been shaped largely by personal experience and by the arbitrary influence of one's own history, society and culture, all points of view are alike subjective, and objective knowledge of reality is an impossibility. For ourselves, while we do affirm the insight that human knowledge is always shaped to some degree by human subjectivity, we differ from the radically relativist point of view in two important respects. In the first place, the subjectivity that informs scholarship is, at its deepest level, religious in nature. That is, the paradigms and worldviews that mould theoretical work have not merely evolved to maturity under historical, social, and cultural influences. Paradigms and worldviews are the products of that fundamental and directing power – the religious impulse – which lies at the very heart of humankind. [Paul notes this most powerfully in his sermon in Athens recorded in Acts 17.] Religion is not merely one more element of human subjectivity standing alongside all the others; it is what shapes and moves them all. Secondly, we reject the relativism that can arise from paying inordinate attention to the subjective elements in human knowledge and knowing. We believe that there is a given order of creation which can be known, and that we are called in our scholarly work to give a faithful account of what we can perceive of that order. [We celebrate the God-given creative capacity of human beings as outlined in Genesis 1. We also celebrate the pathway of reformed critical realism whereby,] though our knowing never occurs in a vacuum, and though our knowledge is always partial and imperfect [epistemic humility], genuine insight into the order of what has been made can be achieved [when perceived from a biblically faithful worldview perspective].

Among Christian academics too[, though we should agree to submit our philosophical constructs to the authority of Scripture and not the other way around,] there are models of scholarship from which we distinguish our own approach. First is a kind of dualism that sees Christian belief as applicable only to the realm of theology, and keeps biblical teaching completely separate from theoretical work in other disciplines. In another approach, often termed biblicism, isolated [and decontextualised passages] of Scripture are brought to bear on specific issues of research and theorizing in the disciplines, but without a proper recognition of the considerable differences in purpose and kind of language which distinguish Scripture from scholarship. A distinctive element of the Reformed tradition of scholarship in which we locate ourselves is its deliberate attention to the inner connection between Scripture and scholarly inquiry, that is, the normative bearing of Scripture on the making of theory. We see it as our responsibility to apply the biblical story and a biblical worldview to the basic religious, ideological, and philosophical assumptions that form the foundations of all academic work. It is these underlying assumptions which come to expression in the creation of a canon of literature, an artistic composition, a conceptual framework, a methodology or a paradigm, and it is on the level of these assumptions that the Scriptures may most fruitfully be brought to bear on the scholarly enterprise. Consequently, it is of great importance for the Christian scholar to have a good grasp of a biblical worldview and some of its philosophical implications, [as well as a credible understanding of the prevailing worldview contours in his/her own discipline. Only then can s/he] critique the assumptions of current secular schools of thought, to recognize valid insights within theories which may not in themselves be derived from a biblical worldview, and reposition such insights within a Christian framework of thought which explicitly recognizes God's revelations in Scripture and creation. Moreover, Scripture is [central in reformational scholarship] not only to shape a Biblical worldview, but also to provide norms and themes that offer more direct guidance and instruction for our [teaching and] theoretical work.

Thus a Christian psychologist or educator might critique behaviourism for its reductionism and determinism, suggesting instead a Christian view of the person which honours the rich complexity of human functioning [in a creation-fall-redemption-fulfilment context and gives due respect to biblical teachings regarding image-bearing, varied giftedness, abnormality, and personal responsibility]. A Christian sociologist might challenge the cultural relativism which shapes most theoretical paradigms in sociology, and argue that normative social structures [such as marriage] are not merely arbitrary in their construction but in fact reflect God's constant and abiding creation order for social life. A Christian historian might take issue with the Marxist view of economic forces as the overriding explanatory force in history, [or the socialist historian's view that all religious movements are essentially social mobility movements. Instead, he might] work out in response a view of the historical process which gives appropriate attention to the multiple causes at work within it, including [the essential] religious[, universal, and irresistible driving force (Acts 17) of seeking after God. A Christian political studies professor will resist the temptation to just affirm the prevailing political ideologies of his age (such as democracy) and instead will subject government and law and order to a biblical critique where all forms of government are held accountable to godly norms for government in contextualised settings. A Christian economics or business professor would explore the religious presuppositions of various approaches to economics/business, in the process dethroning the economy or economic rationalism as the determiner of what is good and what is bad, and also exploring biblical concepts of mutual accountability and the creation of useful goods and services, rather than allowing shareholder profits to dictate economic and business decisions. A Christian IT professor will celebrate technological advances not for their own sake but because of how they can assist in humanising livelihoods for all. In the process she will draw attention to the inequalities caused by unequal access; the unhelpful redefinition of language such as "community" and "friends" caused by new technologies; the blessings and problems created by IT globalisation; and the basic challenge of individualist idolatry (playing God) that is a temptation in much IT development and application. A Christian professor of science] would acknowledge the [religious roots of all scientific inquiry, would resist the ideological fundamentalism of scientism masquerading as neutrality, and would recognize] the tension between a naturalistic explanation of origins and the biblical concept of creation[. In her investigation of] the natural world[, she] would recognize [that all "natural"] phenomena [are] the handiwork of the God who made all things and sustains them [moment by moment through] his word [of power]. A Christian professor of [literature] might encourage the enjoyment of Romantic literature for its celebration of the imagination and of the richness of the world that God has created, while critiquing its individualism and its idolatrous elevation of imagination almost to the place of divine revelation. [He might help students to understand both the liberating and the captivating perspectives of words and language – for example, questioning whether or not a Christian should be happy using the term "The Enlightenment" for a period of history that subjected humanity to the dictatorial constraints of a deified human rationality. He might also explore a postmodern approach to literature which will expose its religious roots, capture its valuable insights, and reject the radical constructivism that it seeks to impose. A Christian journalism professor will explore a biblical concept of truth as a goal for the media, rather than sensationalist incident-bites which can distort but which tend to prevail because they enable managers to increase their ratings and hence their advertising appeal.

Our approach to Christian scholarship within the reformed tradition works out from the biblical] story to an elaboration of a Christian worldview [which is why we maintain that courses in these two core areas should be initial and foundational for any authentic and effective Christian educational program. Seerveld (2014) reminds us that this Christian philosophical systematics needs first to exist in the individual and communal hearts and minds of the faculty, and then become the foundation to which all students are exposed prior to moving into their chosen areas of specialty. From this basis, studies can move out to a philosophical articulation (ontology, epistemology, anthropology) and on to the formulations of the various disciplines.]

As part of a community called to continue the mission of Christ, we commit ourselves to witness to the message of the cross of Christ in higher education. The strength of our particular tradition is an attitude to secular culture which emphasizes simultaneously [ ]the enduring goodness of creation, [ ]the deeply distorting effects of sin, and the restoring power of Christ. In the name of [Jesus,] we wish to say an unequivocal "no" to sin in all its forms and effects . . . across the broad range of human culture. [Starting with ourselves, we] wish to unmask idolatry where[ver we find] it, notably in the academic sphere, and to oppose [every ideology and practice] that compromises academic integrity. But also in the name of Christ we wish to [repeat his] unequivocal "yes" to creation in all its wonderful variety and the goodness that shines in human culture, including academic culture. God gives us all things richly to enjoy (I Tim 6:17), including the gifts of scholarship and of university education. Of that we are witnesses. (*The Cross and our Calling* 2002, 12–16 [amended])

Seerveld (2014, 42) summarizes the witness of the Christian university this way:

. . . when a community of scholars as a body holds the Psalm 24 vision to be true –

The earth with its profuse diversity,
and the world with all its inhabitants
belong to the Lord (Psalm 24:1)

– and when as a body they breathe a holy spirit of inquisitive shalom tempered by "each [scholar's] humbly esteeming the others to be superior to oneself" (Philippians 2:1–11, v.3) as they all together "consider how to provoke! one another to passionately selfless love and good works" (Hebrews 10:19–25, v.24): then you have the heart of a Christian university throbbing with life.

Checkpoints for Faithful Christian Scholarship

The examples noted above illustrate what Christian scholarship and teaching might look like in selected learning areas. Dordt College (Kok 2004) provides several more examples in the disciplines of music, language, psychology, and agriculture. Appendix Two in this book points to what it means to grapple with teaching mathematics from a Christian perspective. Institutions such as Trinity Western University in Canada, at considerable cost, have been prepared to stand up in the public arena for a biblical worldview position in matters such as enrollment and faculty hiring.

Another appropriate entry point into the discussion is to consider key touchstones that should be important for a Christian professor who is seeking to be faithful in his calling in the Christian university. The following ten points are worthy of consideration.

Faithful Scholarship in the Christian University	
1. Know God	6. Practice sacrificial, biblical mentoring with your students
2. Develop a clear and united sense of vision and purpose	7. Implement a regular "critical friend" consultancy in your university
3. Learn how to teach	8. Understand the philosophical foundation of your discipline
4. Abandon tenure as your goal in academic life	9. Restore radicalism, vision, and hope to the university
5. Highlight "No neutrality!" recognizing that God alone sustains your discipline	10. Work hard at Christian scholarship
Suggestion: *after reading the material that follows, try carrying out a personal and institutional self-evaluation in each of the above ten areas.*	

1. Know God

Through Christ and through his Word, God has made himself known. Fundamental to living as a Christian scholar is a personal, pious, and living faith that is nurtured by fellowshipping with God's people, by studying God's word, and by humble prayer. Without this, and without the guidance of God's Holy Spirit who is the inheritance of every believer, the wisdom, discernment, courage and fortitude that are necessary to be a faithful Christian scholar will not be found.

Seerveld puts it this way:

> . . . it is the calling of every [Christian professor] . . . to become intimate with the Bible as God-speaking literature with its true story . . . . To have our teaching consciousness molded by faithful intimacy with the Scriptures . . . to know conversationally the Bible's very idiom (if not its languages), so that one has been outfitted with a biblical *mentalité* . . . such that the Bible provides the a priori for searching the world we live in rather than letting the present culture set the standards and force us to take up a defensive posture, that is, making work of having the Bible so ingrained in our habit of thinking, speaking, and getting things done: all of these makes one a good heir, in my judgment, of the Reformational praxis of Martin Luther and John Calvin. (Seerveld, 2014, 10,8)

2. Develop a Clear and United Sense of Vision and Purpose

We should understand our vocation as Christian university professors to be a clear and present calling from the Lord, and see our research and teaching as a daily offering of worship and service to God who is our primary audience (1 Thessalonians 2). The liberating and empowering blessing of creativity endowed upon humanity as Imago Dei in Genesis 1 and as re-expressed in the Great Commission of Matthew 28, should provide a catalyst for celebratory investigation. We should have a biblically rigorous, clear sense of vision and purpose – personal, collaborative, and institutional – and ensure that our activities are aligned to that vision.

3. Learn How to Teach

Most university professors are appointed to their posts because of their research abilities. Yet teaching usually is an essential component of their responsibilities. We would never think of allowing people to teach at primary and secondary schools without an ever increasing study of and exposure to sustained courses in teaching and learning. Why should it be any different for universities? Sadly, Norton et al. (2013) in a meta-study of teaching quality in higher education, conclude that

> Historically, academics have had little or no preparation for teaching. They

were simply expected to develop into their teaching roles through trial and error, with limited support. Staff relied on deep subject matter knowledge to design curriculum and transmit knowledge to students. . . . It is ironic that the very institutions that exist to provide training for key professions do not yet require similar standards for their own staff. (Norton et al. 2013, 20)

Renowned US philosopher and educator Brian Leiter from the University of Chicago Law School, presumably referring to the wider higher education scene in North America, has concluded that

Teaching counts for nothing. It was a shock to me how dishonest research schools are about teaching: on the brochures, to parents, in official pronouncements the line is that we care about teaching deeply. But in private all my colleagues, even at the official orientation, have said teaching counts for virtually nothing. . . . In other words, there is hardly any institutional concern for teaching. (Leiter 2010, 1)

A major review on quality teaching in higher education conducted across 20 countries by the OECD in 2009 concluded that "initiatives inspired by academic literature and research on the subject [of quality teaching in universities] are rare" (72). Watson (2012, 5) reached the disturbing conclusion that "the proportion of Australian students who report they are satisfied with the quality of university teaching hovers around 50 per cent." Such data would be entirely unacceptable in motor vehicle quality or the success rate of medical procedures, and it should be equally unacceptable in higher educational instruction.

Bexley et al. (2011, 26) report that 37.3 percent of academics have never had even a short course in teacher training, and over 50 percent of academics said they would not give any priority to exploring sustained teacher training opportunities in the future.

Unfortunately, many Christian universities have followed their secular counterparts in not adequately addressing the poor quality of teaching that has beset higher education. Smith and Smith (2011a) put it this way:

A funny thing happened on the way to the Christian university: the central task of teaching almost completely dropped off the scholarly radar. While the conversation was commonly billed as a consideration of the integration of faith and learning, the focus tended to be the role of faith in research and scholarship. . . . Our commitment to Christian scholarship has been significantly more articulate than our commitment to Christian pedagogy. (2–3)

Some teaching insights may be inherent to the individual, but as the Europeans report, "Excellent teachers are made, not born; they become excellent through investment in their teaching abilities. Leaving teachers to learn from trial and error is a waste of time, effort and university resources" (Pleschová et al. 2012, 6).

Christian colleges and universities need to be different, and rise above this unacceptable indifference to quality teaching. Administrators need to encourage faculty to undertake teacher training professional development. Professor quality evaluation needs to go beyond a count of peer-reviewed journals or simplistic student end-of-semester popularity polls. Biblically faithful, academically rigorous, church supporting, and culture engaging are laudable goals for our institutions and their professors. But to these we must add "quality teaching." Concepts such as formative assessment and peer coaching should be understood and practiced in all Christian learning communities. Our institutions must support their professors financially and through time release to engage in sustained, longitudinal, collaborative, evaluated, professional development.

4.   Abandon Tenure as a Goal in Academic Life

> The quest for tenure emasculates people. It turns them into intellectual geldings. They must please the tenured bureaucrats who hand out The Prize. . . . The requirement for tenure is clear: don't rock the boat. . . . The offer of tenure lures intelligent people into lives of high-salaried irrelevance. They write narrow, useless papers for publication in journals that no one reads, except in a quest for footnotes to steal. (North 2013, 1)

Gary North's radical reflection, though controversial, draws attention to the problem of tenure in the modern university. In a time of economic and social uncertainty, and the over-supply of academics in some disciplines, tenure has become a means of securing one's ongoing employment. In many situations, tenure has become more a tool for conformity and mediocrity and misplaced security than an aspect of faithful, dynamic Christian scholarship.

Our confidence should be in the Lord and not some dubious academic device. As long as faculty members are demonstrating in life and scholarship that they are challenging students with a celebration of the lordship of Christ over their discipline, then those professors continued employment should be secure. But when professors lapses into secular/pagan perspectives and practices, then they must be assisted to reform or be ejected from the institution.

5.   Highlight No Neutrality, Recognizing that God Alone Sustains
       Your Discipline

As Christian scholars claim, and as contemporary scholarship agrees, there is no neutrality. Every thought and scholarly endeavor presupposes certain beliefs about life, truth, and the academic task. For the secular scholar as well as for his Christian counterpart, all learning is always faith-committed. As Paul makes clear in Acts 17:27, albeit often unconsciously, faith always is everyone's starting point. Christians therefore should refuse to be embarrassed about the faith foundations of their scholarship as all scholarship is similarly founded. Rather, despite any hostility, we should champion the interdependence between faith and learning, expose the fallacy of neutrality, and assert the universality of Calvin's *sensus divinitatis* or C. S. Lewis's (1984) inconsolable secret, which is that all humanity is seeking after God. To quote Plantinga (1984), "The Christian philosopher is within his right in holding these positions, whether [or not] he can convince the rest of the philosophical world" (269).

In the area of curriculum design for example, something that most academics are engaged in, constructivist academics MacDonald and Purpel (1987) put it very clearly:

> We have argued that any model of curriculum planning is rooted in a cluster of visions – a vision of humanity, of the universe, of human potential, and of our relationships to the cosmos. These visions, though dimly viewed and rarely articulated, nonetheless have a profound impact on our day-to-day educational practices and upon our more theoretical formulations. It is for this fundamental reason that we are so troubled when we encounter the notion that curriculum planning is a separate function divorced from its human, social, economic, political, and religious context. Curriculum planning is but an index, a reflection, an aspect, an activity that emerges from an orientation and vision of who and what we are, where we come from, and where we are going. . . . What is of the most extraordinary import, of course, is which particular vision we decide to choose, for the choosing of a vision allows us to become that vision. (178–9)

6. Practice Sacrificial, Biblical Mentoring with Your Students and Fellow Faculty

Teaching requires the special skills of understanding material, and then also being able to transmit that understanding in a contagious manner that is intelligible to students possessing a wide range of backgrounds and abilities. But the effective teacher also requires personal mentoring dispositions that enhance learning, recognizing that the person of the teacher is an essential part of the teaching and learning process. Teaching has always been as much about relationships at many levels as it has been about information transfer. Paul's reflection on effective teaching in 1 Thessalonians 2:8 makes this point very well: "Because we loved you so much, we were delighted to share with you not only the gospel of God but our lives as well."

Jesus makes the same point when he exclaimed in Luke 6:40, that "The student . . . who is fully trained will be like their teacher." Christian professors, when doing their utmost for his highest, must make themselves available and vulnerable as mentors in the service of their students – the academic equivalent of washing their students' feet. This involves a repudiation of the neo-Confucian, hierarchical, "sage on the stage" model. As Hegeman, Edgell, and Jochemsen (2011) contend, "The moral profile of the teacher is thus the narrative that the student reads" (120).

Elzinga (2012) puts it this way:

> Christian higher education exists because there was once a Galilean who made disciples. His disciples called him Rabbi or teacher. And therein lies a principle by which teachers today are to invite – not coerce, but invite – students to be their disciples, that is, to mentor them. (17)

7. Encourage the Implementation a "Critical Friend" Consultancy in Your University

Most Christian universities submit themselves to regular accreditation and verification investigations that monitor and approve standards in areas such as equipment, faculty qualifications, graduation employment, and so on. This is a good thing, as we all know that an impending evaluation is a strong motivator for self-assessment and improvement. And yet for Christian professors, these standards are all means to achieving a much higher end, which is to mold the hearts and minds of students so that they have a rigorous and compelling perspective on what it means to understand God's world God's way and be equipped to be his ambassadors in every arena of life as they seek the welfare of the city in which they live as servants of the King of kings. However, this godly mission, ... is at our very core, and the activities within the university needed ... never be fully understood let alone be evaluated by secu... whose worldviews (if they are anything like ... upon which we operate.

... our institutions undergo regular ...erstand our motivation and de...assessing the alignment of our ...n our particular mission. More ...f the critical friend concept are

8.   Understand the Philosophical Foundations of Your Discipline

All knowledge is based upon faith convictions. People believe and therefore they know – not the other way around. Therefore, to be able to speak into contemporary academia and also to be faithful to a Christian worldview, Christian academics must understand what lies at the core of their disciplines. Says Craig (2004):

> You really do need to read something on the philosophy of your field. . . . As Christian academics we cannot afford to be unreflective and simply absorb uncritically the common presuppositions of our discipline, for these may be antithetical to a Christian Weltanschauung (worldview). Nor should we allow ourselves to be cowed by the prevailing views in our field or afraid to march to the beat of a different drummer. (23–25)

We will flounder in the wilderness, and like Peter in Matthew 16 we may find ourselves unconsciously doing the devil's work for him, if we do not understand the philosophical presuppositions and their outworkings in our own disciplines. Only then can we begin to distinguish truth from error and, in a reformed critical realist way, assist our students in grappling with our content material and modes of instruction in a manner that honors God.

9.   Restore Radicalism, Vision, and Hope to the University

For those of us from the West who are baby boomers, the student days that we remember are very different from those of the contemporary undergraduate. In our time, "going to 'varsity'" was a total experience of which academic study was just one component. Students expected to engage in big debates, to think about broader issues, and even to protest and be involved in the big "causes" of our day, such as the Vietnam War, racial discrimination, or cultural democratization. Although a few similar issues such as global warming energize some students today, for many the university experience has become little more than the technical acquisition of a specialized set of knowledge and skills in preparation for employment.

Economic rationalism may be partly responsible for this lamentabl development, but perhaps an even deeper reason may be that, in the p modern world, big picture causes rarely exist. What is the point of e ing in discourse about big events or protesting in favor of a cau there is only individual opinion? There are no big causes. P education has taught that there is only the mundane, that tr is a myth, and that commitment to an ideology is philosop Consider music. Where is the folk musical genre about ting an end to war, giving peace a chance, and hamm that was such a powerful cultural force in the mid-twentieth century?

The challenge issued by Wolterstorff (2002a, 170) for the Christian school to be a training ground for dissent and reform in the name of Christ has already been noted. Ntarangwi, the Executive Director of The International Association for the Promotion of Christian Higher Education (IAPCHE), concurs, claiming that a central task of the Christian university is to "challenge social values, policies, practices, and institutions" in the light of a biblical worldview (Ntarangwi 2013a, 3).

Of all people, Christians believe in the most profound metanarrative of all, which is not only the best explanation of reality but which also gives the best vision for life now and in the future. Life that is grounded in a modernist or postmodernist perspective cannot restore a right relationship with God or provide the enduring meaning and purpose that is the fruit of the gospel and a Christian worldview. The Christian university's radicalism is constructive, not destructive; is hope-filled, not hopeless. Exploring the life of the mind in a Christian context should be a wonderfully liberating experience, unsettling in its challenge to the status quo, but full of creative challenge and pregnant with possibility. In the midst of the trials of life, Christian academics have been gifted by a gracious God with the opportunity to lead their students in the exercise of their intellects in a fresh and noble manner to God's glory and for the benefit of the societies in which they live. What a precious endowment.

10. Work Hard at Christian Scholarship

We are not the first group of Christian scholars to be concerned about Christian scholarship. We should use the opportunities (and avoid the pitfalls) of postmodernity to explore our own disciplines, share our insights, and learn from the insights of others. Plantinga (1984) and Kok (2004) provide examples of what biblically faithful scholarship might look like in anthropology, ethics, music, language, psychology, art, and mathematics. After providing some helpful signposts, Goheen (2004, 2008) does the same for science, business, politics, education, sports, and the arts. Eisenbarth and Van Treuren (2004) point the way in engineering. Gould (2007) provides direction with his concepts of "explicit" and "latent" across all disciplines, while Sinnema (2008) provides important insight into what not to do in Christian scholarship. This author has tried to make a small contribution in the area of education. Become familiar with these examples, and others, especially within your own field of inquiry. Contribute to these insights yourself. Lest we descend into that dubious place where our goal becomes to know as much as possible about as little as possible, and also because we are our brother's keeper (Luke

10:25-37), Christian scholarship means having at least some understanding of the potential for good and evil that our profession and research may have on God's world in which we live. For passionate Christian scholars, nothing less will do if we desire to give our utmost for his highest in the area of Christian higher education.

We should also note that quality Christian scholarship does not mean that we restrict ourselves to so-called Christian resources or that we access only material produced by Christian authors. Read the section of this book (Chapter Ten) that deals with resources in the Christian school for more information on this point. We should not be bashful in acknowledging and using scholarly insights from secular scholars. For example, this book has been informed by the work of many secular and Christian academics. In terms of general revelation, all truth is God's truth, and we should happily access it wherever it is found.

CONCLUSION

Ultimately, each individual Christian scholar will have to make up his or her own mind about what constitutes faithful living as a Christian scholar in his or her particular setting. We will encounter opposition, and we will be misunderstood. At times, when we project an image of the nonexistence of any relationship between our scholarly endeavors and our Christian faith, we are our own worst enemies because we perpetuate the myth that Christianity is an anti-intellectual wasteland. Nevertheless, our Heavenly Father, who claims dominion over all creation including the life of the intellect, has not left us to flounder. We have the guiding principles of his Word, and the insights of the fellowship of believers and even secular scholars, to help us on our way. We have a clear belief in truth and purpose, which enables us to devise hope-filled outcomes for our research agendas and for the students whom we teach.

As Christians, we believe that this world is God's world and that all truth emanates from, and belongs to him. Therefore we have a sacred trust, a godly obligation, and a liberating context in which to explore scholarship from a biblically faithful perspective that honors our Creator and seeks the welfare of the time and space in which God has placed us. We want our students to learn about the world this way – and for this to happen, they must see it in us first, and then hear it from us as we teach them in our classes. Bartholomew and Goheen summarize the issue well in the following manner:

> If we are serious about mission, and genuinely concerned that Christian students are trained for a lifetime of service to Christ in whatever area of

life he calls them to, then we urgently need to recover a vision for Christian scholarship. Sending the best and brightest young Christians to study at the feet of the best secular scholars of the day simply will not do.

We need top-rate Christian scholars in every discipline, and we need students to study at their feet . . . developing a Christian understanding of their chosen field. (Bartholomew & Goheen 2013, 8-9)

Chapter 12

Maintaining the Vision I:
Teacher Professional Development

INTRODUCTION[1]

Teacher professional development is that ongoing and reflective equipping process engaged in by educators that enables them to be more faithful and effective in teaching and learning. It involves an awareness of philosophical foundations, an alignment with an institution's vision, collegial cooperation, and the maintenance and updating of knowledge and competencies. It should reflect felt needs, and should be closely related to student nurture, classroom activities, and desired outcomes. Day (1999, 4) offers a similar, alternative definition:

> It is the process by which, alone and with others, teachers review, renew and extend their commitment as change agents to the moral purposes of teaching; and by which they acquire and develop critically the knowledge, skills and emotional intelligence essential to good professional thinking, planning and practice with children, young people and colleagues throughout each phase of their teaching lives.

A few years ago, I contributed to the special edition of a professional journal that focused on the issue of teacher professional development. The overall title given by the editors to that special edition was "A Dangerous Complacency" (Edlin 2008b). A key challenge identified in that issue is as cogent today as it was then: Christian schools that consider sustained, systematic, longitudinal, philosophically consistent, teacher professional development as an *expensive optional extra* run the substantial risk of marginalizing their core reason for existence by entrusting the process of developing pedagogy to professionals whose own training has by and large encouraged them to consign God and understanding the world God's way to the unimportant margins of who they are and how they teach. It's all very well to sing with our students about Christ be-

---

1 This chapter is a revision and extension of materials originally written by the author for *Christian School Education*, 2008, 11(3): 16–21, and Goodlet & Collier, eds. (2014), *Teaching Well: Insights for educators in Christian schools*.

ing Lord over all, but if we are not equipped to ensure that our content and pedagogy inside the key learning areas reflects that commitment, then our words and our singing will fall on deaf ears, and our students will have reason to reject our counterfeit and hypocritical faith. Strong language indeed.

While the clear intention of teacher professional development (PD) is that it should impact and shape classroom practice, given what we know it would seem that much of the teacher development entered into by Christian schools is a waste of time and money. Sadly, as I report elsewhere (Edlin 2014), according to Jayaram, Moffit, and Scott (2012), teachers generally find professional development activities to be of value less than 30 percent of the time. An analysis of PD surveys in several countries involving hundreds of teachers led Archibald, Coggshall, Croft, and Goe (2011) to conclude that teachers report that their professional development experiences have left something to be desired or have been a waste of time almost 50 percent of the time.

Richardson (2001, 2003), in her multi-year investigation into professional development in schools, reaches the disturbing conclusion that educators have practiced pre-emptive capitulation in their approach to professional development, investing in activities that they knew beforehand to be barren of results:

> I have been intrigued, concerned, and frustrated by the fact that while we have had research evidence on characteristics of effective staff development programs for some time, these features are not commonly in practice. . . . Most of the staff development that is conducted with K–12 teachers corresponds with the short-term transmission model, with no concern for what is already going on in a particular classroom, school or school district, little opportunity for participants to become involved in the conversation, and no follow-up. We have been engaged in this form of staff development for years, knowing full well that this approach is not particularly successful. (Richardson 2001, 1)

Once or twice a year, Christian school communities in many countries hold major conventions. Schools close, and entire teams of teachers are transported to a central venue where they listen to keynote speakers, attend workshops, visit exhibition booths, win prizes in competitions, and (sometimes) eat lots of junk food. These events may represent a welcome change from the regular pace of classroom activities. They may provide useful opportunities for social interaction. They may be significant public relations activities that remind media and political pundits that Christian schooling is a significant force in the community. They may even identify new ideas and technologies and provide fresh insights and resources for teachers. But in terms of bringing about redirected perspectives and sustained, systematic classroom renewal, often they are an abject failure. They may *open the door* to new ideas, but without evaluation and subsequent school-based, collaborative, vision-enhancing, measured, and ongoing teacher professional learning to practice and embed those new ideas, these PD days are a colossal misdirection of resources, and they demonstrate a failure to understand the dynamics of effective professional development. This is especially true in the contemporary postmodern educational environment where each semester seems to bury teachers in a cognitive overload of curriculum revisions and/or a barrage of new regulations as governments use schools to try and solve all of society's problems. If new vision-based ideas and practices are to gain traction in this noxious context, then professional development that supports them must stand out as being superior in every respect.

In an attempt to rediscover authentic and faithful teacher professional development in the Christian school, and to justify the necessary funding and time commitment that must accompany it, this chapter commenced with a worldview-consistent definition of professional development. Next, it will examine why positioning PD within a worldview context is a key strategy for effectiveness, especially in Christian education. Widely recognized components of effective professional development are then identified, with focus finally shifting to four associated issues that need to be addressed in order to make PD really work. Many Christian schools and teachers fixate on teacher salaries; but we dedicate too small a portion of our educational budgets to professional development to allow that investment to be used ineffectively.

THE SIGNIFICANCE OF POSITIONING PROFESSIONAL DEVELOPMENT WITHIN A WORLDVIEW CONTEXT

Professional development – be it secular, Christian, or humanistic – is a worldview-dependent activity. Guskey opines that, "professional development programs are systematic efforts to bring about change in the classroom practices of teachers, *in their attitudes and beliefs*, and in the learning outcomes of students" (381). Glanzer and Talbert (2005) make a similar point when they conclude that "the connections between teachers' identities and practices are being recognized and explored more as the two elements are increasingly being seen as interdependent and virtually inseparable" (25).

Recognizing the faith or belief commitments that are inherent in teaching provides a crucial catalyst when shaping PD programs that teachers will value and that will lead to changed practices, procedures, and outcomes in the classroom. Underscoring those convictions allows PD to become a precious aid in reviewing and updating classroom practice. This is particularly so for Christians. Closest to the heart of a Christian is the fervent, heartfelt desire to please our Lord and Savior. A sure way to motivate a Christian is to point to patterns and outcomes that honor God and enhance the gospel. Because Christian schooling seeks to celebrate the lordship of Jesus Christ over all of life, PD activities deliberately and authentically framed by this core value should immediately raise these kinds of opportunities above the ordinary and into the realm of the imperative. In other words, always link PD activities to a school's core purpose, and to teachers' most deeply held beliefs.

The Importance
and Shape of Effective Teacher Professional Development
Effective professional development is indispensable to effective pedagogy:

> If there is anything that the research community agrees on, it is this: The right kind of continuous, structured teacher collaboration improves the quality of teaching and pays big, often immediate dividends in student learning and professional morale in virtually any setting. Our experience with schools . . . bears this out unequivocally. The concurrence among researchers and practitioners in support of this conclusion is both stunning and underappreciated. (Schmoker 2005, xii)

Despite its importance, effective professional development has in practice continued to elude teachers, with many reporting that their PD experiences have had little meaning for them or their classrooms (Finn, Swezey, & Warren 2010, 11). At first blush, this seems puzzling. As Richardson (2003, 401) contends, many of the key features of effective PD have been identified for years; namely, that professional development opportunities should:

- be school wide, with clear links to specific, agreed upon school needs and desired student outcomes;
- be long-term (i.e., longitudinal), with review, evaluation, and improvement feedback loops;
- encourage collegiality through the development of Professional Learning Communities (PLCs) so that the "egg-crate" syndrome of individualism and isolation is overcome;
- foster agreement among participants on goals and vision;
- have a supportive and involved administration (e.g., when the

principal introduces a guest consultant and then leaves the room to attend to "other business," his departure is telling staff that this PD isn't really all that important);

- have access to adequate funds for such things as materials, release time, outside speakers, and substitute teachers.

Richardson (2003, 401) goes on to identify three further components of effective PD that have risen to prominence in more recent years. These are identified below, and we are pleased to note that the crucial nature of beliefs is finally receiving some recognition even in secular circles:

- develop buy-in among participants in problem identification, PD design, and evaluation; including annual personal development reviews, goal setting, and professional portfolio development;
- recognize and link into participants' existing beliefs and practices; and
- make use of an outside facilitator/staff developer.

The nine features identified above could be compiled into a checklist that school-based PD coordinators can use to measure the appropriateness of their professional development offerings. Then, at the conclusion of specific professional development segments, teachers could be asked to rank them in each of the nine areas. This could provide vital summative data concerning the activity itself, and formative data to use in determining future PD priorities and practices.

There are four further issues that need to be carefully considered in developing effective professional development opportunities that is modeled on the worldview and reflective model suggested in the above nine components. These four issues are: (1) tapping into core beliefs, which has already been discussed; (2) creating felt need; (3) the problem of non-transferability; and (4) peer collaboration.

1. Tapping into Core Beliefs (see the earlier discussion). The critical perspective of tying PD into core beliefs can make a huge difference in the efficacy of the PD for any teacher, but it has a special poignancy for Christians and can enable their PD involvement to rise above the other activities clamoring for teachers' precious time and gain real traction in the classroom. The following table provides some examples and suggestions for further reading. Note that this is not the biblicistic idea of struggling to find a verse for every thought, but it is the practice of identifying biblical principles or norms for life that are reflected in God's Big Story, and seeking to

apply these faithfully in our own time and place settings. The figure below identifies just a few of these possible linkages.

In the light of the Son – Examples of Tying Professional Development into Christian Teachers' Core Beliefs	
Subject or Developmental Area being explored in a PD Program	**Christian Belief Tie-in**
Peer collaboration	Example of the Trinity & the Body of Christ
Student evaluation	Parable of the talents
Classroom design	Structuring life and the physical environment so that gifts can be shared with others (Ephesians 4:11–13)
Curriculum development process	Focusing on faithful student outcomes (Philippians 1:9–11)
Social studies	Divine, biblically-based norms for what constitutes a family as a basis for evaluating family patterns in different cultures
Relating mathematical concepts to real-world experience	Jesus' frequent use of story, cultural artifacts, and activity-based learning for his disciples
Fostering responsible land use in geography and agriculture	The authority and responsibility given by God to Adam and Eve (Genesis 1, and as reinforced in Psalm 8)
Encouraging the creative arts and inquiry learning	The cultural mandate wherein the Creator God gave humanity the ultimate blessing by making us in his image as creative (and recreative) creatures
Numerous other examples can be deduced from resources such as MacKenzie (1997), Jones (1998), Drexler (2007), Hollaar (nd), and Smith & Smith (2011a).	

Fig. 12.1 Linking PD with Christian Teachers' Core Beliefs

2. Creating a Felt Need. Teachers (and students) tend to learn better and are more open to change when they recognize within themselves the urgency of the learning they are experiencing and the necessity of the changes that are being advocated. This means that PD should be closely related to classroom needs and practices.

Disequilibrium or cognitive dissonance is a useful strategy in creating felt need. Jesus demonstrated the strategic use of disequilibrium when he told Nicodemus that he must be "born again" (John 3:1–4). Nicodemus had to resolve the cognitive dissonance that this term created and, as a product, became a follower of our Lord – which we understand to have been Jesus' intention. When PD highlights a misalignment between a teacher's thinking and practice, then felt need is created and change is more likely. Caine and Caine, who maintain that complex learning is enhanced by challenge, put it very simply: "To induce change, recognize or introduce disequilibrium" (1997a, 247).

3. The Problem of Non-transferability. As we have noted, one-off conferences are useful in raising morale and in opening the door to new ideas, but they have little value in generating sustained change in the classroom. Effective PD must aim at much more than just exposing teachers to good ideas. In fact, Fullan (1999) suggests that it is extremely difficult for us to adopt and implement someone else's idea when it's presented to us in a one-off conference where we are observers to an expert "sage on the stage" presentation. This is because there is much more to any new concept than just the idea being presented. The idea is just the tip of the iceberg. It is underpinned by a whole panoply of thinking over an extended period of time by the presenter; of tacit knowledge; of presuppositional perspectives; and of fertile preconditions, without which the idea will not flourish. The presenter has probably spent years developing, reviewing, and enhancing the ideas s/he is presenting, and at least some of this process needs to be experienced by others in order to be able to make one's own the patterns being demonstrated by the presenter. The change that is necessary in a teacher's belief structures, cognitive processes, and classroom repertoire takes time to percolate, be reflected upon, be discussed with others, and be trialed before it becomes settled as a part of a teacher's revised teaching practice. This is why effective PD must be longitudinal. Good PD that seeks to engender change must be given the time to address and foster these background pre-requisites, and should carefully con-

sider the process, not just the product.

4.   Peer Collaboration. The team of teachers represents one of the most important groups in an educational community – yet often they function in isolation from each other behind closed classroom doors. Lortie (2002, 14) has called this the "egg crate" mentality. The egg crate mentality is not how it could be or should be for teachers within a school community that is seeking to function faithfully according to biblical norms. As Ferriter recalls,

> In the traditional schools where I spent the first 11 years of my career, teachers were isolated. While they might occasionally have shared ideas and talked about what they were doing in their classrooms, there was no formalized expectation that teachers would work together to identify and amplify best practices. Each individual made decisions, over time falling into predictable patterns using strategies with which they were comfortable. . . . Professional learning communities are different. Teachers agree to work together to reflect, collaborating in ways that are often foreign in our profession. The focus of teacher learning is on identifying what works for students. Shared knowledge is valued above all, and teachers have to be willing to open their practice to review and revision. This collaboration leads to growth and change . . . and holds great power to reform what happens in our schools. (2005, 72–3)

It should come as no surprise to educators with a Christian worldview that teachers working collaboratively in professional learning communities (PLCs) not only create the context for a more worthwhile educational experience for all stakeholders, but also find that this interdependent approach resonates deeply with the core of their own faith commitment. The Holy Trinity is the ultimate example of collegiality where the Bible records one God in three parts working in perfect triune trust and harmony. In the same vein, God in his wisdom gave Adam a helpmate – Eve – because it was not good that man be left alone (Genesis 2:18). The Scriptures are full of "one another" declarations that repudiate egg crate individualism and celebrate the Christian commitment to profound community within the group. Probably the most powerful metaphor in the Bible for the redeemed children of God is the concept of the body of Christ, which is used by Paul to celebrate complementarity, dependence upon one another, and concerned involvement in each other's lives – a spiritual PLC!

This bibliocentric focus on, and call to, vulnerable, joyful, countercultural community within the group should give those with a Christian commitment a special impetus in nurturing professional learning communities in schools. The momentum encouraging Christian educators to adopt the PLC model should be overwhelming since it is a paradigm that is grounded in biblical norms. This is an example of encouraging peer collaboration through tapping into core beliefs that was outlined earlier in the chapter.

A potentially potent tool for enhancing worldview-consistent peer collaboration is the critical friend consultancy. This concept is explored in more detail in the next chapter. Suffice it to note here that activities carried out by secular professional bodies can be strategic in assisting the Christian school in providing professional development assistance. However, secular PD activities can never prioritize, fully comprehend, evaluate, or provide authentic direction concerning the school's or a Christian teacher's core beliefs. The expertise of secular consultants can provide useful assistance and guidance, but because these consultants are beholden to non-Christian presuppositions, their input must be filtered through a Christian worldview lens in order to ensure that the assumptions, practices, and outcomes of their programs are faithful to the school's vision and purpose. This requires the re-examination of secular input by educators with a personal, non-dualistic Christian faith that emanates from the same control beliefs that shape the vision and purpose of the Christian school. An ongoing critical friend consultancy can serve this vital purpose very well.

This is an area in which Edserv International, the vehicle that provides the infrastructure for this author's Christian education support ministry, can partner with schools in a strategic and dynamic way.

CONCLUSION

Despite its cost, good professional development is an indispensable component of effective schooling. When schools face difficult financial times, PD is often an early target of the razor gang. As Hargreaves and Fullan (2012) observe, this is a strategic mistake because: "Getting good teaching for all learners requires teachers to be highly committed, thoroughly prepared, *continuously developed*, properly paid, well networked with each other to maximize their own improvement, and able to make effective judgments using all their capabilities and experience" (3, emphasis added).

Nine strategies and four issues concerning effective professional development have been considered in this chapter. Each should be carefully considered in developing a school community's professional development plan. The foundational feature of ensuring that PD resonates with a school's vision and its teachers' worldview commitments is the best way to ensure its strategic relevance and fidelity. Followed up with a generous and quarantined allocation of time and resources, PD can incorporate the other features noted here to create the environment where genuine and sustained change can occur in classroom practice that enables dynamic, faithful pedagogy on the part of the teachers, and works for the benefit of the students as they learn about the world and their places and tasks in it. Ultimately, of course, the evolving classroom practice that emanates from good professional development will align with the Christian school's vision and mission, and thus will overflow to the honor and glory of our heavenly father, which is every Christian teacher's ultimate purpose and service in life (Romans 12:1).

Chapter 13

Maintaining the Vision II:
Critical Friend Consultancy

The Urgency of the Issue

A recurring theme of this book is that schools and their programs are always philosophically committed. This is the nature of schooling, since all educational institutions seek deliberately to shape the hearts and minds of students according to a prescribed set of values and assumptions. The official direction of that commitment is normally revealed in an institution's mission and vision or goal documents – though it is common to find the practiced philosophical direction to be somewhat at variance with the official statement. This alignment challenge is similar to the disconnect that one might find at times between the "official curriculum" of an institution that is recorded in its published statements, and the "operational curriculum" that one might observe in its individual classrooms. The concept was potently illustrated in the movie *Dead Poets Society* in the misalignment between what occurred in Mr. Keating's classroom (played by Robin Williams) on the one hand, and the values and school mission frequently verbalized by the school's headmaster, and writ large on the school's banners, on the other.

The Value of Accreditations and Audits

Quality educational institutions, either by government mandate or by institutional preference, regularly submit their operations to quality control audits or accreditation procedures by professional bodies. These quality control inspections may:

- act as catalysts for self-improvement;
- assess the performance of an institution against standards identified by the evaluating authority;
- provide reassurance for stakeholders such as funding bodies, denominational leaders, and parents that the institutions involved are adhering to specified standards;

- provide a rich vein of publicity material that the institutions concerned can use when portraying in the public arena the quality of what they offer;
- attempt to verify specifically the alignment between an institution's stated mission and vision and its actual practice.

Though many accrediting authorities claim to be objective, in reality this is not the case, because the accreditation concepts of guiding principles, specified standards, and desired outcomes, make objectivity impossible. In the same sense that schools and their programs are always philosophically committed, so too are the aims and directions of the accrediting and registering bodies that investigate the schools. According to their own beliefs and priorities, accrediting bodies espouse deliberate values and views about what makes up quality education, and what aspects of school life are worth reviewing. Thus they bring their own biases to bear on the process. Even the simple notion of quality assurance, which is central to evaluative activities, assumes a particular screen that separates out some qualities from others, thus reflecting non-objective beliefs about the purpose and nature of effective schooling.

Chapter one of this book is devoted in its entirety to the concept of no neutrality. At this juncture, we will only offer a brief reminder of its meaning and importance. As Bartholomew (2000) notes, "To claim to be free of philosophical presuppositions is simply to be unaware of them" (12). Complete objectivity in the educational process cannot exist, as Jerome Bruner (1996) comments:

> Any choice of pedagogical practice implies a conception of the learner and may, in time, be adopted by him or her as the appropriate way of thinking about the learning process. For a choice of pedagogy inevitably communicates a conception of the learning process and the learner. Pedagogy is never innocent. It is a medium that carries its own message. (63)

J. K. A. Smith (2009) puts it simply: "There is no neutral, nonformative education; in short, there is no such thing as a 'secular' education" (26).

IMPLICATIONS OF WORLDVIEW BIAS

The implications of recognizing a worldview bias in accreditation institutions and instruments are profound for the purpose and quality of investigative procedures entered into by educational institutions, particularly with regard to the fifth purpose identified in the list above ("verify the alignment between an institution's stated mission and vision and its actual practice"). If an accrediting authority's own philosophical assumptions erroneously assume, e.g., that schooling is a secular activity (that is, that religious principles and issues such as divine guidance and responsiveness to biblical principles have little place in policy determination, administrative decision-making, classroom practice, or institutional outcomes), then the investigations and reporting by those assessing bodies may give little emphasis to what they view to be private and extracurricular institutional peculiarities. In so doing, at least as far as an avowedly Christian institution is concerned, the a priori reason for the school's existence, and the most fundamental objectives of the education that it offers, may be largely ignored, seen to be peripheral, and not reported upon. Furthermore, since accreditation priorities and procedures greatly influence a school's operational priorities, then the core reasons for a school's existence can be undermined by the very quality control procedures that are meant to verify and enhance them.

It is instructive to note that, as early as the middle of the twentieth century, Professor William Jellema (1958) at Calvin College warned his own institution that Calvin's curricular structure was more responsive to parameters acceptable to secular external accrediting authorities than it was to the biblical concept of wisdom embedded in Calvin's founding vision. Atwood is the president of a small but influential Christian higher education institution in the US, and he supports Jellema's concern by commenting that "As any one close to higher ed knows, *regional* accreditors have been pressing for secular ideological conformity for years . . . shoving 'diversity' and political correctness down institutions' throats" (Atwood 2012). Cornwell and Johnson (1991) voiced a similar concern when they said that groups shaping school activities "can reify a particular way of seeing – their way of seeing – in the institution of core curricula, to the exclusion or deligitimation of others" (164).

Harvey (2004) presented a significant international study of accreditation and its impact to a conference of the European Network for Quality Assurance (ENQA) in 2003. The address was entitled "The Power of Accreditation: Views of Academics." Harvey does not argue against secular agency accreditation. His research involving a review of existing data plus original survey work among over 50 senior academics and tertiary administrator from across Europe, the US, and Australia sees considerable value in the process. However, Harvey also recognizes that "accreditation is neither neutral nor benign" (Harvey 2004, 5). In recognizing how accreditation takes the focus away from "non-accredited" aspects of a university's operations such as its religious core, Harvey (2003) concludes that both standards-based and outcomes-based accreditations have become principally compliance activities that (1) inhibit innovation; (2) are unnecessarily bureaucratic (especially in Europe); (3) cause institutions to prioritize accredited aspects of their programs over non-accredited aspects; (4) are considered by many professors as leading to a "tail wagging the dog" syndrome where accreditation is the tail that determines what universities value and how universities function. Research by Lingard and Sellar (2013) indicates that not only do external audits shape school priorities, but that some institutions can even be accused of "obfuscating the evidence" (634) in order to demonstrate increased levels of compliance with government external audit criteria.

In recent years in the US, as the federal government has sought to exercise more control over accrediting agencies and denominational colleges (Eaton 2013, Ross 2014), the issue of separation of church and state in the political arena makes the avowedly secular-faith nature of regional accreditation activities more pronounced – a philosophical position that is antithetical to the all-encompassing theistic-faith position of Christian institutions.

It bears repeating: an institution's activities cannot neatly be divided into the nonreligious parts (disciplines, buildings, faculty training, etc.) and the religious parts (values, worship sessions, etc.), because a fundamental presupposition of authentic Christian education is that all of learning is shaped by religious beliefs and pre-existing faith commitments. Even non-Christian academics recognize this reality, also when it comes to such supposedly objective areas as quantitative assessment. For example, as was discussed in Chapter Nine, Derewianka and Ehrich make the case that:

> All testing is based on measures which are not "objective", but which are social constructs. That is, these measures have been constructed at a certain point in time as though they represent a valid measure of things. Such measures are really just human interpretations of certain tasks and reflect current preoccupations, priorities, values and knowledge. They have in fact been constructed by human beings who have the personal and social biases of all human beings. (2013, 8)

THE IMPACT OF THIS BIAS ON CHRISTIAN INSTITUTIONS

The impact of this accreditation bias on Christian institutions needs to be considered in more detail. We accept the contention that one of the most important tasks of members of a school's controlling authority (its Board of Governors or Board of Trustees or Council) is to understand and devise appropriate policies that perpetuate and enhance an institution's mission and purpose, and to verify the percolation of that mission and purpose throughout the school's entire life. The following quartet of couplets embodies concepts that have been used in some form in recent years by Christian educational institutions (Covenant College, Dordt College, Kosin University, Cedarville University, Belhaven University, Taylor University, Wheaton College, Regent University, and many others) at all levels and in several countries to express their God-directed mission and purpose. They seek to be:

- Christ-centered,
- academically rigorous,
- biblically-grounded,
- culturally engaging.

Unfortunately, when an accreditation instrument assumes that education is neutral or secular, then at best, only two of these four couplets that fundamentally define Christian schools and colleges are the subject of deep investigation. Such instruments can provide no biblically-responsive, self-improvement motivation, and no reassurance to governing bodies, that the things that matter most in Christian institutions (the celebration of the lordship of Jesus Christ over all decision-making, all relationships and all subjects of the curriculum, and the equipping of students to function as his ambassadors in every aspect of the culture) are actually occurring. These instruments may give useful feedback in areas such as academic rigor, faculty qualifications, and resource adequacy, but even these areas are not neutral, and the Christian institution will be short-changed if evaluative activities related to them also are not considered in the light of a Christian, rather than a secular, frame of reference.

In such situations, slippage begins to occur in the commitment and practice of a Christian institution with regard to its fundamental raison d'être. To be sure, wonderful statements of Christian commitment and direction might still appear in vision and mission documents (as was the case for many years in the now humanistic Harvard University), but just like the difference between official curriculum and operational curriculum already referred to, the dynamic driving force of these core commitments can become lost, and subordinated in reality to alternative, idolatrous presuppositions and practices. As Harry Blamires (1963) alarmingly observed several decades ago, "We are observing the sly process by which the Christian mind de-Christianizes itself without intending to do so" (69). One would hope that an inquisitive visit to campus by empathetic, fellow Christian scholars who understand the catalytic linkages between Christian worldview and every aspect of the academic enterprise would help avoid this unconscious diminution of Christian witness and enterprise in Christian academia.

An Example from the English Literature Curriculum

It is in part because of this situation, where instruments primarily driven by a secular worldview are used to shape self-study and evaluate many Christian institutions, that the following distressing incident was reported to the author in 2012 concerning an avowedly Christian college. The institution had a significant national profile and international reputation as a determined and respected Christian college. It adhered to the four guiding couplets mentioned earlier. It insisted that all faculty members make a Christian profession and admit an allegiance to popular evangelical statements of faith. But herein lay the tragedy: it was regularly evaluated and accredited *only* by agencies that, though held in high regard in the accrediting community, considered good education to be secular and largely independent of religious bias, and subsequently carried out accreditation practices and priorities in the light of that belief.

Accordingly, there was little incentive in the evaluative and self-improvement process to align educational practice with vision and mission. Despite attempts by its CEO to change the situation, the institution's controlling body was unaware of this misalignment, and, thus, though busy will all manner of things, the council members were failing to carry out their most basic responsibility. One distressing example of this was the situation where, in an undergraduate language course, a very senior professor required the pornographic text *Lady Chatterley's Lover* by D. H. Lawrence to be a basic text. Sadly, this professor operated from a dualistic perspective and, though of a cheerful disposition, showed little capacity to think and teach in a biblically discerning manner. The professor made sections from *Lady Chatterley's Lover* required reading not so that it could be critiqued in terms of the worldview of its contents, but (according to students' responses) because the professor deemed the text to be readily available and a good example of quality English literature of its time.

And, as if the novel's commitment to unbiblical relationships was not enough, the Christian professor concerned seemed oblivious to the fact that Lawrence deliberately mocks Christianity and the Bible as a part of his narrative. His book portrays no holy joy in God-given sexuality as is recorded in the Song of Songs. Lawrence writes gleefully about odious extra-marital coitus that defies God and lampoons Scripture. At the risk of being unseemly, but so as to be clear about its import, the following extract is provided as an example from the text. At this point, in his book, Lawrence tells about an illicit sexual encounter between a man and his married lover. Christian readers will see that it is grossly offensive to God and his Word. It includes a deeply malevolent reference to Psalm 24 as Lawrence applies godly terminology to human urges and male and female sexual organs [caution: the following extract contains explicit material; italics have been added by this author to draw attention to certain features]:

> The man looked down in silence at the tense phallos, that did not change. – "Ay!" he said at last, in a little voice. "Ay ma lad! tha're theer right enough. Yi, tha mun rear thy head! Theer on thy own, eh? an' ta'es no count O' nob'dy! Tha ma'es nowt O' me, John Thomas. Art boss? of me? Eh well, tha're more cocky than me, an' tha says less. John Thomas! Dost want her? Dost want my lady Jane? Tha's dipped me in again, tha hast. Ay, an' tha comes up smi-lin'. –Ax 'er then! Ax lady Jane! Say: *Lift up your heads, O ye gates, that the king of glory may come in.* Ay, th' cheek on thee! Cunt, that's what tha're af-ter. Tell lady Jane tha wants cunt. John Thomas, an' th' cunt O' lady Jane!–"
> . . . Sharp soft waves of unspeakable pleasure washed over her as he entered her, and started the curious molten thrilling that spread and spread till she was carried away with the last, blind flush of extremity.

From the perspective of a secular accrediting authority, the use of *Lady Chatterley's Lover* in an undergraduate literature class might be seen as being slightly risqué, but nevertheless as being acceptable since Law-rence's works rank as famous literature. Because of their secular world-view, these evaluators would have little sense of the profane violation that Lawrence's novel represents to Christians who take the Word of God seri-ously for all of life, including in areas such as literature and the wonder-ful gift of sexuality. They would be ignorant of the dynamic gospel im-pact of the Cultural Mandate, the Great Commandment, and the Great Commission on all of life including academia, for the serious Christian. However, if insightful Christian evaluators were critiquing course design and classroom practice in this Christian college's undergraduate Eng-lish Literature program, they surely would have drawn attention to this course's sacrilegious misalignment with the institution's Christian values, and might even have been able to help with suggestions as to alternative texts and worldview-consistent curricula and resources.

An Example from the Science Curriculum

Without going into too much detail, it seems to be widely accepted by many, that science is purely the result of rational inquiry and therefore religion has no place in the science classroom. In fact, secular accreditation reports in some jurisdictions have required Christian institutions to teach as if this were true, ruling that discussions about such things as beliefs and intelligent design must not intrude into the science curriculum.

But this seemingly factual contention really is the reflection of a secular worldview and is a statement of belief. As was noted in Chapter One, some secular scientists, like David Watson, who one of the greatest evolutionary paleontologists of his day, are gracious enough to acknowledge this reality, explaining, e.g., that, "Evolution [is] a theory universally accepted not because it can be proven by logically coherent evidence to be true, but because the only alternative, special creation, is clearly incredible" (Watson 1929, 95). More is said about this issue in chapter one. What we have therefore, in many science classrooms, at the behest of secular evaluating authorities, is unexamined ideological fundamentalism masquerading as neutrality. Unfortunately, because of the power and bias of accrediting and registering bodies, a number of Christian schools have succumbed to this perspective in their science instruction, in direct contravention to their own core mission and values.

What to Do – The Emerging Value of a Critical Friend

The purpose of this discourse so far has not been to disparage secular evaluations and accreditations, or to suggest that there is no value in some exposure to the works of authors such as D. H. Lawrence. Concerning secular accreditation, there is a host of reasons, often related to public perception and being salt in a pagan world, that might justify their value for Christian schools and colleges. In addition, in some jurisdictions regional secular accreditations provide the validation that unlocks institutional access to government and other research grants and allows for student access to lower cost student loans. However, our contention is that they are singularly unable to provide deep insight into a Christian educational institution's vitality concerning its most cherished purposes. For this to occur, another evaluative stream is important – indeed indispensable – to the faithful operation of such bodies: there needs to be an insightful and reflective audit stream where the core mission of the institution is understood and shared by an experienced and competent visitor or team of visitors.

Seerveld made this point well in an address to faculty at Kosin University, a Christian university in South Korea. Seerveld (2014) claimed that the mission of a Christian university should be to "give able men and women the structured time to experience an intergenerational crucible for reflective shalom, so as to generate the wisdom of God abroad"

(50). It is self-evident that accreditation evaluators who do not share a pervasive commitment to Jesus Christ in their personal and professional lives would have little understanding of what Seerveld is saying, let alone be able to evaluate whether or not an institution's practice aligned with this missional perspective. The secular evaluator also would be powerless to provide biblically-founded concepts and paradigms to assist such a school in any realignment between vision and practice that may be called for. In fact, some of the biblically-derived perspectives and practices that we bring to education will seem like foolishness to our non-Christian friends and secular colleagues (1 Corinthians 1:18; 1 Corinthians 3:19). Therefore, at least for some of its regular evaluations, the evaluator in Christian academia, and the evaluative framework that s/he brings to the task, must have a similar worldview and empathetic sense of purpose to that of the institution s/he is evaluating. And this is where the concept of a critical friend becomes dynamic and important.

THE CONCEPT OF A CRITICAL FRIEND

At first appearance, the concept of a critical friend appears to be an oxymoron – the juxtaposition of two opposites. However, deeper reflection shows that genuine friendship involves both unconditional acceptance and constructive guidance, which are the two concepts that lie at the heart of audits and consultancies involving critical friends. As Brighouse and Woods (1999) comment, the critical friend paradigm lies between the extremes of hostile witness and uncritical lover. Because it seeks the best for the institution under examination, it caringly draws attention to both successes and failures, with the deliberate intention of seeking improvement and the best institutional outcome.

Costa and Kallick (1993) draw attention to the essential nature and benefit of the critical friend relationship:

> The role of critical friend has been introduced in many school systems that see themselves as learning organizations and know that learning requires feedback. A critical friend provides such feedback to an individual – a student, a teacher, or an administrator – or a group. A critical friend, as the name suggests, is a trusted person who asks provocative questions, provides data to be examined through another lens, and offers critique of a person's work as a friend. (49)

The critical friend relationship works best in the following circumstances:

- It is a peer relationship. The critical friend consultancy should be a conversation among equals where a two-way interchange of ideas can flow without the strictures of authoritative difference. The critical friend should be an experienced, analytical, reflective, fellow professional and effective communicator. The responsiveness of each party to the other should not be based upon hierarchical difference, but upon mutual respect, regard, and experience.

- It is a trusted relationship. Vulnerability, openness, and trust should exist between the auditor and the auditee. This happens best when the consultancy occurs in a context unconstrained by hidden agendas, such as any pre-existing desire to change school leadership.

- It involves the commitment of time and energy. An effective critical friend consultancy cannot occur overnight or from a distance. It involves preparation, consultation with key stake-holders, a knowledge of the history and structure of the organi-zation, and a multi-stage investigative and consultative process (see below) ranging from general inquiry to action plan and follow-up.

- In the context of this book, it is indispensable that the critical friend have a deep understanding of the mission and objects of the audited institution, allied to a dynamic working knowledge of what this means for the organization's policy formation, cur-riculum design, faculty appointment, organizational structure, political contexts, self-improvement, and stakeholder relation-ships. To be explicit, and this is at the heart of this proposal, a critical friend relationship that drills down to the core mission and desires of an institution, including their application to its practices and outcomes, requires a critical friend who is expe-rienced and committed to the same core fundamental desires and worldview as the institution s/he is reviewing.

Butler, Krelle, Seal, Trafford, Drew, Hargreaves, Walter, and Bond (2011) claim that the concept of a critical friend is "pivotal in identifying needs, facilitating the process of change, and ensuring a seamless inte-gration with the core business, values, and objectives of the school." As scholars at Canterbury Christ Church University in the UK have noted (2011), a critical friend acts as "a sounding board, a new pair of eyes, is slightly removed from your work but understands it, is trusted and has your best interests at heart but can be relied on to be challenging, is a motivator, is reassuring, and models outcomes" (2).

Let us affirm again: genuine informed reflection and evaluation for the purposes of growth in a Christian institution requires the investigation of an institution's beliefs and procedures by a competent professional who shares those beliefs and procedures but who is independent and sufficiently trustworthy to remark candidly upon what s/he observes, and thus make informed recommendations and reports to appropriate stakeholders. These scholars are the best equipped to powerfully assess and nurture an institution's connection between biblically-formed values and mission and their application in every aspect of the life of the school and its outcomes. It is by adopting this pattern, perhaps in addition to more traditional, secular procedures, that the hallowed mission and direction of Christian educational institutions can best be kept alive and flourish.

For this reason, under the chairmanship of Dordt College president emeritus Dr. Carl Zylstra, a group of leading international Christian education professionals who are committed to an all-of-life-encompassing reformational worldview concurred at a select gathering in the United Kingdom in 2011 that priority should be given to the development of a reformed identity educational consultancy along the lines of the critical friend model. Since then, various participants at that conference have moved forward in the draft development and implementation of this concept, leading to an initial critical friend reformed identity consultancy of the nursing program at Ede Christian University in The Netherlands in March 2012.

Furthermore, organizations such as Edserv International and the Squareinchgroup are equipping themselves as avowedly evangelical, Christian educational resource centers to assist in the development of patterns and provision of expert like-minded personnel who can help schools and colleges in implementing critical friend consultancies in their own institutions. Christian institutions interested in assessing institutional faithfulness and alignment, and also having a desire to confirm and revitalize their core missions and visions by receiving a critical friend consultancy, should check with these groups and commence a conversation with them.[1] The reformed identity consultancy derivative of the critical friend consultancy model is a dynamic program that is under ongoing reflection and review. However, some of the key stages of such a consultancy are identified in the following section.

THE CRITICAL FRIEND PROCESS – AN IMPLEMENTATION MODEL

Very little of the professional literature devoted to the concept of critical friends focuses primarily on the issue of evaluating and strengthening the

---

1   At squareinchgroup@gmail.com for the Carl Zylstra's Squareinchgroup; and at aedlin@edservinternational.org for Richard Edlin's Edserv International.

alignment between mission and practice. There appears to be even less scholarly discussion on using a critical friend's consultancy to achieve this in the context of Christian schools and colleges. Nevertheless, the literature available does provide some useful insights that can be applied to our particular usage of this technique. In their book, *The Critical Friend*, Butler, Krelle, Seal, Trafford, Drew, Hargreaves, Walter, and Bond (2011) provide a fluid and helpful diagram that identifies forty-seven actions that may be a part of a critical friend consultation, correlated against important stages and goals of the entire activity (see Figure 13.1).

Figure 13.1. Framework of Critical Friend Consultancy Action

	Clarifying CONCEPTS	Nurturing RELATIONSHIPS	Facilitating PROCESSES
GETTING IN (introducing, establishing)	Identifying goals and clarifying expectations	Building relationships with and amongst leadership and project teams	Negotiating rules and boundaries of responsibility
	Examining the conceptual framework	Building relationships with and amongst school community	Observing school culture and identifying strengths and opportunities
	Clarifying the aims and objectives of the project	Identifying and meeting other potential stakeholders	Building capacity within the school community
	Acknowledging the complexity of school settings	Building trust and establishing credibility across the school community	Clarifying and negotiating a local agreement or memorandum of understanding
GETTING ON WITH IT (activating, planning, implementing)	Developing shared beliefs and understandings	Demonstrating respect for school culture and ethos	Reviewing [school mission and vision], policies, structures, practices and processes
	Promoting flexibility and adaptability	Cultivating and nurturing	Gathering, interpreting and reflecting on local data

Clarifying CONCEPTS	Nurturing RELATIONSHIPS	Facilitating PROCESSES
Understanding competing demands and modeling collaboration	Building and supporting project teams	Sharing knowledge and expertise
Reiterating goals and expectations	Paying attention to staff wellbeing and morale	Fostering critical inquiry
Exploring evidence-based practice	Consulting with the broader community	Developing a strategic plan with targets and timelines
Using local data for insight into local issues	Encouraging enabling and supporting project teams	Building expertise through professional learning
Challenging assumptions and orthodoxies	Acknowledging the interests and recognizing the strengths of different staff	Identifying barriers and enablers to progress
Advocating active reflective practice	Facilitating deep conversations	Resourcing though information, ideas and insights
Promoting change as a dynamic process	Planning for and negotiating departure	Monitoring the progress of strategies and any other changes
Planning for transition and building sustainability	Openly acknowledging and appreciating relationships among the team	Developing ways for maintaining momentum
Identifying unexpected learning	Recognizing contribution of individuals and collective effort	Reviewing processes and evaluating strategies
Celebrating achievement and milestones		Embedding changes into policies, structures, practices, and processes

GETTING OUT (embedding, sustaining)

$\longleftarrow \qquad\qquad\qquad\qquad \longrightarrow$

Figure from Butler, Krelle, Seal, Trafford, Drew, Hargreaves, Walter, & Bond (2011, 33).

A distillation of Butler et al.'s (2011) suggestions and other references points to five key stages in the critical friend's model as a catalyst for missional faithfulness in the Christian school. The stages are broadly linear in nature, but may also apply in a nonlinear sense with feedback loops linking each stage with all others. For the purposes of clarity, the discussion below examines their primary linear character only. The stages, as represented in the following diagram, are:

1. Establishment, Clarification, Orientation, and Self-study;
2. Verification;
3. Report & proposals;
4. Implementation; and
5. Follow-up.

Figure 13.2. Activity Flow for Critical Friend Consultancy as a Catalyst for Missional Faithfulness in Christian Schools.

© R. J. Edlin, 2013

Stage 1. Establishment, Clarification, Orientation, and Self-study
Subsequent to an initial inquiry by a responsible leader from the target organization, the potential critical friend will lay the groundwork for the later stages. The critical friend should ensure that the organization's CEO and controlling body are fully supportive of the process so that, as Du-Four, Eaker, and DuFour (2005) assert, the critical friend process and its

product can assist the administrator in developing habits of mind and practice among faculty members in mission-aligned ways. Ideally, stage one should involve the construction of a formal agreement or contract concerning the consultancy. Questions that will need to be discussed at this stage include the following:

1. What factors caused the institution to consider a critical friend's consultancy in the first place?

2. What are the desired outcomes from the critical review process when the activity has concluded?

3. What qualities is the institution looking for in the philosophical orientation and experience, and in the professional background and experience, of the critical friend?

4. What is the institution's history, specifically with regard to the origin and maintenance of its mission and goal?

5. What initial reflections can the CEO and members of the controlling body make about the goals and desired outcomes of the institution's current stakeholders and current student body compared to those of its founding stakeholders and students?

6. To what degree do the members of the governing body view alignment between mission and practice to be their responsibility or to be a responsibility of the CEO?

7. In what ways are the mission and values currently celebrated and nurtured by and among
   - The controlling authority and CEO?
   - Existing and prospective faculty members in their personal understanding and classroom practice?
   - Parents?
   - Existing and prospective students?

8. What is the proposed timeline for the consultancy?

9. What proposed activities will be included in the consultancy (e.g. document review, stakeholder interviews, classroom observations, nature of the written and oral reports, future strategic planning, faculty professional development sessions, etc.)?

10. What is the agreed cost and fee structure for the consultancy? Activities such as this are resource-intensive and, including the professional services of the critical friend, could cost in a range from between US$800 to US$1500 per day plus expenses for a two-to-six week single-consultant commitment including follow-up, a substantial portion of which might be spent by the critical friend onsite in the institution.

Self-Study – An aspirational expansion across stakeholders of the mission and vision

Prior to the conclusion of this stage, the institution should undertake a significant survey of its stakeholders, and then produce a controlling-body approved, expanded explication of its mission and vision. This self-study will be different from standard accreditation documents. It will not explore existing school practice – that comes later. It will focus upon the *desired* nature of the relationship between the mission and vision statement on the one hand, and the institution's governance, enrollments, teaching, learning, reporting, relationships, promotions, forward planning, general administration, and outcomes on the other.

Remember that this should be an aspirational document that is reflective of the school community's ideals. It is to be hoped that actual practice is aligned with these aspirations, but one of the purposes of the critical friend consultancy is to investigate the extent of that alignment. Examples of statements that fit this model (all available online) that could be consulted to aid in this process include:

- *The Cross and Our Calling*, produced by Redeemer University College (2002);
- Dordt College's *The Educational Framework of Dordt College* (1993);
- The statements on Covenant Christian School's *Why Christian Schools* website;
- Bellevue Christian School's *Educational Confession* (Hagan 2003, 97–105).

As the following diagram illustrates, it will be a primary purpose of the critical friend: (1) to review the accuracy of this aspirational document in the light of the institution's mission and vision; (2) to assess the degree of its actual implementation within the community; and (3) to recommend strategies that will enhance the alignment between aspiration and practice in a manner that reflects and celebrates the mission and vision of the institution.

Fig. 13.3. Stage 1 and 2 Components

Components of Stage 1		One Component of Stage 2
Mission and Vision Identification and Clarification ➡	Aspirational self-study including an expanded, ➡ contemporary understanding of mission and vission	Review by the critical friend of the nature and accuracy of the linkage and alignment between (1) mission and vision; (2) aspirational self-study; and (3) on-the-ground practice

Stage 2. Verification

Now that the ground rules have been confirmed, a clear idea of the actual meaning of the written mission and vision direction of the institution has been developed, and the aspirations of the educational community in the light of the mission and vision ascertained, the time has come for the critical friend to make an extended visit to the institution. The primary purposes of this second stage are to:

1. Establish the degree to which the words and import of the mission and vision statements are actually understood across the school community. As was outlined earlier, this requires the critical friend to be a follower of Jesus Christ; be experienced in educational leadership; possess a strong, biblically-grounded frame of reference; be profoundly cognizant of the all-of-life character of the mission and vision statements; possess an analytical mind; be a clear communicator; be empathetic but provocative; have a dynamic concept of historical continuity; not be distracted but remain outcome-focused; be robustly personable; and, true to the character of a critical friend, be seen to be clearly dedicated to the ultimate increased faithfulness and vitality of the institution s/he is reviewing.

2. Determine how close to reality are the aspirational claims made in the self-study document and its summary, as developed in stage 1.

3. Engage in significant interactions with a sample of members from stakeholder groups through direct means (group or individual interview, classroom observations, interactions with

governing body members, teachers, students, and alumni) and indirect means (such as Likert scale surveys, reading of accreditation documents, and school report cards). Note that it could be written into the contract that secretarial help be made available to the critical friend in order to facilitate this task.

4. Be able to access all records and files that may relate to his/her task, with the assurance that material of a sensitive nature will be treated with appropriate confidentially.

5. Be conducted in a manner such that the essential relational character of education is celebrated. The informing and forming of students that occurs in Christian schools is based as much on the lived-out witness and example of teachers and consultants as it is on the contents of a textbook, computer package, or curriculum. Therefore, understanding the way the faculty comprehend and unpack a Christian worldview in their own disciplines and lives must be an integral aspect of the investigative work of the critical friend.

Stage 3. Report and Proposals

The strongly interactive character of stage 2 now gives way to a mix of interaction and report preparation in stage 3. Much of this stage will still be carried out in an on-campus manner, though some of the report presentation may be finalized from a distance. In the previous stage, the critical friend completed data-gathering, and in this stage s/he now synthesizes this material into a report that includes clear evaluative comments, both of commendation and criticism.

As well as including a review aspect, the report will look to the future, and should contain specific recommendations or proposals concerning further permeation and celebration of the mission and vision throughout the entire institution.

The report should be made available to the board and principal/ administrator, who should jointly determine the timing and extent of its subsequent distribution. The report should be clear, honest, and constructive, demonstrating the unique blend of unconditional support and frank challenge that characterizes the critical friend concept.

It is recognized that a critical friend's report, however empathetic, inevitably will cause some unease within the institution being critiqued. It should challenge the status quo and indicate areas of thinking and operation that need revision. The uncertainty thus created should be explained and treated as a creative force – a motivator for development and improvement. Critical friends and institutional leaders would do well to become familiar with the literature concerning the role of cognitive dissonance or disequilibrium in promoting communal vision, missional alignment, and institutional change in educational settings. Caine and Caine (1997b), Harmon-Jones (1999), Williston (2005), and Carter (2008) are among the many who recognize the strategic role of creating measured disequilibrium in causing growth. Jesus himself (John 3:7) used it when he issued Nicodemus with the challenge that he "must be born again." Edlin (2009a) provides a schema whereby disequilibrium can promote growth and an increased affinity among stakeholders with a Christian institution's core purpose.

Despite its considerable value however, one must be especially careful about using disequilibrium strategies in "shame and honor" or Confucian cultures where harmony and at least surface consensus, allied to an unquestioning acceptance of authority, shape educational patterns. In these contexts, the extensive use of disequilibrium or cognitive dissonance can create an unanticipated volatility.

Stage 4. Implementation

The degree to which the critical friend consultancy extends into developing and implementing an action plan for strategic change will have already been addressed in stage 1 where the parameters for the consultancy were established. However, in line with the best practice blend of summative and formative evaluation in education, and if the critical friend (individual or team) has developed an empathetic rapport with institutional stakeholders, then the external consultant(s) could become strategic catalysts in assisting teachers and others in the realignment of their beliefs and practices with the institution's core mission and values.

This could involve working as a member of the professional learning community teams that could be established at this stage to examine the critical friend report, celebrate its commendations, and work hard on responding to its recommendations so that the mission and vision's Christian worldview priorities continue as the deliberate and overt directing force in the life of the Christian school or college.

This could involve assisting in the revision of core school documents such as policy documents, procedures and agendas for Board meetings, report cards, publicity brochures and websites, recruitment resources and employment contracts, curriculum scope and sequence documents, parent newsletters, student guidance counseling documents, discipline procedures, etc.

At the elementary and high school level, and since parents play a key role in shaping institutional patterns, the critical friend and his/her report may help in the development and delivery of mission-focused parent vision conferences that involve the whole school community.

Stage 5. Follow-up

It is all very well to submit to a critical friend consultation process and peruse the resulting report and recommendations. The positive impact will only reach its constructive potential if specific action plans are developed, trialed, evaluated, and revised again as a part of an ongoing cycle, always actively monitored in the light of the institution's mission and goals or values. As previously discussed, the uncertainty created by the critical friends consultancy, if handled well in a culturally appropriate context, can be channeled in creative directions and can result in a more cohesive community that understands and champions its mission, values, and purpose.

By agreement, the critical friend may or may not be involved in the follow-up stage. It does, however, need someone to coordinate it and give it a sense of overall direction and purpose.

A Word about Alumni

As well as involving teachers, board members, and existing students, this longitudinal activity should also involve alumni. Graduates are the living report cards of an institution. The way they live, work, recreate, and socialize in the world at large some years after graduation could be surveyed and correlated against the mission and vision of the school. If the institution has been true and successful to its gospel mandate of being Christ-centered, academically rigorous, biblically-grounded, and culturally engaging, then this should be obvious in the mindset and lifestyles of a significant number of its graduates. The degree to which they have not conformed to this world but have been transformed by the renewing of their minds in their day-to-day cultural formation will at least partly be a reflection of their education. Our institutions' true heroes should not necessarily be those who have risen to prominence in the public arena, but should be those who, like the faithful in Hebrews 11, have understood their gospel calling and have remained true to it whatever the cost in the areas of life in which God has placed them. We need to celebrate God's goodness in keeping them faithful, encourage them in their witness, hold them up as humble examples, and enlist our faithful alumni's support in maintaining the biblical dynamic of our Christian educational institutions.

Conclusion

External reviews or accreditations can be disruptive, time-consuming, expensive, and unsettling. And yet they are not an optional extra. They are vital to validate what our schools are about and to provide a platform for institutional improvement. They also are philosophically committed. This means that their investigations and reports are only able to be valid within the context of the expertise and worldviews of the investigators.

In many countries, the norm is for school and college evaluations to be conducted just by secular authorities – either government-appointed, or established as a result of the consensus of the professional bodies involved. If it is true, as Seerveld (2014) maintains, that Christian educational institutions "are communal human responses to God's call for educating a younger generation in the wonders of God's world" (39), this paper maintains that any profound institutional review that seeks to validate that missional commitment in the life of a school, or that seeks to provide stakeholders with an informed estimate of how faithful an institution is being to that vision, of necessity requires investigators who personally understand and have experience with that definition and goal.

Secular accreditations are important, and joint secular/Christian accreditations also have their place. But a regular, overtly Christian and foundational investigative procedure is indispensable for the vitality and faithfulness of a Christian educational institution that wants to maintain its godly vigor, its biblical direction, and its purpose of equipping young people to be God's culturally-engaging agents of hope and shalom in the twenty-first century global community. Only then can we know, as Henry Zylstra (1951) affirmed, that our education "will be both education and Christian if it is to justify itself and successfully meet the secular challenge" (39).

This chapter has made the case that a critical friend consultancy provides a way wherein the faith distinctives of a school, which are embodied in its mission and values, can be investigated and strengthened in every aspect of the life of the school. Such an activity can be a part of a school's broader reflective, self-improvement program. It will be not just an event, but more a part of an ongoing process, and so will be both formative and summative in nature. It can help counter an institution's succumbing to the often subtle pressures of a dualistic, secular culture in academia, as well as providing the school with a platform for the intellectual and practical pursuit of godly cultural formation among its administration, faculty, and students in every area of life.

Chapter 14

Christians Teaching
in the Public School

MYTHS AND LEGENDS

Many amusing and memorable incidents occurred during my ten years of teaching in public (i.e., government) schools. I well remember the interchange that took place one day with Anthony, a teaching colleague and friend. Anthony made no claim to be a Christian. He was a high school science teacher, but one of his extra responsibilities was to supervise textbook purchases. As a part of this task, he regularly received sample texts for evaluation from publishers of educational materials. He would give these sample books to faculty members working in the subject area of the book and ask for their input and evaluation. Another one of my colleagues at this school was Geoff. He was a Christian, and he taught a social studies class that included a section on comparative religions.

One day, Anthony received a sample textbook, entitled *Myths and Legends*, to evaluate. As I was working at my desk in the teacher study area, Anthony came into the room to talk to Geoff, whose desk was next to mine. Anthony extracted *Myths and Legends* from the pile that he was carrying, and gave it to Geoff. Anthony, in all seriousness, said to Geoff, "Here Geoff, could you have a look at this book for me? I think that it's something that you might be able to use in your comparative religions course." Being on good terms with both of these two men, I picked up the book and returned it to Anthony with the comment, "Going by its title, Anthony, I would have thought that it was ideal material for your science classes!"

We all laughed as Anthony took my remark in the good-natured spirit in which it was given, but he knew very well what I was suggesting. From our previous discussions, he realized that my comment implied that I considered the approach to science in public schools to be just as bound by a faith commitment to an idea (in science's case it is the idolization of the scientific method) as any other subject. Furthermore, as Anthony knew, I was suggesting yet again that science and its faith assumptions were inadequate of themselves (in fact, often myths and legends) in their attempts to explain reality and prepare young people to learn about God's world and their places and tasks in it.

A PRINCIPLE FROM THE STORY OF NAAMAN AND ELISHA:
THE CHRISTIAN TEACHER HAS A KEY ROLE IN PUBLIC SCHOOLING

The argument of this book has been that all schools are religious institutions and that Christians are called to act in a distinctively Christian manner in their practice of education. However, this contention raises difficulties for the Christian teacher in the public school. Current law in most Western countries allows non-Christian secular humanist teachers in the public school to encourage children to adopt their secular religious way of looking at life but denies the Christian teacher from doing the same.

This situation where the Christian teacher is denied the opportunity of coherently presenting the truth has led some Christians to question the whole issue of whether or not Christian teachers should be involved in public schools at all. The argument is that if the Christian is forced to hide his faith, then how can he function? Is this restriction not obliging him to deny the lordship of Christ over creation and thus teach from the spiritual enemy's point of view? I have been in conversations where Christians have argued this position and where they have exhorted Christian teachers to remove themselves completely from the disobedient arena of public education.

There does seem to be a logic to this position – until it is examined in the light of Scripture. When looking at the involvement of the Christian in the public school, we should consider the issue in the context of the principle found in the story of Naaman and Elisha in 2 Kings 5:1–19. Let us review the story. In the section preceding the verses quoted below, God had used Elisha to direct heathen Naaman to the Jordan River where God miraculously cured this great Syrian military leader and confidant of the Syrian king of his leprosy.

> Then Naaman and all his attendants went back to the man of God. He stood before him and said, "Now I know that there is no God in all the world except in Israel. So please accept a gift from your servant."

> The prophet answered, "As surely as the LORD lives, whom I serve, I will not accept a thing." And even though Naaman urged him, he refused. (2 Kings 5:15–16)

Here, Naaman is declaring his faith in the God of Israel. In modern terms, we would say that he had become a Christian. But he had a real dilemma. Listen to what it was and to the counsel that God's prophet gave to him.

> "If you will not," said Naaman, "please let me, your servant, be given as much earth as a pair of mules can carry, for your servant will never again make burnt offerings and sacrifices to any other god but the LORD. But may the LORD forgive your servant for this one thing: When my master enters the temple of Rimmon to bow down and he is leaning on my arm and I have to bow there also – when I bow down in the temple of Rimmon, may the LORD forgive your servant for this." (2 Kings 5: 17–18)

Naaman's problem was that now that he was a believer, what was he to do when he had to accompany his heathen king into temples dedicated to a false god and appear to join with him in worship? Obviously, Naaman's heart would not now be in it. What would Elisha counsel him to do? We wait with bated breath for the prophet's answer. Probably, we think, he would tell Naaman that he had no place going to this evil temple and that, despite the cost, he should get out of there. That is not Elisha's answer, however. What he said was at the same time very simple and very profound: "Go in peace [Shalom]," Elisha said (2 Kings 5:19).

The word *shalom* is pregnant with meaning. It does not just mean "Do not worry about it." Rather, it involves the whole concept of the rich peace, security, and blessing of the almighty God going with you. Naaman had already declared that he would never worship his king's god again. The "bowing" mentioned by Naaman in verse three obviously was not to be interpreted as an act of worship but perhaps as a ceremonial act in the presence of the Syrian king. Elisha understood this. Elisha's response indicated to Naaman that his responsibility to the Syrian king was God-given and that even if it involved him in entering the very temples of false gods, God's peace and presence would go with him! What a radical and dynamic answer.

Elisha's answer also is full of meaning for the Christian teacher in the state school that, like the Syrian king's temple, is dedicated to the service of a false god. If this is where the Lord has clearly led the Christian teacher to work, then God's blessing and peace can go with him. In fact, as we shall see later, the responsibility of the Christian teacher to be salt and light in the state school has exciting and dynamic implications, for the state school is important missionary territory. It's also important to establish that the schooling debate for Christian teachers is not a competition between those who serve in Christian faith schools and those who serve in government secular faith schools. There is a great opportunity here for godly, brotherly love to flourish and for both sets of educators, as members of the body of Christ, to assist, encourage, and pray for each other in their respective callings.

We must be sure to differentiate between the involvement of the Christian teacher in the non-Christian state school and the involvement of the Christian child who is a student there. Some might suggest that this argument for the presence of Christian teachers in government secular schools should apply to Christian children as well. If the Christian teacher can operate as a missionary for God's cause there, then should not Christian children be there as well doing the same thing? Nicole Baker Fulgham, e.g., from the Expectations Project, in her worthy drive to encourage Christians to consider the issue of social justice in education, suggests that it would be "fabulous" for Christian families to send their children to the local public school (Beaty, 2012).

To address this question aright, we have to consider why teachers and students go to school. There is a different answer to this question for each group. The primary purpose for Christian *teachers* being at the state school is to teach. As much as possible, as with any teacher there, they should do this in a way that is consistent with what they believe to be right and true but, ambiguously in the state school context, like Naaman, the teacher also is contractually bound to work within the secular vision and mission of the school.

On the other hand, the primary purpose for the presence of the *child* in the school is to learn. They are not there as pawns to achieve otherwise noble purposes. As a Christian, the child should be salt and light before his classmates, but he is not sent to school primarily to proselytize. If his main function is to learn, then his parents should be careful to immerse him in a learning environment that is consistent with, not antithetical to, their own religious view of life, the world, and learning.

Perhaps the example of sending a child to the dentist will help to illustrate the point. What do we expect of our children when we send them to the dentist? Do we expect them to interrupt the dentist while he is treating them and explain the four spiritual laws? Of course not. We hope they will display Christian manners and their trust in the Lord as and when the situation arises. However, they have been sent to the dentist for dental treatment, not to turn the situation into an evangelistic soapbox. The same is true of school. We hope that our Christian children will be

to say No to all others. And indeed any act of selection is simultaneously an act of exclusion. . . . It underscores the fact that the [public] school system in its entirety is a kind of closed forum and not a genuine marketplace of ideas at all. (1987, 4)

Ultimately, plurality of belief in democratic societies demands a diversity of equally-accessible schooling options – as has been successfully implemented in schooling systems in the Netherlands for decades.

POSSIBILITIES FOR CHRISTIAN WITNESS IN THE PUBLIC SCHOOL

Stronks & Stronks (1999) repeat Schwartz's model (1998) in identifying three categories of Christians involved in teaching in public schools. They are: (1) agents for good who completely mask their Christian commitment from public view; (2) agent provocateurs who admit to their Christian faith and seek to provide Christian insights whenever allowed to do so; and (3) truth-seekers who ask worldview questions in the staffroom and classroom as they encourage peers and pupils to be aware of worldview presuppositions and deliberately shape their lives in the light of them. Often, Christians teaching in public schools may find themselves moving between these three positions. For example, a sympathetic principal or school board might allow the gentle recognition of Christianity in some school districts (such as talking about "Christmas," or explaining the meaning of Easter, or talking about intelligent design in the science classroom, e.g.), whereas in other more rigidly secularized settings these activities might not be allowed.

In many settings however, I think there is a fourth (and sadly, perhaps the most common) alternative that might be added to Schwartz's schema. We might call this the "schizophrenic" category. This describes the teacher who is happy for colleagues and students to know that he is a Christian, and whose private piety is unquestioned, but who tries (unsuccessfully) to divide life between a personal spiritual dimension and a public non-spiritual dimension. For him, school activities fall into the latter category, thus releasing him to structure and teach the curriculum in the same secularized manner as his dedicated non-Christian colleagues. He keeps his faith where he mistakenly thinks it belongs – on the Sunday and personal devotions shelf – quarantining it from his professional and cultural life. This is the dualist approach, often reinforced from the pulpit and in seminaries, that has so infected and disempowered the broader Christian church today.

The perspective of this chapter is that there is no such thing as a sacred/secular divide, and that Christians should always be prayerfully and pro-actively seeking the welfare of the place where God has put them (Jeremiah 29:7). This means that pattern (3) above should be the prevailing pattern for Christians teaching in public schools, tempered with epistemic humility and, when the opportunity is permitted, a quiet acknowledgement of the lordship of Christ over everything. This is similar to what Brian Hill elsewhere (2003, 2005) has called "committed impartiality," and which Fennema describes as a combination of silent witness and legally sanctioned verbal witness. As Fennema comments, particularly where there is a sympathetic community, "it may be surprising how much of God's truth can be taught within a public school system" (2008, 4).

The table below, and the explanatory notes that follow, indicate some of the ways that Christian teachers in government schools can fulfill their calling to be witnesses to the truth, to be harbingers of grace as they seek to live out the image of God in a secular environment (Graham 2011).

POSSIBILITIES FOR CHRISTIAN WITNESS IN THE PUBLIC SCHOOL
The Christian teaching in the public school is God's witness in a temple dedicated to false Gods.
The Christian teaching in the public school should expose competing worldviews and the religious foundations of knowledge.
The Christian teaching in the public school should winsomely challenge colleagues with the "Why?" question.
The Christian teaching in the public school should be an influence for good.
The Christian teaching in the public school should be especially supportive of Christian children.

Fig 14.1 Possibilities for Christian witness in the public (i.e., government) school

THE CHRISTIAN TEACHING IN THE PUBLIC SCHOOL IS GOD'S WITNESS IN A TEMPLE DEDICATED TO FALSE GODS

The first way a Christian teacher can be salt and light in the public school is by being God's witness in that place. She can pray regularly for her students and for the administration over her, as well as model a Christian lifestyle. This means that:

- She will be concerned for all of her students and colleagues as individuals and not just view them as all the same.
- She will make herself vulnerable to her students, as Christ was to us. Her students' fears, joys, and sorrows will become her

fears, joys, and sorrows as she ministers to her children.

- Her service in the school will not be just within the classroom but will extend to the lunchroom, the bus line, the playground, and in consultation with the parents. Guy Doud noted that some of the best teaching he ever did was in the lunchroom and on the playground.

- Her motivation will not be her paycheck, but she will be teaching to the best of her ability in order to please her Heavenly Father.

- She will give her students the freedom to make decisions and will hold them accountable for the consequences of those decisions.

- She will strive to exhibit Christ-like patterns in all her relationships, exhibiting personal piety, hard work, concern for others, and a collaborative spirit.

Some of these qualities are shared with teachers who are committed to other faiths. At times, as with inquiry learning, it will be the radical constructivists who share our perspective. At other times, such as the valuing that we place on meaningful memorization, we will find our allies in the content-centered, positivist camp. These co-belligerencies are valuable and help build bridges, and Christians teaching in public schools should heartily embrace them. Indeed, at times expressing one's motivation in commonly accepted language such as "the common good," "social justice," or "moral purpose" is viewed by some as an imperative to the survivability of Christians in the public arena. Nevertheless, situational alliances do not create worldview commonality. There is a legitimate and important exclusivity to the Christian faith, a "sacred particularity," as Mouw (2011) reminds us, which is to be held sacrosanct in a clear but humble way. It is only the Christian who has the primary aim that students will learn about the world and their places and tasks in it in a way that points to the discerning hope that comes through knowing and serving Jesus Christ. It truly has been said that in today's post-Christian world, Christians will be the only Bible that most people will ever read. This is true in the public school as well.

THE CHRISTIAN TEACHING IN THE PUBLIC SCHOOL SHOULD EXPOSE COMPETING WORLDVIEWS AND THE RELIGIOUS FOUNDATIONS OF KNOWLEDGE

Educators of any merit generally recognize the religious foundation of teaching. It is logically impossible to teach all of the knowledge that exists in any subject area. Every teacher *selects* what to teach and how to teach it. This selection is guided by the curriculum and is based upon what teachers *believe* to be important about the world and the subject matter with which they are dealing. In other words, this selection process is based upon teachers' worldviews or religious convictions.

For example, I well remember studying the English Civil War on two different occasions during my student days. On the first occasion, at high school, we learned about the English Civil War as if it was primarily a political event, with dates, places, and all sorts of fascinating political intrigue. God was not relevant to the issue, as it was then taught. The second time that I was taught this period of history, while at university, it was taught as a social event. The professor was a socialist who followed his personal religious persuasion and selected his information to highlight the socio-economic climate and working-class struggle of the period. Again, God was irrelevant.

As I consider the English Civil War today, I can only marvel at how revisionist and distorted were both perspectives that I was being taught by my teachers. More than anything else, this was a war about fundamental religious beliefs and their application to individual freedom and liberty. An authentic history would highlight the fact that many of the central players were more motivated by key religious questions, as they affected our relationship to God, authority structures, and society, than they were by anything else. How can one read the writings of Oliver Cromwell, John Owen, and other contemporary Puritans and come to any other conclusion? The answer, of course, is that if we do not believe that a relationship to God is of any importance, then our own biased personal religious perspective forces us to screen out anything to do with such a relationship, and so we attempt to present the events of that time to our students in purely secular worldview terms. Accordingly, the fundamental religious perspective of Oliver Cromwell and the Puritans was considered irrelevant by my non-Christian professors in earlier years.

The example of the English Civil War is a simple reminder of the axiom that all teachers appear to teach according to what they believe – that is, in accordance with their own religious prejudices. The example of *Dead Poets Society*, as considered elsewhere in this book, highlights this reality. It is a task of the Christian teacher in the public school to unmask this idolatry. The interchange with Anthony at the beginning of this chapter records just one little example of this activity.

George Counts' reflection, cited in Chapter One, is worth repeating here. Counts was one of the great American educators and writers of the twentieth century. He was not a Christian, but the wisdom of some of his writings on education is a profound and timely confirmation that all educators always spin education in a particular worldview direction. He wrote:

> The formulation of an educational program is a . . . long series of complex creative acts . . . embracing analysis, selection, and synthesis. It likewise involves the affirmation of values and the framing of both individual and social purposes. Inevitably, education conveys to the young responses to the most profound questions of life – questions of truth and falsehood, of beauty and ugliness, of good and evil. These affirmations may be expressed in what an education fails to do as well as in what it does, in what it rejects as well as in what it adopts. (Counts 1952, 36)

> To a very large degree, education was actually the handmaiden or midwife of catastrophe. . . . [Education] may serve any cause. . . . [I]t may serve tyranny as well as freedom, ignorance as well as enlightenment, falsehood as well as truth, war as well as peace, death as well as life. It may lead men and women to think they are free even as it rivets upon them the chains of bondage. (28–29)

THE CHRISTIAN TEACHING IN THE PUBLIC SCHOOL SHOULD WINSOMELY CHALLENGE COLLEAGUES WITH THE "WHY?" QUESTION

Whenever possible, the Christian teacher in the secular school should be challenging his or her colleagues to acknowledge and review their own religious commitments, which determine the way that they view reality and govern the way that they teach in their classrooms. The topics considered in this book, such as student assessment or curriculum development, are structured in the public school as a consequence of the commitment to non-Christian religious principles. By frequently asking "Why?" questions and by seeking to point to the presuppositions that undergird these educational structures, the Christian teacher can expose this idolatry and indicate its inadequacies. After all, if the Christian position is the only true and adequate explanation of reality, then the Christian teacher can learn how to use the beliefs of those committed to a non-Christian perspective to show the impotence of their position. This is what Paul did in Acts 17:27–30 when he quoted the writings of non-Christian philosophers right back at their supporters when he was challenging them about the inadequacy of their view of the world and presenting them with the Christian alternative. This was a strong motivator in much of the writing of Francis Schaeffer. We should learn from and follow the patterns set by these heroes of the faith.

Discipline in schools is an interesting example of how the Christian can challenge the status quo and suggest positive remedial action for the current increasingly violent nature of schools. I should preface my remarks with the comment that, although in all my years as director of Carachipampa Christian School corporal punishment was only used once, I, nevertheless, believe that it is biblically sanctioned and can be appropriate in the right cultural and educational circumstances where it is legally permissible.

Corporal punishment was deemed to be politically incorrect by the educational establishment a few years ago and thus has been progressively outlawed from public schools in many countries. It was claimed that corporal punishment gave official sanction to child abuse and that it needed to be abolished if the general rise of violence in society was to be reduced.

In many western nations, several years have now gone by since the abolition of corporal punishment in public schools, and Christian teachers in that arena should be holding their anti-corporal punishment colleagues accountable. The abolition of corporal punishment in schools has not lead to a reduction in concern about youth violence, as deeply disturbing incidents such as schoolyard bullying or the Columbine High School massacre in 1999 remind us. Instead, according to the material published by the Australian Psychological Society, "many indicators reveal youth violence has been rising . . . in recent decades" (Toumbourou et al. 2013, 1). The original argument given for abolishing the paddle, the strap, or the cane has not been sustained. Although the re-introduction of judicious corporal punishment may not be possible, misconceptions about it being the origin of society's ills can now be refuted.

The broader issue of behavior modification is another example of an area in which the Christian teacher in the public school can challenge existing patterns and offer real alternatives. Much of the general discipline in public education is concerned primarily with humanistic, Skinnerian behavior modification. Eliminating disruptive behavior is not a bad thing and, particularly with smaller children whose reasoning capacities are not yet well-developed, it can be an appropriate technique. However, ultimately, the Christian point of view is that unless the *heart* is affected, it is unlikely that there will never be long-term change for good in the behavior of a wayward student, and the opportunity to address core heart issues in the child also will be lost if we focus purely on behavior. For all its horrific themes and visual images, Kubrick's movie *Clockwork Orange* makes the point very clearly, of the barrenness of mere behavior modification.

This might provide an opportunity for Christian teachers to point to acceptable discipline alternatives that are consistent with one's own faith position, and also consistent with the beliefs of many of one's secular colleagues and school jurisdictions. For example, one could draw attention to the benefits of a restorative justice approach in the classroom. Some applications of this approach incorrectly portray it as an alternative to personal accountability, and Wolterstorff (2007) is right when he reminds us that a true understanding of the person is only ultimately possible on the basis of a biblical view of humanity and God's big story of creation, fall, redemption, and fulfillment. Nevertheless, the precious balance of accountability, justice, and mercy in the context of community that underlies effective restorative justice patterns (Marshall 2012), when consistent with the overall atmosphere cultivated in the classroom by the teacher, is a dynamic, biblically authentic pattern that Christian teachers can advocate in every educational context.

Accompanied by a Christ-like concern for the wellbeing of others, the process of challenging the myth of religious neutrality, and highlighting worldview foundations, should apply in the faculty lounge in the public school and also in the classroom. In her own room, the Christian teacher can be encouraging all students to identify the religious foundations that underpin what they believe about the world. In science, asking "Why?" questions about issues such as conservation will achieve this goal. Why conserve the environment? Conservation, like any issue, is deeply rooted in religious commitment. Humanist answers to this question will lead to a concept of pantheism or scarcity of resources. These essentially are religious views behind some people's (and textbooks') support of conservation. This should be pointed out in the classroom. For the Christian, both of these reasons are inadequate. Our primary reason for conservation has to do with good stewardship and accountability to the Creator! Although the secular religious commitment in the public school will restrict Christian teaching there from being able to express this in any detailed manner, the Christian teacher should at least be able to acknowledge it and encourage the students to examine their own beliefs for the attitudes that they hold on this issue. If she is challenged on the matter, she might be able to seek the support of humanists on the faculty because what she is doing is "values clarification," one of those buzz-word ideas that is politically acceptable today in the educational vanguard.

We should hold our humanist colleagues in education accountable to their own set of beliefs. We should enlist their support in changing the *status quo* so that in academia, Christians are granted once again the same liberty to express their beliefs and philosophical assumptions that seems to have been granted to everyone else! For example, secular academia claims to champion tolerance, and we should hold secular educators accountable to this claim, castigating them for their inconsistency when they restrict such "tolerance" just to those who are politically correct!

In civics classes, a review of what students believe about the separation of church and state, and why we believe this, will again highlight religious convictions. There is no neutrality. In social studies, when we are teaching about the family with all the different types of families – including the homosexual family – that are often accepted today, "Why?" questions will lead us to the issue of what society in general, and our students in particular, really believe about the definition of a family. Is the family a cultural, man-made institution, or is it more than that? What is the basis for our belief? How adequate is it? What are the implications of our belief about the family when we consider the future of society? These are all good and important questions to raise. If the proponents of "values clarification" and "outcome-based" education are being consistent, they should be very comfortable with, and supportive of, this approach.

In none of these discussions will the Christian teacher in the public school have the freedom to cogently and systematically explain her Christian worldview basis for belief about the family or conservation or the origins of the English Civil War. In today's world, this constraint on free speech is one of the key differences between the entrenched, public secular humanist school system and a Christian school, where the latter encourages exploration and analysis of all viewpoints in the light of the school's acknowledged commitment to God's Word. Nevertheless, in that same spirit of free thought and individual expression that our humanist friends claim to espouse, the Christian teacher in the public school should at least claim the right to ask questions that expose the religious foundations of what is believed and taught. In classical humanist terms, to allow anything less is to deny the children the right to choose which set of "equally valid" beliefs that they will adopt as they construct their own views of the world and their places and tasks in it.

THE CHRISTIAN TEACHING IN THE PUBLIC SCHOOL
SHOULD BE AN INFLUENCE FOR GOOD

One aspect of what occurs when Christians take seriously the calling to be the salt of the earth is that those around them, both Christians and non-Christians alike, benefit. We see this happening throughout history both within the Bible and outside of it. When Joseph, for example, exercised his role responsibly as Pharaoh's most senior advisor, the whole nation benefited from his food conservation program when the famine came. When William Wilberforce and his Christian friends strove to abolish horrible child labor and slavery, the whole nation benefited once again. The amazing example of the godly philanthropy and care for employees displayed by the Cadbury brothers in nineteenth century industrial England also is worthy of being studied in schools, as is the sacrificial story of young Christians involved in the White Rose group in Nazi Germany during World War II.

There are myriads of examples where Christians in public office and in leadership in industry, medicine, and science often have acted in a manner that benefits Christians and non-Christians alike. The Christian educator, by being salt and light in the secular public school, can have the same effect. For example, the current pattern of assessment and accountability in many public school systems across the Western world is doing a disservice to children in schools because it is based upon a false view of self-esteem and often fails to recognize individual effort. Grade inflation means that often a majority of students receive an "A" grade for their work lest we damage their self-image by awarding a lesser grade. Chapter Nine explores the issue of student evaluation and assessment in the Christian school in more detail, and many of the reflections there can also be of value in the public school context, particularly with regard to valuing effort (see Jesus' parable of the talents) and encouraging the flourishing of a broader curriculum, and not just one determined and shaped by the jobs market. The Christian teacher has a salt-and-light capacity to be involved in the forums that chart educational policy and direction in public schools in order to identify inadequacies such as these and to suggest constructive alternatives.

A further example is in the area of labor-management relations. In many countries, relationships between educational controlling authorities such as boards or departments of education and public schoolteachers, as represented by their trade unions, have become polarized and divisive. Where Christians have risen to prominence on one side or other of this divide, without compromising their beliefs, they have been able to bring healing, reconciliation, and a cooperative spirit back to these relationships as well as real wisdom to their deliberations.

Christians will not always be loved by those with whom they work because the values and perspectives by which they function are often contrary and offensive to those around them. Yet, we are told that the beauty and attractiveness of the Lord Jesus Christ to the despairing and lost should be evident in us. When this is so, there will be a grace, meekness, and comeliness about the Christian that often will make him or her irresistible to the world. That is partly why, at first, the crowds welcomed Jesus into Jerusalem. That is why Guy Doud was selected as Teacher of the Year in the US. The lifestyle example of the Christian teacher in the public school has been the vehicle used by God many times to draw people into a personal relationship with Jesus Christ. In all senses, the effective Christian teacher, as salt and light, is the very best hope for public education.

THE CHRISTIAN TEACHING IN THE PUBLIC SCHOOL SHOULD BE ESPECIALLY SUPPORTIVE OF CHRISTIAN CHILDREN

Not all Christian children, or children from Christian homes, are going to be attending Christian schools any time soon. Although the numbers of Christian schools in many countries are rapidly rising, there are still far too few of them. In addition, as long as some Christian schools continue to fund their programs from a poorly understood concept of tuition, they will remain elitist and many youngsters will be excluded from their ranks because their parents cannot afford to pay the fees. Perhaps setting tuition as a proportion of income would be a more biblically authentic alternative – Luke 12:48. Furthermore, there are still many Christian parents who do not send their children to Christian schools because they aren't convinced of the biblical mandate for such institutions (though, hopefully, as they prayerfully consider books such as this one, they may be open to revisiting the issue).

All of these factors mean that there are millions of Christian children in schools right now who daily spend five hours or more inside the portals of public schools dedicated to the glory of a foreign god. These children need refuge, and they need Christian role models of fine, vibrant Christian teachers who are living as effective, Christian teachers in this same environment. Many public schools allow Christian groups to meet on their premises during breaks or after school. Christian teachers must be involved in using these opportunities. As Paul did with his friends in Thessalonica, they should use these times to encourage and comfort the Christians in their care. In his day-to-day activities in the class, in the gymnasium, in the lunchroom and on the sports field, the Christian teacher must prayerfully be conscious of the fact that his actions and words are being used as patterns to follow by the young Christians around him.

This is not to say that the Christian teacher can be accused of being any less attentive to his or her non-Christian students. In fact, s/he is the very best hope for them as well, both for successful living in the present world, and in pointing them to the Creator of the world and his Son in whom there is to be found fulfilled life now and for eternity.

CONCLUSION

The calling to be a Christian teacher, in either the Christian school or the public school, is a noble and responsible calling. The purpose of this book has been to focus on the nature and task of the Christian school, but the invaluable contribution and ministry of the Christian teacher in the public school must not be overlooked (Parker 2012). The Christian community in general needs constantly to be uplifting to the Lord in prayer Christians in both these two arenas. In a very real sense, they hold the future in their hands. Is it possible to teach in the same holistic, Christian way in the public school as it is in many Christian schools? Is it possible to "look at everything in the light of the Son?" No, it is not. Might the Christian who teaches in the public school suffer special persecution and a concern about a loss of identity? Yes she might (Anna 2008). Can a Christian's lifestyle example and love for her pupils and colleagues point students and faculty to Christ? Absolutely. May God bless and encourage all teachers in this unique and blessed discipling task. May God also encourage the children in their care so that they too will come to know him personally and then realize the exciting challenge of celebrating his Lordship over all that they learn about God's world and all that they do in the lives that lie before them.

STUDY GUIDE

Study Guide Questions

Responses to earlier editions confirm that *The Cause of Christian Education* is widely used in ways that reflect its threefold intended purpose:

- to be used by teachers in schools and universities to give focus and direction to faculty-wide professional development that reflects a Christian worldview;
- to be used in Christian universities as a set text in undergraduate and graduate teacher education courses – we are also aware that some Christian schools use the introductory chapters with their year 12 [i.e., grade 12] students; and
- to be used as an invitation to biblical thinking by Christian parents, grandparents, pastors, and concerned others who are grappling with the issue of what is involved in making discerning schooling choices for children. For example, a number of Christian schools use the book in parent vision conferences, and/or give the book to every newly-enrolled family, to help parents become committed to the vision and direction of the school.

In all of these contexts, many have suggested a chapter-specific study guide to assist in individual reflection and/or community discussion. Accordingly, starting with the 3rd edition, now updated for the 4th edition, a study guide has been included as well.

Typically, each chapter's study guide consists of three types of questions. The first two or three questions assist in the review of the chapter's content; a couple encourage readers to extend their thinking on important issues; and then there are some designed to provoke readers to apply the concepts in their own settings and Christian walk.

Sometimes, a special question is added, pointing to other resources that readers may wish to explore to further develop their thinking, understanding, and application of the concepts covered in that chapter. Also, don't forget to sift through the List of References at the end of the book for other resources that the author has found worthy of note.

Chapter 1. No Neutrality, and Why It Matters

1. What do we mean when we say that schooling is never neutral? What is the link between this statement and Paul's declaration in Acts 17:27? Why is such a claim important in education for citizens of any faith perspective?

2. Define secularism, and explain why it is a religious position.

3. Provide three examples to illustrate Counts' claims that schooling "involves the affirmation of values and the framing of both individual and social purposes," and that "Education may serve any cause. . . . It may serve tyranny as well as freedom, ignorance as well as enlightenment, falsehood as well as truth, war as well as peace, death as well as life. It may lead men and women to think they are free even as it rivets upon them the chains of bondage."

4. Have someone read aloud the extract from John Dunphy. Like most non-Christian, postmodern educators, he rejects the notion of educational neutrality. What does Dunphy consider to be the real battle in educational thinking today, and how does this concur with the reflections of Richard Rorty? Discuss the implications of this perspective.

5. What is the difference between science and scientism?

6. In the text, Dr. Arthur Jones from the UK, referring to science teaching, is quoted as saying "That which is presented as a scientific conclusion based upon the rational analysis of empirical evidence, may, largely and primarily, flow from (unrecognized) philosophical and religious commitments." Put Dr. Jones' comments in your own words, and discuss the validity and significance of his claim.

7. At what point, and why, did the young people in the Forum interview lose their biblical anchor?

8. Why do you think that the myth of neutrality in education is so pervasive – especially among Christians?

9. If you were teaching a social studies class of 14-year old children, how could you use the Survivors Role Play (1) in a Christian school, and (2) in a secular school?

Chapter 2. Foundations of Christian Schooling

1. Why is the placement of furniture in a classroom described as a religious activity?

2. Explain what the second characteristic of Christian schooling (*Christian education does not spend all its time looking at the Son; instead, it looks at the world and our places and tasks in it in the light that the Son provides*) might mean for a science classroom, or for a mathematics classroom (hint: check out Mrs. Alhborn's thoughts in Appendix Two).

3. This chapter gives two definitions of schooling. Discuss the similarities and differences between them. The two definitions are:
    a. Schools are social institutions in which children learn about the world and their places and tasks in it.
    b. Schooling from a Christian perspective involves challenging children with the celebration of the lordship of Christ over all of creation.

4. Borrow a church hymnal and look at the wonderful old hymn *How Great Thou Art.*
    a. Why does the author of this book suggest in Chapter One that we might want to add a few verses to that hymn?
    b. Try writing a couple of verses to reflect what Edlin is talking about.

5. Read the quotation from Redeemer University College (2007) recorded in the book and repeated below.

    We are called to witness to the victory of Jesus Christ in our whole lives, to make known the good news of God's renewed reign over creation (1 Corinthians 10:31; Colossians 3:17). Since the kingly authority of our risen Lord extends to the whole world, the mission of his people is equally comprehensive: [to teach our children about the world and their places and tasks in it in such a way that we] embody the rule of Christ over marriage and family, business and politics, art and athletics, [science and history,] leisure and scholarship (Matthew 28:18–30; Romans 12). Thus the work of [the Christian school] must be understood as a part of the call of God to [learn about and] proclaim [the all-of-creation breadth of] the good news of his kingdom; [a kingdom with the exclusive, reconciling cross of Jesus Christ at the centre;] a kingdom which is in our own day both present and yet-to-come.

    a. Is there a similar commitment in your own school's vision statement?
    b. If not, why not?
    c. If so, how is the school implementing it first in the community within the school and second in the community around the school?

    d.   How is the school equipping children to exercise a missional salt-and-light responsibility after they leave the school? How is this evaluated?

6.   How do you suggest a Christian school could use the *White Rose* story?

7.   How do you nurture your school community in the perspective outlined in this chapter? It is important that not only teachers but prospective parents, existing parents, and board members as well all are continually discussing and celebrating this biblical perspective. Two suggestions:

    a.   Purchase a copy of *The Cause of Christian Education*, give it to every prospective enrolling family, ask the parents to read chapters one and two before they come for their initial interview, and then use it as a foundation for the discussion about what the school is like and what it seeks to achieve.

    b.   A board's primary role is to protect and enhance the vision and life of the school. Therefore board members must be able to speak passionately about why the school exists and what it is seeking to achieve. To help equip them for this task, provide a copy of *The Cause of Christian Education* for every board member. Covenant together to read one chapter between each board meeting, appoint a facilitator, and then start each board meeting with a discussion of the set chapter and its relevant questions. (You might like to have pre-allocated questions to various members at the conclusion of the previous meeting.)

    c.   Look at the List of References at the end of the book. Consider purchasing some of the books listed there for your faculty professional library – or even giving one to each teacher and board member as a Christmas gift.

Chapter 3. Why We Think the Way We Do

1.   What did Harry Blamires mean when he said that, "We are observing the sly process by which the Christian mind de-Christianizes itself without intending to do so?" Can you think of examples from your own Christian walk that illustrate what Blamires is trying to say?

2.   Using whatever sources are available to you, see how many of the philosophers depicted by Raphael in "The School of Athens" you can actually identify.

3.   Draw a picture of the situation described by Plato in "The Cave."

4. How has Platonic thinking infected (1) the Christian church; and (2) education?

5. The chapter does not attempt to explore the entire historical record of factors that have shaped contemporary Western thought. Discuss the impact of the Renaissance and the Enlightenment on why we think the way we do today. Explain why, for Christians, the word "Enlightenment" is an unfortunate term to use to describe that period of human intellectual development.

6. If it is inadequate to say that to "know" consists solely of comprehending it in the world of the mind, what is a biblically faithful understanding of what it means to know something? Support your answer from Scripture. What implications does this have for a Christian approach to schooling?

7. Read Appendix Three, Mark Greene's essay. What implications does this have for the Christian church in general, and for education in particular?

Chapter 4. The Place of the Bible in the Christian School

1. What are the three categories of usage of the Bible in the Christian school?

2. Take the extract from Douglas Wilson in Chapter 4 and rephrase it in your own words.

3. How is a proper view of the place of the Bible in the Christian school different from "proof-texting"?

4. Why is it inadequate to describe the Bible as merely a filter that helps us to screen out what is wrong?

5. What might be an example of the permeative function of the Bible?
    a. In a business studies class;
    b. In a Christian school's human relationships and development program;
    c. In a Christian school's attitude to student sports and cultural interaction with surrounding secular and Muslim schools.

6. What biblical insight underlies the decision of some Christian schools not to describe their extension program as a "Gifted and Talented Program"? Do you agree with this?

7. Discuss the issue regarding which translation of the Bible should be used in the Christian school.

8. Suppose your school was offered sufficient funds by a benefactor to give every student, as they reach the fifth grade, a hard copy of the NIV Study Bible, OR to give every fifth grade student an iPad. Which option would you choose, and why?

9. What biblical principle underlies the decision of some Christian schools to retain whole class photos rather than using an IT-created montage of individual photos? Do you agree with this?

Chapter 5. The Integrity and Vision of the Christian School

1. What is the difference between a creed and a confession? Which term best describes the foundational expression of belief in the Christian school?

2. Describe the importance of the church pulpit and the Christian teacher-training college in assisting in developing and maintaining a vibrant and applied mission and purpose in the Christian school.

3. What is Jay E. Adam's concern, and is it true of your school? What can be done in school communities (i.e., among teachers, parents, and board members) to correct the situation?

4. How can regular external audits by avowedly Christian groups assist in the task of strengthening a Christian school's vision and purpose? Can this be achieved just as effectively through a secular accreditation or audit? Why / why not?

5. Compare the sample Confession in this chapter with the one in a Christian school with which you are familiar. Identify and account for similarities and differences.

6. Several issues are listed in the chapter under the heading "Maintaining the Integrity and Vision." They are repeated below. Imagine that the sample Confession recorded in this chapter is that one that guides your particular school. What responses would you give to each of the issues, and how has the sample Confession guided you in developing these responses. The issues are:
   a. The suggestion from a parent at the PTA meeting that the school should focus upon being a college preparatory school.
   b. Is it appropriate for the church pastor to be the chairman of the school board?
   c. Shouldn't we offer manual arts courses just to the less academically able students, since they will go to a community/technical college, whereas the brighter ones will go on to university?

d. What is wrong with saying that Christian need not worry when an outside publishing company determines the curriculum, as long as it is a Christian company?

e. Why do we pay different salaries to high school teachers from those paid to equivalently qualified grade school teachers?

f. Should we or should we not have uniforms for students?

g. What is a good balance between Christian and non-Christian children in our student population?

h. What is our basis for giving prizes at the end of the year?

i. Why do some people object to outcomes-based education?

j. What is the significance of the notion (Smith 2009) that we are involved in "forming" as much as "informing" in the Christian school?

k. What should our report cards look like?

l. Should we require all children to attend chapel?

m. What should we do when some parents and teachers object to a "spiritual emphasis" week?

n. Should we accept government financial aid – isn't this "accepting money from Caesar"?

7. What specific steps can your school take to enhance an understanding and application of your vision and mission?

a. Among parents;

b. On the school Board or Council;

c. Among students;

d. In the broader Christian community;

e. In the broader non-Christian community;

f. Among Department of Education officials;

g. Among local politicians.

Chapter 6. Responsibilities and Relationships in the Christian School

1. State the United Nations declaration, signed by most Western countries, that affirms parental responsibility in education.

2. Explain the concept of "office," and describe why and how it is important in the context of Christian schooling.

3. Identify and resolve:

a. two ways in which the profession of teaching can disenfranchise parents.

b. two ways in which parents can fail to recognize the calling and authority of teachers.

4. What is the role of a school's vision or mission statement in resolving conflict between teachers and parents?

5. If Christian day-schools and Christian home schooling both can be authentic expressions of parental responsibility in education, discuss the relationship that should exist between the Christian day school and Christian homeschoolers.

6. Consider the following scenario. You are the principal/administrator of McDonaldtown Christian School. A class of eight year olds is intending to present a choreographed version of "Shine Jesus Shine" during the Christmas Concert. A small group of concerned parents has made an appointment to meet with you to discuss this issue. Some of them have children in the class and this group feels that dancing is not an appropriate activity for a Christian school. What are the issues involved in this question, and how could it be resolved?

7. From the list under "Parents," identify what you consider to be the most important point in that list. How would you make it become a part of the practice of your school community?

8. From the list under "Teachers," identify what you consider to be the most important point in that list. How would you make it become a part of the practice of your school community?

9. How might the appointment of a School Commissioner work, and how could it make membership of school boards more attractive to busy parents?

10. How should Christians inform the political community about their views on education?

11. Review the concept of "office" as explored in this chapter. If a particular Christian school is linked to a specific local church, what office should or should not that church's pastor hold in the life of the school?

Chapter 7. The Teacher as Mentor and Role Model

1. What evidence exists to suggest that teachers are important mentors and role models?

2. What caution is issued in the chapter about viewing Jesus primarily as a role model?

3. What is meant by the term "inferential teaching"?

4. Explain what David Smith means when he says, as is quoted in this chapter, that, "Education is not primarily a heady project concerned with providing *information*; rather, education is most fundamentally a matter of *formation*, a task of shaping and creating a certain kind of people." What implications does this have for the teacher as mentor and role model?

5. How has ICT re-shaped mentoring and role modeling in today's classrooms?

6. Have each person in your group recount a personal story from their schooling experience. How many of these stories highlighted the impact of a teacher as mentor?

7. How does Jesus' parable in Luke 6 weave together the content and relationship aspects of teaching? How is this similar to the comments of Paul in 1 Thessalonians 2:6–12?

8. What implications for teacher training and selection are involved in the concept of the teacher as mentor?

9. How does your Christian school balance encouraging students to celebrate the lordship of Christ over all of creation on the one hand with allowing for the God-given freedom to defect from this commitment on the other?

10. Explain the relationship between imagination/creativity and being made in God's image. What is the impact of this relationship for Christian school classrooms?

Chapter 8. Foundations for Curriculum in the Christian School

1. Which examples are given in this chapter that support the contention that curriculum is based upon the religious commitments and assumptions of its developers?

2. What is "perspective consciousness" (Hanvey), and why is it important in curriculum design?

3. Although the Christian school is God-centered rather than content-centered or child-centered, it nevertheless is very concerned about its students. How do we apply Jesus' example of contextualized instruction in our schools? Give specific examples.

4. Edlin's Curriculum Development Flow Chart is exemplified in the area of social studies. How would you apply it to another subject of your choice?

5. How would you respond to the Christian teacher who comments "Don't bother me with all this theory. I'm too busy for all that. Just give me step-by-step instructions about how to teach Christianly that I can straightforwardly implement in my classroom."

6. Describe a Christian approach to teaching grammar.

7. Discuss *either* Ahlborn's approach to teaching mathematics (see Appendix Two) *or* Ireland's comments concerning literature.

Chapter 9. Student Evaluation and Assessment in the Christian School

1. Read Matthew 25:14–30. What implications does this parable have for student evaluation?

2. What is meant by the term interactive evaluation?

3. How can we avoid assigning worth to children on the basis of their in-class performance?

4. Reread the discussion about Mary and Martha from John 11:1–44 and the ensuing comments in this chapter. What implications do these readings have for how we cope with individual differences in our classrooms (consider learning styles, cultural differences, personality types, socioeconomic backgrounds, life experience, and religious commitment)?

5. Examine a (blank) student report card and evaluate it in the light of the principles in this chapter.

6. How does your school ensure consistency in student evaluation among teachers?

7. What lessons can we learn from Asian educational patterns?

8. Review key ideas concerning evaluation and assessment suggested by Alfie Kohn (www.alfiekohn.org), and critique them from a Christian worldview perspective. For example, how does his statement that "the reward is in the task" unwittingly reflect a biblical view of the value of creation and work?

Chapter 10. Resource Selection in the Christian School

1. List three reasons people often give for selecting resources in a Christian school and identify where these reasons can be inadequate.

2. What should be the connection between a school's vision or mission statement and its resource selection process?

3. Can a Democrat be a Christian? Explain your answer.

4. With regard to resource selection, what is the relevance of Wilson's comment that, "The Christian educator's job is not to require the students to spend all their time gazing at the sun. Rather, we want them to examine everything else in the light the sun provides."

5. Explore the following statement in the context of resource selection in the Christian school: "We should be doing just what the Bible does – looking at the world the way it really is in all its fallenness and promise, and giving our students God's handles to live with confidence in it."

6. What questions need to be addressed in the Christian school when it is devising its Information and Communication Technology (ICT) policy?

7. Review the "Snake Alley" example.
   a. Would you have invited the senior students to join the teachers in witnessing in Snake Alley? Why/Why not?
   b. What are some of the "snake alleys" surrounding your school community?
   c. As you train students to be God's responsive salt-and-light disciples, how does your school help students relate to the "snake alleys" around it?

Chapter 11. Christians in Higher Education

1. What observations would you make about the openness and effectiveness of the witness of Christian professors in secular universities with regard to their academic disciplines? Is Craig right when, as quoted in this chapter, he maintains that, "Most Christian scholars today fail to make a meaningful contribution because either they are intimidated by the hostile [secular university] environment or they have uncritically accepted a post-Enlightenment liberalism where their faith at best provides only qualitative enrichment to secular ideas while ignoring the contradiction between the two."

2. Do you agree with Edlin's comments about tenure? Why/why not?

3. The table below is taken from the chapter, and identifies 10 touchstones Edlin claims should be important for an academic seeking to be true to his Christian faith in his profession. Conduct an informal personal and institutional self-assessment in each area, identifying action steps that need to be taken where necessary.

Faithful Scholarship in the Christian University	
1. Know God	6. Practice sacrificial, biblical mentoring with your students
2. Develop a clear and united sense of vision and purpose	7. Implement a regular "critical friend" consultancy in your university"
3. Learn how to teach	8. Understand the philosophical foundations of your discipline
4. Abandon tenure as your goal in academic life	9. Restore radicalism, vision, and hope to the university
5. Highlight "No neutrality," recognizing that God alone sustains your discipline	10. Work hard at Christian scholarship

4. What articulation has your institution produced concerning the relationship between the Christian faith, the life of the mind, and the task of the Christian university? How widespread across administration, faculty, and student body is an awareness and practice of this articulation?

Chapter 12. Maintaining the Vision I: Teacher Professional Development

1. There are nine features plus four core issues that are identified in this chapter that together make for effective teacher professional development. Construct a table of these thirteen characteristics and conduct an ongoing survey where teachers are asked to evaluate every PD activity in which they are involved, identifying how many of the thirteen characteristics were present in each activity. Review and discuss the results, and use them to help identify the best PD activities in which to invest in the future.

2. How highly does your school value ongoing professional development?

    a. Is there a widely understood PD prioritization (i.e., which areas of school life are we going to give priority access to PD for this semester) that includes input from faculty?

    b. What percentage of the school budget is allocated and quarantined for PD – if it is less than 1 percent of expenditure, then it is too low?

    c. Do teachers have the opportunity and requirement to report on PD activities to the rest of the staff?

d. Is there any long-term follow-up on PD activities to ensure that they have influenced classroom patterns and student outcomes?

e. Is PD linked to each teacher's personal professional development plan?

3. Explain Fullan's concern about non-transferability, and suggest mechanisms that can be used to overcome this challenge.

4. When did you last make an extended visit to another teacher's classroom with the express purpose of collaborating together in a professional development goal? When did you last have a peer make an extended visit to your classroom for this purpose?

Chapter 13. Maintaining the Vision II: Critical Friend Consultancy

1. Identify implications for institutional audits of Smith's claim that there is no such thing as a "secular" education.

2. How does the movie *Dead Poets Society* illustrate the misalignment between institutional mission and purpose on the one hand and classroom practice on the other? What are potential implications of this misalignment in the movie in particular, and in schools in general?

3. How does the story of *Lady Chatterley's Lover* illustrate the misalignment between a Christian institution's mission and vision on the one hand, and the practice in its undergraduate English instruction program on the other? What would you do in this situation?

4. What is the meaning of the term "tail wagging the dog" when it comes to institutional audits? Do you agree or disagree? Explain your answer.

5. Why might it be argued that not only are secular accreditation authorities philosophically unable to validate a Christian institution's mission and values, but that we do not want them to attempt such a task?

6. How might a critical friend consultancy work in your school?

7. What role might disequilibrium play in the efficacy of a critical friend consultancy?

Chapter 14. Christians Teaching in Public Schools

1. Why is it important to have Christian teachers in government schools?

2. Why does the chapter differentiate between the involvement of the Christian teacher in the government school and the presence of Christian students there?

3. How can Christian teachers in government schools teach biology in a way that is both consistent with curriculum requirements and yet is also an authentic expression of their worldview?

4. The following comment is by Brian Hill as he wrestles with the best way forward concerning the nurturing of values for a Christian who takes up a teaching position in a public or state school. As is mentioned in Chapter 14, Hill settles on a position that he calls "committed impartiality." What is Hill actually suggesting, and discuss with colleagues your response to his model, particularly in the light of the usual intention that state education authorities have of requiring that public schools maintain a secular religious stance.

    > The way ahead is what I have called "committed impartiality." Here's how it works. The teacher [who is a Christian] does not try to exclude values discussion, but encourages it. In doing so, students are helped to understand the different world views and value traditions prominent in the life of their communities, and to learn skills of empathy and evaluation which will enable them to make wise personal choices. . . . At the same time, we don't, as teachers, pretend that we are neutral umpires without any value preferences of our own. That would be a misleading model to present to our students. We need to be seen as committed citizens; committed at the least to the values spelled out in the agreed values framework of the school. It is therefore acceptable and helpful to give an honest answer to the typical student question, "But what do *you* think?" at some stage in our teaching. (Hill 2003, 2–3)

5. Carefully examine the activities in the list below in which Christian teachers in a government school could be involved. Which of these activities would you consider to be appropriate? Why/Why not?
    a. Identifying and exposing the worldview presuppositions in the curriculum by constantly asking the "why?" questions.
    b. Actively proselytizing students in the classroom.
    c. Actively proselytizing students on an individual basis outside the classroom.

d. Bringing an overtly Christian perspective to faculty-wide discussions on the curriculum development process.

e. Starting class with public prayer.

f. Evangelizing colleagues in the staffroom during lunchtime.

g. Displaying a Bible (prominently?) on the teacher's bookshelf in the classroom.

h. Giving extra special attention and concern to Christian students in their care.

i. Publically challenging the sinful actions of other staff.

j. Explaining the "real meaning" of Christmas or Easter at the appropriate time of the year.

k. Determining to be the hardest working teacher in the school whatever the cost.

l. Offering a prayer on behalf of the school at school functions.

m. Holding up the Christian students as a special example to others.

6. Suggest strategies that can increase cooperation and mutual support among Christian educators in government and independent schools.

Appendix One

A Letter to my Daughter
on her Graduation from Christian High School

by Glenn Oeland, May 2012[1]

Dear Katie,

Graduation Day at last! Congratulations! Bravo! Well done! Hurrah! I'm so filled with love and pride right now I'm about to burst. Many times I've come into your room late at night and found you toiling over algebraic equations, or struggling to plumb the depths of Dostoyevsky, or trying to think clearly and Christianly about the big questions of life. I commend you, my dear daughter, for being faithful to your calling as a student these past twelve years. You've been a delight to me – well, most days – and I am deeply grateful to God for entrusting so precious a gift to so imperfect a parent.

As you celebrate this joyous day, I urge you not to forget all the people who built this Christian school – from the visionaries who founded it in borrowed rooms at church, to the teachers who've given you high standards of study, character, and service.

I think of dear Mrs. B, your first grade teacher. What a saint she was, radiating the love and joy of Jesus despite being crammed into a tiny classroom with 16 squirming six-year-olds. Remember her ancient guitar, the one she called Old Glory? I'm sure you'll never forget her lilting arrangement of 2 Timothy 3:16 – "All scripture is God-breathed and is useful for teaching, rebuking, correcting and training in righteousness. . . ." That chorus sounded the keynote for your education.

Then I remember fourth grade, and the move from the church to the beautiful new campus. Remember walking into those bright, spacious classrooms for the first time? What a gift it has been to me – and to you, I hope – to see what God can do when his people join together in faith, prayer, sacrificial giving, and hard work.

But enough about me. What are *you* feeling on this momentous day? Elation, I'm sure. And relief. And maybe a twinge of anxiety about your future. I've shared this with you before, but it's worth repeating,

1 Reprinted with permission from www.cardus.ca/comment/article/3251/

even memorizing: "'For I know the plans I have for you,' declares the Lord, 'plans to prosper you and not to harm you, plans to give you a hope and a future'" (Jeremiah 29:11). This is not, of course, the kind of *carte blanche* promise the prosperity preachers make it out to be, but I think you already understand that. For twelve years you've been learning how to accurately understand and faithfully apply the Bible. You know religious snake oil when you smell it.

I suspect you also know the main reason your mother and I decided to enroll you in Christian school in the first place: to give you the opportunity to gain a life-transforming grasp of God's truth. When the body of Christ is ignorant about the Bible, it becomes feeble, and no Christian can grow up strong in the faith without a diet rich in Holy Scripture. We also wanted you to come to see all God's world through the lens of God's word, and to understand the relevance of Jesus Christ to every subject of study.

Most importantly, perhaps, we wanted you to learn the truth about you: that you are not the unplanned product of a purposeless universe, the random offspring of time, chance, and biochemistry. You are instead the masterwork of the majestic Creator, the Divine Artist whose mind and imagination infuses the cosmos with meaning, order, and beauty. As an image bearer of this infinite, personal God, you have intrinsic and incalculable worth, regardless of your GPA, your earning power, or your place in the social pecking order.

And never forget that the truest measure of your worth is the price Christ paid to liberate you from sin and selfishness and bring you into a love relationship with your Heavenly Father. The King of Glory has paid your ransom and adopted you into his royal family. As you launch out into the next season of life, I pray that you will hold fast to your true identity and destiny.

I don't have to remind you, of course, that some of the students and professors you'll meet at college will urge you to grow up and stop clinging to comforting myths and infantile fairy tales. Hasn't science shown us the cold, hard facts about the universe and our place in it? Likewise, the story of Christianity, as you'll hear it told in some classes, is a shameful chapter of Western history that brought us the Dark Ages, the Crusades, and the Salem witch trials.

Faced with such assaults on their beliefs – combined with the temptations of the campus hook-up culture – it's little wonder that the faith of many young Christians flatlines during their college years. I don't pretend that you will be immune to the challenges and temptations, but at least you'll not be going into battle without essential training and equipment. Your study of apologetics, church history, and ethics has informed and fortified your faith, and I know you will be a strong ally in the struggle to win hearts and minds.

I'm aware that Christian school hasn't always been a church picnic, and there have been times when you've missed some of the perks of public school. And we've all felt the financial pinch – *squeeze* might be the better term – of paying private school tuition. The trip to Disney we never made, the pets we couldn't afford, the bigger house, the newer car – I hope you'll remember these as good things we gave up to gain something much better.

And if, in God's good providence, you eventually marry and become a mother, please remember this as well: *All* education is religious education. Place a child in an environment where God is never mentioned, and what will she conclude? Either God isn't real, or he's irrelevant. Either way, the conclusion is that he can safely be ignored.

But you know, and I know, that ignoring God has profound consequences for how we think, feel, and act. The opposite is true as well. I'm greatly heartened by research showing that graduates of Protestant Christian schools are more generous with their time and money, are less likely to divorce, are more committed to their churches and communities, and possess greater hope and optimism about the future than alumni of other schools. By my accounting, that's a good return on investment.

And I can't help but note in passing that the good accrues not only to Christian school graduates, their families, and their churches, but also to society at large. As you learned when you studied our country's history, democracy depends on the cultivation of virtuous citizens. Christian schools are making an important contribution to that cause.

Finally, I'll remind you that to whom much is given, much is expected. Jesus calls us to be salt and light, preventing moral decay and dispelling the darkness in the world. So how can you make a difference at this stage of your life?

You might start by reading *Do Hard Things* by Alex and Brett Harris. It's full of inspiring stories of young people who are taking action to change their corners of the world. Christian thinkers such as James Davison Hunter and Andy Crouch have also written probing books examining how Christians can best bring their influence to bear for the greater good of society. While only the most gifted among us will ascend to the commanding heights of culture, we can all pursue our callings with passion and excellence. We can learn to write and speak clearly and persuasively. We can spend less of our time and energy chasing empty prosperity and devote more of our lives and resources pursuing the Kingdom. We can ask Christ to give us his vision of the good life and replace our misguided measures of blessedness with his beatitudes.

Katie, my dear Katie, I know you want to live a life pleasing to Christ your Lord. I am so grateful for all that God has done, and is doing, and will do, in and through you. And so I'll sign off for now with St. Paul's words to the Christ-followers in Philippi: "being confident of this, that he who began a good work in you will carry it on to completion until the day of Christ Jesus."

I love you.

Dad

Appendix Two

A Christian Philosophy of Mathematics

Patricia L Ahlborn[1]
Head of Mathematics
Delaware County Christian School
Newtown Square, Pennsylvania

INTRODUCTION

What can be Christian or non-Christian about mathematics? Two plus two equals four in all classrooms, both Christian and non-Christian. Cornelius Van Til (201) refers to mathematics education as the "black beast of Christian instruction" due to its oft-misunderstood role in the Christian school. He asserts that most people, both Christian and non-Christian, see mathematics as neutral to religion. Christian parents want mathematics taught by a Christian teacher only so that a Christian atmosphere will surround their children. They do not expect that the instruction will be fundamentally any different than it would be in a public school. Rarely are there any calls to censor mathematics textbooks because seldom is there any obviously objectionable material in even the newest mathematics books – unless one disapproves of word problems where *Mr.* Jones bakes a cake and *Mrs.* Jones drives a truck. Nowhere in the textbooks is there any statement of philosophy about mathematics. Page after page has "just the facts."

During the last forty years of mathematics education, however, we have seen much change. In the early sixties we saw traditional mathematics instruction give way to *new math*. In the seventies the back-to-basics movement took over. In the eighties mathematics educators were championing the *problem-solving* approach. In the nineties it became *standards based learning*. These changes alone ought to suggest that there is more to mathematics education than "just the facts."

The challenge for the Christian teacher is to develop a biblical phi-

---

1 This paper (2001) represents my personal philosophy for teaching mathematics in a Christian school. It has been developed over 25 years of teaching mathematics in Christian schools and reading a variety of Christian scholars. A complete bibliography follows the text. PLAHLBORN@gmail.com

losophy by which to anchor his own teaching and to respond to the changes surrounding him. That is not to say that having developed such a philosophy, he will be able to teach without change. We are all sinners living in a fallen world. Just as we are continually on a path of sanctification that reforms our personal lives, so we should also be on a path of sanctification that reforms our professional lives, bringing both our curriculum and teaching methods into greater conformity with the will of God. As Van Til so humbly expressed, "Ah how large a portion of the grace of God it requires to be a teacher of the children of the covenant!"(202).

NATURE AND ORIGIN OF MATHEMATICS

Let us begin our discussion of the nature of mathematics by discussing what mathematics is and what it is not. To give an admittedly simplistic definition, mathematics is the study of the numerical and spatial aspects of the universe (Van Brummelen 4). The concept of number is used to count and the concept of space is used to measure. "How much?" "How many?" "How long?" are all questions for which mathematics has the answer.

Where did these concepts originate? When we think of God's creation, we often think only of physical objects – trees, animals, people, mountains, and oceans. Too easily, we overlook the many nonphysical aspects of these objects. Objects are hot or cold because God created temperature. Objects have a beginning and an end because God created time. Similarly, objects are countable and measurable because God created the many parts of the universe with a numerical and spatial aspect. We can count because God made objects in a discrete, countable form. We can measure because God made objects to take up measurable space.

Over the years, as man observed God's creation, he began to see more of the patterns built into it. An early observation would have been of two rocks, two trees, two horses – from which man abstracted the concept of twoness. When man selected a name for this concept he began to form the discipline of mathematics (Van Brummelen 5–6). In different regions of the world different names were chosen for the concept of twoness and different symbols were chosen for writing it, but the concept was universal. The concept was of God.

Once man had given names to different numbers, the arithmetic operations followed naturally. At some point man would have observed that putting three sheep in a pen with two sheep would always make a total of five sheep, and from this he abstracted the concept of addition. Mathematics is then the discovery and organization of patterns that are built into the creation. All the arithmetic facts, all the geometric formulas, and all the algebraic properties that we teach are merely abstractions of God-created patterns in the universe.

Though all will agree that man has had an important role in the development of mathematics, the Christian and the non-Christian will disagree on the nature of that role. To the non-Christian, man's role is that of originator, or creator. John Dewey, a prominent humanist of the twentieth century, said that humans do not discover truth, they make it (Greene 16). That philosophy is apparent in the title of a college textbook from the early seventies titled *Mathematics: The man-made universe*. If one starts with the assumption that there is no God, then the only reasonable conclusion is that man is the creator of mathematics. This secularist view tends to glorify man and his intellect. It considers man able, with his reason, to make sense out of the world and control his future (BJU 8)

The Christian, however, recognizes God as the ultimate creator of all things both physical and nonphysical. God is the source of knowledge, and the mind of man is but a gift from God (BJU 8). Consequently, the Christian defines man's role as that of discoverer and developer of mathematics, rather than of ultimate creator. Indeed, since mathematics has been an important tool for understanding and thereby ruling over the earth, the development of mathematics can be viewed as an act of man's obedience to the cultural mandate: "Be fruitful and increase in number; fill the earth and subdue it. Rule over the fish in the sea and the birds in the sky and over every living creature that moves on the ground" (Genesis 1:28).

And after all of the labor of discovering and writing out principles of mathematics, how do we know that these same principles will still hold true tomorrow? The non-Christian has no answer for such a question. He can only hope for the best. The Christian knows that the same God who created the universe sustains it day in and day out. Harro W. Van Brummelen summed it up well in his statement, "Laws of mathematics are dependable not because man with his logical reasoning created a fool proof system, but because God in His constant faithfulness embedded these unchangeable laws in His creation" (Steensma 139).

In order to use mathematics properly we must also understand its limitations. Mathematics is a tool for describing the creation, not the creator. Every attempt to define a mathematical model for the triune God fails in some respect. When we count each personage of the Godhead as a discrete entity, we have three gods. When we illustrate God as a whole divided into three parts, each personage becomes only one-third god. These are both very unsatisfactory models! This should not surprise the thoughtful Christian, as the creator is never bound by his creation. "Can you fathom the mysteries of God? Can you probe the limits of the Almighty?" (Job 11:7).

Even within the creation, mathematics is only one aspect of a multi-faceted universe. It *does* help us describe such aspects as temperature, position, and time. It *does not* help us describe such aspects as emotion, beauty, and commitment. We can never reduce all of creation to a mathematical model. Interestingly enough there have been attempts to do just that, which we will discuss in the next section.

SECULAR INFLUENCES ON TWENTIETH CENTURY MATHEMATICS EDUCATION

Two non-Christian philosophies that have influenced mathematics education in the United States in the second half of the twentieth century are Logicism and Formalism. Though their influence in the present day curriculum is waning, they are of particular importance to me because they were most prominent during the sixties when I was in high school and college. My education from Kindergarten through graduate school was entirely from secular institutions. Hence, my own personal training in mathematics was permeated by these philosophies and it carried over heavily to my early years of teaching. Only by studying these philosophies in the light of Scripture have I been able to move my own teaching along that path of sanctification.

Logicism is the mathematical outworking of rationalism, which traces its roots back to the Enlightenment of the eighteenth century. It holds that reason, or analytic thought, is the source of all truth (Van Brummelen 10–11). The logicist begins with a small number of truths that are recognized to be unverifiable, but are accepted on faith. From these assumptions is logically deduced all of mathematics and all of accepted reality (Greene 6). Thus, human reason, rather than Biblical revelation, becomes the source of all knowledge.

In mathematics, these unverifiable truths originally centered on real numbers. In the late nineteenth century through the work of Giuseppi Peano and Georg Cantor the foundations of mathematics were pushed down to the more basic system of natural numbers. In the early twentieth century Ernst Zermelo put forth a set of axioms, which has come to be called set theory, for describing the system of natural numbers in terms of concepts of sets. Bertrand Russell and Alfred Whitehead took it one step further in their *Principia Mathematica* by trying to show that all of mathematics can be made to rest on propositions of logic. Ultimately,

Logicism is an inherently flawed system. The work of Kurt Gödel in 1931 demonstrated that a logical system could never be both complete and consistent, and hence Logicism could never adequately serve as a philosophical foundation for all of mathematics, much less for all of reality (Eves 369).

Formalism is the mathematical outworking of Postmodernism. The postmodernist does not believe there is any final truth (Greene 17). Thus the formalist begins with basic assumptions that are set forth by man, regardless of whether they have any relationship to reality. He then logically deduces a system of statements that are never true or false, only valid or invalid based upon the original assumptions. He has no interest in trying to apply these results to the real world because he considers reality unknowable (Van Brummelen 11).

Formalism originated in the writings of David Hilbert who asserted that the basic objects of mathematical thought are the mathematical symbols themselves. The mathematician should not, he believed, be concerned with attaching any meaning to those symbols. A strong adherent to this philosophy was the mathematician Godfrey Hardy who believed that a mathematical topic was only to be considered pure mathematics if it was utterly useless. He even boasted that: "I have never done anything 'useful.' No discovery of mine has made, or is likely to make, directly or indirectly, for good or ill, the least difference to the amenity of the world." The false nature of this philosophy has been exposed by the work of other mathematicians who took Hardy's work and demonstrated its roots in God's creation. Hardy's Law became central in the understanding of Rh-blood groups and in the treatment of hemolytic disease in newborns. In addition, his investigations of Riemann's Zeta function have formed a foundation for the theory of pyrometry (temperatures of furnaces) (Neuman 2026).

Throughout history God has used both Christians and non-Christians to unfold the mysteries of his creation. Adherents of both Logicism and Formalism have had positive effects on the development of mathematics. The emergence of set theory brought unification to many diverse branches of mathematics and introduced elegant notation for expressing certain concepts (Eves 370). Due to the influence of Formalism on mathematics education, more emphasis was placed on the understanding of the foundations of the number system, its algorithms and properties. For more able students this produced a broader understanding of the nature of mathematics and provided a better foundation for more advanced study.

A negative consequence was that, in some textbooks, set theory became the basis for introducing mathematical concepts at the lowest grade levels. Instead of presenting numbers and operations as abstractions of patterns seen in God's creation, a number was taught to be a name of a class of sets and addition was introduced as the union of disjoint sets. Throughout the grades, application of mathematics to the real world was de-emphasized. The number of pictures and word problems diminished in the textbooks. Sets, rather than God's created world, became the motivational source of mathematics. This level of abstractness especially harmed less able students. Many failed to learn basic skills or to see any relevance in the study of mathematics.

For the past ten years the most dominant influence on mathematics education in the United Sates has been the *Principles and Standards for School Mathematics* published by the National Council of Teachers of Mathematics first in 1988 and revised in 2000. There is much good to be said for these standards. They have championed the need to have mathematical understandings grow out of a student's experiences in the real world. They have discarded the straightjacket of formalism for an approach that seeks to engage the student in meaningful problem solving at every level. They have also called for a change in the often-shabby approach to educating the less able students in our schools.

However, one does not have to read far to experience the unbiblical philosophies of humanism and rationalism that pervade the standards. We are boldly told that: (1) reasoning is the standard of truth in mathematics (Mathematical Sciences Education Board and the National Research Council 47) and (2) a major goal of school mathematics programs is to create autonomous learners. By "autonomous" educators mean students who will construct their own ideas about mathematics and decide their own truth without having to be told (National Council of Teachers of Mathematics 21). In a special report to the nation prepared by the National Research Council in 1989 we find these supporting statements: "Mathematics does provide one of the few disciplines in which the growing student can, by exercising only the power inherent in his or her own mind, reach conclusions with full assurance. More than most other school subjects, mathematics offers special opportunities for children to learn the power of thought as distinct from the power of authority" (4).

BROAD OBJECTIVES OF CHRISTIAN MATHEMATICS EDUCATION

As a young teacher in a Christian school, I struggled with the question, "How do I put God into my mathematics class?" I listened to many lectures on the integration of the Bible and learning, but they did little to help. I always felt that I was trying to impose something artificial on mathematics. Yes, there were numbers in the Bible, but pointing that out hardly made my teaching distinctively Christian. I finally began to make progress along that path of sanctification in my profession when I came to realize that I did not have to *put* God into mathematics. He is already there! My role is to *reveal* him to my students. I should be helping students to remove the blinders that sin puts on their eyes so that they can see the character of God revealed in every part of the creation (Kienel 79). "For in him we live and move and have our being" (Acts 17:28).

Furthermore, the content in my classroom may well be the same as the content in a secular school not because I am failing to teach Christianly, but because that content is rooted in God's creation wherein all Christians and non-Christians function. The difference is rather in what I *do* with that mathematical content. Students need to experience mathematical content in the context of its true meaning. They need to be shown the proper place of mathematics in God's creation. They need to understand that it is only as we combine human reasoning with a faith commitment to the God of the Bible that we will come to know truth. And God's truth is not passive; it calls people to respond to him in love and service. Hence, for me to teach with meaning requires that I give direction to the development of students' lives (Greene 168).

Teaching mathematics with meaning is summarized in the following three broad goals.

The study of mathematics should reveal the God of the heavens and earth by whose Word all things were brought into being and are sustained moment by moment (Greene 273).
Everything God created reveals his nature. "For since the creation of the world God's invisible qualities – his eternal power and divine nature – have been clearly seen, being understood from what has been made, so that men are without excuse" (Romans 1:20). However, when man fell into sin, he lost the ability to see God plainly in the creation. In God's love, he gave man the scriptures to more clearly reveal who he is and what his claim is on us. Finally, in the ultimate act of love, God gave his only son to restore the bond between God and man that was broken by sin. Once the student comes to know God through Christ, his eyes will be opened to see the truth of God in creation. As the student explores the depths and details of that creation in the classroom, he will be adding depth and detail to his understanding of God.

The study of mathematics should call the student to a life of service, using his God-given gifts to glorify his creator and help his fellow man (Greene 275).

God's truth is distinguished from the world's idea of truth in that it is not neutral or value-free. Neutral facts make no claim on the student. Indeed the autonomous student is free to not only construct his own truth, but to decide to act or not act on that truth. God's truth is never neutral. God's truth is centered in the person of Christ. "I am the way and the truth and the life" (John 14:6). God's truth calls for a response. "And he died for all, that those who live should no longer live for themselves but for him who died for them and was raised again" (2 Corinthians 5:15). God has given man responsibilities in this creation, both as keepers of the creation and as reconcilers of this fallen world to him. As the student grows in his knowledge of the truth of God through his study of the creation, he will grow in his commitment to serve him in the everyday activities of life. "We know that we have come to know him if we keep his commands" (1 John 2:3).

The study of mathematics should lead the student into a deeper unity with the Lord that has its outworkings in increased love, praise, and worship of God (Greene 276).

> Ascribe to the LORD the glory due his name; worship the LORD in the splendor of his holiness. The voice of the LORD is over the waters. . . . The voice of the LORD breaks the cedars. . . . The voice of the LORD strikes with flashes of lightning. . . . The voice of the LORD shakes the desert. . . . And in his temple all cry, "Glory!" Psalm 29:2–9

In creation we see a God who out of love formed a world marvelously attuned to our needs. He placed the earth at just the right distance from the sun. He surrounded it with the perfect atmospheric conditions needed by our bodies. He daily provides the sunlight and rain to grow our food. He gave us a mind with which to investigate that world. Indeed, he is a loving God, and his love calls forth a response in us of love towards him. "We love because he first loved us" (1 John 4:19). When the student comes to see that the earth really is the Lord's, his response cannot help but be to love him and give him the glory due his name.

IMPLICATIONS FOR THE CURRICULUM

The implications of these goals for the mathematics curriculum in a Christian school are far-reaching. In some of these areas we will find ourselves in concert with the best of secular education around us, because all truth is God's truth and common grace abounds. In other areas we will be distinctively different.

Mathematical principles must be presented as generalizations of man's experiences in the creation, not as brilliant creations of the human mind.

In the study of geometry, it was traditional to present each new theorem as a logical deduction from previous theorems or postulates. Such teaching gave the impression that someone in days past sat down and developed the whole of geometry by placing one logical precept upon another. Nothing could be farther from the truth. Most theorems in geometry originated as the result of inductive reasoning based on experiences of everyday life in the creation and came to be proven deductively only well after their general acceptance.

Teaching in the classroom should mirror this reality. A student should normally be given time to explore a topic intuitively before it is handed to him in polished form. This will give him the opportunity to discover and organize mathematical patterns for himself. Such opportunities will both improve his problem-solving skills and help him to appreciate how mathematics has been developed in the past and will continue to be developed in the future.

The proper role of reasoning should be discussed. It is not, as the Logicist would claim, "an autonomous guide capable by itself of leading us to truth. Our reason always follows our heart" (Greene 200). Our heart is either committed to the true God of Scripture or to some idol. All the theorems of mathematics rest ultimately on assumptions that remain unverifiable except through faith (Gaebelein 58–9). The Christian student must be taught to use his reasoning in concert with God's revealed Word to find truth (Greene 200).

Mathematics must be taught in a way that reflects the unity of all things in the creation (Steensma 145).

Christ is the light in which we see and understand everything around us. The Christian school must teach all subjects as parts of an integrated whole that is bound together at its core by the Word of God. In the mathematics classroom, we must show that every part of creation has a numerical and spatial aspect. Classroom activities and projects should illustrate the use of mathematics in fields of economics, science, history, politics, art, music, language, health, athletics, business, etc. Care should be taken to distinguish non-Christian views that man or even mathematics is the source of unity in these diverse fields from the Christian view that it is a reflection of God's unity. "They exchanged the truth of God for a lie, and worshiped and served created things rather than the Creator – who is forever praised. Amen" (Romans 1:25).

At the same time, the student must be shown that mathematics itself has many different aspects. There is a language of mathematics that must be mastered by the student so that he can accurately share his mathematical understandings with others. There is an aesthetic aspect to mathematics that can be seen in the elegant solution to a difficult problem.

There is a history to mathematics that enables us to see how man has lived out God's command to have dominion over the earth. Students should be shown how in the historical development of mathematics the level of complexity of mathematics was related to the needs of the society. They should be exposed to the variety of philosophies that have emerged through the ages. They should be challenged to look for ways in which mathematics has influenced our modern culture and how our culture has influenced the development of mathematics (Van Brummelen 18).

Mathematics education must be a dynamic discipline.
As our culture changes, the topics covered in the classroom must be re-evaluated and modified to ensure that the student will be prepared to serve God in *today's* world (Van Brummelen 23). Mathematics must never be taught as an end in and of itself. Christian teachers are in danger of doing just that when they cling to favorite topics of the past and refuse to recognize that God's world is not static. The use of calculators and computers has fundamentally changed what mathematics people need to know for everyday life and how new mathematical ideas are discovered. New educational research, when it is demonstrated to be valid, should help the Christian teacher to better understand how students learn. The Christian teacher's own desire to know God more fully should keep him exploring more deeply into the creation in ways that continually renew his teaching.

Mathematics and values must be taught together.
It is not possible to separate religious values from true education. Learning to do statistics, for example, gives the student a tool for functioning in the creation. But how is he to use that tool? If we do not teach that, we have not truly educated the student. Used properly, statistics can convey complex data in easy to understand visual formats that enable oth-

ers to make informed, intelligent decisions. A well-known book among mathematicians is titled *How to Lie with Statistics* by Darrell Huff and Irving Geis. It exposes the common methods for using statistics to mislead the public. When we teach mathematics as value free, we open the door for just such misuse. Indeed our present day advertisement industry has raised the skill of lying with statistics to the level of high art. Godly education instructs the student in how to use his skills to honor God and to expose the abuses of others. It produces a changed heart and an altered life, growing in the fear of God (Greene 167).

Learning mathematics will require hard work on the part of the teacher and the student.
We live in a fallen world and sin rears its ugly head at every turn. Our attitudes towards work are no exception. Children have a God-given curiosity, but that is not the same as a love of learning. Adults are increasingly pleasure oriented rather that work oriented. Hence, we often see a decline in a student's enthusiasm with school as he progresses up through the grades, a decline that is frequently caused by the sin of laziness on the part of the teacher or student, or both. As Christian teachers, we seek to give students not only the tools to learn about God's creation, but the desire to use those tools. Love is a powerful motivator. We love God and our fellow man because God first loved us (1 John 4:7,19). When our teaching is permeated with our love for mathematics and the God who created it, we inspire our students to delve more deeply into that which gives us so much joy. Love requires sacrifice. God so loved us that he sent his only son to die for us (John 3:16). Teaching with love and learning with love will require the teacher and the student to give of themselves wholeheartedly, sacrificing worldly pleasures to his purposes (Wilson 73).

Mathematics must be taught by a Christian teacher who knows God and knows himself.
God's Word teaches that we cannot begin to build a new life in Christ until we have first broken down the old life of sin. That is true for both the student and the teacher. The Christian teacher is one whose eyes have been opened to see the depths of his own depravity and has acknowledged his complete unworthiness to merit God's grace. He has been redeemed by the substitutionary death of Jesus Christ and brought to faith and repentance through the renewing work of the Holy Spirit. He is daily kept in faith by the almighty power of God and enjoys the security of knowing that nothing can separate him from the love of Christ (Steele 16–18).

The Christian teacher understands that the Word of God has spoken all of creation into being. He recognizes that his ability to acquire reliable knowledge about that creation is based on the faithfulness with which God keeps his covenant promises and maintains his creation (Van der Laan 60). He understands that by studying the creation he can learn to know God more fully and be brought into even deeper communion with him. He views work and the study of the creation as a form of praise and worship of God.

The Christian teacher knows that his worldview, Godly or otherwise, will gradually condition the worldview of his students (Gaebelein 37). He does not fool himself into thinking that his teaching or his life witness will bring his students to Christ. He knows that salvation is the province of God alone. Nevertheless, he expects that God can and will use him to prepare the way for the working of the Holy Spirit in the lives of his students. In the words of Cornelius Van Til, "The Christian teacher knows himself, knows the subject, and knows the child. He has the full assurance of the absolute fruitfulness of his work. He labors in the dawn of everlasting results" (207).

GLORIFYING GOD IN MY CLASSROOM

Anyone who has spent significant time in Christian education has found himself trying to explain and defend the role of the Christian school to those who do not see the point of its existence. To some of our critics we should teach Bible non-stop because knowing Christ is all there is. To others of our critics we should confine the teaching of religion to our churches and send our children to the local public school to learn an objective view of the world. In *Recovering the Lost Tools of Learning*, Douglas Wilson presents a charming analogy to explain the role of Christian education using the sun to represent Christ as the light of the world (John 8:12). Wilson likens the first criticism to a person who ignores the world and spends all day staring at the sun. He likens the second criticism to a person who blocks the sun and attempts to study the world in the darkness that results. By contrast, the student in a Christian school studies the world in the light of the sun. "In [Christ] are hidden all the treasures of wisdom and knowledge" (Colossians 2:3).

In this last part of the paper, I will describe how I attempt to bring Godly meaning to the study of mathematics at Delaware County Christian School, using the light of Christ. I am encouraged by the realization that sanctification is a lifelong process. What follows is a description of where I perceive that I am on the path of sanctification in my profession.

Mathematical principles must be presented as generalizations of man's experiences in the creation, not as brilliant creations of the human mind.

For students to see the reflection of God in mathematics, they have to see that mathematics is rooted in God's creation. In geometry, we discuss the fact that lines and circles and polygons are simply abstractions of the shapes that God used in building his creation. As a result of my reading for this paper, I have come to realize that I must be more careful in such discussions not to hold up the mathematical model as the ideal and the God-created object as an imperfect representation. Rather, it is the mathematical abstraction that imperfectly attempts to describe the great complexity of God's world.

Geometry also provides an ideal backdrop for discussing the role of reasoning in mathematics as well as in doctrine. Inductive reasoning consists of drawing a general conclusion based on the observation of a pattern. It is perhaps the primary tool God has given the mathematician for discovering patterns in his creation. In the computer laboratory, my students have the opportunity to discover geometric patterns for themselves. By constructing a variety of isosceles triangles on the computer and measuring their angles, for example, they can observe the pattern that the base angles of such triangles are congruent. However, it is a leap of faith to say that something observed in three or four examples is necessarily true for all such items. Hence, we then proceed to apply deductive reasoning to support such a hypothesis.

Deductive reasoning consists of drawing a general conclusion by logical inference using only accepted facts. Supporting our observation from the laboratory by writing a deductive proof then strengthens our confidence in the truthfulness of our observation. However, the important realization for the Christian student is that he is *still* making a leap of faith. Our definition of deductive reasoning above refers to "accepted facts." How are we to establish these "facts," since they cannot be proven? They are, in fact, faith agreements. In geometry, one of these accepted facts is that "two points determine a line." This "fact" is improvable. Nevertheless, it is such an obvious statement, that our inability to prove it takes nothing away from our certainty that it and anything we deduce properly from it are true.

We then discuss how this relates to the way we reason in doctrinal matters. "The Bible says that Christ died to save sinners. I am a sinner. Hence Christ died for me." That is deductive reasoning. But its validity is rooted in the faith agreement that there is a God and that the Bible is truly his Word. We cannot logically prove that God exists any more than we can logically prove that two points determine a line. Yet with the eyes of faith both are fully believed. Through a discussion of these issues in the classroom, I want my students to understand that reasoning by itself cannot bring us to an understanding of truth in mathematics or in doctrine. Truth comes only when reasoning is rightly applied by faith to that which God reveals to us in his Word and in his creation.

Mathematics must be taught in a way that reflects the unity of all things in the creation.

To demonstrate the unity of God's creation, I bring to my courses problems that illustrate the role of mathematics in the investigation and understanding of many different fields of study in the creation. In calculus we just recently finished an assignment where students analyzed data about the distribution of income in the United States over the past 70 years. They used methods of calculus to quantify the degree of income inequity year by year and computer generated graphs to visually display the patterns of change. Earlier in the year, the class did a computer laboratory activity with skydiving. (They begged me to make it a field trip!) Using computer generated graphs to model the fall of the skydiver, we were able to analyze the perfect time to pull the rip cord so as to enjoy the most free-fall while preserving just enough time to float gently to a safe landing. Throughout the course, I try to bring in non-standard examples where calculus helps us to understand or predict human or physical phenomena. We model traffic flow on a freeway. We determine the frequency of drug doses needed to maintain a certain safe level of a drug in the body. We calculate the number of years needed to remove pollutants naturally from a body of water based on its rate of outflow. With the eyes of faith, each example becomes one more piece of evidence of the divine unity behind the creation and one more glimpse into the depths of God's genius.

In geometry students research a variety of mathematical patterns to see how they are evidenced in the creation. They study spirals and learn how they describe the shape God gave to the chambered nautilus and the horns of the Barbary sheep. They learn about the Fibonacci sequence and how it describes the arrangement of petals on a flower or the ancestors of a honeybee. They investigate the elliptical paths God gave to the planets and comets as they orbit the sun.

Equally important is to help students see how God gave many different aspects to mathematics and each is important in understanding, using, and appreciating God's gift of mathematics fully. Of utmost importance is God's gift of language. God created mankind to live and work in community with each other and language is one of the tools of community living. I require students to learn the vocabulary of mathematics so that they can read and comprehend mathematical explanations written by others. Especially in algebra, I stress learning to use mathematical symbolism properly so that students can communicate their mathematical ideas with others. God's gift of language also gives clarity and organization to the student's own thinking. Thus by teaching students the language of mathematics, I am laying a foundation for the learning of more complex mathematical ideas in the future.

Because God created time, mathematics has a history. When I teach trigonometry, I discuss how God enabled the ancient Babylonians to develop a working knowledge of geometry and trigonometry to help them control the floodwaters of the Tigris and Euphrates Rivers. In calculus, we discuss the historical significance of the discovery of the Fundamental Theorem of Calculus and some of the all-too-human jealousies among mathematicians that harmed the development of mathematics. In algebra and calculus, we talk about how the rise of computers and calculators is actively changing the nature of mathematics in our own society. By presenting mathematics in its historical context, I try to help my students see that mathematics results from man's obedience to the cultural mandate and from God's goodness in opening up to him more of the mysteries of his creation.

Because God is beautiful, we see that he has imbedded great beauty in mathematics. In the classroom we see the marvelous way in which different branches of mathematics are intertwined and how exciting it is to see a complex idea made simple by the application of the proper theorem. Though not every student sees the same beauty in mathematics, I take great delight in seeing the acknowledging smiles on even a few faces when our class discussion brings us to a moment of great clarity on a mathematical idea.

Not only is there an aesthetic aspect to mathematics, but we also see a mathematical aspect to aesthetics, or fine arts. Teaching geometry gives a wonderful opportunity to use mathematics to create art. After discussing the mathematical properties of tessellations, students get to create their own tessellations, first by using colored shapes on the computer and later by cutting them out of construction paper. We also study the mathematics behind drawing in perspective, and learn how to use the computer to facilitate such drawings. Each year several students in geometry research the golden ratio and present to the class the influence this mathematical concept had on classical art and architecture.

Mathematics education must be a dynamic discipline.
God is alive and at work in his world. New mathematics is constantly being developed, and the widespread use of computers enables old mathematics to be applied in new ways. I have added an introduction to fractals in my geometry course so that students will better understand the developing nature of mathematics. We learn how fractal ideas are used in understanding the measure of a coastline and in describing the dimension of new kinds of curves. In calculus we use direction fields and Euler's Method to work with differential equations that would be unsolvable by more traditional methods. Assisted by calculators and computers, Euler's Method enables us explore problems with stable and unstable equilibriums, and to carry out the skydiving activity discussed earlier.

As we enter the twenty-first century, we find that employers now seek different mathematical skills than in years past. To respond to these changes I have been continuing to shift the emphasis in my algebra and calculus classes away from the predominance of analytic skills to a broader based approach that involves teaching concepts graphically, numerically, and analytically. For example, in previous years the primary means of solving an equation was to follow a pencil and paper algorithm. Though I still teach such algorithms, we spend less time perfecting these skills on complex equations, because computers and even calculators are capable of performing these computations quickly and accurately. Instead, we spend more time learning how to use graphs to solve equations, how to evaluate the reasonableness of a proposed solution, and how to interpret the solutions. In addition I give students more opportunities to discuss their ideas with a classmate and to work cooperatively towards the solution to a problem. These are all skills that are important in the way mathematics is being used in God's creation today.

Mathematics and values must be taught together.
Douglas Wilson uses the phrase that a sinner educated apart from the Bible simply creates a cleverer sinner (Wilson 72). As mathematics is taught in a Christian school, it needs to be coupled with direction for using that knowledge in God honoring ways. As we study percents in algebra and their application to calculating investments, we discuss wise investment principles and good stewardship of the money God gives us. In completing the calculus project discussed earlier on income inequity

in the United States, my students are asked to document the historical events and government policies that may have contributed positively or negatively to the level of inequity. In this way they can begin to see how mathematical knowledge can be used to guide the formation of government policy and bring about positive changes in our society.

The project my students do in geometry opens the opportunity to discuss academic integrity so that they learn to give proper credit for the use of information they have gotten from others. Everyday activities of turning in homework and taking tests give opportunities to discuss personal honesty. In the enforcement of school rules, I have the opportunity to teach students the difference between a begrudging, half-hearted obedience to authority and the humble, wholehearted obedience that the Bible teaches.

However, the strongest voice for teaching values is not the classroom discussions or even the individual counseling, but the silent witness that my own life presents. It is a challenge that I take very seriously even as I admit my failings. To teach students obedience to authority, I must model the same in my responses to administrative authority over me. To teach students to treat each other with kindness and forgiveness, I must respond to them with love and forbearance. To teach students responsibility in their daily work, I must demonstrate responsibility in my teaching – being prepared for class every day, grading student papers promptly, and carrying out administrative instructions fully and on time. To teach students honesty, I must be honest before my students, admitting my mistakes and taking responsibility for my failures. The most powerful teaching is accomplished when teacher and student travel together down the road of discipleship (Greene 220).

Learning mathematics will require hard work on the part of the teacher and the student.

I love teaching and doing mathematics. It is my passion. It is also my living sacrifice to the Lord. To do it well requires that I spend much time outside of school learning more about mathematics and developing better ways to teach it to my students. I will summarize here a few of my most recent advances in mathematics. A few years ago I started learning about fractals and how to interweave them in the curriculum. I have used them to advance students' understanding of complex numbers and to experience some of the thrill of discovering new mathematical ideas for themselves. Two summers ago I attended a conference where we explored ways to teach students to tackle more real-world problems in mathematics, problems in which students have to wrestle with social and economic values in their solution of the problem. I have been using some of these examples to enrich the curriculum in our Mathematics Club. Last summer I learned to use the Geometer's Sketchpad program as a tool to dynamically illustrate concepts of calculus. My students responded very enthusiastically this year to lessons where I used these demonstrations to teach new concepts. This past Christmas vacation I had my son show me how to construct a web page. I worked for the following two months to create a web page that now serves as a homework resource for my students and a communication link with their parents.

Through my love for God and his creation, particularly the mathematics of that creation, I desire to inspire in my students a similar love for the Lord and the world in which he has placed us. That love will call for a response of sacrifice from them. I expect them to invest themselves wholly in the task of learning. "Whatever you do, work at it with all your heart, as working for the Lord, not for human masters" (Colossians 3:23). Students cannot learn mathematics by sitting idly in the classroom, however quiet and well-mannered their behavior. Hence I prod them with questions, solicit their ideas, and encourage them to challenge results that do not make sense to them. Students cannot learn mathematics when they neglect homework. Consequently, I check their homework daily and use every means at my disposal to "force" them to be diligent. They also cannot learn mathematics when they approach it as a mindless task of repeating processes demonstrated in the classroom. This is a much more difficult problem to deal with because educators themselves are often at the root of this problem. Too frequently, teachers reward students with high grades when they can successfully perform mathematical algorithms, but are unable to apply them to the meaningful solution of real-world problems. This is unfortunate. Mathematics is a tool for doing God's work in the creation. If the student cannot properly apply mathematical processes to meaningful problems, he has no true knowledge. I am constantly confronting students with problems that require them to think about the meaning and application of what they are doing. I also work to develop tests that measure student's ability to use mathematics in meaningful ways.

Mathematics must be taught by a Christian teacher who knows God and knows himself.

The Lord took me, a self-centered sinner, and for his glory changed my heart to seek his will. He taught me through the words of scripture that

Jesus died for me, to pay the penalty for my sin (Ephesians 1:3–12). His Spirit brought renewal to my being. He gave me purpose and direction in life. He holds me in his loving arms and assures me of spending eternity in his presence.

He called me to a life of service as a mathematics teacher. I am encouraged by the promise that his strength is made perfect in my weakness (2 Corinthians 12:9). Being a Christian teacher requires that I remain close to the Lord. The Lord can only work through me as I allow his standards to be my standards. "Be holy because I, the LORD your God, am holy" (Leviticus 19:2).

In the classroom I strive, however imperfectly, to model the example of Christ as the great teacher. He used a variety of teaching methods to reach the audience at hand. He made time for every person who sought knowledge from him. He held up the highest of standards. He showed compassion when appropriate and judgment when necessary. His love was always evident.

Most of all I seek to teach that Christ is the truth in everything. It is he to whom all of creation points. Numbers and space exist because God spoke them into being for his purposes. His power upholds them, moment by moment. All of mathematics is but one of the wonderful gifts of God's love (Greene 189–190). It is his truth and his creation that we study. It is his name that we praise for all that exists. And it is for his glory that we live.

For from him and through him and to him are all things. To him be the glory forever! Amen. (Romans 11:36)

BIBLIOGRAPHY

BJU – Bob Jones University – Department of Mathematics. *The Christian Teaching of Mathematics*. Greenville, South Carolina: Bob Jones University Press, 1982.

Eves, Howard. *An Introduction to the History of Mathematics*. New York: Holt, Rinehart, and Winston, 1964.

Gaebelein, Frank E. *The Pattern of God's Truth*. New York: Oxford University Press, 1954.

Greene, Albert E. *Reclaiming the Future of Christian Education*. Colorado Springs, Colorado: Association of Christian Schools International, 1998.

Kienel, Paul A., editor. *The Philosophy of Christian School Education*. Whittier, California: Association of Christian Schools International, 1986.

Mathematical Sciences Education Board and the National Research Council. *Reshaping School Mathematics: A philosophy and framework for curriculum.*

Washington, DC: National Academy Press, 1990.

National Council of Teachers of Mathematics. *Principles and Standards for School Mathematics*. Reston, Virginia: National Council of Teachers of Mathematics, 2000.

National Research Council. *Everybody Counts: A Report to the Nation on the Future of Mathematics Education*. Washington, DC: National Academy Press, 1989.

Neuman, James R., editor. *The World of Mathematics*, Vol. IV: *Machines, Music and Puzzles*. New York: Simon and Schuster, 1956.

Steele, David N. and Curtis C. Thomas. *The Five Points of Calvinism Defined, Defended, Documented*. Philadelphia: Presbyterian and Reformed, 1965.

Steensma, Geraldine and Harro W. Van Brummelen, editors. *Shaping School Curriculum*. Terre Haute: Signal Publishing, 1977.

Van Brummelen, Harro W. *Mathematics in the Christian School*. Toronto: The Association for the Advancement of Christian Scholarship, 1971.

Van der Laan, Harry. *A Christian Appreciation of Physical Science*. Ontario, Canada: The Association for Reformed Scientific Studies, 1966.

Van Til, Cornelius. *Essays on Christian Education*. Phillipsburg: Presbyterian and Reformed, 1979.

Wilson, Douglas. *Recovering the Lost Tools of Learning*. Wheaton: Crossway Books, 1991.

Appendix Three

Mark Greene – The Real Dilemma of Workplace Ministry. Cape Town. 2010.
[Capetown Address Transcript – transcribed with permission]

I work for a place called the London Institute for Contemporary Christianity, which was founded by John Stott, affectionately known as Uncle John. I want to discuss the nature, for contemporary Christians, of the workplace challenge. It is my conviction that the church's failure to embrace the workplace challenge is a symptom of a much deeper problem that affects almost every area of the church's mission to the world. And I think that, unless we address the deeper theological problem, neither workplace ministry nor the church's mission will flourish as it might do.

Simplistically put, I think there are probably two main strategies for reaching the world.

- The first one is to recruit the people of God to use some of their leisure time to join the missionary initiatives of church-paid workers. Now, how many people would say that's probably the model of missions in your country? Just put your hands up if that's basically the model of mission that you have in your country. Most people here. OK.
- The second model is to equip the people of God for fruitful mission in all of their life.

The reality is that strategy number one is *the* strategy for most people in the world, as we've just seen. That is dominant. And the result of that strategy is this: That the 98 percent of Christians who are not in church-paid work are, on the whole, not equipped or envisioned for mission except in the two to ten hours that they might spend in church-related activities every week. That is the reality. That is the implication of strategy number one.

So the workplace agenda is not some little thing on the side. It goes right to the heart of the potential of the world evangelization movement. In other words, 98 percent of Christians have neither been envisioned nor equipped for missions in 95 percent of their waking lives. What a tragic waste of human potential.

But there was good news for workplace ministry in the Manila Manifesto of 1989. The 12th affirmation reads this way: "We affirm that God is committed to the whole church and every member of it, the task of making Christ known throughout the world. We long to see all," it says, "all of the world mobilized and trained for the task." However, in church practice and in daily life, that affirmation has been primarily understood and pursued as training lay and ordained people for neighborhood witness and neighborhood evangelism. Similarly, we can affirm the 14th affirmation. "We affirm that every congregation must turn itself outward to its local community in evangelistic witness and compassionate service." Yes and Amen. But interestingly, it does not say, "We affirm that every congregation must turn itself outward to its *members'* communities and networks in evangelistic witness and compassionate service." In other words, when I was in advertising, I knew the first names of probably a 150 people in an organization of, say, 750. And I knew the names of over 30 clients. But I probably knew the names of only two people in my apartment block. Now, what might happen if every congregation started to pray, by name, for the people its members already know in the networks and communities they're already in?

In reality, for whatever reason, the basic psychological model we have of the church is this: The dots are in the corner. In the ghetto. And every now and then we scuttle out to do some mission, and then we scuttle back in. But in reality, the people of God are Monday through Saturday out in the world, touching hundreds sometime – some people, thousands of people in a given week – taking traces of grace out there.

The most effective action against poverty is the creation of decent jobs. But the poor do not just need jobs. They need a vision for their job, when they get one, that goes beyond provision. We all need an understanding of how our job might be an intrinsic component of God's mission in time and eternity. Indeed the manifesto is much stronger on what we are saved *from* than what we are saved *for*. Thy kingdom come, Thy will be done on earth as it is in heaven. In my workplace as it is in heaven. In my sweatshop as it is in heaven. In my kitchen as it is in heaven. In my school as it is in heaven. And so on. Who? Who's going to influence multinationals to maximize the good – outsiders or insiders?

So in sum there is much to affirm about the Manila Manifesto but nothing really, from my perspective, that grips the heart or captures the full-orbed richness of God's mission to renew the world through the high calling of our daily work. So perhaps there are some additions to be made to the manifesto there.

But I think if we stop there, we might miss a bigger issue. The question is why, despite the enormous evangelistic opportunity and transformational opportunity the workplace presents, why, on the whole, has the church not envisioned her people for fruitful engagement? Why, despite the fact that the Bible is brimming with material on work, have so few churches found a way to teach, envision, and support their people for where they spend most of their time? Well, the reason, as you might expect, is theological. Our actions are always shaped by our ideas. And the reason is the Sacred-Secular Divide [SSD, or dualism, or *enwhanron* (Korean)]; the belief that some things are important to God – church, prayer meetings, evangelistic outlook, social action – but other things – work, college, school, sports, music, the arts, sleep, rest . . . they don't really matter to God.

Now, examples abound of SSD in every aspect of church life. Who are our heroes here this week? We honor, celebrate, and tell stories about pastors, preachers, missionaries, in the narrow sense worship leaders, and – praise God – social activists. But we almost never tell stories about school kids or cleaners or bus-drivers or lawyers or bankers or politicians. And then we wonder why our institutions and businesses lack heart.

So, we may know in our heads that the Gospel embraces every area of life, but this is not the gospel that we have been teaching people to live or celebrate when we do. It is not the *lived* gospel. We're not making disciples for the places people find themselves in. There is a crisis in disciple-making, which is leading to a crisis in evangelization. So we rejoice in the progress that the marketplace movement has made, but the reality is we have a systemic issue. The Sacred-Secular Divide, S.S.D., is a systemic issue. The soil is toxic. The good seed of the marketplace movement, the workplace movement, the people of God movement, is being planted in poor soil. So it will not matter how much we water that soil, how diligently we seek to nurture the seed, how we protect the plant from disease. The soil is deeply affected by the Sacred-Secular Divide. So the people of God will not, can not, yield their full potential. And it seems to me that neither the Manila Manifesto nor the [Lausanne] Covenant have named this issue or dealt with it.

So the key missiological challenge is not only that we have failed to regard work as significant. The key problem is that we have failed to regard the whole of life as significant. The key challenge is not that the local church has not discipled people for daily work. The key challenge for the local church is that, on the whole, they have not, we have not, discipled one another for ordinary, daily life. We have not given people a vision for the adventure that it is to go out in Jesus Christ, in the power of the Spirit, into the world day by day and participate with him.

So the good news is not that Jesus came to redeem our leisure time, but that he came to redeem all of our time. The good news is not that Jesus said, "Come, take up your cross and follow me . . . when you get home from work or school." The good news is that Jesus calls us to follow him every nanosecond of the day. The good news is that God, in Christ, not only created all things, but seeks to reconcile all things to himself. Now you all know this.

Here is the bad news: Although the church has identified this problem in every generation of the last century, we have not yet found a way to put this whole-life, disciple-making Gospel back where it belongs: at the heart of our thinking and practice. And the result of that is to take us back to where we started.

There are two strategies to reach the world. The first one is to recruit the people of God to use some of their leisure time to join the missionary initiatives of church-paid workers. And the second one is to equip the people of God for fruitful mission in all of their life. Strategy One is what we have. I plead with you that it will not be what the next generation will have as well.

In the name of the Father, and of the Son, and of the Holy Spirit.

Used with permission.

BIBLIOGRAPHY OF WORKS CITED

Adams, J. 1982. *Back to the Blackboard: Design for a biblical Christian school.* 2nd ed. Woodruff, SC: Timeless Texts.

Alphonso, C. 2013. The one-room classroom could make a comeback in Hamilton. *The Toronto Globe and Mail,* 21 November. http://www.theglobeandmail.com/news/national/education/ontario-education-director-eyes-multi-age-classrooms/article15556227/

Andreu, R., L. Canos, S. de Juana, et al. 2003. Critical friends: A tool for quality improvement in universities. *Quality Assurance in Education* (11)1: 31–36.

Anna. 2008. What is a Christian teacher anyway? Blog. http://christianteacherforum.wordpress.com/2008/05/31/what-is-a-christian-teacher-anyway/

Ansalone, G. 2010. Tracking: Educational differentiation or defective strategy? *Education Research Quarterly* 34(2): 3–17.

Archibald, S., J. Coggshall, A. Croft, and L. Goe. 2011. *High quality professional development for all teachers: Effectively allocating resources.* Washington, DC: National Comprehensive Center for Teacher Quality.

Aristotle. 330BC [1995]. *Politics: VII.* Trans. E. Barker, R. Stalley, ed. Oxford: World Classics.

ASCD. 1996. ASCD calls for members' views on key issues. *Education Update* 38(2). http://www.ascd.org/publications/newsletters/education-update/mar96/vol38/num02/ASCD-Calls-for-Members'-Views-on-Key-Issues.aspx

Atwood, R. 2012. *On higher ed.* Blog. http://royatwoodonhighered.wordpress.com/category/accreditation/page2

Aubry, M. 2102. Alternative school grads more civic-minded: report. *Ottawa Sun,* 17 October. http://www.ottawasun.com/2012/10/17/alternative-school-grads-more-civic-minded-report

Authentic Assessment. 2007. What is authentic assessment? http://www.deakin.edu.au/itl/assets/resources/pd/tl-modules/assessment/authenticassessment.pdf.

Auty, J. 2008. Curriculum in the classroom of a Christian school. *Christian School Education* 11(3): 28–30.

Baer, R. 1987. American public education and the myth of value neutrality. In R. Neuhaus, ed. *Democracy and the Renewal of Public Education.* Grand Rapids: Eerdmans.

Bartholomew, C. 2000. Uncharted waters: Philosophy, theology and the crisis in biblical interpretation. In C. Bartholomew, C. Greene, and K. Möller, eds. *Renewing Biblical Interpretation.* Carlisle: Paternoster Press.

Bartholomew, C., & M. Goheen. 2013. *Christian Philosophy: A systematic and narrative introduction*. Grand Rapids: Baker.

Baumann, Z. 1997. *Postmodernity and its Discontents*. New York: New York University Press.

Baus, G. 2008. Dooyeweerd's conception of societal sphere sovereignty with an application to the question of the status and tax-based support of education. Princeton Theological Seminary Conference: Princeton, NJ. https://docs.google.com/document/d/1mgOUeW5N9g6ri6ZtuPOBWqSiB1kEeNzU pxy8Yzbvv3E/preview?pli=1

Beaty, K. 2012. Public Education: The next moral issue for today's evangelicals. *Christianity Today*, April 17. http://www.christianitytoday.com/thisisourcity/7thcity/publiceducation.html?paging=off

Becker, G. 2013. Higher education from a (reformed) global missions perspective. In *Proceedings of the 6th International Conference on Christian Higher Education and Scholarship*. Gyeongju, Korea.

Beech, G. 2013. *Researching the Teaching Context: Faithful practice*. Penrith, AU: National Institute for Christian Education. http://www.nice.edu.au/resources/Documents/ResearchingtheteachingcontextBEECH.pdf

Belz, J. 1993. Editorial, *World Magazine*. 19 June.

Berkhof, L. 1990. Being reformed in our attitude toward the Christian school. In Dennis Johnson, ed. *Foundations of Christian Education*. Phillipsburg, NJ: P&R.

Berry, E. 1989. Invitation to relationship: The teacher as role model, *Faculty Dialogue* 11: 83–92.

Bexley, E., R. James, and S. Arkoudis. 2011. *The Australian Academic Profession in Transition*. Melbourne, Australia: Centre for the Study of Higher Education.

Bishop, S. 1996. Beliefs shape mathematics. *Spectrum* (28)2: 131–141.

Blamires, H. 1963. *The Christian Mind*. London: SPCK.

Blomberg, D. 1991. The integral curriculum. *Christian Educators Journal* 31(2): 7.

——. 2007. *Wisdom and Curriculum: Christian schooling after postmodernity*. Sioux Center: Dordt College Press.

Blue, T. 2009. Mentor-teaching in the English classroom. http://gradworks.umi.com/34/05/3405836.html

Bluestein, J. 1995. Mentors, masters, and Mrs. MacGregor. Albuquerque: Instructional Support Services.

Borich, G., & M. Tombari. 1997. *Educational Psychology: A contemporary approach*. New York: Longman.

Bradley, J., & R. Howell. 2011. *Mathematics through the Eyes of Faith*. New York: Harper Collins.

Bradley, W. 2007. On being a Christian professor in the secular academy. In W. Lane & P. Gould, eds. *The Two Tasks of the Christian Scholar*. Wheaton: Crossway.

Braunschweig, M. 2012. It ain't necessarily so: Textbooks around the world. *The Economist*, 13 October. http://www.economist.com/node/21564554/print

Brighouse, T. & D. Woods. 1999. *How to Improve Your School*. London: Routledge.

Brinkman, S. 2013. Teen video denounces rising anti-Christian sentiment in schools. http://www.womenofgrace.com/blog/?p=21234

Brock, P. 2006. *Occasional Address*. Speech (8 April) at the Graduation Ceremony, University of New England, AU.

Brooks, D. 2001. The organization kid. *The Atlantic*. (April). http://www.theatlantic.com/magazine/archive/2001/04/the-organization-kid/2164/

Brown, H. & P. Abeywickrama. 2010. *Language Assessment: Principles and classroom practices*. Whites Plains: Pearson Education.

Bruner, J. 1996. *The Culture of Education*. Cambridge: Harvard University Press.

Buckingham, J. 2010. *The Rise of Religious Schools*. Sydney, AU: Centre for Independent Studies.

Butler, H., A. Krelle, I. Seal, et al. 2011. *The Critical Friend: Facilitating change and wellbeing in school communities*. Camberwell, AU: ACER Press.

Caine, R. & G. Caine. 1997a. *Education on the edge of possibility*. Alexandria, VA: ASCD.

——. 1997b. *Unleashing the Power of Perceptual Change: The promise of brain based teaching*. Alexandria, VA: ASCD.

Caldwell, R. 2003. How to get real. *Philosophy Now* 42: 106.

Carson, D. 2002. Maintaining scientific and Christian truths in a postmodern world. *Science and Christian Belief* 14(2): 107–122.

——. 2008. *Christ and Culture Revisited*. Grand Rapids: Eerdmans.

——. 2012. *The Intolerance of Tolerance*. Grand Rapids: Eerdmans.

Carter, S. 2008. Disequilibrium and questioning in the primary classroom. *Teaching Children Mathematics*, (15)3, 134–137.

Ch'ng, A. 2012. Discrimination isn't always such a bad thing. *The Drum: ABC Radio*, AU. http://www.abc.net.au/unleashed/3945628.html#

Chadwick, R. 1990. *Christian School Curriculum: An integrated approach*. Winona Lake, IN: BMH Books.

——. 1992. *Candidacy Handbook for Overseas Schools*. Colorado Springs: ACSI.

Chaplin, J. 2010. *A Christian view of the role of government*. Paper presented (13 November) at the Theos God and Government Conference, Westminster, UK. http://www.wheaton.edu/CACE/CACE-Print-Resources/~/media/Files/Centers-and-Institutes/CACE/articles/ChristianViewRoleGovernment.pdf

Chua, S. & R. Edlin. 2010. The seductive advent of information technology. Wollongong, AU: *Edserv International*. https://dl.dropboxusercontent.com/u/68052584/Technology.pdf

Cimbala, J. 2004. A "closet Christian" steps out: A Christian professor explains how he was motivated to begin sharing his faith with students and colleagues. http://www.leaderu.com/real/ri9601/cimbala.html

Claerbaut, D. 2004. *Faith and Learning on the Edge: A bold new look at religion in higher education*. Grand Rapids: Zondervan

Collier, J. 2010. Christian Education Excerpts. Unpublished report.

——. 2012. A School that is Authentically Christian. Unpublished manuscript.

Colson, C. & N. Pearcey. 1999. *How Now Shall We Live?* Wheaton: Tyndale House.

Comenius, J. 2008. Retrieved 4 July 2008 from Wikipedia: http://en.wikipedia.org/wiki/Comenius

Cooling, T. 2005. Curiosity: Vice or virtue for the Christian teacher? Promoting faithfulness to Scripture in teacher formation. *Journal of Education and Christian Belief* 9(2): 87–103.

——. 2010. *Doing God in Education*. London: Theos.

Cornwell, G. & B. Johnson. 1991. The conflict of postmodern and traditional epistemologies in curricular reform: A dialogue. *Studies in Philosophy and Education* 11: 149–166.

Costa, L. & B. Kallick. 1993. Through the lens of a critical friend. *Educational Leadership* 51(2): 49–51.

Counts, G. 1932. *Dare the School Build a New Social Order?* New York: John Day. [reprinted in Flinders, D., & Thornton, S., eds. 2009. *The Curriculum Studies Reader*. 3rd ed. New York: Routledge.]

——. 1952. *Education and American Civilization*. New York: Teachers College Press.

Craig, W. 2004. *On Being a Christian Academic*. Addison, TX: Lewis & Stanley.

Crick, F. 1994. *The Astonishing Hypothesis: The scientific search for the soul*. New York: Touchstone.

Day, C. 1999. Developing Teachers: The challenges of lifelong learning. London: Falmer Press.

De Kool, R. 2009. *The Essence of Christian Teaching*. Gouda: Driestar Educatief.

Dean, K. 2010. *Almost Christian: What the faith of our teenagers is telling the American church*. New York: Oxford University Press.

Delbanco, A. 2001. *Writing New England: An anthology from the puritans to the present*. Cambridge: Harvard University Press.

Derewianka, B. & J. Ehrich. 2013. *EDGT983 Assessing and evaluating in TESOL environments: Types of assessment*. [Class Handout]. Wollongong, AU: University of Wollongong.

Dewey, J. 1976 [1899]. *The School and Society*. Carbondale: Southern Illinois University Press.

Dinan-Thompson, M. 2005. (Non)neutrality of curriculum in Queensland. In C. Harris & C. Marsh, eds. *Curriculum Developments in Australia: Promising initiatives, impasses and dead-ends*. Deakin West, ACT: Australian Curriculum Studies Association.

Doud, G. 1990. *Molder of Dreams*. Colorado Springs: Focus on the Family.

Drexler, J., ed. 2007. *Schools as Communities*. Colorado Springs: Purposeful Design.

DuFour, R., R. Eaker, & R. DuFour, eds. 2005. *On Common Ground: The power of professional learning communities*. Bloomington, IN: Solution Tree.

Dunphy, J. 1983. A religion for a new age. *The Humanist* 43: 23–26.

Eaton, J. 2013. *Challenges and opportunities ahead for accreditation*. Washington, DC: Council for Higher Education Accreditation. (podcast at http://cheanews.org/)

Edlin, R. 2006a. In pursuit of an authentic Christian paradigm: The place of reformed critical realism. In R. Edlin & J. Ireland, *Engaging the Culture*.

——. 2006b. In pursuit of an authentic Christian paradigm: The place of reformed critical realism. In R. Edlin & J. Ireland, *Engaging the Culture*.

——. 2006c. Inhabiting the mindfield. In R. Edlin & J. Ireland, *Engaging the Culture*.

——. 2008a. Christian education and worldview. *ICCTE Journal* 3(2). http://icctejournal.org/issues/v3i2/v3i2-edlin/

——. 2008b. Making professional development work. *Christian School Education* 11(3): 16–21.

——. 2009a. Disequilibrium as a teaching strategy. Paper presented at the International Symposium, Yanbian University of Science and Technology, Yanji City, China.

——. 2009b. Keeping the faith: The Christian scholar in the academy in a postmodern world. *Christian Higher Education* 8(3): 203–224.

——. 2014. Teacher training and professional development. In K. Goodlet and J. Collier, *Teaching Well: Insights for educators in Christian schools*. Barton, AU: Barton Books.

Edlin, R., & Ireland, J., eds. 2006. *Engaging the Culture: Christians at work in education*. Blacktown, AU: National Institute for Christian Education.

Eisenbarth, S. & K. Van Treuren. 2004. Christian worldview and the engineering context. Proceedings of the 5th Christian Engineering Education Conference, Salt Lake City.

Elliot, D. 2012. Toward an agenda for teacher education in Christian colleges and universities. *ICCTE Journal* 7(2). http://icctejournal.org/issues/v7i2/v7i2-elliott/

Elzinga, K. 2012. Christian higher education vs. Christians in higher education. In E. Davis, ed. *A Higher Education: Baylor and the vocation of a Christian university*. Waco: Baylor University Press.

Etherington, M. 2008. Is Christian schooling really at loggerheads with the ideas of diversity and tolerance? A rejoinder. *Education Research and Perspectives* 35(2): 112–137.

Etherington, M., ed. 2014. *Foundations of Education: A Christian vision*. Eugene, OR: Wipf and Stock.

Evangelical Manifesto Steering Committee. 2008. An evangelical manifesto: A declaration of evangelical identity and public commitment. http://www.anevangelicalmanifesto.com/docs/Evangelical_Manifesto_Summary.pdf.

FAQ. 2005. University of Washington Office of Educational Assessment. http://www.washington.edu/oea/services/research/program_eval/faq.html

Farrell, J. & D. Tanner. 2002. Textbooks. *Encyclopedia of Education.* http://www.encyclopedia.com/topic/Textbooks.aspx

Fennema, J. 2006. Transforming education: Parents. In R. Edlin & J. Ireland, *Engaging the Culture.*

——. 2008. Teaching Christianly and legally within public schools. Paper presented at the ICCTE Conference, Gordon College.

Fenton, J. & M. Gould-Drakeley. 2012. Embedding a Christian worldview in Indonesian at Macarthur Anglican School. In B. Cowling, ed. *From Vision to Venture: The integration project.* Sydney, AU: Anglican Education Commission. http://www.aec.edu.au/resources/Projects/The%20Integral%20Project/Integral%20Dinner%20Booklet.pdf

Fernhout, H. 1997. Christian schooling: Telling a world view story. In I. Lambert & S. Mitchell, eds. *The Crumbling Walls of Certainty.* Sydney: Centre for the Study of Australian Christianity.

Ferriter, B. 2005. The day I was wrong: a lesson in professional development communities. *Journal of Staff Development* 26(3): 72–3.

Finn, D., J. Swezey, and D. Warren. 2010. Perceived professional development needs of teachers and administrators in PS-12 Christian schools. *Journal of Research on Christian Education* 19: 7–26.

Fischer, M. 2004. Is differentiation the answer to the tracking debate? *Education World.* http://www.educationworld.com/a_curr/voice/voice124.shtml

Fletcher, W. 1971. *Humanity of man – The language animal.* Wellington, New Zealand: Hicks Smith and Sons.

Fowler, S. 1980a. Contemporary thought: Religious antithesis. In J. Mechielsen, ed. *No Icing on the Cake.* Mt. Evelyn, AU: Brooks-Hall.

——. 1980b. The Bible in the school. In J. Mechielsen, ed. *No Icing on the Cake.* Melbourne, AU: Brooks-Hall.

——. 2006. *Living World Views.* Eltham, AU: Amani Educational Services.

Fullan, M. 1999. *Change Forces: The sequel.* Philadelphia: Falmer.

Furst, L. 1992. State control of non-government schools: A comprehensive review of case law. *Journal of Research on Christian Education* 1(1): 103–115.

Gaebelein, F. 1954. *The Pattern of God's Truth.* Chicago: Moody Press.

Gatto, J. 2005. *Dumbing Us Down: The hidden curriculum of compulsory schooling.* Gabriola Island, CA: New Society Publishers.

Glanzer, P. 2012. The missing factor in higher education. *Christianity Today.* March.

Glanzer, P. & T. Talbert. 2005. The impact and implications of faith or worldview in the classroom. *Journal of Research in Character Education* 3(1): 25–42.

Glenn, C. 2012. Disestablishing our secular schools. *First Things* 23 January. http://www.firstthings.com/article/2011/12/disestablishing-our-secular-schools

Glionna, J. 2011. Seoul's intellectual pressure cooker. *Los Angeles Times*, 21 August. http://articles.latimes.com/2011/aug/21/world/la-fg-south-korea-exam-village-20110822

Godfrey, K. 2011. *Investigating grade inflation and non-equivalence*. New York: The College Board.

Goheen, M. 2002. The organism of revelation. In J. van der Meer, ed. *Facets of Faith and Science: Vol. 4, Interpreting God's action in the world*. Lanham: University Press of America.

——. 2004. The gospel and the idolatrous power of secular science. In Ireland, Edlin, & Dickens, *Pointing the Way*.

——. 2006. Delighting in God's good gift of sport and competition. In R. Edlin & J. Ireland, *Engaging the Culture*.

——. 2010. Dethroning the idols. *Australian Presbyterian* (August): 4–9.

Goheen, M. & C. Bartholomew. 2008. *Living at the Crossroads: An introduction to Christian worldview*. Grand Rapids: Baker.

Goldsworthy, G. 2006. *Gospel-centered Hermeneutics: Foundations and principles of evangelical biblical interpretation*. Downers Grove: InterVarsity.

Good, T. & J. Brophy. 2008. *Looking in Classrooms*. 10th ed. Boston: Pearson.

Goudzwaard, B., M. Vander Vennen, & D. Van Heemst. 2007. *Hope in Troubled Times: A new vision for confronting global crises*. Grand Rapids: Baker.

Gould, P. 2007. The two tasks introduced: The fully integrated life of the Christian scholar. In W. Craig & P. Gould, eds. *The Two Tasks of the Christian Scholar*. Wheaton: Crossway.

Graham, D. 2003. *Teaching redemptively: Bringing grace and truth into your classroom*. Colorado Springs: Purposeful Design.

——. 2011. *Making a difference: Christian educators in public schools*. Colorado Springs: Purposeful Design.

Greidanus, S. 1982. The use of the Bible in Christian scholarship. *Christian Scholars Review* 11(2): 138–147.

Guskey, T. 2002. Professional development and teacher change. *Teachers and Teaching* 8: 381–389.

Hagan, L. 2003. *Second Sight: Renewing the vision of Bellevue Christian School for a new century*. Bellevue, WA: Bellevue Christian School.

Hankins, B. 2007. "I'm just making a point": Francis Schaeffer and the irony of faithful Christian scholarship. *Fides et Historia* 39(1): 15–34.

Hanvey, R. 1975. An Attainable Global Perspective. Center for Teaching International Relations, University of Denver.

Hargreaves, A. & M. Fullan. 2012. *Professional Capital: Transforming teaching in every school*. New York: Teachers College Press.

Harmon-Jones, E. & J. Mills, eds. 1999. *Cognitive Dissonance*. Washington, DC: American Psychological Association.

Harris, C. 2009. Instructor's philosophy of education. [syllabus] Harrisonburg, VA: James Madison University.

Hart, D.B. 2009. *Atheist Delusions: The Christian revolution and its fashionable enemies*. New Haven: Yale University Press.

Hart, D.G. 1997. What's so special about the university anyway? In Kuklick & Hart, *Religious Advocacy and American History*.

Hartzell, J. 2006. *In the Name of Purpose: Sacrificing truth on the altar of unity*. Bloomington, IL: Exlibris. http://www.inthenameofpurpose.org/page2.html

Harvey, L. 2004. The power of accreditation: Views of academics. In P. Nauta, P. Oma, et al., eds. *Accreditation Models in Higher Education*. Helsinki: European Network for Quality Assurance in Higher Education.

Hegeman, J., M. Edgell, H. Jochemsen. 2011. *Practice and Profile: Christian formation for vocation*. Eugene: Wipf and Stock.

Hekman, B. 2007. Schools as communities of grace. In J. Drexler, ed. *Schools as Communities*. Colorado Springs: Purposeful Design

Hénard, F. 2009. Learning our lesson: review of quality teaching in higher education. *An OECD Report*. www.oecd.org/edu/imhe/44058352.pdf

Henderson, P. 2004. Aristotle: A man for our times. *Evidence* 9: 53–56.

Henry, C. 2012. The crisis of the campus. *Renewing Minds: A journal of Christian thought* 1: 51–66.

Henry, D. & B. Agee, eds. 2003. *Faithful Learning and the Christian Scholarly Vocation*. Grand Rapids: Eerdmans.

Higton, M. 2012. *A Theology of Higher Education*. Oxford: Oxford University Press.

Hilgemann, T. 1993. *The Selection and Use of Textbooks in an MK School*. MKOA Conference, Quito, Ecuador.

Hill, B. 2003. Send reinforcements. We're going to teach values. *Curriculum and Leadership Journal*. http://www.curriculum.edu.au/leader/send_reinforcements._were_going_to_teach_values,4617.html?issueID=9691

——. 2005. Whose house do you live in? A brief for religious education in schools. *Journal of Christian Education* 48(2): 9–17.

Hoekema, D. 2003. Keeping the faith in the Christian college, past and present [Review of *Building the Christian Academy* and *Quality with Soul*]. *Perspectives*. January. http://www.rca.org/page.aspx?pid=3161

Hollaar, L. nd. *Christian Pathways for Schooling*. Langley: Society of Christian Schools in British Columbia.

Holland, R. 2011. *Chaplains and Biblical Studies: Is it time for a new paradigm*. Sydney: Anglican Education Commission.

——. 2012. Livewire: An innovative curriculum approach for Anglican schools. In B. Cowling, ed. *From Vision to Venture: The integration project*. Sydney: Anglican Education Commission. http://www.aec.edu.au/resources/Projects/The%20Integral%20Project/Integral%20Dinner%20Booklet.pdf

Holmes, A. 2003. The closing of the American mind and the opening of the Christian mind: Liberal learning, great texts and the Christian college. In Henry & Agee, *Faithful Learning*.

Horne, H. 1978. *Teaching Techniques of Jesus*. Grand Rapids: Kregel.

Horton, M. 1992. My father's world. *Christ and Culture* 1(2). http://web.
archive.org/web/20001010081657/http://www.alliancenet.org/pub/mr/
mr92/1992.02.MarApr/mr9202.msh.fathers.html.

Hughes, A. 2003. *Testing for Language Teachers.* 2nd ed. Cambridge: Cambridge
University Press.

Hughes, R. 2005. *The Vocation of a Christian Scholar*, rev. ed. Grand Rapids:
Eerdmans.

Ireland, C. 2012. 5 days in Finland. *Education Forum* 38(1): 30–35.

Ireland, J. 2001. Literature selection in schools: A Christian worldview
perspective. *Christian Teachers Journal* 9(1): 4–7.

——. 2004. The Christian mind and children's literature. In Ireland, Edlin, &
Dickens, *Pointing the Way.*

Ireland, J., R. Edlin, & K. Dickens. 2004. *Pointing the Way: Directions for
Christian education in a new millennium.* Blacktown, AU: National Institute
for Christian Education.

Irish Educators: There's no value-neutrality school. 2011. *Zenit News Bulletin,*
6 April. http://www.zenit.org/en/articles/irish-educators-there-s-no-value-
neutral-school

Jackson, D. 2011. Developing a biblical studies curriculum in a Christian
school. *Journal of Christian Education* 54(2): 63–75.

Jackson, P. 1992. Conceptions of curriculum and curriculum specialists. In P.
Jackson, ed. *Handbook of Research on Curriculum.* New York: Macmillan.

Jayaram, K., A. Moffit, & D. Scott. 2012. Breaking the habit of ineffective
professional development for teachers. https://mckinseyonsociety.com/

Jeffrey, D. & C. Evans, eds. 2007. *The Bible and the University.* Grand Rapids:
Zondervan.

Jellema, W. 1958. The curriculum in a liberal arts college. In D. Oppewal,
ed. 1992. *Voices from the Past: Reformed educators.* Grand Rapids: Calvin
College Press.

Jensen, B., A. Hunter, et al. 2012. *Catching Up: Learning from the best school
systems in Asia.* Carlton, AU: Grattan Institute.

Johnson, T. 2003. Dutch reformed philosophy in North America: Three varieties
in the late twentieth century. *Communio Viatorum* 45(2): 117–133.

Jones, A., ed. 1998. *Science in Faith: A Christian perspective on teaching science.*
Romford, UK: Christian Schools' Trust.

Kanitz, L. 2005. Improving Christian worldview pedagogy: Going beyond mere
Christianity. *Christian Higher Education* 4(2): 99–108.

Keenan, D. 1993. *Curriculum Development in the Christian School.* Colorado
Springs: Purposeful Design.

Keller, T. 2009. *Counterfeit Gods.* London: Hodder & Stoughton.

Keyes, R. 1995. *True Heroism in a World of Celebrity Counterfeits.* Colorado
Springs: Navpress.

Kienel, P. 1988. Patterns of organization and procedure for Christian school
boards. Colorado Springs: ACSI.

Kinney, P. 2012. Student-led conferences support learning. *Principal Leadership* 13(3): 55–57.

Kitching, G. 2008. *The Trouble with Theory: The educational costs of postmodernism.* Sydney: Allen & Unwin.

Kohn, A. 1999. *Punished by Rewards: The trouble with gold stars, incentive plans, A's, praise and other bribes.* New York: Houghton Mifflin.

Kok, J. 1998. *Patterns of the Western Mind: A reformed Christian perspective.* Sioux Center: Dordt College Press.

——, ed. 2004. *Celebrating the Vision: The reformed perspective of Dordt College* Sioux Center: Dordt College Press.

Kopple, W. 1991. Toward a Christian view of language. In L. Ryken, ed. *Contemporary Literary Theory: A Christian appraisal.* Grand Rapids: Eerdmans.

Kuklick, B. & D.G. Hart, eds. 1997. *Religious Advocacy and American History.* Grand Rapids: Eerdmans.

Lee, I. 2009. Situated globalization and racism: An analysis of Korean High School EFL students. *Language & Literacy* 11(1).

Leiter, B. 2010. Teaching counts for nothing. *Leiter Reports.* May. http://leiterreports.typepad.com/blog/2010/05/you-finally-get-that-tenuretrack-job-and-then-you-discover-this.html

Lennox, J. 2007. *God's Undertaker: Has science buried God?* Oxford: Lion.

Leo, J. 1992. Schools to parents: Keep out. *U.S. News & World Report.* 5 October.

——. 1993. A for effort – or for showing up. *US News & World Report.* 18 October.

Levin, B. 2007. Does curriculum matter? *EQ Magazine.* Spring: 15–16.

Lewis, C.S. 1980. *The Weight of Glory.* New York: Harper Collins.

Lewis, N. 2004. The intersection of post-modernity and classroom practice. *Teacher Education Quarterly* 31(3): 119–134.

Lewontin, R. 1997. Billions and billions of demons. *The New York Review* 44(1): 25–33.

Lincoln, Y. & G. Guba. 1985. *Naturalistic Enquiry.* Newbury Park, CA: Sage.

——. 2103. *The Constructivist Credo.* Walnut Creek, CA: Left Coast Press.

Lingard, R. & S. Sellar. 2013. Catalyst data: Perverse systemic effects of audit and accountability in Australian schooling. *Journal of Education Policy* 28: 634–656.

Lopez-Otero, A. nd. Be humble, but daring: A non-Christian professor offers advice and encouragement for Christian faculty. http://www.leaderu.com/real/ri9702/adolfo.html

Lortie, D. 2002. *Schoolteacher: A sociological study.* Chicago: University of Chicago Press.

Lynch, B. 2001. Rethinking assessment from a critical perspective. *Language Testing* 18: 351–372.

MacDonald, J. & D. Purpel. 1987. Curriculum and planning: Visions and metaphors. *Journal of Curriculum and Supervision* 2: 178–192.

Machen, J. 1951. *What is Christianity?* Grand Rapids: Eerdmans.

MacKenzie, P. 1997. *Entry points for Christian reflection within education.* London: CARE for Education.

Marsden, G. 1997a. Christian advocacy and the rules of the academic game. In Kuklick & Hart, *Religious Advocacy and American History.*

——. 1997b. *The Outrageous Idea of Christian Scholarship.* New York: Oxford University Press.

Marshall, C. 2012. Divine Justice as Restorative Justice. In Baylor University, *Prison: Christian reflection.* Waco: Baylor University. http://www.baylor. edu/content/services/document.php/163072.pdf

Mathewes, C. 1999. The academic life as a Christian vocation. *The Journal of Religion* 79(1): 110–121.

McCabe, N. 1995. Twelve high school 11th grade students examine their best teachers. *Peabody Journal of Education* 70(2): 117–26.

McCarthy, R., D. Oppewal, et al. 1981. *Society, State, & Schools: A case for structural and confessional pluralism.* Grand Rapids: Eerdmans.

McMillan, J. 2013. *Classroom Assessment: Principles and practice for effective instruction.* 6th ed. Boston: Pearson.

Mellichamp, J. 1997. Focused research/teaching. In *Ministering in a secular university: A guide for Christian professors and staff.* http://www.leaderu.com/ msu/chapter6.html.

——. 2002. The Christian professor in the secular university. http://leaderu.com/ cl-institute/xtnprof/secintro.html

——. 2004. How to restore Christian thought to the university. http://leaderu. com/real/ri9702/mellichamp.html

Mill, J. S. 1859. *On Liberty.* London: Parker (reprinted 2002; New York: Dover).

Millay, E. 1988. *Collected Sonnets.* New York: HarperCollins.

Miller, D. L. 2012. *Emancipating the world: A Christian response to radical Islam and fundamentalist Islam.* Seattle: YWAM.

Miller, L. 2010. Why Harvard students should study more religion. *Newsweek.* 3 March. http://www.newsweek.com/why-harvard-students-should-study-more-religion-75231

Mills, K. 2003. The culture of the school. *Journal of Education and Christian Belief* 7(2): 129–142.

Minor, L., A. Onwuegbuzie, et al. 2002. Characteristics of effective teachers. *The Journal of Educational Research* 96: 116–127.

Mission Statement. 2013. Brisbane, AU: Christian Heritage College. http:// www.chc.edu.au/index.php/about-us/mission-statement/

Moroney, K. 1999. How sin affects scholarship: A new model. *Christian Scholar's Review* 28: 432–451.

Moscrop, D. 2013. Grade inflation and the cult of self-esteem. *Ottawa Citizen.* 10 October.

Mouw, R. 1996. Tolerance without compromise: Christian engagement in an era of political rancor. *Christianity Today* 40(8): 33–35.

——. 2011. The civility mandate. *Capital Commentary*. 1 April. http://www. capitalcommentary.org/politics/civility-mandate

Mouw, R. & S. Griffioen. 1993. *Pluralisms and Horizons: An essay in Christian public philosophy*. Grand Rapids: Eerdmans.

Murphy, J. 1987. *Quintilian on the Teaching of Speaking and Writing: Translations from books one, two, and ten of the Institutio Oratoria*. Carbondale: Southern Illinois University.

Myers, J. 2004. U.S. Supreme Court denies review of Bishop: Academic freedom stumbles in wake of 11th Circuit Court ruling. http://www.leaderu.com/ real/ri9203/court1.html

Nagel, T. 2012. *Mind and Cosmos: Why the materialist neo-Darwinian conception of nature is almost certainly false*. New York: Oxford University Press

Nash, R. 1990. *The Closing of the American Heart*. Plano, TX: Probe.

Neuhaus, R. 1996. The Christian University: Eleven theses. *First Things* 59: 19–22. http://www.firstthings.com/article.php3?id_article=3799

Newbigin, L. 1986. *Foolishness to the Greeks: The gospel and western culture*. Grand Rapids: Eerdmans.

Niebuhr, H.R. 1937 [1988]. *The Kingdom of God in America*. New York: Harper and Row.

——. 1951. *Christ and Culture*. San Francisco: Harper.

Noll, M. 1994. *The Scandal of the Evangelical Mind*. Grand Rapids: Eerdmans.

——. 2011. *Jesus Christ and the Life of the Mind*. Grand Rapids: Eerdmans.

——. 2012. The Bible, Baptists, and the challenge of Christian higher education. In E. Davis, ed. *A Higher Education: Baylor and the vocation of a Christian university*. Waco: Baylor University.

North, G. 2013. Tenured Austrian Economists vs. Murray Rothbard. http:// www.garynorth.com/public/10768.cfm

Norton, A., J. Sonnemann, et al. 2013. *Taking University Teaching Seriously*, Carlton, AU: Grattan Institute. http://grattan.edu.au/static/files/assets/ aa7940a6/191_Taking-Teaching-Seriously.pdf

Ntarangwi, M. 2013a & b. What makes a Christian university Christian (I & II). *IAPCHE Contact* 25(1 & 2): 2–3.

O'Neill, G. 2010. *Programme Design: Overview of curriculum models*. Dublin: University College Dublin.

Oeland, G. 2012. A letter to my daughter on her graduation from Christian high school. http://www.cardus.ca/comment/article/3251/.

Ogden, S. M. 2001. Academic freedom and Christian scholarship [Review of the book *Academic freedom and Christian scholarship*] *Academe* 87(3): 74–75. http://proquest.umi.com

Orchard, J., ed. 2013. *Religious Education: Draft programmes of study*. London: Religious Education Council of England and Wales.

Our desire. 2013. Sydney: Covenant Christian School. http://www.covenant. nsw.edu.au/uniqueness.html

Our goal. 2013. Seattle: Bellevue Christian School. http://www.bellevuechristian. org/

Ozmon, H. 2012. *Philosophical Foundations of Education.* 9th ed. Boston: Pearson.

Paksuniemi, M. 2013. Teacher education in Finland: What are Finnish teachers made of? 25 November. http://www.edutopia.org/blog/teacher-education-in-finland-merja-paksunie

Parkay, F. 2013. *Becoming a Teacher.* Boston: Pearson.

Parker, D. 2012. *Christian Teachers in Public Schools: 13 essentials for the classroom.* Kansas City: Beacon Hill Press.

Piirto, J. 1999. Implications of postmodern curriculum theory for the education of the talented. *Journal for the Education of the Gifted* 22: 324–353.

Plantinga, A. 1984. Advice to Christian philosophers. *Faith and Philosophy* 1(3): 253–271.

Plantinga, C. 2002. *Engaging God's World: A Christian vision of faith, learning, and living.* Grand Rapids: Eerdmans

Pleschová, G., E. Simon, et al. 2012. *The Professionalization of Academics as Teachers in Higher Education.* Strasbourg: European Science Foundation.

Poe, H. 2004. *Christianity in the Academy: Teaching at the intersection of faith and learning.* Grand Rapids: Baker.

Postman, N. 1995. *The End of Education.* New York: Knopf.

Rampel, C. 2011. A history of college grade inflation. *New York Times.* 14 July. http://economix.blogs.nytimes.com/2011/07/14/the-history-of-college-grade-inflation/?_r=0

Raschke, C. 2004. *The Next Reformation: Why evangelicals must embrace postmodernity.* Grand Rapids: Baker.

Redeemer University College. 2003. *The Cross and our Calling.* Ancaster, Canada. http://www2.redeemer.ca/about/The-Cross-and-our-Calling.pdf.

Religion. 2013. *Merriam-Webster Dictionary.* http://www.merriam-webster. com/dictionary/religion.

Religion. 2013. *Oxford Dictionary.* http://oxforddictionaries.com/definition/english/religion.

Religious Education. 2013. London: The British Humanist Association. https:humanism.org.uk/schools-and-education/school-curriculum/religious-education/.

Rice, T. 1999. *Oh What a Circus.* London: Hodder & Stoughton.

Richardson, V. 2001. *Alexis de Tocqueville and the dilemmas of professional development.* Ann Arbor: Center for the Improvement of Early Reading Achievement

——. 2003. The dilemmas of professional development *Phi Delta Kappan* 84(5): 401–406.

Ripley, A. 2011. Teacher, leave those kids alone. *Time Magazine.* 3 October.

Roberts v Madigan, United States, Court of Appeals, Tenth Circuit, 17 December 1990, 921 *Federal Reporter,* 2nd Series: 1056.

Roehrig, G. & R. Kruse. 2005. The role of teachers' beliefs and knowledge in the adoption of a reform-based curriculum. *School Science and Mathematics* 105: 412–422.

Roques, M. 1989. *Curriculum Unmasked: Towards a Christian understanding of education.* Eastbourne, UK: Monarch.

Rorty, R. 2000. Universality and truth. In R. Brandom, ed. *Rorty and His Critics.* Malden: Blackwell.

Ross, B. 2014. What happens when schools cut denominational ties. *Christianity Today.* January 7. Retrieved from http://www.christianitytoday.com/ct/2014/january-february/what-happens-when-schools-cut-denominational-ties.html

Rouse, J. 2006. Review of *Christianity in the Academy: Teaching at the intersection of faith and learning.* http://www.amazon.com

Roys, J. 2013. *Wheaton College corrects course.* Blog. http://www.julieroys.com/2013/07/wheaton-college-corrects-course.html.

Runner, H.E. 1982. *The Relation of the Bible to Learning.* Jordan Station, ON: Paideia.

Schaeffer, F. 1982. *The Complete Works of Francis Schaeffer.* Westchester: Crossway.

Schmoker, M. 2005. Here and now: Improving teaching and learning. In R. & R. DuFour & E. Eaker, eds. *On Common Ground: The power of professional learning communities.* Bloomington, IN: Solution Tree Press.

Schofield, K. 2010. *The Purpose of Education.* Queensland, AU: Queensland State Education.

Schrontenboer, P. 1989. *Man in God's World: The biblical idea of office.* Pittsburgh, PA: Radix Books.

Schuman, R. 2012. Grading time: I give up, you're all exceptional. 20 March, *Huffington Post.* http://www.huffingtonpost.com/rebecca-schuman/grading-time-i-give-up-yo_b_1489430.html

Schwartz, J. 1998. Christians teaching in the public schools: What are some options. *Journal of Education & Christian Belief* 2(1): 53–64.

Schwartz, Z. 2013. High-school grade inflation balloon ready to pop. *The Globe and Mail.* March 29. www. Theglobeandmail.com/news/education/high-school-grade-inflation-balloon-ready-to-pop/article10452197/.

Scott, D. 2002. A vision of veritas: What Christian scholarship can learn from the puritan's "technology" of integrating truth. http://www.leaderu.com/aip/docs/scott.html

Seerveld, C. 2014 [2000]. Why should a university exist? In J. Kok, ed. *Cultural Education and History Writing.* Sioux Center: Dordt College Press.

——. 2014 [2002]. Reformational Christian philosophy and Christian college education. In J. Kok, ed. *Cultural Education and History Writing.* Sioux Center: Dordt College Press.

Sehorn, G. 2013. Preparing for the crossfire: Equipping evangelical leaders for service in public schools. *ICCTE Journal* 8(2). http://icctejournal.org/issues/v8i2/v8i2-sehorn/

Sinnema, D. 2008. How to use the Bible in Christian scholarship. *Contact Academic Insert*. June. http://www.iapche.org/insert194.pdf

Sire, J. 2009. *The Universe Next Door: A basic worldview catalog*. 5th ed. Downers Grove: InterVarsity.

Slavin, R. 2013. What are the pros and cons of grouping kids for reading instruction based on test results? *Reading Today Online*. 13 September. http://www.reading.org/reading-today/archive

Sloane, A. 2006. *On Being a Christian in the Academy: Nicholas Wolterstorff and the practice of Christian scholarship*. Eugene: Wipf & Stock.

Smart, S. 2012. Faith in the infallibility of the mind is the atheist's delusion. *Sydney Morning Herald*. April 12. http://www.smh.com.au/.

Smith, D. 2007. Kuyers Mathematics Online. Grand Rapids: Kuyers Institute for Christian Teaching and Learning. http://www.calvin.edu/kuyers/math/index.html

Smith, D. & J. Shortt. 2002. *The Bible and the Task of Teaching*. Nottingham: Stapleford Centre.

Smith, D. & J. Smith. 2011a. *Teaching and Christian Practices: Reshaping faith and learning*. Grand Rapids: Eerdmans.

——. 2011b. Practices, faith, and pedagogy. In Smith & Smith, *Teaching and Christian Practices*.

Smith, J. 2009. *Desiring the Kingdom: Worship, worldview, and cultural formation*. Grand Rapids: Baker.

——. 2013a. *Discipleship in the Present Tense: Reflections on faith and culture*. Grand Rapids: Calvin College Press.

——. 2013b. *Naturalizing "Shalom": Confessions of a Kuyperian secularist*. http://www.cardus.ca/comment/article/3993/naturalizing-shalom-confessions-of-a-kuyperian-secularist/.

Snook, I. 2005. Graduate teachers warned of strife. *New Zealand Herald*. May 16, A5.

Spurgeon, C. 1855. The power of the Holy Ghost. Sermon. 17 June. http://www.spurgeon.org/sermons/0030.htm

Spykman, G. 1977. The place and role of the Bible in the school. In Steensma and Van Brummelen, *Shaping School Curriculum*.

——. 1985. Christian higher education in a global perspective: A call to ongoing reformation. In D. Van Halsema & G. Spykman, eds. *Thinking and Acting Globally*. Sioux Center: Dordt College Press.

Stanford University. nd. Assessment: FAQ. http://www.stanford.edu/dept/pres-provost/irds/assessment/faq.html

Stark, R. 2011. *The Triumph of Christianity: How the Jesus movement became the world's largest religion*. New York: HarperCollins.

Steensma, G. & H. Van Brummelen, eds. 1977. *Shaping School Curriculum: A biblical view*. Terre Haute, IN: Signal Publishing.

Stemler, S. & D. Bebell. 2012. *The School Mission Statement: Values, goals, and identities in American education*. Larchmont: Eye on Education (Routledge).

Stenhouse, L. 1967. *Culture and Education*. New York: Weybright and Talley.

Stevens, M. 2012. *Anglican Schools as God's Culture-Makers*. Sydney: Anglican Education Commission.

Stronks, G. & D. Blomberg, eds. 1993. *A Vision with a Task: Christian schooling for responsive discipleship*. Grand Rapids: Baker.

Stronks, J. & G. Stronks. 1999. *Christian Teachers in Public Schools*. Grand Rapids: Baker.

Tan, D. 1995. Perceived importance of role models and its relationship with minority student satisfaction and academic performance. *NACADA Journal* 15(1): 48–51.

Tarnas, R. 2010. *The Passion of the Western Mind*. London: Pimlico.

Teale, W. 1996. Editorial. *Language Arts* 73(5): 295.

Templar, M. 2003. *Constructivism*. http://www.angelfire.com/az3/mercury_templar/construct.html

Thompson, R. 2005. *A Biblical Introduction to Worldview*. Auckland: Masters Publishing.

——. 2008. *God is One God: He wants us to live in community*. Whangaparaoa, NZ: Interact Curriculum Press.

Toufexis, A. 1993. The Right Chemistry: Evolutionary roots, brain imprints, biological secretions. *Time Magazine*. February 15. http://content.time.com/time/magazine/article/0,9171,977754,00.html

Toumbourou, J., G. Baksheev, et al. 2013. The role of psychology in the prevention of youth violence. *InPsych,* June. http://www.psychology.org.au/publications/inpsych/2013/june/toumbourou/

Tovey, J. 2013. Gone are the days of the old school yard. *Sydney Morning Herald,* August 24. http://www.smh.com.au/data-point/gone-are-the-days-of-the-old-school-yard-20130823-2sh09.html

Tyler, R. 1949. *Basic principles of curriculum and instruction*. Chicago: University of Chicago Press.

United Nations. 1948. *Declaration of Human Rights*. http://www.un.org/en/documents/udhr/.

Van Brummelen, H. 2002. *Steppingstones to Curriculum: A biblical path*. Colorado Springs: Purposeful Design.

—— 2009. *Walking with God in the Classroom*. 3rd ed. Colorado Springs: Purposeful Design.

Van Dyk, J. 1985. *The Beginning of Wisdom: The nature and task of the Christian school*. Grand Rapids: Christian Schools International.

——. 2000. *The Craft of Christian Teaching*. Sioux Center: Dordt College Press.

——. 2007. *The Maplewood Story: Fostering a reflective culture in the Christian School*. Sioux Center: Dordt College Press.

Vardy, S. 2011. Critical friend guidance pack. Canterbury: Canterbury Christchurch University. See: http://www.canterbury.ac.uk/education/quality-in-study-support/TrainingCourses/critical-friend-pdp/key-documents.aspx

Viadora, D. 1995. Against all odds. *Teacher Magazine* 6(8): 20–22.

Wang, J. & X. Lv. 2011. Western "Marxist study": The myth of value neutrality. *Advances in Education* 1(1): 1–5.

Watson, D.M.S. 1929. Adaptation. Paper in a Report by the British Association for the Advancement of Science. http://archive.org/stream/ reportofbritisha30adva/reportofbritisha30adva_djvu.txt

Watson, L. 2012. Quality and performance in Australian higher education. http://www.atn.edu.au/Documents/2012/2012%20Conference%20 Quality/Watson.pdf

Watts, R. E. 2007. The restoration of rhetoric: Rethinking the categories of Christian education. http://www.altavistaseattle.org/avs/b/archive2/Watts_ RestorationOfRhetoric_2007.pdf

Wax, T. 2013. Science, too, calls for a leap of faith. *New York Times*. 15 August. http://www.nytimes.com/roomfordebate/2013/08/15/should-creationism-be-controversial/science-calls-for-a-leap-of-faith

Webb, S. H. 2001. Review of *Academic Freedom and Christian Scholarship*. *The Christian Century* 118(5): 64.

Wiggins, G. & J. McTighe. 2005. *Understanding by Design*. Alexandria, VA: Association for Supervision and Curriculum Development.

Willhoite, M. 2000. *Daddy's Roommate*. Los Angeles: Alyson Publications.

Williston, J. 2005. From Dream to reality: Today's teachers preparing for future schools. *Childhood Education* (81)5: 286–291.

Wilson, D. 2012. The biblical antithesis in education. http://www. cambridgestudycenter.com/the-biblical-antithesis-in-education/

Wilson, W. 1991. *Recovering the Lost Tools of Learning: An approach to distinctively Christian education*. Wheaton: Crossway.

Wolters, A. 2005. *Creation Regained: Biblical basics for a reformational worldview*. 2nd ed. Grand Rapids: Eerdmans.

——. 2007. No longer queen: The theological disciplines and their sisters. In D. Jeffrey & C. Evans, eds. *The Bible and the University*. Grand Rapids: Zondervan.

Wolterstorff, N. 2002a. *Educating for Life: Reflections on Christian teaching and learning*. Grand Rapids: Baker.

——. 2002b. *Educating for Shalom: Essays on Christian higher education*. Grand Rapids: Eerdmans.

——. 2007. *Justice: Rights and wrongs*. Princeton: Princeton University Press.

Worthen, M. 2010. The reformer. *Christianity Today*. October. http://www. christianitytoday.com/ct/2010/october/3.18.html

Wright, A. 2013. *Christianity and Critical Realism: Ambiguity, truth, and theological literacy*. New York: Routledge.

Yancey, P. 1995. *The Jesus I Never Knew*. Grand Rapids: Zondervan.

Yelland, N. 2012. Learning by rote: Why Australia should not follow the Asian model of education. *The Conversation*. http://theconversation.com/ learning-by-rote-why-australia-should-not-follow-the-asian-model-of-education-5698

Young, B. 2007. The collaborative school community. In J. Drexler, ed. *Schools as Communities*. Colorado Springs: Purposeful Design.

Zammito, J. 2013. The Nagel flap: Mind and cosmos. *The Hedgehog Review* 15(3): 1–6.

Zuck, R. 1995. *Teaching as Jesus Taught*. Grand Rapids: Baker.

Zylstra, H. 1951. Christian education. In D. Oppewal, ed. 1992. *Voices from the Past: Reformed educators*. Grand Rapids: Calvin College Press.

Index

CPSIA information can be obtained
at www.ICGtesting.com
Printed in the USA
FFOW03n2058040914
7196FF

9 781940 567099